SSB
INTERVIEWS

SECOND EDITION
REVISED & UPDATED

SSB
INTERVIEWS

SECOND EDITION
REVISED & UPDATED

Maj (RETD) Ravindran Vasudevan, MBA

JAICO PUBLISHING HOUSE
Ahmedabad Bangalore Bhopal Bhubaneswar Chennai
Delhi Hyderabad Kolkata Lucknow Mumbai

Although there are a plethora of books written on achieving success at Services Selection Boards, no book has been penned from candidates' point of view as to how to succeed. The pictorial figures highlighted have simplified understanding the art of achieving success in all the techniques of assessment at SSB. ...A must-read for those who are aspiring to be leaders in the Defence Forces.

Maj Gen (Retd) Jaideep Mittra
Ex-Centre Commandant, SCS Bangalore &
Ex-President, SCS Bangalore

Maj Ravindran Vasudevan raises critical questions that have long concerned those of us in the field of educational tools. How do instructional uses of technology relate to or influence students' learning? Ravi's book while primarily addresses preparation for facing SSB interviews, the psychometric is applicable to any student preparing for challenging professions, both public and private sectors. Anyone involved in the development of teaching tools for career development and preparation for challenging roles will treasure this book because it provides another avenue to help students become reflective, observant and introspective – the professionals they wish them to become.

Dr Raveendran Pottathil
PhD CEO, AccuDx Corporation
Visiting Professor, Rutgers University NJ, USA
Northwest Agriculture and Forestry University, Yangling, China
Florida International University Miami, Florida, USA

...A must-read for all those aspiring for a career in the Defence Services. Every aspect of the SSB procedure is lucidly explained. ...A treasure trove of information which will interest both the lay person as well as military buffs alike.

Maj Gen (Retd) S. Sunder, AVSM
Ex-Selection Centre Commandant
Ex-President of Selection Board

This book on Services Selection Board Interviews outlines various facets involved in the selection process at The Selection Board. The author has chronicled it in a very simplistic manner for one and all to understand. As such it enables the reader to effectively assimilate the nuances of the selection process. A thorough grasp of its contents will surely empower the potential candidates looking forward to join as officers in the Armed Forces and Para Military forces.

The author, Maj Ravindran Vasudevan, besides his experience of having served in the Army, has the expertise and a unique distinction of training and grooming the potential candidates not only for facing SSB but also Corporate interviews. He has successfully handled this task for over two decades. The chain of training academies by the name, 'Cavalier India, and 'The Excel Training Academy'. which are known brands today, bear testimony to the excellence in this field. I dare say with professional conviction that this book is the only of its kind which goes all the way to groom the personality of its readers rather than provide cut and dry short cuts to face the challenges of a Services Selection Board.

Indeed a 'prize possession' for all leaders in making who are vying to 'ace the Services Selection Board or any interview for corporate management.

Brig MS Dadhwal, SM, VSM, Retd
EX President, 19 SSB Allahabad

Although the book is titled for a specific audience, the reach is enormous and breaks all barriers and boundaries to inspire each and every one who wishes to lead a positive life. Possessing a copy of this book by itself enhances one's patriotic value, and written by someone who has experienced life in the Armed Forces and has continuously put it into practice as a civilian and been successful, this book is a must-read. Academic organizations and the training divisions of the Corporate Sector can take a cue from this book in developing their curriculum.

Dr. Joseph V.G.
Honorary Consul of the Republic of Maldives in Bangalore
Trade Commissioner – ASEAN Region of Karnataka Regional Economic Trade Organization
Chairman – Garden City Group of Institutions

This is a brilliant book distilled from the vast teaching experience of Maj. Ravindran. Over two decades of his interactions with thousands of potential young defence leaders irrespective of gender and socio-economic background led to the emergence of this very unique book. This fills the vacuum of the existence of practical and actionable ideas in print form to clear SSB interviews.

Brig (Retd) F.B. Khatri
Ex SSB Board President, Interviewed over 15000 Candidates
Ex Dy GOC Delhi Area

Kudos to the author for bringing out a comprehensive and easy-to-understand compendium on SSB procedures... This book is an astute analysis of the procedures and techniques involved in the Services Selection Board combining strong practical reality and theoretical perspectives.

Col (Retd) George Thomas
MSC, PGDCA, ISSFP, Sr. Psychologist

A very comprehensive, captivating and practical book on ALL that happens in the SSB. The book is unique in many ways – right from defining the procedure at the SSB in a different manner to having exclusive points related to armed forces. The pictorials add clarity to the text and the "success mantras" for each task are very good. A MUST HAVE book for aspirants who wish to crack the SSB Interview.

Col (Retd) H.S. Grewal
Ex GTO 34 SSB Allahabad & SSB Bangalore

The Testing Procedures at Services Selection Boards to identify potential leaders have remained an area of mystery to most people. This book aims to simplify and educate the student regarding the fundamentals of leadership and also instil confidence to perform well in these tests. The author utilizes all his experience to dissect, analyze and explain various methods to handle these tests successfully. His articulate yet simple style of writing is certain to appeal to the readers.

A book strongly recommended for all aspirants wanting to join the various branches of the Indian Armed Forces.

Wg Cdr (Retd) R. Mohan Chand
Ex Senior Interviewing Officer SSB Mysore and Ex AF Pilot

This is an excellent book, adequate resources are provided to succeed. Every aspect of SSB Selection has been explained in detail. It is easy to understand and follow. It exposes the candidate to what happens in the SSB as also prepares them to face the tests and the unfamiliar situations with confidence and conviction.

Captain (Indian Navy) K.K. Nair
Ex-Senior GTO 12 SSB

I am sanguine that in the light of concrete realities this book focuses on how to enter the most honorable and most adventurous profession in first go. This book will be a milestone in the history of all the SSB books and will be as a beacon for times to come.

Col (Retd) M.Z.U. Siddiquie, SM
Wound Medal, COAS Commendation Card and recipient of over 25 other medals.
Author of seven books published internationally

Acknowledgements

There are many experts in the field of SSB training, who have encouraged and helped me in writing this book and I have mentioned a few of them here.

Firstly, Cdr S Prakash N M, Phd, PGDIRPM, PSC Ex-interviewing officer Bangalore SSB, who has interviewed over five thousand candidates at the SSB, and trained over nine thousand candidates to clear the SSB interviews. I express my thanks to him whose whole-hearted support is worthy of mention.

My sincere thanks to Brig P C Joseph, Ex senior GTO Allahabad SSB, who has examined over five thousand candidates at the SSB and trained over two thousand candidates to clear SSB while being with Cavalier India as the head of GTO training activities. His contribution to this book is invaluable.

Also I would like to thank all those candidates whom I trained during the course of last two decades and a good number of them are officers today. It has been a two-way learning process for me and my students.

Preface

"There is no such thing as a self-made man. You will reach your goals only with the help of others."

George Shinn

As the founder of Cavalier India and Excel Training Academy, the past two decades have been a continuous learning process for the training team as well as me. During this period we have interacted with, as well as trained thousands of defence career aspirants. Based on their feedback after their success/failure in the SSB, also our continuous research and analysis of results we modified and evolved a training program to match the dynamics of the SSB selection procedure. We created an innovative training program which would enable an average candidate to understand and follow at the SSB.

In this new and innovative SSB training procedure, all the three SSB selection techniques have been integrated and designed into one training module that covers all the aspects of Services Selection Procedures. It includes interviews, psychological tests and group testing. It has been the biggest breakthrough in SSB training and it's the first of its kind. This book explains all the relevant concepts in detail and with a lot more material which is required to clear such an important career interview.

I have also created an iconic SSB training network in the country which caters to the needs of thousands of defence career aspirants. However, it is evident that a good percentage of students, due to other commitments, are not able to attend SSB coaching classes and they give the interviews without the necessary preparations. When a good candidate gets rejected, the nation loses a good, potential, commissioned officer.

Therefore, I am compelled to write this book along with my team of trainers. Whatever is mentioned in this book, if followed at the SSB, success is guaranteed.

A career in the defence forces as an officer is one of the most prestigious and elite ones in the country. Youngsters who aspire for a career in the defence forces need to be highly focused and committed. They need to start preparing well in advance for the written examinations as well as the interviews. The power of proper training and proper tool should never be underestimated.

To prove this point, I have many experiences to share. In one of my batches, I had 18 candidates and 16 of them got selected. That was the highest ever SSB success for Sainik School, Bijapur, where Cdr S. Prakash and myself handled the training. So was the case in Sainik School, Trivandrum, where Wg. Cdr. R Mohan Chand and I did the same. Here too, 22 candidates out of 28 got selected. Knowing what to do in each test is extremely important. This book primarily deals with the self-learning tools and techniques that will help candidates face the SSB with confidence and pass with flying colours.

Changing adult behavior is a difficult thing and that is what I have been doing for the past two decades. All the principles and theories that were used to do so have been put in print form in this book.

These are not just SSB selection techniques but also actionable ideas crafted and distilled out of my experiences of training thousands of candidates from different parts of the country. However, this is not a book explaining the SSB testing procedure or a few theories. I cannot tell you the effort required at each step. Teaching and updating is a two-way process. It has been a long journey of mending, training and self-learning. What I am offering is a product that has evolved from the dynamics of intellectual interactions of many bright minds. Training candidates from different socio-economic and cultural backgrounds and moulding them to match the required standard has been a very challenging yet satisfying task. The organizations I have created have produced many efficient officers for our defence forces. Some of them even took up their second career as senior civil servants.

While writing this Preface, I received a call from Mr. Ajay Kumar (a candidate whom we trained recently) informing me that he got selected on his 20th attempt! As far as I know, it is the first time that a candidate who has attempted this 20 times has gotten selected. There is no better example than this.

This book is based on evidence and conviction. If you follow the recipes for success that I have explained in this book, you can make it at the first attempt itself.

MAJ (RETD) Ravindran Vasudevan

For clarification, contact:
Website: www.ravindranvasudevan.com
e-mail ID: info@ravindranvasudevan.com

Contents

Acknowledgements ix
Preface xi

Section A: Introduction
1. Promise 80 and Deliver 120 — 3-4
2. Are you a Cricket Addict? — 5-7
3. Knowing Yourself – Important for Progress — 8-14
4. Indian Armed Forces – A Great Career Option — 15-17
5. Reasons for Joining the Indian Armed Forces — 18-21
6. Sample of PIQ Form — 22-26
7. Wrong Perceptions held by Candidates/Parents — 27
8. Officer-like Qualities — 28-29
9. Do you have it in you? — 30-32
10. Shade Cards used by Assessors at SSB — 33-39

Section B: Achieving Success at SSB
1. Selection Techniques at SSB — 43-47
2. Screening Test — 48-78
3. Facing Interview — 79-112
4. Clearing Psychological Tests — 113-195
5. Cracking GTO Tasks/Tests — 196-296
6. Pilot Aptitude Battery Test (PABT) — 297-304
7. Conference Procedure — 305-310
8. Medical Examination Procedure of the Recommended Candidates — 311-316

Section C: Defence Awareness
1. India's Foreign Policy from Nehru to Modi — 319-323
2. Indo-China Relations (Past, Present and Future) — 324-337
3. Indo-Us Relations & India's Takeaways — 338-352

4.	Indian Ocean–Hub of Political & Economic Activities	353-359
5.	Digital India Project	360-361
6.	Smart Cities Mission and Amrut	362-365
7.	India Building Relationship: PM Modi's Visit Abroad	366-375
8.	ISIS–Terror Tentacles	376-379
9.	Nuclear Treaties & Disarmament	380-388
10.	Goods and Services Tax-GST	389-390
11.	Military Awards	391-394
12.	Defence Organisatin – Army/Navy/Air Force	395-407
13.	Types of Entry & Eligibility for Armed Forces	408-410
14.	Call up letter / Certificate	411-413
15.	SSB Preparation By Services Candidates: ACC/SL/SCO	414-416
16.	If you got rejected at the SSB then there is some thing Special about you.	417-420
17.	Why SSB selection is not perfect	421-426
18.	SSB Interview Training & Development	427-430

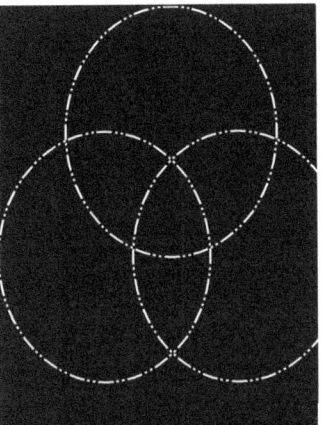

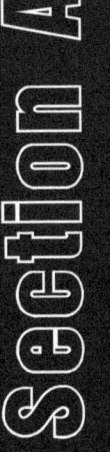

Section A

Introduction

Chapter 1: Promise 80 and Deliver 120
Chapter 2: Are you a Cricket Addict?
Chapter 3: Knowing Yourself – Important for Progress
Chapter 4: Indian Armed Forces – A Great Career Option
Chapter 5: Reasons for Joining the Indian Armed Forces
Chapter 6: Sample of PIQ form
Chapter 7: Wrong Perceptions held by Candidates / Parents
Chapter 8: Officer-like Qualities
Chapter 9: Do you have it in you?
Chapter 10: Shade Cards used by Assessors at SSB

1
Promise 80 and Deliver 120

The reasonable man adapts himself to the world: the unreasonable one persists in trying to adapt the world to himself. Therefore all progress depends on the unreasonable man."

– George Bernard Shaw

In this book, I have explained few aspects that go beyond the scope of SSB preparations. I have given glimpses of few challenges that a young person like you will face at some point in your life. Whether you clear the SSB or fail it, both the teams will have the same challenges ahead. Neither one is superior. The future is a leveller for everyone. If you understand a bit of this world, how it works and changes, you will take it as a wake-up call. There is no guarantee for anything. The world changes in an unimaginable way. Hollywood films of space expeditions are becoming a possibility.

Millions of people become unemployed because new technologies are taking over what initially required manpower. Artificial intelligence will rule the word and would become powerful than human and already they are.

Living in space will be a reality. The earth may not be able to sustain life. Water and food shortage already persists in many parts of the planet.

Present-day education system in our colleges and universities is obsolete; those graduates will have no jobs. The computers will have all the answers. Facebook and Google will answer your queries about mental health.

With Amazon, mega retailers around the world shut down. People prefer shopping online, thereby jeopardizing the job of a mall. Google has brought all the required information under one domain. In the future, the earth may be powered from space. Unmanned fighter planes could carry nuclear warheads. Solar powered drivers less transportation system will change the real estate market and many other domains of daily living. Robots will replace human. If you do not adapt to the changing world, you will be left out. You may know about how every sport works, or who the latest heartthrob in Hollywood is. But you will get nowhere in life if this knowledge is not directly helpful in the field you want to pursue. We have to understand the difference of seeing and observing, and only by observing can you learn. You will learn to see the world differently.

The qualities that the SSB is looking for are very simple and can be developed over time. Our closest cousins – chimpanzees and Bonobos – have them, Incidentally the DNA difference between human beings and them is only 1%. They communicate effectively with in the group and lead a social life. They co-operate well, raise children and protect one another from dangers. The leaders are well defined. Everything seems to be in control in their group. If these animal can have these qualities what is wrong with educated human? All these qualities can be developed to perfection. There is no limit how you can horn those skills. The bottom of these skills are yet to be found by people. "Conventional wisdom hold that some people are innately creative, while most have few original thoughts. Some people can have real impact but majority can't."

The word personality itself came in to existence during the 18th century. How much some body's personality can be developed nobody can predict. For a potential leader of 21st century can't afford to act like somebody from the 18th century. The concept of personality has already travelled so far and reached to the present level. Modern world is not very old. Even the common use of tooth brush and paste started only in the early 19th Century.

"Personal development is a process of developing more what you have as a latent potential with in". Reaching full potential consists of two different process.

"One the process of acquiring new characteristics and attitude such as patience, courage, determination self confidence and trust worthiness. The 2nd process is correcting old habits the wearing away of rough edges of your personality" Essentially personality development is a two way process.

If you have understood whatever I mentioned above clearing the SSB is not a problem for you. You will be a winner in the changing world any ways.

> "Pay attention to your thoughts because they become words
>
> Pay attention to your word because they become actions
>
> Pay attention to your actions because they become habits
>
> Pay attention to your habits, because they become your character.
>
> Pay attention to your character because it is your fate"
>
> – From the Talmud

2

Are you a Cricket Addict?

Easiest way to increase happiness and creating depth in knowledge is to control your time. Time is the key in your overall success. Where do you invest your time? Are you getting enough sleep? I want you to take a sheet of paper and write three lines about the following.

(a) India Cricket Captain
(b) Cable NEWS net work
(c) Your Favorite Hero
(d) Watson
(e) How many friends you have in facebook
(f) Ted talks
(g) Indian newspaper. How much time you spend on reading new paper
(h) Your favorite TV Channel
(i) Stephen Howking
(j) A1 stand for? Give two answers
(k) Future energy
(l) Future Jobs
(m) How many whatsapp groups you are in
(n) Your favorite pass time
(o) Latest movie you have seen
(p) Elon musk
(q) Latest Cricket match you seen live and who was the man of the match and write few lines about him.
(r) Your role model
(s) Where do you see yourself in five years
(t) Astrology an aid to deal with future

If you had diffculites in answering questions B.D.F.I.J.K.L,P,S then there in something drastically wrong. Also there is trouble if you have answered other Questions without any difficulties because they are already stored in your memory deeply and brain access them easily. Information about these question are easily available and brain keep getting reminders about them all the time. Let us take the example of Cricket. Cricket addiction is spreading the Indian Social Canvas like Cancer it takes away the precious time of millions of people in India, time is at scarcity for people. Cricketing rogues are the role model for millions of young people in India. Cricketing activities have exploded and continue to expand in every possible way.

Front pages of new paper covers Cricket news, over all Cricket is a dominating features, in the newspaper, TV channels, radio and in every social media billions are being pumped in to it. There are Cricket scientists who will predict every aspect before the matches and after it. Even one six hit or a catch dropped can be an agenda for Cricket gurus to speak endlessly. That doesn't stop there next day newspaper will carry the news in many forms and major discussion point among friends and colleagues. In college campus, work place, at home, restaurants, bars, clubs and everywhere including social media. This set the tone for the next match and people remain glued to the TV for hours together. Potato Chips are available for Company, if your role model is a Cricketer who with all kinds of tattoos and other religious concoctions all over his body behaves like a rowdy in the field or score a century you are in a bliss. Face book, Whatsapp and other social media connections will do the rest. The entire nation seems to have got infected by this disease. Appointing a Cricket coach can be projected as an event bigger than the election of American President.

Besides this, you need to watch your favorite film stars movie and get all details about their daily activities especially their dating details, then came the favorite serial that is full of suspense. It doesn't stop here what about the face book comments on the picture you have posted posing with your girlfriend/boyfriend? Your new car and other cosmetic possessions? The picture of that great place where you went and had dinner?

Also the responses of your comments and posts? You are on an emotional trap. Your friends have one thousand friends and you have only 900, so there is fire on, you have to beat the number. There is hell out there.

Then comes google GOD he will tell you what you like and keep showing you every time you hit the internet.

Have you ever realized that the biggest competitor for Google, Facebook, Cricket, Netflix, WhatsApp, YouTube, TV Serial, Cinema theatre etc. is your SLEEP. They want you to remain there where they want you to be. If you do not sleep better it is.

Reasonable entertainment I am not against it but you should not entertained to death.

I would like to make an honest confession. I have a reasonably big TV and I have not switched it on for the past two months. Newspaper I do not spend more than five to Ten minutes, I have not watched a Cricket match for the past 6 years. Is there something wrong with me? But I found time to write this book. Cricket is a virus it can affect anyone. Recently a news appeared in Times of India, projected as an event of extreme important that a young lady CEO called Poonam Gupta, a British entrepreneur purchased a painting of an Indian Cricketer for 2.9 million pounds. Cancer can hit Steve JobS also mental cancer has no cure and it can infect any one. Look at the newspaper what it was trying to convey to the public?

It is time to do advance thinking and advance planning Stephen Hawking, the most intelligent man on the planet says "start vocating the earth" if that be the case should we waste billions of dollar and many lives for a piece of land? Future of human beings on the earth is bleak and space will decide if they have any future at all. Option of living in Space /Other planets is a reality and the road map is already drawn. Such things no newspapers or TV/other medias will cover newspaper is full of Crickerters/ Film stars pictures, Astrology and other religious connected news which can offset social unity of the nation. Newspaper is another waste of time that channelizes human minds to a particular direction mostly negative.

3
Knowing Yourself – Important for Progress

"Our daily objectives should include an honest effort to improve on yesterday."
- Zig Ziglar

Getting to know yourself is a lifelong process. An individual needs to remove all of the multiple personalities (masks) that he puts on for different people and at different times. He needs to get down to the core of his essence and get rid of his own false self-images and delusions.

Identify Your True Self

To know one's self is to know one's true identity. Our personalities are made up of many facets that we pick up and reflect from our experiences. Sometimes they are strong and cover the real you. Still it is possible to know it to a greater extent by knowing yourself, your strengths, weaknesses, fears and so on.

How you manage your life, guide others, take charge, perform and behave in relationships really depends on how effectively you use your strengths and identify your weaknesses which you will discover when you truly know your "self".

Defence life has become complex. You need to work with people of different region, religion, language and culture. Therefore to understand others you need to understand yourself first. It is impossible to understand others unless a person has understood himself/herself.

You therefore need to discover and become your own true person, not what others perceive you to be; also not who you believe you must be, but the person that you truly are.

To summarize, knowing yourself is to know your true identity. So to know oneself is being true to oneself and living one's purpose.

THE POWER OF TRAINING

The key to human development is training and learning in a way that can change your thinking and your life. Majority of candidates undermine the power of learning and face the SSB interview without any preparations; this is the main reason why the average selection rate is below 10%. I have asked many candidates as to why they gave the SSB interview without proper training. The most common answer has been that they were told that the SSB is looking for originality. So if they prepare for the interview, they would lose that uniqueness. This has been the opinion of majority of assessors, GTOs, Psychologists & IOs.

For example, a new-born child has no knowledge; it is the continuous teaching and learning that formulate the qualities of that child. It is all about education, self-learning and training; they transform the individual into a better human being. It is not advisable to face the SSB interview, which is spread over a period of six days and involves various tests, without any preparations. What is the harm in practicing giving a good lecture to an audience of 10 to 14 individuals? What is the harm in learning how to effectively contribute in a group discussion? What is the harm in writing a report in a logical and systematic manner? What is the harm in preparing for any question that may be asked in an interview? The SSB is looking for the demonstrated performance. You do not perform, you get no result. It is definitely not a good idea to face the SSB without knowing what is lined up for you and how to excel in every test. Had I not trained that group of 18, the success of the 16 candidates would not have been possible. I can narrate thousands of such examples where training and learning helped candidates to pass with flying colours.

Why preparing for SSB Interview is easy and success is almost certain

It is the only selection procedure in the world where almost everything is explained to the candidate in advance. Isn't this like getting the question paper well in advance of the examination? Where can you get such a golden opportunity? Whenever I take classes I tell my students to follow what is being taught; this will not only help them to get selected but also put them among the top in the order of merit. The onus of following what is taught in the class lies with the student. If I teach you how to effectively take part in group planning exercises and at the SSB you do not contribute how can you be selected? It is the same when it comes to this book: whatever is mentioned here you need to understand it. If you put in adequate practice and do extensive homework, success is yours. You need to go deep into all the tests/tasks with 100% preparations and then face the tests at the SSB.

When conducting the training sessions, I sometimes designate candidates as assessors. They are asked to design questions for each test and then test the given group as an assessor. The catch here is: how well-prepared are you? It depends on the level of your preparation and the depth you have gone into. You have to go that extra mile. Extraordinary preparation will produce extraordinary result. There is a category of candidates who feel that they know everything, which is one of the laziest positions a modern man can be in. This world is changing fast, and if you do not keep up learning with the same pace of change you will be left out.

The content of this book is an one-window solution to your success at the SSB, provided you perform the post-mortem of each line and decode it in your brain.

The I-know-everything attitude comes mostly from the service candidates and people from military background families. The rejection rate at the SSB for this category is the highest. '*What I know*' is not important; '*what is it that I do not know*' is important. The concentration should be on the depth of my knowledge and all that I do not know.

In fact, as per my opinion, it is very easy for an average person to clear the SSB tests. The reason being, all the tests are given to them in advance. These are simple tests and, if practiced to perfection, can deliver a sterling performance at the SSB. I program my candidates not to just clear the SSB but to aim for the top slot in the order of merit. It is a realistic and achievable goal. I am absolutely convinced that it is possible. My experience has not only turned the dreams of thousands of students into reality but also trained numerous, qualified officers to become expert trainers. Today many of them are running successful SSB coaching centers in various parts of the country.

There is no shortcut to learning; perseverance is the only way to thrive and move forward.

When I interact with unsuccessful candidates, a majority of them expressed their frustration saying that they were capable of giving better answers and perform better. "I could have done better." Nothing can be more frustrating than this. But why does this happen? Did the candidate not prepare and went to face the SSB interview without a game plan?

Importance of Knowing Yourself

If you know yourself, you will be able to know your strengths and weakness. Subsequently, you will be able to conquer your weakness. You must know yourself in order to be useful to yourself and others.

1. **Helps to control emotions:** Everything you do is based on your emotions and, often, emotions lead to miscalculations. Knowing yourself helps you to take control of your emotions and helps in decisions.
2. **Helps to reach your goal:** Knowing yourself is a very important task that you have to undertake and the most challenging as well. When you know who you are, and clearly understand what you want, you have a better chance of reaching your goal, personal fulfillment and happiness.
3. **Helps to reach better decisions:** Knowing yourself is important because it will help you to make better decisions and be a better person. The more aware you are of your faults, the less detached you will feel. You will also feel more at ease with yourself and try to improve those things that you want to and let go of the things that you don't.
4. **Helps to improve relationship:** Knowing your true and inner self will be of great help when working to reach your goals. It will guide you along the path to success and take you to such calmness that it will improve your attitude as well as your relationships with others.
5. **Helps to realize and improve your full potential:** Knowing yourself will enable you to develop your full potential and be happy, contented and fulfilled. Knowing yourself ensures success in business, friendship, love, sports, or altogether.
6. **Helps to experience happiness and joy:** Knowing yourself enables you to discover and attain your goals and then when you reach your goals you turn out to be a happy person. This not only fills you with more happiness, but also improves your mindset. And that is happiness in its truest sense.

SWOT Analysis

A SWOT analysis – acronym for Strength, Weakness, Opportunity and Threat – is an effective mind-tool, helping with self-awareness of strengths and weakness, in relation to the external environment. It is important to identify them in relation to your classmates/colleagues. For example, you may be good in communication skills, but if you are pursuing a marketing career, then it's not strength, but a necessity. In the same way, if you have high energy levels, it is strength in most careers, but not in defence careers, where it becomes a requirement. The analysis of opportunities and threats enables you to take advantage of your strengths and minimize the threats arising out of your weaknesses.

As a student, you may have many fears about taking decisions regarding a new course or a career. Most fears cannot withstand the test of careful scrutiny and analysis. When we expose our fears to thoughtful examination, they usually just evaporate. Thus, SWOT analysis eliminates fears and apprehensions, boosts your confidence level, which is crucial to implement your plans. That is, your arm to form a defence career.

SWOT analysis is a critical thinking process, which can be applied to any situation or issue, and therefore, an analytical tool in problem solving and decision-making. It's also an enlightening process of self-discovery, which empowers your mind to consider viable alternatives and take the right decisions about academics, career or personal life.

USING SWOT ANALYSIS: When using SWOT analysis, be realistic about your strengths and weaknesses. Distinguish between where you are today, and where you would like to be a few years down the line. Be specific by avoiding grey areas and always analyze in relation to the actual situation. Finally, keep your SWOT analysis short and simple, and avoid complexity and over-analysis. Use it as a guide and not a prescription.

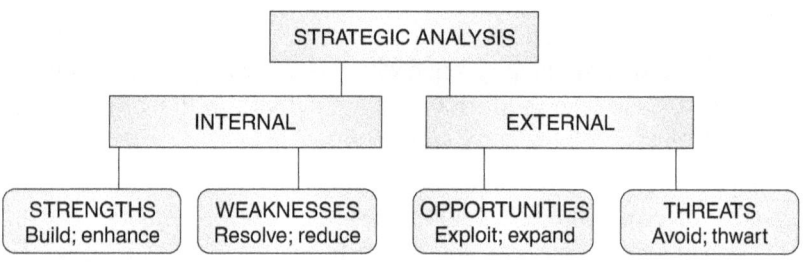

ANALYSIS-FITNESS FOR DEFENCE FORCES CAREER

STRENGTHS – Build, Enhance
1. Effective writing/Speaking skill in English
2. Pleasing personality
3. Values in life (ethics, integrity, sincerity)
4. Self-motivation and initiating
5. Leadership qualities
6. Team spirit
7. Projecting positive style
8. English vocabulary
9. Working under stress and complexity
10. Logical and systematic in approach

OPPORTUNITIES – Exploit, Expand
1. Academic opportunity
2. Career opportunity
3. Any mentor to guide you
4. Networking and facilities available
5. What strength helps to achieve the opportunity?

WEAKNESSES – Reduce, Overcome
1. Low fluency in English
2. Getting confused and taking time to recollect
3. Being disorganized
4. Hesitant, tending to remain behind
5. Avoidance
6. Lazy and taking time
7. Stressful and nervous
8. Low self-esteem/confidence
9. Inadequate defence knowledge
10. Inadequate CA and GK

THREATS – Avoid, Thwart
1. Obstacles in your way of plan
2. Competition from others
3. Over-supply
4. Clash with other exams
5. What threat can arise out of your weakness?

PREPARATIONS TO GO BEYOND THIS BOOK

If you think the Services Selection Board Interview result is a herculean task for you, then do not proceed to the SSB. You should face the board with an I-am-a-worthy-candidate-and-I-am-here-in-front-of-you attitude. I do not mean to say that you have to be arrogant, but only that you have to prepare very well. I am talking about your individual brand and net worth. First, the outside needs to be sorted out. The way a person presents himself will speak volumes about his nature; it will never be the other way around. It won't take more than 30 seconds for the interviewer to judge you. So clean up and dress well. This will go a long way in branding yourself, which is a key component for a positive recommendation in the SSB.

Now coming to the software: install the right kind of software inside. This includes increasing the depth of knowledge, avoiding low-level inputs, feeding only high level inputs and having your role model. Why not have, as your role model, the most powerful man on the earth? Does he spend time watching TV serials? You have to build your brand value like Apple Inc. does with their products. You have a choice today; be extremely careful while making them; they will control you and your life. There are thousands of channels on TV; which one you prefer?

One click of a mouse and the Internet can open everything. What would you like to watch? Do you have a personal goal in life? Are you accountable for each day of your life? Have you created depth in anything in your life?

You should not move into the future blindly; create your future and walk into it – that is what I did when I created the iconic SSB network in the country.

Be a powerhouse of knowledge and a self-motivator. Be accountable to every day of your life and add value to your own brand every day. You will be a winner forever. No SSB can stop you from succeeding.

Coaching is soft-skills training for personality development, enhancing group dynamics, interpersonal relationships, team morale and performance, motivation, responsibility, contribution and productivity. It includes team building, consensus building, understanding, implementing group values and the visioning of future goals.

Evidence-based Approach

In this book I have narrated my experience, which is based on evidence. The methods and tools I have used in teaching thousands of students during the last two decades are the evidence to state that, if one follows what is written in this book, success at the SSB is guaranteed.

4

Indian Armed Forces – A Great Career Option

The Indian Armed Forces have a reputation of being one of the finest in the world and offers a very challenging and attractive career for Indian youth, both men and women. The Indian armed forces, after induction, imparts required training to ensure that the individual becomes fully capable of handling difficult and complex situations that arise in operational and administrative spheres.

SERVICES ENVIRONMENT

(u) The armed forces offers a very healthy work culture and a challenging and result-oriented environment. It is best suited for an honest and upright person to serve the nation.

(v) A person becomes a true nationalist and stops distinguishing individuals based on religion, caste and regional basis. It is the only career which demands and teaches supreme sacrifice for the country.

(w) Armed forces is a major setup, which provides reasonably good and fast career growth. Career growth in armed forces depends on performance and skill. Certain courses entitle you to additional pay and allowances.

(x) Life in armed forces is regimented and it takes priority over normal life and builds up *esprit-de-corps*.

Nature of Work

- Indian Armed Forces render invaluable service to the nation, both in times of war and peace. Though the primary task is defending our nation against external aggression, many times it is called to restore internal strife and help in natural calamities.
- Nature of work in armed forces is diverse and also demands serving in most difficult terrain and weather conditions throughout the country, hence there is a need for constant physical fitness of highest order.

Work Demands

- Service in armed forces demands a spirit of adventure as well as unflinching loyalty and integrity for nation and readiness to lay down one's life for the nation when required. Work involves defending territorial, coastal and air space integrity of our country against all external and internal threats. It also involves man management of highest order, continuous development of leadership qualities and on the job training to achieve required perfection for these jobs.

Job Description

- Service in the armed forces requires training for war and peace time in trying conditions and sacrifice and bravery of highest order to save the pride and integrity of the nation at the time of war. A brief description of works of all three branches of the Armed Forces is as follows:-

    (a) **THE INDIAN ARMY:** The Indian Army is responsible for defending the territorial integrity of the country against all external aggression and internal disturbances. During war the army is responsible for protecting the nation against external aggression, whereas, during peace time also it provides aid to the civil authorities during natural calamities, and helps in maintenance of law and order when required. The Indian Army is mainly divided into combat arms and services. The combat arms are the infantry, the artillery, and the armoured corps, the corps of engineers and corps of signals. Whereas, services include army service corps, army ordnance corps, army postal services, army medical corps, army education corps, intelligence corps and so on. The latter provides logistics support to the fighting arms. Combat arms are responsible for actual combat, whereas, services ensure continuous flow of required ordnance including food and clothing for men, varied vehicles, tanks, arms and ammunition.

    (b) **THE INDIAN NAVY:** The Indian Navy is responsible for defending the extensive coastline of the country in times of war and peace. The navy is also responsible for safeguarding our maritime interests including defence of off-shore oil and gas installations, coastal shipping and fisheries rights, and to protect the vital trade links. The navy has three main branches:

    (i) The **Executive Branch** which manages the navy's warships and submarines as instruments of tactical warfare.

    (ii) The **Engineering Branch** which is responsible for the maintenance and service of engineering equipment, the propulsion systems on board the ships including electrical and electronic systems, weapon systems, missiles, radar and radio communication systems.

    (iii) The **Education Branch** ensures that the officers and men are updated in their technical knowledge and tactics.

(c) **THE INDIAN AIR FORCE:** The Indian Air Force is responsible for the air defence of the country, ensuring both offensive and defensive roles. It is a responsible for the air defence of vital installation of strategic importance to the country. The air force has three main branches:

   (i) **Flying Branch:** The flying branch includes fighter pilots who fly combat or fighter planes carrying ammunition and missiles; transport pilots who fly planes which carry men and materials, and helicopter pilots who provide air support to a moving army, or are used for para-dropping men and supplies.

   (ii) **Technical Branch:** The technical branch gives engineering support and is responsible for the engineering equipment and weapons systems of the air force.

   (iii) **GDO Branch:** The GDO branch includes all the departments that provide logistical, meteorological, educational and administrative support to the flying and technical branches.

5
Reasons for Joining the Indian Armed Forces

A Noble Profession: A career with the Indian armed forces is a noble and secular profession and provides opportunity for direct service to the nation. It is a challenging and thrilling career, gazetted and non-political in nature. One joins an institution having camaraderie.

Early Career with Growth: If you are a studious person, this is the place for you to be. By the time you retire in the normal course of your career, you end up doing masters (M.Sc) degree, M.Phil, MBA and PhD (Optional). No company in the world gives so much paid leave and pays its employee to pursue this quantum of studies.

Technical Officers have the opportunity to pursue M.Tech from IIT Delhi, Chennai or Mumbai in the course of their career in the seats which are reserved for armed forces.

Job Security: Nowadays in India, private companies do not offer as much job security as they did to our parents and grandparents. In an economy where nothing is certain, having a government job is the best because we will never be asked to leave from a government job. Best of all, there are no pay cuts but only increments throughout our life. Whether the economy or rupee falls, no one will be sent home jobless from a government job.

Foreign Assignments: The MNCs send their employees to foreign destinations for temporary assignments that last only a few months long. Whereas in the armed forces officers are sent with diplomatic visas to foreign countries as defence attaches in the embassy and also on peace-keeping posting.

The officers even pursue Masters in reputed defence colleges. Every year, the navy sends a handful of officers to the Royal War College, London or the US Marine Staff College, etc. The kind of facilities and luxury these officers receive in those countries are unmatched.

Respect Wherever You Go: You might wonder why I have included this point here, because in the present world not many people care a lot about it. But actually speaking the respect you will command from your soldiers, subordinates, the society and even your family is something you will never be able to get in any profession. Most of the time you will (even if you don't wish to) end up being a role model to your children.

Style/Charisma and Camaraderie: Not many people understand the style and charisma that sticks with the men in uniform. Believe me, there is nothing more appealing than a smart officer turning up in a crisp uniform. You can never buy that outfit outside. Like the Bourneville ad, you have to earn it to understand it. The pride which comes along with wearing the uniform is out of this world and you must experience it to understand it.

High Priority to Physical Fitness: Today no one thinks along these lines before joining a company – whether the job will allow him to stay fit, play a sport, do some physical exercises or indulge for some fun time in physical activity/adventure activity. But a job in the armed forces is all about what is mentioned above. Your physical fitness is paramount. You can assure yourself a healthier lifestyle in this place.

Comparable Pay and Allowances: If you are a freshly passed out and commissioned officer in the armed forces you will make about Rs. 42,000 per month, and which is likely to be more after seventh pay commission. Additionally the allowances that you will get are flying pay, high altitude allowance, sailing allowance, island allowance, pilotage allowance, diving allowance, submarine allowance, commando allowance, etc. Allowances vary between Rs. 6,000 to Rs. 16,000 plus DA every month.

Facilities for You and Your Family: The facilities include free education for children, free medical facilities for dependents, canteen facilities, car for senior officers, loan facilities, excellent accommodation wherever you are posted, free air tickets for you and your family anywhere in India once in a year. Recreational facilities like swimming pool, tennis court, squash courts, golf courses, etc.; provision for ration supply and life-time pension and medical benefits are part of the compensation.

Memberships to prestigious clubs, gyms and golf courses are so cheap that they are as good as free.

Post-Retirement Options: On retirement, apart from the handsome amount that you will receive, you will get a pension throughout your life. Today an officer with 22 years of service after retirement will get a pension of approx. Rs. 50,000 per month. Post retirement, officers of the armed forces are the most sought-after for leadership roles in big companies because of their experience and knowledge base. The armed forces nurtures each officer into a leader which becomes his second nature. Hence a second innings post-retirement is very probable and equally attractive.

REASONS FOR SERVICE CANDIDATES TO BECOME OFFICERS

The service candidates of Army, Navy & IAF may find the following statements more suitable when replying to interviewing officer on the question of why they want to become a commissioned officer in armed forces:

1. Provides continuous higher platform for serving nation directly
2. Scope for growth in life
3. Great responsibilities and decision making vested and one can exercise freely
4. Effective utilization of one's defence experience and expertise gained in service
5. Better understanding of PBOR (Personnel below Officer rank) and uncovering their potentials
6. More respect and status in society being a gazetted officer
7. Style and charisma attached to a commissioned officer will always be there
8. Enhances post-retirement benefits including re-employment opportunities.

9. Higher education possibilities
10. There is an average of five people with whom you spend your maximum time with, so when you join the office cadre it makes a big difference in your personal growth

6

Sample of PIQ Form

PERSONAL INFORMATION QUESTIONNAIRE

OIR..........................

1. Selection Board　　Batch No.　　　Chest No.　　　UPSC Roll No.
   (No. and Place)

2. Name in CAPITALS (As in the Application form) ....

3. Father's Name ....

4. (A) Place of maximum residence ....
   (B) Present Address (with approximate population
       of the city/town/village ....

5. Fill in the details below:

State & District	Religion	Whether SC/ST	Mother Tongue	Date of Birth	Married/Single/Widower

6. (A) Parents alive　　　　　　　　　　　　　Yes/No
   (B) If not alive, your age at the time of father's/mother's death.....................
   (C) Parents Occupation/Income (as applicable)

Particulars	Education	Occupation	Income per month
Father			
Mother			
Guardian			

7. Education Record (Commencing from Matriculation/Equivalent Examination)

Sl. No.	Qualification Acquired	Name of the Institution	Year	Division & Marks %	Medium of Instruction	Boarder/ Day Scholar	Outstanding Achievement if any
A.	Matric / Hr Sec						
B.	10+2 equivalent						
C.	B.A / B.Sc / B.Com Others						
D.	Professional						

8. Age (Years/Months) .... Height (in mtrs) .... Weight (in kilogram) ....

9. Present Occupation and personal monthly income, if any

10. (a) N.C.C. Training Yes/No

    (b) Total (yrs). (If yes, give details below)

Total Training	Wing	Division	Certification obtained

11. (a) Participation in games & sports:-

Games/Sports	Period or duration of Participation	Represented School/ College University	Outstanding achievement if any

(b) Hobbies/Interest ....

(c) Participation in extracurricular activities:

Name of the activity group   **Duration of participation**   **Outstanding achievement if any**

(d) Position of responsibility/Offices held in NCC/Scouting:

Sports team/Extracurricular group & other fields _____

12. (a) Nature of Commission:

(b) Choice of Service:

13. Number of chances availed for commission in all three Services:

14. Details of last interview, if any by (Air/Navy/Army Selection Boards)

Type of Entry	Place and SSB No.	Date	Batch and Chest No	Recommended/Not Recommended

PERSONAL INFORMATION QUESTIONNAIRE

1. Selection Board No... City..

2. UPSC Roll Number..

3. Entry .... 4. Batch No. .... 5. Chest No. ....

6. Choice of service..

PERSONAL & FAMILY

1. Selection Board No... City..

2. UPSC Roll Number..

3. Entry..................... 4. Batch No......................... 5. Chest No.........................

6. Choice of service..

7. Name (in block letters) as in the application form...

8. Date of birth day.................................. month...................... year........................

Sample of PIQ Form 25

9. Age years.........................months............................ 10. Gender Male/Female
11. Height............................. cms 12. Weight............................. kgs
13. Marital Status Married/Single/Widower
14. Religion (Hinduism/Christianity/Islam/Sikhism/Others)............................
15. Mother Tongue.. 16. Community General/OBC/SC/ST
17. Place of maximum residence (with State)..
18. Present address (including state) with approximate population (in lacs) of city/town/village
   ....
   ....
   .... (Population in lacs) ....
19. Permanent address (including state)
   ....
   ....
   .... (Population in lacs) ....
20. Particulars of parents/guardian/brothers/sisters

Relations	Name	Age (yrs)	Education	Occupation	Income per Month

21. Parents alive? Yes/No   If parents not alive your age at the time of their death..................years
22. Candidate's present occupation Govt./Private/Self employed Income per month Rs.. Designation/appointment............................
   Department/Firm..
23. **EDUCATIONAL QUALIFICATION (COMMENCING FROM MATRICULATION/ EQUIVALENT EXAMINATION) Matric/Higher Secondary**
   Name of the Institution (In full, no abbreviations)..
   ....
   Location of Institution (City/Town/Village)   Name of the Board..........................
   CBSE/ICSE/State Board/Others...........................

Type of Institution Govt/Private   Medium of Instruction English/Hindi/regional..............
Year of passing............... Overall percentage of marks obtained................ Division............
day scholar/boarder

Subject	Theory			Practicals / Assignments			Total			Outstanding achievements (if any)
	Max marks	Max obtained	%	Max marks	Max obtained	%	Max marks	Max obtained	%	

24. Senior Secondary/10+2/Equivalent

Name of the Institution (In full, no abbreviations)...
....

Location of Institution (City/Town/Village)   Name of the Board ....
CBSE/ICSE/State Board/Others...

Type of Institution Govt/Private Medium of Instruction English/Hindi/Regional...................

Year of passing......... Overall percentage of marks obtained............ Division.................
day scholar/boarder

Subject	Theory			Practicals / Assignments			Total			Outstanding achievements (if any)
	Max marks	Max obtained	%	Max marks	Max obtained	%	Max marks	Max obtained	%	

7

Wrong Perceptions Held by Candidates/Parents

Candidates should NOT have or hold some common wrong perceptions, on the selection system which is generally prevalent. Some of these wrong perceptions or myths held are given below.

WRONG PERCEPTIONS

- Bribe matters and people involved in selection need to be approached.
- Repeater candidates have some disadvantage at SSB.
- Recommended candidates will always clear SSB.
- Revealing if one has undergone training/coaching puts candidates to disadvantage.
- Candidates of defence personnel have advantage over that of civilians in selection.
- Candidates from rural background have disadvantage.
- Performance at conference matters.
- There is something called original quality.
- Leadership qualities can't be acquired.
- Qualities are fixed from birth and cannot be changed.

8

Officer-like Qualities

The SSB looks for certain Officer-like Qualities (OLQs). These qualities, fifteen in all, are grouped under various factors; each factor is enumerated in the succeeding pages. You may not have all these qualities in matured forms; however, as long as you exhibit the grains of these qualities while attending each technique you are likely to be selected and then sent to an academy where these qualities are further polished and strengthened. Eventually, you are commissioned as an officer.

You have to be extremely aware that you need to demonstrate these qualities during each test – in written, verbal and in physical action. You might have come across an advertisement released by the Indian Army with the tagline *Do you have it in you*? These fifteen qualities – do you have them? If you don't have these qualities this book will help develop them and clear the SSB. Keep these qualities with you all your life and keep improving them – the biggest personal asset that you will ever possess. You will be a leader for life, no matter which domain you get into. In this regard the mind, heart, limbs & body are central to these 15 OLQs that are explained in succeeding pages.

You might have won the national competition in drawing and painting. These got you a national award also; when you report at the SSB you consciously or unconsciously demonstrate your artistic qualities in excess and fail to demonstrate these fifteen qualities even though you might have them. The end result is that in spite of being a national award winner in the field of art you get rejected at the SSB.

Therefore, it is very crucial for you to understand these qualities and design your own game plan to demonstrate them at the SSB. You can have a road map created to suit your capabilities and a personalized method to show to the assessors. This method what you may devise may be a very personalized one and the same may not be applicable to other candidates.

There is no point in asking a candidate what question the Interviewing Officer had asked him. This happens very often at the SSB. Candidates waiting to go for the interview take inputs from the candidate who has already given it. What question the IO has asked and what answer the candidate gave has no relevance to the person who is next.

The Officer-like Qualities (OLQs) are shown below.

Planning and organization
1. Effective Intelligence
2. Reasoning Ability — HEAD
3. Organizing Ability
4. Power of Expression

Social adjustment
1. Social Adaptability
2. Co-operation
3. Sense of Responsibility — HEART

Social effectiveness
1. Initiative
2. Self-confidence
3. Speed of Decision
4. Ability to influence the group — BODY
5. Liveliness

Dynamic
1. Determination
2. Courage
3. Stamina — LIMBS

9

Do you have it in you?

"You must begin to think of yourself as becoming the person you want to be."
—David Viscott

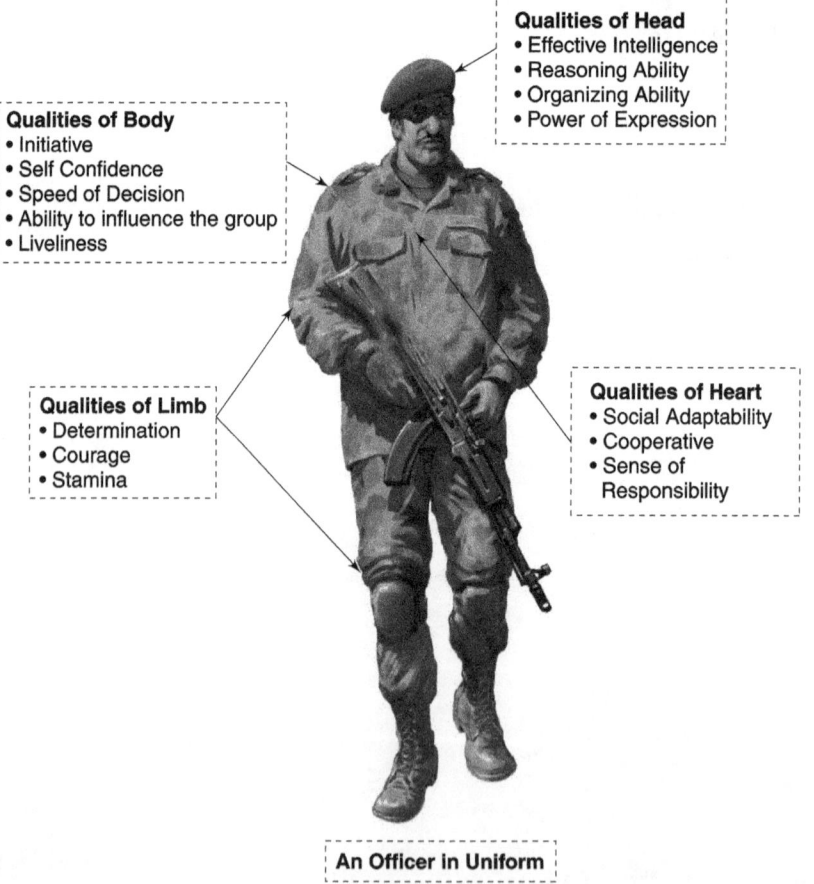

An Officer in Uniform

From trainability point of view, these 15 OLQs may be classified as deep-rooted qualities, trainable qualities and less trainable qualities.

1. DEEP-ROOTED QUALITIES
1. Effective intelligence
2. Reasoning ability
3. Co-operation
4. Sense of responsibility
5. Stamina (half) – mental stamina

2. TRAINABLE QUALITIES
1. Organizing ability
2. Power of expression
3. Initiative
4. Self-confidence
5. Ability to influence a group
6. Stamina (half) – physical stamina

3. LESS TRAINABLE QUALITIES
1. Courage
2. Liveliness
3. Social

The SSB has the above viewpoint that certain qualities are less trainable; however I am a firm believer in power of training. Today we are living in a world where DNA is being modified and I am absolutely convinced that all these qualities can be trained to perfection and can form part of life assets. The first step in solving any problem is recognizing that there is a problem. Building of your individual branding has to be a constant effort. You need to be aware of all the good, bad and ugly of your personality traits.

Life improvement has two major aspects: the first is adding new values to your life that you do not possess, and the other is improving upon those negative aspects of your life which are constantly pulling you down in spite of your best effort in other departments – a two-way approach to success. I do not want to categorize this book as a tool only for only clearing the SSB. But I suggest that this book be used as a life-improvement guide. In fact, you should read this book at least once again after getting into a career path as a commissioned officer or any other.

MARKS AND RECOMMENDATIONS

1. Total Marks:
    - (a) IO   - 225
    - (b) GTO   - 225
    - (c) Psychologist - 225

2. Candidates who score 90 marks (40% at least) or more in each technique are recommended candidate in that technique (IO/Psy/GTO).
3. **Overall Present Rating:** Each assessor after assessing the candidate on the basis of his performance has to give the grading which is known as Overall Present Rating but this rating is not the final one.
4. **Overall Predictive Rating as an Officer:** Whether the training would help the candidate to improve further, if he gets recommended and goes for training or whether the individual would take the benefit to improve or not. Is he trainable? This trainability depends on the following factors and that much additional weightage is given to that candidate. Trainability marks given by each assessor are generally higher for technical entry (NDA & TES) and are lower for direct entry (IMA/OTA/AFCAT) and least for service candidates of Army, Navy & IAF.
5. A person who is comparatively young and has longer training period at the academy, for example, NDA entry candidate has higher trainability as compared to a 24-year-old technical graduate with one year pre-commissioned training period.

10

Shade Cards used by Assessors at SSB

HOW ASSESSORS MEASURE OLQS

- On completion of every task/technique the assessing officer forms an impression about the candidate in terms of various officer-like qualities.
- Every individual has his/her own and unique personality. Therefore, it should be appreciated that personality needs to be described individually and no generalization made.
- At present, assessors at SSB follow a ten-point rating scale. Therefore, a number of attempts have been made to give a shade card with ten point scale as reference. An example of the shade card currently used by assessors is given below for understanding the various OLQs that are assessed.

FACTOR-I PLANNING AND ORGANIZING

Effective Intelligence

i. Is able to effectively handle complex problems. Is quick in improvisation. An impasse-breaker.
ii. Effectively handles even difficult situations. Is quick in improvisation.
iii. Can convincingly handle situations of moderate difficulties. Is able to improvise and put to use available resources.
iv. Is able to effectively handle simple and familiar situations, shows tendency to improvise.
v. Is able to handle simple and familiar situations. Can tackle simple problems.
vi. Is able to handle simple and familiar situations, but gets stuck when faced with problems.
vii. Tries to handle most of the familiar and simple situations. Gets puzzled with problems.
viii. Shows some ability to handle simple and familiar situations. Is unable to face problems.
ix. Is shaky when faced with simple situations.
x. Is unable to handle even simple and familiar situations. A non-starter.

Reasoning Ability

i. Is extremely quick in grasping. Has wise understanding and is able to analyse systematically and arrive at conclusions.
ii. Is quick in grasping. Has a methodical approach and is logical in reasoning.
iii. Is quick in grasping. Has a discerning mind. Is quite logical in his analysis and approach.
iv. Is fairly quick in understanding the complexities of a situation. Tries to reason out the solutions, logically understands and can arrive at conclusions for simple situations.
v. Can differentiate between essentials and non-essentials. Tries to reason out before arriving at a solution.
vi. Understands and can arrive at conclusions for simple situations. Strives to distinguish between essentials and non-essentials.
vii. Makes effort to analyse a situation and tries to understand the priorities.
viii. Gets mixed up in allotment of priorities, unable to reason out the situations.
ix. Gets carried away by trivialities. Jumps to conclusion without understanding.
x. Fails to understand even simple situations. Gets easily emotional and confused.

Organizing Ability

i. A systematic planner with forethought and fertile ideas. Makes precise use of the resources. Is prepared to meet any eventuality.
ii. Is systematic. Uses his resources correctly. Maintains proper perspective. Is an effective planner and organizer. A good planner and organizer who makes judicious use of resources.
iii. Plans and organizes fairly effectively. Is capable of handling problems.
iv. Plans and organizes resources in simple situations. Makes effort to handle problems. Has limited foresight. Can plan and organize simple tasks. Gets stuck when faced with a problem.
v. Shows some sense of planning in familiar situations only. Uses trial-and-error method.
vi. Is haphazard. Fritters resources, shows disproportionate sense of perspective. Cannot visualize priorities. Easily perplexed when required to organize even familiar situations. Cannot make use of available resources. Totally puzzled and confused. Unable to get along with the job.

Power of Expression

i. Has lucid, fluent and precise expression. Can engage attention and leaves impact on others.

ii. Expresses himself with ease and clarity. Makes himself easily understood. Creates impact on the listeners.
iii. Expresses himself fluently and makes himself understood.
iv. Conveys his ideas reasonably well.
v. Conveys his ideas and makes himself understood.
vi. Manages to put across his ideas.
vii. Speaks hesitatingly. Is sketchy.
viii. Verbose, lacks substance. Others find it difficult to understand him.
ix. Has strained expression. Finds it difficult to arrange words while putting them across.

FACTOR-II SOCIAL ADJUSTMENT

Social Adaptability

i. Extremely considerate. Displays compassion. Puts others at ease; maintains harmonious and warm relations.
ii. Likeable. Has warmth in relationship with others. Possesses mature understanding of others' feelings.
iii. A ready mixer who is at ease with others.
iv. Mixes easily with others. Is considerate.
v. Generally gets along with others without any difficulty.
vi. Maintains working relations with others, has limited spontaneity and warmth.
vii. Is choosy and sometimes unconcerned about others.
viii. Is ill-at-ease in the company of others, is generally a passive spectator.
ix. Is temperamental, withdrawn, self-centered.
x. Aloof, selfish, quarrelsome.

Co-operation

i. Does not mind going out of his way to help others.
ii. Volunteers help in all situations.
iii. Volunteers help in most situations.
iv. Willingly co-operates.
v. Lends a helping hand.
vi. Co-operates as and when required or asked for.
vii. Co-operates occasionally, preferring his interest rather than group objective.
viii. Un-cooperative. Is neither concerned nor bothered about group objective.

ix. Is a hindrance to others. Puts obstructions in attainment of group goals.
x. Proven dissident. Disrupts group activities, will himself not work and won't let others either.

Sense of Responsibility

i. Willingly shoulders his responsibilities even beyond the call of duty. Extremely conscientious.
ii. Seeks responsible roles willingly. Performs assigned tasks with dedication and zeal.
iii. Happily comes forward to accept responsible roles. Is conscientious.
iv. Dutiful. Keen in accepting responsible roles.
v. Performs the assigned task diligently. Likes to shoulder responsibilities.
vi. Performs assigned tasks.
vii. Has limited awareness of his duties and obligations.
viii. Grudgingly undertakes the assigned task. Hesitates to take responsibility.
ix. Casual in performing his duties. Shirks responsibilities.
x. Refuses to shoulder any responsibility. Reluctant to perform even assigned tasks.

FACTOR-III SOCIAL EFFECTIVENESS

Initiative

i. Self-starter. Can handle unforeseen situations and events effectively with ease and resourcefulness.
ii. Quick in taking effective action in practically every situation. Improviser.
iii. Takes necessary and appropriate action in diverse situations.
iv. Takes necessary action on his own in a new situation.
v. Generally takes necessary action on his own. Requires guidance sparingly.
vi. Generally takes necessary action on his own, and often gets stuck up.
vii. Awaits instructions to start. Fumbles to make a headway.
viii. Talks boastfully but hesitates in initiating any action.
ix. Avoids taking action even in known situations.
x. Does not act without guidance even in simple situations; gets stuck up and seeks help at every step.

Self-confidence

i. Has full faith in his own abilities to handle situations which are even unfamiliar and stressful.

ii. Is usually self-reliant under normal and stressful situations.
iii. Is at ease while handling a variety of situations. Retains composure under stress.
iv. Capable of handling various situations including those which are stressful.
v. Handles day to day situations appropriately but gets a bit shaky under stress.
vi. Tries to handle familiar situations. Feels diffident when faced with difficulties.
vii. Likes to meet simple and familiar situations only. Gets upset when faced with even minor difficulties. Looks for support/guidance/encouragement.
viii. Shows off, brags in order to cover up his inadequacies; breaks down under stress.
ix. Shaky, has doubts about his own ability, is pessimistic.
x. Is unable to stand on his own, even in a simple situation.

Speed of Decision

i. Is quick in taking decision correctly.
ii. Is able to arrive at a correct decision expeditiously.
iii. Is quick in deciding; the decisions are generally correct.
iv. Is able to arrive at reasonably correct decisions without undue delay.
v. Deliberates and arrives at a workable solution.
vi. Takes a workable decision but at times has wavering after-thoughts.
vii. Decisions taken by him are generally workable, but arrived at after delay and deliberation.
viii. Hasty in taking decisions; tends to overlook its correctness.
ix. Ponders unduly over to-do or not-to-do without arriving at any decision.
x. Painfully slow and vague. Unable to decide what to do in a given situation.

Ability to Influence the Group

i. Has a charismatic bearing; others willingly rally around him.
ii. Is a go-getter with willing support from others.
iii. Persuades others by his personal example and understanding of others feelings and capabilities.
iv. Is able to persuade others by his pleasant manners and sound arguments.
v. Capable of persuading others for achievement of a group task.
vi. Tries to persuade others and is generally partly successful.
vii. Has ideas but is too mild to put them across and persuade others.

viii. Impresses initially but bursts like a bubble, resorts to shouting, turns aggressive, runs down others.
ix. Has some ideas but is too rigid and quarrelsome.
x. No one listens to him in a group.

Liveliness

i. Bubbling with life, exudes enthusiasm and cheer, undeterred by difficulties.
ii. Keeps his cool even under adverse conditions, is optimistic.
iii. Enthusiastic, takes things in his stride. Is cheerful.
iv. Has a zest for living. Is not easily perturbed under adverse conditions.
v. Is cheerful under normal conditions. Generally retains composure under stress.
vi. Is generally cheerful under normal conditions. Gets slightly serious under stress.
vii. Loses his cheer quickly when faced with minor difficulties.
viii. Indulges in buffoonery. Poses to be optimistic, treating even serious things lightly.
ix. Loses his heart easily. Gives up hope at the slightest pretext.
x. Sees doom everywhere. Pessimistic, morose.

Determination

i. Persists in achieving his goal in spite of all odds.
ii. Tenacious, persistent in his approach.
iii. Strives hard to achieve his goal. Does not give up easily.
iv. Is consistent in putting a sustained effort to achieve his goal.
v. Makes some attempt, but is unable to sustain.
vi. Inconsistent and haphazard in putting efforts. Gets easily disturbed.
vii. Gives up easily when faced with difficult situations. Takes the path of least resistance.
viii. Gives up without putting any efforts.

Courage

i. Undaunted by hazards. Appreciates situations and willingly takes risks.
ii. Appreciates difficult situations. Strives to meet them even at the cost of physical inconvenience and even if chances of success are low.
iii. Understands the pros and cons of a difficult situation.
iv. Appreciates the gravity of a situation. Takes risks in situations where chances are even.

v. Willingly takes risk in familiar situations. Likes to take chance when success is in sight.
vi. Tries to take risk in familiar situations only.
vii. Generally tries to avoid and wriggle out of situations involving risks.
viii. Unable to face risky situations. Resorts to bragging, indulges in bravado.
ix. Timid. Keeps away from situations involving risk.
x. Foolhardy. Jumps into a situation without understanding.

Stamina

i. Is a reservoir of energy. Puts in sustained hard work without impairing the quality. Knows the art of relaxing.
ii. Puts in sustained hard work under diverse situations. Tough, will not rest till he achieves the goal.
iii. Has capacity to work under sustained pressure, is able to put in required effort.
iv. Puts in goal-oriented efforts, does not get tired easily.
v. Works well under normal conditions. Can work under minor pressures.
vi. Works under normal conditions. Makes reasonable effort and likes to face minor pressure.
vii. Works when made to, but is not able to sustain.
viii. Talks tall without putting any effort.
ix. Gets tired very easily, gives up at the slightest pretext.
x. Lazy, even the thought of putting effort scares him.

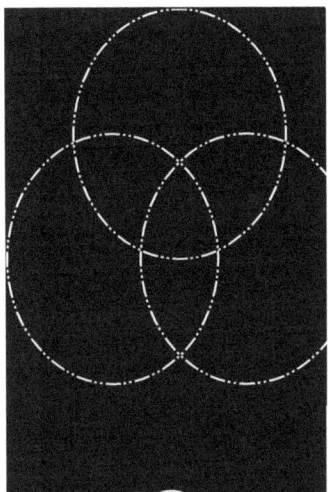

Achieving Success at SSB

Chapter 1: Selection Techniques at SSB
Chapter 2: Screening Test
Chapter 3: Facing Interview
Chapter 4: Clearing Psychological Tests
Chapter 5: Cracking GTO Tasks / Tests
Chapter 6: Pilot Aptitude Battery Test (PABT)
Chapter 7: Conference Procedure
Chapter 8: Medical Examination Procedure of the
Recommended Candidates

Selection Techniques at SSB

The SSB assesses the personality and intelligence of candidates and the process is spread over 5 days. The assessment scientifically analyses each candidate's potential and compatibility for commission into the Armed Forces of India.

The interview is mainly an overall Assessment of the personality of the candidate, to gauge his/her potential as a future Officer in the Armed Forces. The tests conducted by the SSB aims at selecting individuals with OLQs (Officer Like Qualities).

These qualities include effective intelligence, sense of responsibility, initiative, judgement (under stress), ability to reason and organize, communication skills, determination, courage, self-confidence, speed in decision-making, willingness to set an example, compassion and a feeling of loyalty to the nation (India).

Most of the tests require natural responses from the individuals. The tests are graded into various categories of both individual and group variety and each batch of candidates goes through the subtle testing pattern in the course of a few days. They are under observation not only while they perform in various tests but even as they conduct themselves during the course of their stay at the SSB centres, where they are billeted for that duration.

The SSB Board is not concerned with the number of vacancies. Its responsibility is to assess and then, recommend. After recommendation, the candidates appear for Medical Examination and after that is the Merit List. Those who finally make the grade join for training and become Commissioned Officers.

Origin of this type of testing belongs to the First World War era. During the First World War, a large number of casualties on battle fields necessitated recruitment of best fighting talent in Armed Forces. For this need, psychologists designed some scientific tests to assess candidate's Officer Like Qualities (OLQs). Over the years, SSB testing has been improved based on feedback and has proved to be an effective and accurate way of selecting candidates who are capable of being at least an average officer after training, although SSB is the world's well-planned and exhaustive selection technique.

SERVICES SELECTION BOARD INTERVIEWS

- Facilities for candidates at SSB
- Pick-up and drop from reporting railway station.
- Furnished accommodation.
- Messing.
- Medical facilities.
- Games, magazines and newspapers are other facilities provided to candidates to ensure that they feel at home.

Procedure Followed

Candidates who are declared by UPSC as having cleared the written exam or recommended by Preliminary Interview Board (PIB) in case of Territorial Army (TA), as well as those shortlisted Direct Entries are called through Call Letters to appear for SSB(Allahabad/Bangalore/Bhopal/Dehradun/Mysore/Varanasi/ Coimbatore/ Vishakapatnam/Gandhinagar) at the Centre allotted to the candidate. There have been instances when the call letter fails to reach the candidate and the onus lies on the candidate to be alert and contact the office after a reasonable amount of time if the call letter is not received when UPSC written has been cleared. For navy there are four selection centres all over India, i.e. Bhopal, Bangalore, Coimbatore and Vishakhapatnam. For air force the selection centres are situated at Dehradun, Mysore, Varanasi and Gandhinagar. For army the selection centres are at Allahabad, Bangalore, Bhopal, Kapurthala.

• Day of Reporting

Reporting at the centre is usually one day before first day of testing. Time of reporting varies from centre to centre. Sometimes the candidates need to report on the same day of testing, i.e. Day 1 or Stage I. On the day of reporting, the candidates are required to verify their educational documents from assigned staff. Candidates are then allotted chest numbers or a vest on which a number is printed. This vest or chest number becomes the identity of a candidate, as it is easier to identify a person by a number than his/her name. The chest number is also used while interacting with fellow candidates during testing. The results are also announced by calling the chest numbers of recommended candidates. Candidates have to return their chest numbers whenever they leave the campus of a selection centre.

SSB is a two-stage process. To qualify for Stage II, a candidate needs to clear Screening Test or Stage I. On the day of reporting, the candidates are picked from the railway station and during the evening, certain forms and travelling allowance forms are filled. Candidates are also briefed on testing schedule and general instructions, which must be followed throughout the duration of stay at selection centre.

• Day 1 (Screening Tests)

On the next day, is the Stage I, in which candidates are given Intelligence Test (Verbal and Non-Verbal), then there is a Picture Perception test, in which a slide (hazy or clear) is shown for 30 seconds;, the candidate has to observe it very carefully and in the next one minute he/she has to mark number of characters seen in the picture in a box made in the sheet provided to them and the main theme of their story. First the mood of the character – whether the character is in positive, negative or neutral mood, then approximate age and sex of the character is to be jotted down. Candidates also need to identify one character which they saw first, which is often termed as central character or main character of story they are going to write; this character's details should be encircled so that assessor can identify which character has been observed by the candidate as the main character. The candidate is given four minutes time to write the story; it is expected that the candidate should write a story in 70 words or more. Candidates are advised to write the story on the picture shown to them but some candidates describe the picture which puts them at a disadvantage over others.

Once the written part is over, the second part follows in which candidates are told to sit in a semicircular fashion for a Group Discussion. First one by one each candidate will narrate his/her story in one minute to the rest of the candidates, in the duration of one minute. Often the candidates take more than one minute to narrate their story, in that case the assessors give chance to next candidate. As individual narration of stories ends with the last candidate, it is expected that the group start the discussion and come to a common story, as it is obvious that all candidates can perceive the same picture with different themes or backgrounds, and different stories from each another. This sequence is popularly called PPDT – Picture Perception and Discussion Test.

After the completion of these tests, results are announced and those who do not make it in this attempt are dropped back to the railway station and the successful candidates are retained for 4 days of detailed assessment. A certain number of candidates are short-listed based on their performance in screening round, the rest are sent back. The screened candidates are required to fill the bio data forms known as "Personal Information Questionnaire" (PIQ). PIQ is very important – there must be no cutting and inconsistency in each of the three copies of PIQ you fill. PIQ is also the basis for the individual candidate interview, which is scrutinized by the Interviewing Officer before the interview.

• Day 2 (Psychological Tests)

1. **Thematic Apperception Test (TAT)** – Commonly known as Picture Story writing. TAT is very similar to PPDT, but here the candidates are shown clear pictures, in which the candidate has to observe it for 30 seconds and then needs to write a story on it in four minutes. There are total 12 slides shown, 11 slides will be shown one by one; i.e. after 4 minutes

and 30 seconds the next slide will appear. There will be only one answer booklet for all the psychological tests, and will be provided only once, no supplementary sheets are provided. The 12th slide will be a blank slide where a candidate is supposed to write any story of his own choice. In TAT here candidates will not be marking the number of characters and related information; also there will be no group discussion on it.

2. **Word Association Test (WAT)** – WAT is the second psychological test of SSB selection process. In this test the candidates are shown a word on a screen for a period of 15 seconds; in this time duration the candidate has to write the first thought that comes in his/her mind for that word. Total 60 words will be shown one after another (i.e. between each word the gap will be of 15 seconds). The answer sheets will be provided to candidates only once; candidates are required to make no mistakes such as unnecessary cutting or scribbling. The words shown will be very simple and of day to day use. This test will not assess a candidate's proficiency in English language. If a candidate is not aware of meaning of a certain word, he can skip that word and wait for next word to be flashed, and write the response for the next word. The main idea is to maintain the sequence of responses given to the word; the maintenance of sequence is important, as assessor can derive the result systematically for the respective response.

3. **Situation Reaction Test (SRT)** – Applications to various unknown situations are assessed. Sixty situations are given, each to be tackled in 30 seconds. Write specific two/three actions that could be taken for each situation.

4. **Self-Description Test (SD)** – A variation of this like description from the point of view of parents, teachers, colleagues, neighbours, etc. Total 15 minutes are given to write the responses.

• Day 3 and Day 4 (GTO Tasks)

The following tests are conducted in this category:

1. Group discussion
2. Group Planning Exercise (sometimes known as Military Planning Exercise)
3. Progressive Group Tasks
4. Half Group Tasks
5. Individual Obstacles
6. Group Obstacles Race or Snake Race
7. Command Task
8. Lecturette
9. Final Group Task

Note: Interviews are held during afternoon/evening hours on 2nd/3rd/4th day.

• Day 5 (Conference)

On the final day, all the assessors sit together and have a chat on demonstrated performance of the candidate. The fate of the candidates for that SSB is decided by the assessors collectively there. The candidates are required to appear before the complete Board of Examiners composed of President, Deputy President, all the psychologists, all the GTOs, and Technical Officer.

After the board meeting of every candidate is over, the final result is declared immediately. Selected candidates are required to stay back for their medical examination (takes about three to five working days) in the Military Hospital nearby or at a different place and the remaining candidates are dropped at the railway station.

PABT

- Candidates appearing for commission in the 'Flying Branch' Entry have to undergo the Pilot Aptitude Battery Test (PABT).

All the above tests are explained in detail in the subsequent chapters of this book.

2

Screening Test

"No one can make you feel inferior without your consent."

—Eleanor Roosevelt

The screening test (ST) is conducted on the first day of the selection process. The ST comprises of Intelligence test leading to Officer Intelligence Rating (OIR) and Picture Perception and Description Test (PPDT). These tests are aimed to find out the analytical ability of the candidate and to eliminate unsuitable candidates for the next stage of testing.

What is Intelligence & why is it measured?

Intelligence is:
- The innate ability to solve problems
- An inborn mental efficiency
- The capacity to solve new unknown problems of varying complexities
- A measure to indicate trainability of candidates at training establishments

COMPOSITION OF SCREENING TEST

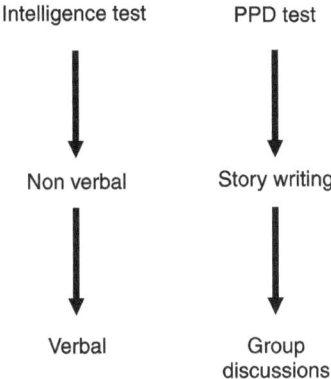

IMPORTANCE OF INTELLIGENCE TEST (IT)

The marks obtained in the IT is important since Officers Intelligence Rating (OIR) computed from marks obtained helps in screening candidates for phase II process. Candidates securing OIR 5 will have no chance of screening in unless all the assessors, i.e. IO, GTO & Psy recommend. The reasons for conducting IT are:

- A defence officer is confronted with complicated situations.
- To be critical and analytical.
- He is required to make quick decisions.
- To face/react to modern warfare warranting not only physical strength but also mental capacity.
- To seek competitive advantage.
- To determine OIR (officer intelligence ratings) at SSB & to assess trainability.

TYPES OF QUESTIONS ASKED IN INTELLIGENCE TEST

There are two types of intelligence tests from where OIR is computed. These measure the candidate's innate ability and are as follows:

Verbal Test: These tests are used with the language and consist of:
- Analogy and classification
- Coding-Decoding
- Number series
- Blood relations
- Direction
- Seating arrangement

- Puzzles
- Basic mathematical aptitude

Non Verbal Test: These tests are conducted with use of graphics, geometrical figures or sketches.

- Analogy and classification of figures
- Complete and incomplete pattern of figures
- Cubes and dice
- Venn diagram (simple one)
- Paper Folding
- Figure for Motion & Analysis

QUESTION PATTERN

Verbal Test

Analogy and classification

In this part, a word and its related word is given, then another word with four options are given. We have to find out the related word from the options given.

Example: Phone: Cell phone :: Computer :: _____? (a) Speaker (b) Keyboard (c) Theatre (d) Laptop

In this (d) Laptop is the answer. Since Cell phone is the derivative of Phone, so Laptop is the derivative of Computer.

Coding-decoding

In this part, a word is coded to a number/ alphabet and vice versa, and we have to decode it accordingly. The basic technique to follow is write numbers for the alphabets quickly in the rough sheet provided.

Example: A-1, B-2, C-3, D-4, E-5, F-6, G-7, H-8, I-9, J-10, K-11, L-12, M-13, N-14, O-15, P-16, Q-17, R-18, S-19, T-20, U-21, V-22, W-23, X-24, Y-25, Z-26

As shown in the above example, write the alphabets and their corresponding numbers as soon as you get the rough sheet.

For example, if the question has the word FROG, then you decode it as:

F R O G - 6 18 15 7

Suppose the word given is DOCTOR, we have to decode it as:

D O C T O R - 4 15 3 20 15 18

Number series

In this a series of numbers is given and we have to find out the next number. The series given may be of squares, cubes values or simple odd or even numbers also.

Example: 555, 666, 777, 666, 777, 888, _____?_____, 888, 999

In the above example the answer is 777. If we take the first three numbers and compare with the next three, we find that 111 is added to every number. In this way we have to analyse and give the correct answer.

Blood relations

The blood relation questions are easy to solve if we are thorough with understanding relationships.

Example: The husband of your brother's mother is whose husband?

Ans: The husband of your brother's mother is your father. So he is your mother's husband only.

Like this, questions are twisted a little bit, but it's easy if we practice well.

Direction problems (DP)

In DP, the candidates are advised to find the direction.

Example: You are facing towards east and if you move left for 10 metres then turn left for 15 metres and then take right turn for 25 metres then which direction you will face?

Ans: North (Draw the direction on the paper then solve it.)

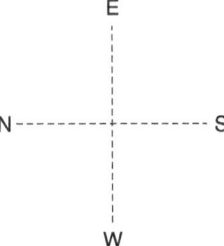

Seating arrangement

In the seating arrangement, an example of questions asked is given below:

Example: A group of five people are sitting at a round table such that A is to the left of D, C is to the right of E. Then write the sequence from A towards left.

Ans: ABEDC. These types of questions are asked rarely, but if asked it is time consuming, so practice it well before.

Puzzle and basic mathematical aptitude

In puzzle you will get simple puzzles and in mathematical aptitude, you will get time and distance, work, basic numerical problems etc.

Conduct of Non-verbal Test

- Conducted by a psychologist
- Does not require proficiency in language
- Requires imagination
- No negative marking for wrong answers
- 60 questions to be attempted in 30 minutes
- Even if 40 questions are solved appropriately, would suffice

QUESTION PATTERN

Analogy and classification of figures

Analogy refers to finding the same type of figure.

Example: There will be two figures given which are related to circle and another two figures given which are related to squares. We have to find which figure is related to square.

Question Type: (a) {figure with circle}: (b) {figure with circle} :: (c) {figure with square} (d) {_____?_____}

In this we have to find the figure from the given options, that is, which figure is related to square.

This question is an easy one and with little practice we can solve it very easily.

Complete and incomplete pattern of figures

This type of question is also easy, that some part of the figure is missing. We have to find out from the given option that part which is missing.

Cubes and dice

This question is little bit tough, but it needs a lot of practice and it is time-consuming; so practice this well. Usually cube problems are rarely asked but dice problems appear frequently.

Venn diagram

This type of question is very easy to answer. There are two types of questions related to Venn diagram part. One is with numerical data and another one is pictorial representation.

Example

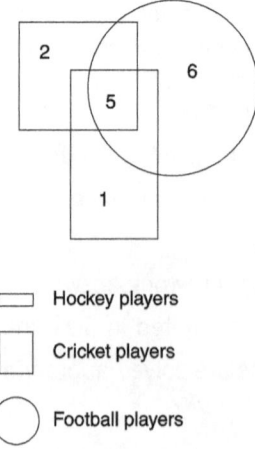

Screening Test 53

Note: Follow the R.S. Aggarwal verbal and non-verbal books to practice these type of questions well. Since it is easy to write the test, it is better to do well to get OIR Rating within 1-4. OIR 5 will lead you to get eliminated unless all three assessors have agreed with YES remarks in Discussion after the PPDT.

After the end of the Verbal & Non-verbal intelligence test, there is some time break for the next level of the process. The next test is Picture Presentation & Description Stage (PPDT).

Picture Perception and Description Test (PPDT)

Picture Perception is a projection test, which is a part of the screening. In this, the candidates are shown a hazy picture for duration of 30 seconds and the candidate has to write down a story in 4½ minutes by noting down the basic seven parameters such as

- Age
- Sex
- Character
- Mood
- Past (what he has done)
- Present (what is going on in the story)
- Future (what he will do)

Conduct of Picture Perception (Story Writing)

The candidates are advised to sit in a big auditorium. Then the psychologist gives instruction about the PPDT. A hazy/blurred picture is projected deliberately from the projector for 30 seconds by switching off the light. In this hazy picture the candidate has to note down the basic seven parameters as described above. Then they should think of a constructive/positive story in mind to write.

Mood = Positive (+)
Character-male/female

- Age
- Sex
- M

Before writing, there is a need to fill up certain details; a square box is printed in the psychological answer sheet. In this box the candidate should fill in the following: who is the central character, what's his age, what's his mood, what led to the situation (past), what is going on in the situation (present), and what will happen at the end (future).

You will get a clear idea about this after going through the example given below.

Picture Story Writing Phase

In the above picture, a boy is standing in front of the queue with a cap on his head. So he may be a service person. So this is to be marked in the psychological paper i.e. in that square box as a male (M), age 22, his mood is positive (+) and his character is helping mind. Also marked is a point at the left corner of the rectangle because one has chosen that person from picture who is in that exact location. So we should be able to make it clear to the psychologist that is the person we are choosing from the picture.

After marking this, how to project or write the story

The story in which we are going to write should be of positive nature and the result should also be positive. The hero should be of same age and same sex as yours. If you find no hero in the story then create a hero of same sex and age. Write the story with little introduction i.e., what led to the situation (past), then what is happening in the situation (present) and what is the result (future). The story should be in past tense only.

Example

Prakash was a newly posted officer, in Uttarakhand which is prone to landslides. He was an above average student from childhood but showed lot of interest in extracurricular activities such NSS, NCC etc. One day while he was at home, he suddenly heard people shouting and understood the situation quickly that people in the nearby apartments were trapped under the small landslides. So he engaged himself by calling the fire service and rescued most of the people up to an extent. He saved many people and then joined hands with fire service people also. Later he arranged for the affected people food and shelter with the help of the local panchayat.

(In this story, we are showing his quality from childhood as a good boy (past), landslide and rescue operation scenario (present) and arranging shelter and food (future). Like this the story should be a positive one with positive end.)

Remember to:

> Fill personal details on answer sheet.
> Pay full attention to instructions given to you.
> Work very fast and quickly.
> Blurred picture displayed deliberately.

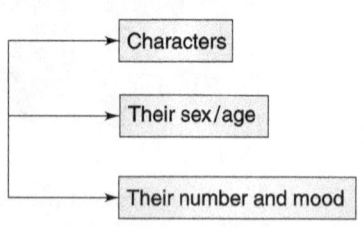

- Total time for seeing and writing is 5 minutes.
- Interpret and write the story as per your imagination.
- There should be relevance
- Identify characters
- Write down what led to the story (proper beginning)
- What is happening presently in the screen (effective body)
- What is going to happen ultimately (healthy conclusion)
- May or may not write the title of the story.

Group Discussion Phase

Group discussion phase is a very important phase at the screening on Day 1 since the selection for the four days and rejection (screened out) are based on this performance only, this is the MOST Important Test of all tests at SSB - it is do or die situation. At the GD candidates are made to sit in a semicircle before the Interviewing Officer (IO), GTO and the psychologist based on their chest numbers. The candidates are ordered to narrate their individual story before the group while sitting. After the individual narration, the group starts to discuss about the picture. During discussion phase, candidates must participate two to three times before coming to conclusion by giving facts/figures and points of views/ideas. A final conclusion may not be arrived at (generally inconclusive).

Guidelines for Group Discussion on Picture
- Conducted by a GTO
- Candidates will be called in batches of 15 to 20 for discussion and will be seated in semicircle before three assessors, as shown above.

Procedure

1. In this test a vague, sketchy, unstructured picture is shown for 30 seconds and the candidate is asked to answer 06 (six) questions on a paper sheet provided by the testing officer:
    (a) Total number of characters with their position.
    (b) How many of them are Male - Female (F, M)
    (c) Approximate age of each character.
    (d) Mood of each character Positive - Negative (P, N) or (+, –)
    (e) The character you saw first and then circle it.
    (f) Action or activity going on in the picture.
2. Perceive the picture very carefully and answer the above six questions accordingly. If there is a character that is of your sex and age group, put a circle around that character and treat him as the main character (hero) and give him a proper name and job. If there is no character of your sex or age group, in that case bring the main character from the outside.
3. **Action:** Write one or two words about the theme/scene. This means the story must be based on any situation concerning that theme only.

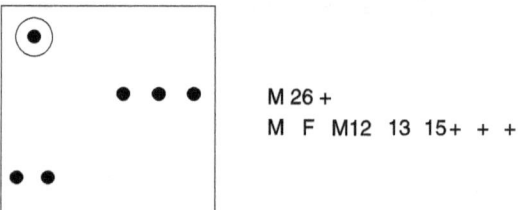

4. Once above six questions are answered, each candidate has to write a story in 04 (four) minutes time keeping point Nos. 5 & 6 in mind. So it means approximate length of the story should be 70-80 words and also the story should be achievable and believable. The situation should not be of routine or average nature, rather it should be little difficult or demanding. Then, in 40-50 words, 06-07 qualities are to be displayed, i.e. how has he solved and handled that situation, and then sum up or conclude the story in a positive manner.
5. After four minutes the sheet is taken back and candidates are called for Group Discussion where each candidate narrates their story one by one and after narration the GTO asks to start the discussion and to give the Common Group Story.

Narration of Story - Examples

Candidate 1: A very good morning to all of you. Gentlemen, after perceiving the picture I see 06 characters – 04 males and 02 females. The character whom I saw first is a male person of 26 years of age. He is in (+) mood. Rest of the characters are between the age group of 12 to 40 years and all are in (+) mood. The Action of my story is A Birthday Celebration Party and my story goes like this:

Ranjit, after discussing with his parents, decided to organize the birthday party of his younger brother on coming Sunday evening. He, with their consultation decided to invite his friends, neighbours and few relatives. He got readymade eatables & drinks from the market. He also organized few party games to make the party memorable. He also arranged music system and decorated the house properly. Due to his full involvement, the party proved to be a great success and everyone enjoyed the party.

OR

The birthday party of Nitin was organized by his elder brother Anurag. The children while playing some game suddenly touched the live wire left behind the sofa by the electrician. One of the children got a shock and cried loudly. All the people attending party were shocked and unable to take any action. Anurag, the elder brother happened to enter the house at that moment. Seeing everybody lost and confused, he immediately switched off the mains and separated the boy from the wire. He assured him his welfare. Seeing this, others came to his help. He gave him first aid and after little rest, the party again resumed.

Candidate 2: Friends, in the picture shown I perceive four males and two females in age group of 20-22 years and in positive mood. They seem to have lined up for submitting forms for passport at the passport office. Swati is my above character, aged around 21 years, who plans to proceed to the USA for higher studies as she has been given scholarship by one of the Universities in America.

Swati plans to join DRDO or Defence Forces as a technical officer and contribute her knowledge and expertise. Subsequently she got her passport and proceeded to the USA for higher studies and joined the law branch of the Navy.

Candidate 3 (during discussion): Gentlemen, we all agreed that we identified 06 characters in the picture shown to us. It appears as if a group of people was involved in a birthday party celebration as one of the boys was wearing birthday cap. As young dynamic candidates we can make many stories on the picture like chest No. _____ has written the story on _____ and chest No. _____ has written on _____, so it is quite difficult for us to give one story till we compromise with each other.

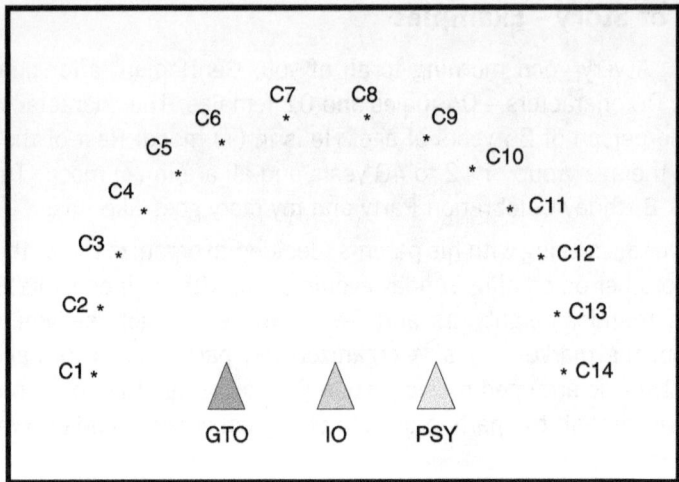

Seating Arrangement for Picture Discussion

- ➢ Narrate your story clearly and confidently with smart disposition.
- ➢ Scan through the candidates.
- ➢ Be natural and give positive story.
- ➢ Not to take more than one to one and half minutes while narrating.
- ➢ During discussion go by the best story. Don't harp on your story only.
- ➢ Story to have proper beginning, effective body and healthy conclusion.
- ➢ Take active part but do not dominate.
- ➢ Be adaptive and active.
- ➢ All three assessors, viz GTO, psychologist and interviewing officer will be assessing candidates simultaneously.

Conclusion

Candidates to discuss their stories together and finally come to a common conclusion on a single story, which is unlikely.

Time allotted is 20 to 25 min.

On arriving at a common story, which is quite unlikely, candidates are told to proceed out.

REMEMBER

- ✓ Three assessors present, decide jointly on final recommendation for stage II.
- ✓ A gap of half hour to two hours available before starting the group discussion.
- ✓ In this period mentally prepare the story that is going to be narrated by you and practice yourself.
- ✓ You may complete the story if the same was not done while writing, keeping the relevance.

REMEMBER

> ➢ Smart turn out and alertness
> ➢ Hair cut/shave/shoes polished
> ➢ Military bearing and pleasant disposition
> ➢ Stress freeness and general etiquettes

"aid to decision making in your favour"

Decisions by Assessors

- Y - YES for stage II
- D - DOUBTFUL for stage II
- N - NO for stage II

RELATIONSHIP BETWEEN OIR & DECISIONS-SOME EXAMPLES

Candidate	OIR	GTO decision	Psych decision	IO decision	Final decision for next stage
1	4	DDD	DDD	DNY	YNY
2	2	NNN	NDN	YNN	YYN
3	1	NYD	NND	NND	NYY
4	3	DDD	DDN	DNN	YYN
5	5	YYD	YND	YND	YNN

STAGE I SCREENING
BENEFIT OF DOUBT, IF ANY, GOES IN FAVOUR OF THE

CANDIDATES

Tips for Overall Success in PPDT

- Ensure you are smartly seated, presenting military bearing and smart body language.
- Never look at the assessors while narration of the story or while engaging in the discussion.
- Never question group members, give facts and figures to support point of view.
- Try to talk at least three times during discussion phase, then surely you will succeed. It's not necessary to talk all the time in PPDT.
- Also don't argue with others. Give your points clearly and listen patiently.
- Keep pleasant disposition – it's the key to success in PPDT.
- Be cool in narrating your story, participate in subsequent discussion and facilitation of thoughts and ideas.
- Show concern and attention while others are talking.
- After dispersing from the PPDT walk with head held high and upraised chest. This shows that you are confident in your participation.

These are about screening on Day 1 of SSB. After this the students will go for lunch and come to the auditorium for the results. The results will be declared and screened in students will be given new chest numbers and further procedure for their stay.

SAMPLES OF INTELLIGENCE TEST

SOLVED INTELLIGENT TEST

1. Choosing the Odd Word

Direction: Choose the word which is least like the other words in the group.

1. (a) Carrot (b) Potato (c) Tomato (d) Ginger (e) Beetroot

Sol: Here, all except Tomato grow underground. Hence, the answer is (c).

2. (a) Chameleon (b) Crocodile (c) Alligator (d) Locust (e) Salamanders

Sol: Here, all except Locust are reptiles while locust is an insect. Hence, the answer is (d).

2. Series Completion Number Series

Completing the Given Series

1. Which is the number that will come next in the following sequence?

    4, 6, 12, 14, 28, 30, (....)

    (a) 32 (b) 60 (c) 62 (d) 64

Sol: The given sequence is a combination of two series:

(i) 4, 12, 28 (....) and (ii) 6, 14, 30.

Now the pattern followed in each of the above two series:

+8, +16, +32.

So, missing number is = (28 + 32) = 60 Hence the answer is (b).

Elementary idea of progressions

1. **Arithmetic Progression (A.P.):** The progression of the form $a, a + d, a + 2d, a + 3d$ ... is known as an A.P. with first term = a and common difference = d.

    Example 3, 6, 9, 12 ... is an A.P. with $a = 3$ and $d = 6 - 3 = 3$.

    In an A.P., we have nth term = $a + (n - 1) d$.

2. **Geometric Progression (G.P.):** The progression of the form **a, ar, ar^2, ar^3** ... is known as a G.P. with first term = a and common ratio = r.

    Example 1, 5, 25, 125 ... is an G.P. with $a = 1$ and $r = 5/1 = 25/5 = ... = 5$.

    In a G.P., we have nth term = ar^{n-1}

    Example How many terms are there in the series 201, 208, 215 ... 359?

    (a) 23 (b) 24 (c) 25 (d) 26

Sol: The given series in an A.P. in which $a = 201$ and $d = 7$

Let the number be n.

Then, $369n = 201 + (n - 1) \times 7$ or $n = 25$.

Hence the number is (c).

3. Coding-Decoding

A CODE is a 'system of signals'. Therefore, Coding is a method of transmitting a message between the sender and the receiver without a third person knowing it.

The Coding and Decoding Test is set up to judge the candidate's ability to decipher the rule that is used to code a particular word/message and break the code to decipher the message.

Example 1 In a certain code, SIKKIM is written as THLJJL. How is TRAINING written in that code?

    (a) SQBHOHOH   (b) UQBHOHOF
    (c) UQBJOHHO   (d) UQBJOHOH
    (e) None of these

Sol: Clearly, the letters in the word SIKKIM are moved alternately one step forward and one step backward to obtain the letters of the code.

Example 2 If in a code, ALTERED is written as ZOGVIVW, then in the same code, RELATED would be written as

    (a) IVOZGVW   (b) IVOZGWN
    (c) IVOGZVW   (d) VIOZGVW

Sol: Clearly, each letter of the word ALTERED is replaced by the letter which occupies the same position from the other end of the English alphabet, to obtain decode. Thus, A, the first letter of the alphabet is replaced by Z, the last letter. L, the 12th letter from the beginning of the alphabet, is replaced by O, the 12th letter from the end. T, the 7th letter from the end of the alphabet is replaced by G, the 7th letter from the beginning of the alphabet and so on.

Similarly, in the word RELATED, R will be coded as I, E as V, L as O, A as Z, T as G and D as W. Thus the code becomes IVOZGVW. Hence the answer is (a).

4. Blood Relations

Example 1 X introduces Y saying, "He is the granddaughter of the father of my father". How is Y related to X?

    (a) Brother   (b) Son
    (c) Brother-in-law   (d) Nephew
    (e) Son-in-law

Sol: The relation may be analyzed as follows:

Father's father _____ Grandfather, Grandfather's Grandfather, Granddaughter – Sister, Sister's husband – Brother-in-law.

So, *Y* is X's brother-in-law.

Hence the answer is (c).

Example 2 Pointing out to a lady, Rajan said, "She is the daughter of the woman who is the mother of the husband of my mother". Who is the lady to Rajan?

(a) Aunt
(b) Granddaughter
(c) Daughter
(d) Sister
(e) Sister-in-law

Sol: The relation may be analyzed as follows:

Mother's husband – Father, Father's Mother – Grandmother, Grandmother's daughters, Father's sisters, Father's sister – Aunt.

So, the lady is Rajan's Aunt. Hence the answer is (a).

5. Puzzle Test

Directions: Study the following information and answer the question given below it:

(1) Kailash, Govind and Harinder are intelligent.
(2) Kailash, Rajesh and Jitendra are hard-working.
(3) Rajesh, Harinder and Jitendra are honest.
(4) Kailash, Govind and Jitender are ambitious.

1. Which of the following person is neither hard-working nor ambitious?
    (a) Kailash
    (b) Govind
    (c) Harinder
    (d) Rajesh
    (d) None of these

Sol: We may prepare a table as under:

	Intelligent	Hard-working	Honest	Ambitious
Kailash	✓	✓		✓
Govind	✓			✓
Harinder			✓	
Rajesh		✓	✓	
Jitendra		✓	✓	✓

2. C: Harinder is neither hard-working nor ambitious.

6. Direction Sense Test

In this test, the question is a sort of direction puzzle. A successive follow-up of directions is formulated and the candidate is required to ascertain the final direction or the distance between two points. The test is meant to judge the candidate's ability to trace and follow correctly and sense the direction correctly.

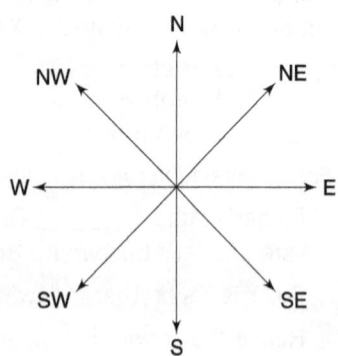

The adjoining figure shows the four main directions (North N, South S, East E, West W) And four cardinal directions (North East NE, North West NW, South East SE, South West SW) to help the candidates know the direction.

Example 3 A child is looking for his father. He went 90 meters in the east before turning to his right. He went 20 meters before turning to his right to look for his father at his uncle's place 30 meters from this point. His father was not there. From there, he went 100 meters to his north before meeting his father in the street. How far did the son meet his father from starting point?

(a) 80 meters (b) 100 meters
(c) 140 meters (d) 260 meters

7. Logical Venn Diagrams

Example TABLE, CHAIR, FURNITURE

Clearly, table and chair are separate items but both are items of furniture. So, they would be represented as shown in fig. 1, with circle 'A' representing Table, circle 'B' representing Chair and circle 'C' representing Furniture.

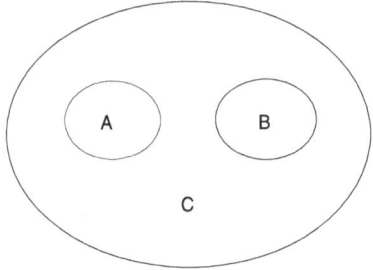

Fig. 1

Example MALES, FATHERS, BROTHERS

Clearly, some fathers may be brothers. So, Fathers and Brothers would be represented by two intersecting circles. Also both father and brother are males. So, the diagrammatic representation would be as shown in fig. 2, with circle 'A' representing Fathers, circle 'B' representing Brothers and circle 'C' representing Males.

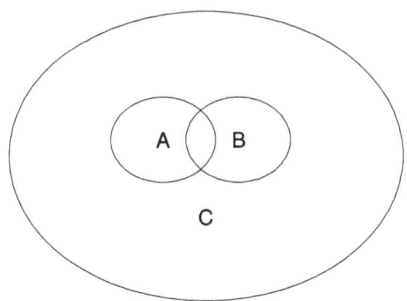

Fig. 2

Example DOGS, PETS, CATS

Clearly, some Dogs and some Cats are Pets. But, all the Pets are not dogs or cats. Also, dogs and cats are not related to each other. So, the given items would be represented as shown in fig. 3, with circle 'A' representing Dogs, circle 'B' representing Pets and circle 'C' representing Cats.

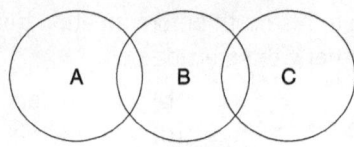

Fig. 3

Example CLERKS, GOVERNMENT EMPLOYEES, EDUCATED PERSONS

Clearly, some Clerks may be Government Employees and some may be educated. Similarly, some Government Employees may be Clerks and some may be educated. Also. some Educated Persons may be clerks and some may be clerks and some may be Government Employees. So, the given items may be represented as shown in fig. 4 with three different circles with 'C' denoting the three classes.

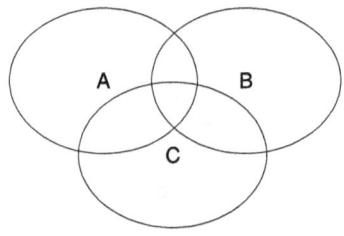

Fig. 4

Example ENGINEERS, HUMAN BEINGS, RATS

Clearly, all engineers are human beings; this would be represented by two concentric circles, but the class of rats is entirely separate from these two. Thus, these items would be represented as shown in fig. 5 with circle 'A' representing Engineers, circle 'B' representing Human Beings and circle 'C' representing Rats.

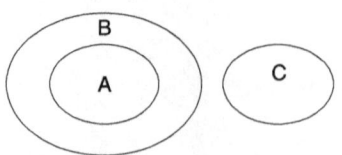

Fig. 5

1. Which in the following diagrams correctly represents Elephants, Wolves, and Animals?

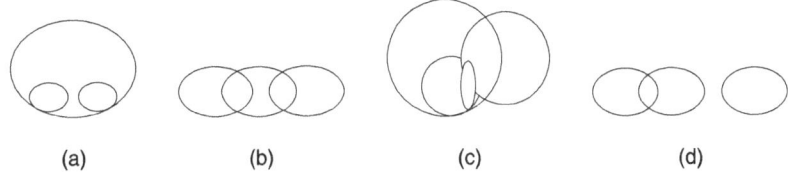

(a)   (b)   (c)   (d)

8. Alphabet Test

1. Alphabetical order of words

In this type of questions, certain words are given. The candidate is required to arrange them in the order in which they appear in the dictionary and then state the word which is to be placed in the desired place.

How to arrange the words in Alphabetical Order?

First consider the first letter of each word. Arrange the words in the order in which these letters appear in the English alphabet.

Example Consider the words: Alphabet, Torture, Payment, Fossil, Shark.

These words begin with the letters A, T, P, F, and S respectively. Their order in English alphabet is A, F, P, S, and T.

So, the correct alphabetical order is:

Alphabet, Fossil, Payment, Shark, Torture.

In some cases, two or more words may begin with the same letter. Such words should be arranged in the order of second letters in the alphabet.

Example Consider the words:

Client, Castle, Face, Viper, Dazzle.

Here, as in the above example, the words can be arranged as:

$$\left.\begin{array}{l}\text{Client}\\\text{Castle}\end{array}\right\} \text{Dazzle, Face, Viper.}$$

What remains now is how to arrange 'Client' and 'Castle'.

Consider the second letter i.e., *l* and *a*

Arrange these words accordingly; 'Castle' comes before 'Client'.

Thus, the correct alphabetical order is: Castle, Client, Dazzle, Face, Viper.

If both the first and second letters of two or more words are the same, arrange these words, considering their third letters and so on.

9. Number, Ranking & Time Sequence Test

Number test

In this type of question, generally you are given a long series of numbers. The candidate is required to find out how many times a number satisfying the conditions, specified in the question, occurs.

10. Illustrative Examples

Example How many 5's are there in the following sequence which are immediately followed by 3 but not immediately preceded by 7?

8 9 5 3 2 5 3 8 5 5 6 8 7 3 3 5 7 7 5 3 6 5 3 3 5 7 3 8

    (a) One   (b) Two
    (b) Three   (d) Four
    (e) More than four

11. Mathematical Operations Problem-Solving by Substitution

In this type, you are provided with substitutes for various mathematical symbols, followed by a question involving calculation of an expression or choosing the correct/incorrect equation. The candidate is required to put in the real signs in the given equation and then solve the question as required.

Note: While solving a mathematical expression, proceed according to the rule BODMAS- i.e., Brackets, Of, Division, Multiplication, Addition, Subtraction.

    e.g., $(36 - 12)/4 + 6/2 \times 3$ (Solving Brackets)

        $= 6 + 3 \times 3$ (Solving Division)

        $= 6 + 9$ (Solving Multiplication)

        $= 15$ (Solving Addition)

12. Logical Sequence of Words

In this type of question a group of words is given. The candidate is required to arrange these words in a meaningful order such as the sequence of occurrence of events, sequence from a part to the whole, sequence accordingly.

Example 1 Arrange the following in a meaningful sequence:

    1. Consultation   2. illness   3. Doctor   4. Treatment
    5. Recovery

        (a) 2, 3, 1, 4, 5   (b) 2, 3, 4, 1, 5
        (c) 4, 3, 2, 1, 5   (d) 5, 1, 4, 3, 2

Sol: We know that illness occurs first. One then goes to the doctor and after consultation with him, undergoes treatment to finally attain recovery.

    Thus, the correct order is 2, 3, 1, 4, 5.

    Hence, the answer is (a).

Example 2 Arrange the following in a meaningful order, from particular to general:
 1. Family   2. Community   3. Member   4. Locality
 5. Country
  (a) 3, 1, 2, 4, 5   (b) 3, 1, 2, 5, 4
  (c) 3, 1, 4, 2, 5   (d) 3, 1, 4, 5, 2

Sol: Clearly, a member is a part of a family, which in turn is a part of community. The community lives in a locality which lies within a country.

Thus, the correct order is 3, 1, 2, 4 and 5.

Hence, the answer is (a).

13. Arithmetical Reasoning

1. Calculation-based problems

Example 1 In a group of cows and hens, the numbers of legs are 14 more than twice the number of heads. The number of cows is
  (a) 5   (b) 7
  (c) 10   (d) 12

Sol: Let the number of cows be x and the number of hens be y. Then,

Number of legs in the group = $4x + 2y$.

Number of heads in the group = $x + y$.

So $4x + 2y = 2(x + y) + 14$ or $4x + 2y = 2x + 2y + 14$ or $2x = 14$ or $x = 7$.

Number of cows = 7.

Hence, the answer is (b)

Example 2 A worker may claim Rs. 15 each km which he travels by taxi and Rs. 5 for each km which he drives his own car. If in one week he claimed Rs. 5000 for travelling 80 km, how many km did he travel by taxi?
  (a) 10   (b) 20
  (c) 30   (d) 40

Sol: Let the distance covered by taxi be x km.

Then, distance covered by car = $(80 - x)$ km.

$15x + 5(80 - x) = 500$ or $15x = 400 - 5x = 500$ or $10x = 100$ or $x = 10$.

Distance covered by taxi = 10 km.

Hence, the answer is (a).

14. Inserting the Missing Character

In such type of question, a figure, a set of figures or a matrix is given, each of which bears certain characters, be it numbers, letters or a group of letters/numbers, following a certain pattern. The candidate is required to decipher this pattern and accordingly find the missing character in the figure.

Example 1

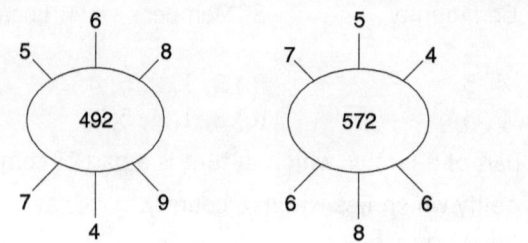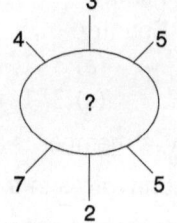

(a) 115 (b) 130
(c) 135 (d) 140

Sol: Clearly, the number inside the circle is equal to the sum of the product of the upper three numbers and the product of the lower three numbers. Thus the anwer is (b).

Example 2

6	18	15
3	2	5
4	3	?
8	27	9

(a) 11 (b) 6
(c) 3   (d) 2

Sol: Clearly, in the first column, 6 × 4/3 = 24/3 = 8.
In the second column, 18 × 3/2 = 54/2 = 27.
Then, 15x/5 = 9 or 15x = 45 or x = 3. Hence, the answer is (c).

Example 3

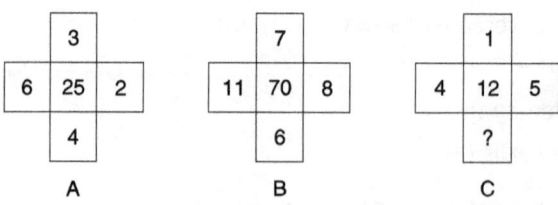

(a) 10 (b) 6
(c) 2   (d) 1

Sol: The arrangement is as follows:
In fig. (A), (32 + 62) – (22 + 42) = (9 + 36) – (4 + 6) = 45 – 20 = 25

In fig. (B), $(72 + 112) - (82 + 62) = (49 + 121) - (64 + 36) = 170 - 100 = 70$
In fig. (C), let the missing number be x. Then, $(12 + 42) - (52 + x2) = -12$ Or $17 + 12 = (52 + x^2)$ or $x^2 = 29 - 25 = 4$ or $x = 2$. Hence, the answer is (c).

15. Data Sufficiency

This section consists of problems in which a question on any topic such as Coding-Decoding, Puzzle Test, Blood Relations, Mathematical calculations etc., is put forward, followed by certain statements containing facts providing clues to solve the question. The candidate is required to find out which of the given statement is/are sufficient to answer the given question.

Example Out of six lectures of one hour each - A, B, C, D, E and F scheduled between 10 a.m. to 4 p.m., which one will be third?

Statement: I. Lecture F is preceded by A and is followed by C.

II. There is only one lecture before A and there is no lecture afte B.

Sol: From I, we get the sequence as A, F, C.

Also, it is given in II that there is only one lecture before A and no lecture after B.

Clearly, F is the third lecture.

Thus, both I and II are required to answer the given question.

16. Assertion and Reason

The test is meant to judge the candidate's knowledge and with it, his ability to reason out correctly. In this test, two statements referred to as the Assertion (A) and Reason (R) respectively are provided. Five alternative comments on these are given and the correct one is to be chosen.

Examples

Direction: For the Assertion (A) and (R) below, choose the correct alternative from the following:

(a) Both A and R are true and is the correct explanation of A.

(b) Both A and R are true but R is NOT the correct explanation of A.

(c) A is true but R is false.

(d) A is false but R is true.

(e) Both A and R is false.

1. **Assertion (A):** Bulb filament is made of Titanium.

   Reason (R): The filament should have low melting point.

   Clearly, the answer is (e) since both the statements A and R are false.

17. Verification of Truth of the Statement

In this type of questions, the candidate is required to stress only on truth of the facts that always hold. Questions are asked in context of a particular thing or factor that is always characterized by a specific part. The alternatives other than the correct answer also seen bear a strong relationship with the thing mentioned. So, absolute truth is to be followed.

Example 1 Atmosphere always has

    (a) Oxygen   (b) Air

    (c) Germs   (d) Moisture

    (e) Dust

Sol: Clearly though all the alternatives may form a part of the atmosphere, the air is the most vital part, without which there can be no atmosphere. So, the answer is (b).

Example 2 Which one of the following is always found in 'Bravery'?

    (a) Courage   (b) Experience

    (c) Power   (d) Knowledge

Sol: Clearly, 'bravery' is a quality exhibited only by a person who possesses courage so, the answer is (a).

18. Part II – Non-Verbal Reasoning

Detecting the relationship and choosing the correct substitute

This type of question contains figures A, B, C and D in the Problem Set and figures 1, 2, 3, and 4 in the Answer Set. It is required to select a figure from the Answer Set which best substitutes fig. D of the Problem Set such that element D is related to the element C in the same way as element B is related to element A. If none of the answer is suitable then answer is 5.

Example

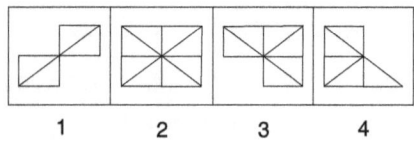

PROBLEMS FIGURES   ANSWER FIGURES

A   B   C   D   1   2   3   4

Sol: Here, two triangles from fig. (A) are lost to form fig. (B). With this relationship we find that with the loss of two triangles from fig. (C), fig. (3) will be formed. So, fig. (3) is the answer.

Direction: Each of the following questions bears four figures numbered A, B, C and D which constitutes the Problem Set and four other figures numbered 1, 2, 3, and 4 which constitute the Answer set. Figure A and B are related in a particular way. Establish a similar relationship between figure C and D by choosing a figure from the Answer set that would best substitute fig. (D) in the Problem set. In case if none of the figure of the Answer set is suitable then answer is 5.

Screening Test 73

PROBLEMS FIGURES   ANSWER FIGURES

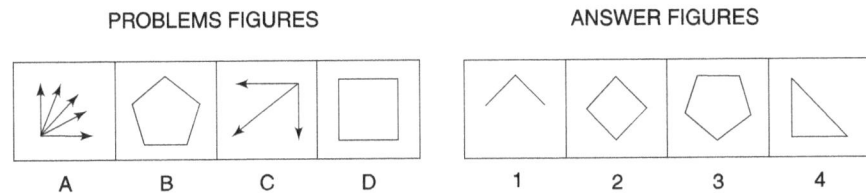

A   B   C   D   1   2   3   4

Sol: The number of sides in (B) is equal to the number of arrows in (A).

19. Classification

In the section on classification, we deal with problem of Odd-Man-Out type. In such problem, we are given a set of figures, such that, all except one have similar characteristics/features. We are required to select the figure which differs from all other figures in the given set. Several other types of problem based upon classification are also discussed in details in this section.

1. Choosing the odd figure

Under this heading, we study problems in each of which we are given five/four figures, out of which all except one are alike in some manner. We have to select the exclusively different figure in the given set.

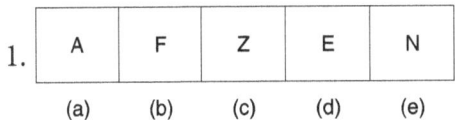

Sol: Answer is (d). It is the only letter having four lines, rest all have three lines.

20. Choosing a Similar Figure

The problem in this type of classification involves four un-numbered figures followed by five other figures numbered as 1, 2, 3, 4 & 5. The four un-numbered figures forming the Problem Set are alike in a certain manner. A figure, from amongst the numbered ones forming the Answer Set, is to be chosen such that it is similar to the Problem figures in that manner.

PROBLEMS FIGURES   ANSWER FIGURES

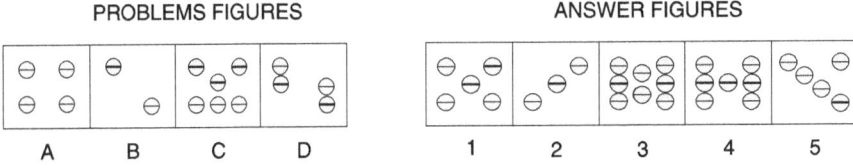

A   B   C   D   1   2   3   4   5

Sol: Answer is 3. There are even numbers of dots in all other figures.

21. Analytical Reasoning

The section on Analytical Reasoning involves the problem relating to the counting of geometrical figures in a given complex figure. The systematic method for determining the number of any particular type of figure by the analysis of the complex figure would be clear from the examples that follow.

Example What is the number of straight lines in the following figure?

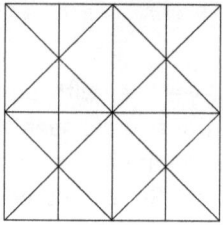

(a) 11   (b) 14
(c) 16   (d) 17

Sol: The figure is labeled as shown.

Clearly, there are 3 horizontal lines namely AE, LF and KG.
There are 5 vertical lines: AK, BJ, CI, DH and EG.
There are 6 slanting lines: LC, KE, IF, LI, AG and CF
Thus, there are 3 + 5 + 6 = 14 straight lines in the figure.

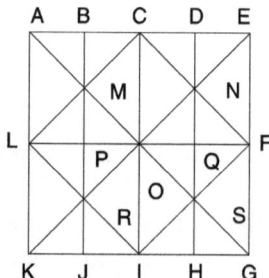

22. Mirror Images

Direction: In each one of the following question, you are given a combination of letters or I and numbers followed by four alternatives (a), (b), (c) and (d). Choose the alternative which most closely resembles the mirror-image of the given combination.

1. BRISK
    (a) BRISK   (b) B RIK
    (c) K RBB   (d) BRISK

Sol: (d)

2. WHITE

a) ⊒⊥IHW
b) ƎTIHM
c) ƎTIHW
d) ETIHW

Sol: (c)

Direction: In each one of the following questions, choose the correct mirror-image of the figure (x) from amongst the four alternatives (a), (b), (c), (d) given along with it.

1.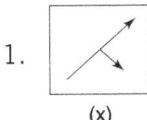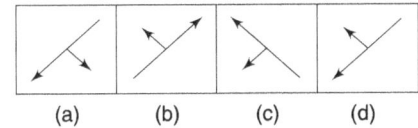

Sol: (c)

Direction: In the following question, you are given a combination of letters and numbers followed by four alternatives (a), (b), (c), (d). Choose the alternative which most closely resembles the water-image of the given combination.

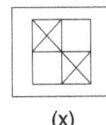 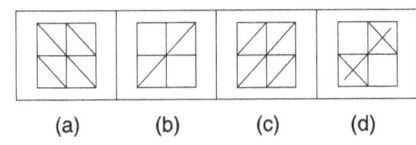

Sol: (d)

23. Paper Folding

The problem based on paper folding involves the process of selecting a figure which would most closely resemble the pattern that would be formed when a transparent sheet carrying design on either side of a dotted line, is folded along this line. The figure has to be selected from a set of four alternatives.

Direction: In each one of the following example find from amongst the four response figures, the one which resembles the pattern formed when the transparent sheet, carrying a design is folded along the dotted line.

Example

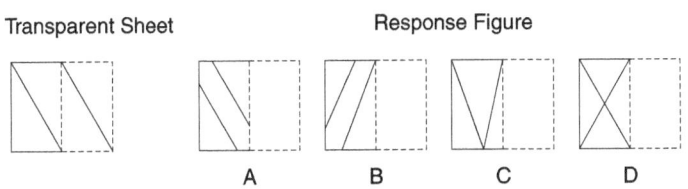

Sol: The right halves of the response figures being dotted indicate that the right half of the transparent sheet has been folded and placed over the left half. Visualizing the combination of the design on the two parts, we obtain fig. (D).

Hence, fig. (D) is the correct answer.

Directions: In each one of the following problems, a square, and a square transparent sheet with a pattern is given. Figure out from amongst the four alternatives as to how the pattern would appear when the transparent sheet is folded at the dotted line.

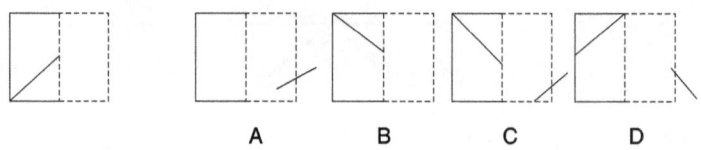

A   B   C   D

Sol: (C)

24. Paper Cutting

Example

Consider the following three figures, marked X, Y, Z showing one fold in X, another in Y and cut in Z. From amongst the answer figures (a), (b), (c) and (d), select the one showing the unfolded position of Z.

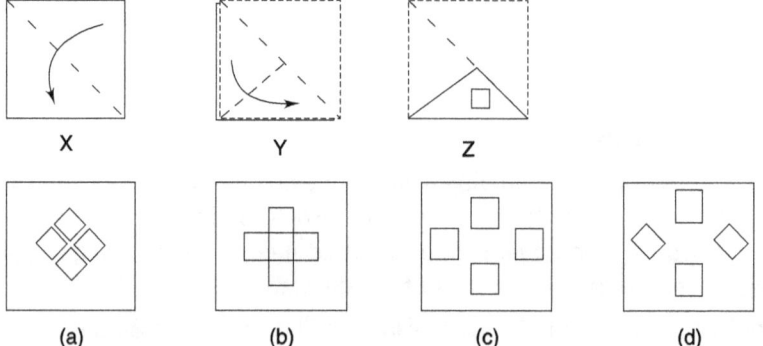

Sol: In fig X. the upper triangular half of the paper has been folded over the lower half.

In the fig. Y, the paper refolded to the quarter's triangle.

In the fig. Z, a square has been punched in the folded paper.

Clearly, the square will appear in each of the triangular quarters of the paper.

Thus, when the paper is unfolded, four squares will appear symmetrically, over it and it will resemble fig. (c).

Direction: The figure (x) given on the left hand side, in each problem, is folded to form a box. Choose from amongst the alternatives (a), (b), (c) and (d), the boxes that are similar to the box formed.

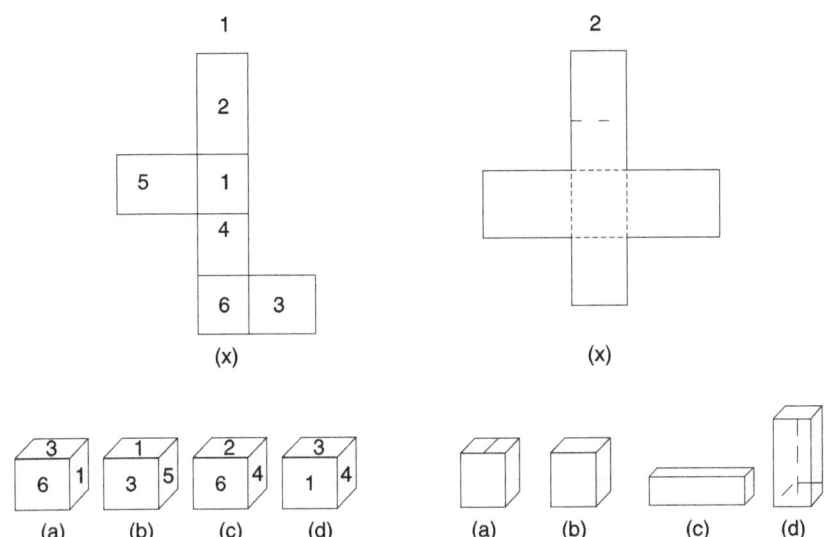

Sol: (d). Fig. (x) is the same as form 3, so when cube is formed, 2 lies opposite 4, 1 lies opposite 6 and 5 lies opposite 3. Hence, the pairs 2 and 4, 1 and 6, 5 & 3 cannot occur at adjacent faces. So, only cube (d) can be formed.

25. Problem on dice

Sometimes we are given figures of the same die in various positions. After observing these figures, we have to find the number opposite a given number on the die. The procedure to be adopted for solving such problem will be clear from the following examples:

Example A dice is thrown four times and its four different positions are given below. Find the number on the face opposite the face showing 2.

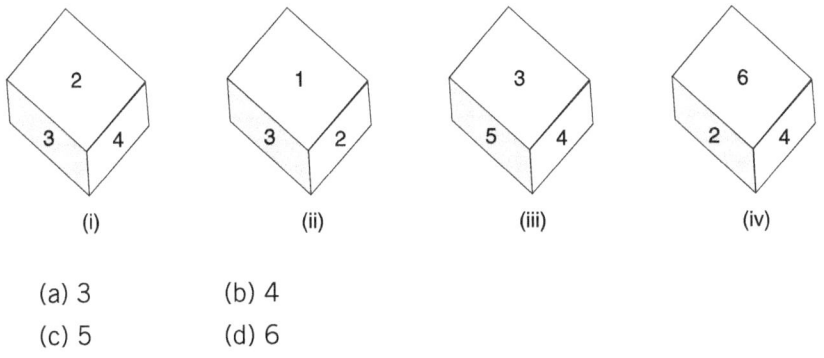

(a) 3   (b) 4
(c) 5   (d) 6

Sol: Here, the number 2 appears in three dice, namely, (i) and (ii) and (iv). In these dice, we observe that the number 2, 4, 1 and 6 and appears adjacent to 3. So, none of these numbers can be present opposite 2. The only number left is

Hence, 5 is present on the face opposite 2.
The answer is (c).

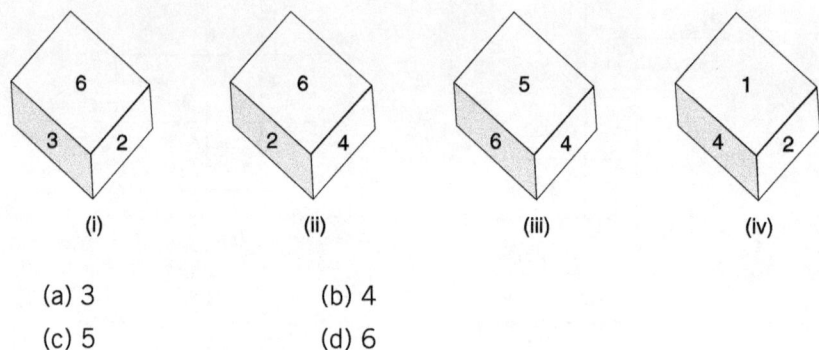

(a) 3   (b) 4
(c) 5   (d) 6

Example Which number is on the face opposite 6?

Sol: From fig. (i), (ii) and (iii), it is clear that the numbers 3, 2, 4 and 5 lie adjacent to the number 6. So, 1 lies opposite 6.

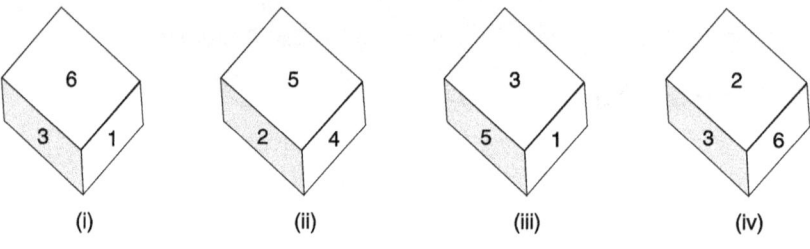

Example What number is opposite 3?

Sol: From fig. (i), (iii) and (iv), it is clear that the numbers 6, 1, 5 and 2 lie adjacent to 3. So, 4 lies opposite 3.

Facing Interview

"The acquisition of knowledge is hard...... Our minds are prone to illusions, fallacies and superstitions......"

– *Steven Pinker*

General

Interview is an interaction between the Interviewing Officer and the candidate, through which the IO checks the same qualities which are being checked by the Psychologist & the GTO respectively. He asks general questions related to individual's service, family, schooling, friends, hobbies, interests, sports and about information furnished by the individual in his PIQ Form. Most of the questions are preset and the rest are predictable. Based on your responses he decides your fate.

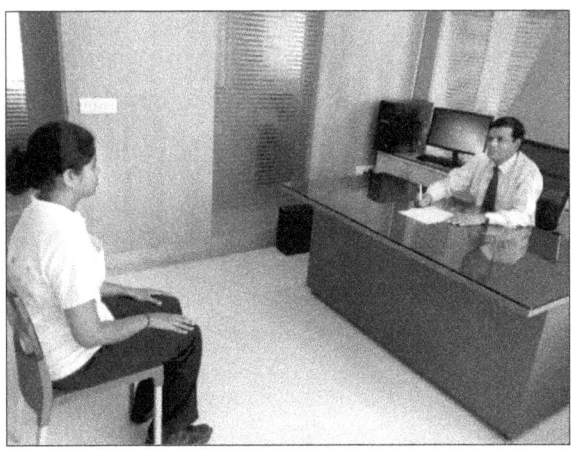

Here too the catch is preparation; take each question and give out your answer. If you can record your answers and listen again you will realize that you are in a position to generate a better answer. Repeat this process time and again, and weed out all the unwanted low level responses. If possible make your professor to take an interview for you. It could be any of your mentors. If you prepare well at the SSB the IO will be too glad to grade you with high marks. The IO being the senior-most testing officer, his grading will go a long way in deciding your fate. Here too, I reiterate that the success formula is preparation and homework.

The interview is intended to judge the mental calibre, attitude and outlook of the candidate along with his leadership qualities and character traits. Thus, it would be an assessment not merely of his academic proficiency and intellectual qualities but also of his social traits and interest in current events. Some of the personality traits to be judged can be listed as:

- Mental alertness and grasping power
- Power of expression and presentation
- Balance of judgment
- Systematic and logical exposition
- Variety and depth of interests
- Ability for social cohesion and effectiveness
- Intellectual and moral integrity

The Aim of the SSB Interview

The IO at the SSB tries to assess the leadership or officer-like qualities of the candidate by means of direct or purposive conversation during the interview. He also tries to evaluate the training potentialities of the candidate. The questions at the interview will be so directed as the candidate may automatically emit enough light on his leadership ability in his answers.

Two important factors of the interview which play a decisive role are the candidate's level of knowledge and his power of expression. He should be able to speak fluently and express himself clearly, then he will score high marks. While answering the candidate should take the lead and cover as much as possible. In other words, simply saying "YES" or "NO" to a question will not suffice. The candidate should explain convincingly why he agrees or disagrees to a given proposition. He must logically and forcefully substantiate his views with valid arguments.

INTERVIEW PROCESS

The Personal Interview (PI) is the mental, physical & social assessment of the candidate by the IO, usually in the rank of Colonel/Captain (IN), GP Captain, i.e. who is the president or deputy president of the board. Board Presidents are generally Brigadier/Air Commodore/Commodore.

PIQ Filling & Recapitulation

The IO reads well the PIQ filled by the candidate before the candidate is called inside the room. Thus the IO just cross checks with the candidate by triggering some asic questions, also triggering the series of questions at a stretch that is called as Rapid Fire Questions (RPF). With these replies he notes down the response and checks whether the candidate is truthful with his answers and he notes down the qualities of the candidate. So ensure that PIQ is filled up neatly and completely as it creates first impression about the candidate on IO and Psychologist.

ROLE OF BODY LANGUAGE IN INTERVIEWING

What is Body Language?

1. Psychologists describe body language as a language of signals. Every day, we unconsciously send out many signals through our body. Body language reveals lot about your personality and the truth of what you are saying.

2. Everyone knows, right from school days that banging fists, narrowed eyes, puckering lips and clenched teeth are signs of anger and one need not scream to display it. Thus, you may be sporting a wide grin, telling a person how happy you are to see him. But if you are doing so while leaning back in your chair, tightly holding your hands together and at the same time avoiding looking at the person in the eyes, it indicates only too clearly that you wish you two had never seen each other. In any job, which involves interaction with people, body language plays an indispensable role.

Relevance of Body Language in Interviewing

3. A person releasing body language signals is usually unaware that he is expressing his true feelings through gestures as movements are controlled by the subconscious. This can prove to be a boon for interviewing officers.

   Experts comment that non-verbal communication is expressed through a series of "gesture clusters". The way you carry yourself, sit, stand, talk and move your hands or feet conveys more than a thousand words and reflects your state of mind. One may use a lot of words and yet fail to get his point across, but to anyone who can read signs, the body 'speaks' in a simple yet straightforward way. Body language is perhaps more eloquent than spoken words. The science of body language has always been fascinating and intriguing. After all, one has always wanted to know as to what people mean by a glance, blush or a twitch of an eyebrow.

4. Understanding body talk calls for both close observation and interpretation. Through reading non-verbal signs, an interviewer can be reasonably accurate in assessing a candidate's personality as well as his innermost thoughts. It is clearly evident that body language is 'Personal Psychology' today, adding a whole new dimension to what you can understand about people and their behaviour.

Body Language Clues

5. To analyse a personality reasonably effectively, one must be able to clearly identify as to what he is looking for. Some important elements of body language are listed below:

    (a) Facial Expression: Personality clues are often obtained by noticing permanent facial lines and structure. A number of personality traits leave their mark on the face of the person and therefore, could be used for correlation. Moreover, facial expression also indicates what a person feels or thinks under various circumstances.

    (b) Overall Appearance: A person's gender, age, cultural background, geographical origin etc. can be assessed by his/her overall appearance. Appearance would include height, body, shape and size, colour of the skin/hair etc. If someone is an easy-going person and very relaxed, his body posture will be loose and fluid because this is how his muscles are. Conversely, if the person is nervous and tightens his muscles he would show tense raised shoulders and so on.

    (c) Movements and Gestures: The way a person moves his/her various body parts and displays personalized gestures also conveys considerable meaning in terms of body language. These would include hand/limb movements, head nods as well as gestures expressed through various body parts.

    (d) Movements of Eye: It is widely believed that our eyes are the most expressive parts of our body. Various moods and relationships are reflected through our eyes. While a person is telling a lie, he would generally avoid eye contact. A person expresses various sentiments by using his eyes and eyebrows. In this context, angry eyes, lover's gaze, scared eyes etc., are some of the very common examples.

    (e) Voice: While expressing himself, a person uses his voice to display his age, sex, race etc. Subtle changes in pitch, volume and rhythm also indicate how one feels about something.

    (f) Physical Functions of Body: Numerous body functions such as breathing patterns, heart rate, blood pressure, sweating levels etc., also indicate a person's feelings and reactions to a given situation.

GUARDING AGAINST POOR NON-VERBAL COMMUNICATION

It is now common knowledge that much more than words, it is our body language that speaks volumes. In this regard, the way you place or use your hands, carry yourself and use your eyes etc., assume critical importance. It is felt that the following handy tips would help candidates a great deal to adopt suitable and positive body language while facing interview.

- **Body Posture:** The posture of sitting with your head erect and shoulders back, generally reflects your alertness. A slight lean forward would also indicate that you are keen for the discussion. On the contrary, an extended lean backwards would reflect your disinterest in the proceedings and should, therefore, be avoided under all circumstances.
- **Facial Expressions:** A pleasant look on your face goes a long way to convey that you are a relaxed as well as a confident person. In this respect, furrowed brows, tense jaw and nervous twitches should be scrupulously avoided. Although, a certain amount of anxiety cannot be kept away, a relaxed look does go in your favour and indicates that you can take a substantial amount of stress in stride. In this regard, reading some light material and having a good sleep during the previous night would generally help.
- **Eye Contact:** Our eyes reflect the general state of our mind. A good eye contact with the IO indicates your attention and interest in that person. Consequently, during discussion, it would be prudent to keep an eye contact with the IO. However, it must be clarified that keeping an eye contact with the IO, does not imply staring at him. Of course, breaking the eye contact occasionally would be in order to ensure an occasional glance away. Looking at the tip of the nose of the IO gives an impression of eye contact, at the same time you will feel at ease.
- **Voice Modulation:** While conveying ideas, candidate should appropriately modulate his/her voice. Speaking loudly does not bring about the desired impact. Moreover, subtle changes in pitch, volume and rhythm also indicate how one feels about something. A candidate having a mature and balanced outlook would maintain the required modulation to convey and lay emphasis on certain significant aspects.
- **Head Movements:** It has been experienced that anxiety makes a candidate nod his head rather excessively. On the other hand, not moving one's head at all may sometimes indicate disinterest in the ongoing discussion. It is, therefore, recommended that nodding of head should be done in a subtle manner but never excessively or vigorously.
- **Movement of Hands:** While expressing yourself verbally at interviews, keep a deliberate check on excessive movements of both your hands. Vigorous and frequent movement of hands reflects your limitations in verbally expressing yourself. Slight movement of hands once in a while may be acceptable, but pointing fingers towards would undeniably amount to bad manners on the part of the candidate. A palm-closed finger gesture reveals aggression.
- **Movement and Gestures:** Our gestures reveal a lot about our state of mind. Constant fidgeting and yawning create a negative impact on the formal set up of a group discussion. A candidate should consciously avoid certain unnecessary movements and gestures such as tapping of feet, repeated

touching of hair, fiddling with the ring, jewellery or spectacles, lip-biting etc. These movements are distracting and indicate that a candidate is either bored or nervous or has become impatient. Consulting one's watch frequently or looking outside the window should also be avoided as these gestures suggest a lack of interest on the part of the candidate. Narrowing of the eyes is a particularly strong negative gesture that is indicative of disagreement and even resentment. Similarly, raised eyebrows convey disbelief and communicate that you do not trust.

The above paragraphs clearly indicate that small changes in one's body language make a big difference in terms of flow of information between the candidate and IO and create a substantial impact on the proceedings of interview or discussion or any other talk needing conversation with assessors. The indications through your body language could be:

1. Are you sweating or perspiring, indicating nervousness?
2. Are you shaking legs or fidgeting, showing instability?
3. Are you closing eyes too often or looking one side and talking other side, indicating shyness or short memory?
4. Are you often pausing or giving breaks in your conversation, indicating inadequate communication skills etc.?
5. Your facial expressions, if you are natural in responses or otherwise.
6. Your fast movements of hands or head, or high pitched voice, indicating aggressiveness.

Remaining Calm & Cool during Interview

To make the whole process as a cake walk, the only way is to be honest and natural – since it is not an easy task to tell a lie or bluff the IO. As he is very much trained he would know if a person is lying.

What the interviewing officer expects from the candidate is not an all-rounder or a well knowledgeable person, but a person who adapts to all situations, one who can handle and work under pressure, who is able to move with a group of people, who has an eye over the world and national issues, is able to give solution to the national issues etc. So put yourself to these points and assess yourself (a jack of all trades but master of none).

Interview Preparation

- Appearance
- Entry & First Impression
- Body Language during the process
- Clarity of thought and explanations
- No beating around the bush

- Pleasant Disposition
- Holding ground in tough questions
- Being Logical & Analytical
- Interview Questions and How to Tackle

Appearance

It is better to wear a light-coloured shirt and a dark-coloured pant. If you have your school/college blazer, wear it, as this gives a decent professional look. Ensure you have a decent haircut, shaved, polished shoes. Also wear a tie which matches the shirt and pant colours. Women should not wear tight or revealing clothes. Salwar suits/pants and shirts should suffice. You should look smart & pleasant.

Entry & First Impression

Enter the interview room with a smile and calm face, as this shows that you are cool. Also have a proper dress code. Walk with head held high, with upraised shoulder and chest. This gives a positive, confident look. Also before entering into the hall ask for permission and wait for the response; if you got the response from IO, open the door with smiling face (the smile should be true) and march ahead into the room with confidence, and wish the officer as per the time (good morning, evening etc.). Also stand behind the chair meant for the candidate and don't stand in front of the chair, as it shows that you have a thought in your mind that you will be granted to have a seat. It's wrong; the candidate should stand behind or by the side of the chair and wait for permission from the IO to sit. If the permission is granted he should thank the officer and sit comfortably without shaking or changing the position of the chair.

Body Language during the Process

Body language plays a vital role in the process as highlighted earlier. Experts say that above 93% of non-verbal communication plays a main role in the process. Sit in proper manner; also don't shake your hands, fingers, or legs during the process. The IO matches the response from your mouth to the body language what you are showing at that time. Also try to have a proper eye contact. Keep your breath normal. Do not get distracted or look here and there; it would be like *looking London, talking Tokyo (LLTT)*. For these things to be normal, the one and only way is to be truthful to yourself and to the IO. If you are honest, then your reply will be bold.

Clarity of Thought and Explanations

The thought and answers coming from the candidate should be crystal clear. When the IO asks a question it means the candidate has to think about that clearly and make a clear answer with explanations. Never give Yes/No type of replies as this shows your confidence level is low. If you explain your answer with positive points, it gains you more credits in the process. So please avoid the yes/no type responses.

Also if you have only little knowledge about that topic, tell the IO that 'Sir, I know these things about this question', or 'Sorry sir, I am not getting more points about this topic at this moment'. This shows your honesty and the IO likes this only. He doesn't expect the candidate to be an encyclopedia. Be polite and confident in your answer.

Not Beating Around the Bush

Be truthful & natural to the IO. If you don't know, tell him openly, 'Sorry sir, I am not fully aware of it'. It's better to tell the truth than beat around the bush. Also the important point is, don't say immediately after the question is asked by the IO, that sorry sir I don't know. Just try to give at least a single point of answer to the question, i.e. think for a while and if you really don't get the answer, say then politely sorry sir I don't recollect it.

Pleasant Disposition

It is the key to success. Never be a Sad Man in front of the IO. Try to give smiling posture all through the process, i.e., from entering the room and till the end of the process. To keep smiling, you should be free by mind, to be free, be honest to the IO. Else your artificial smile will be recognized as a fake smile. So you may reduce your chance of getting selected. Be calm and truthful in your replies. Be natural in your behaviour.

Holding Ground in Tough Situations

Losing the ground with the IO is common for all candidates. Since this is an oral war between the IO and the candidate, it's not an easy thing to win over the oral war with the IO, as they have real war experience. To avoid this situation, don't argue with the IO. The IO expects that the candidate should not lose his ground and face all the situations tactfully. If you have sound knowledge in subjects and positive replies you never lose your ground. Tackle the questions with presence of mind and show your knowledge and positive approach with the replies.

Logical & Analytical Ability

The analysing capability is one of the important qualities of an officer. Most of the candidates have the analysing capability, but what the IO expects is whether you are using your analysing capability even under pressure or tough situations. So the IO cross-checks this quality with the candidate throughout the process by triggering various questions at different situations.

Interview Questions & How to Tackle

The pattern is a four-step process usually followed at all SSB boards. The SSB interview is different than what is followed in the corporate world. Unlike corporate interviews which are semi structured or unstructured, SSB PI are fully structured and the same type of questions are asked to all the candidates. So the question paper is known to the candidates. It is the most appropriate answer which will give credit to the candidates. Sequence of questions asked by IO is pictorially shown below:

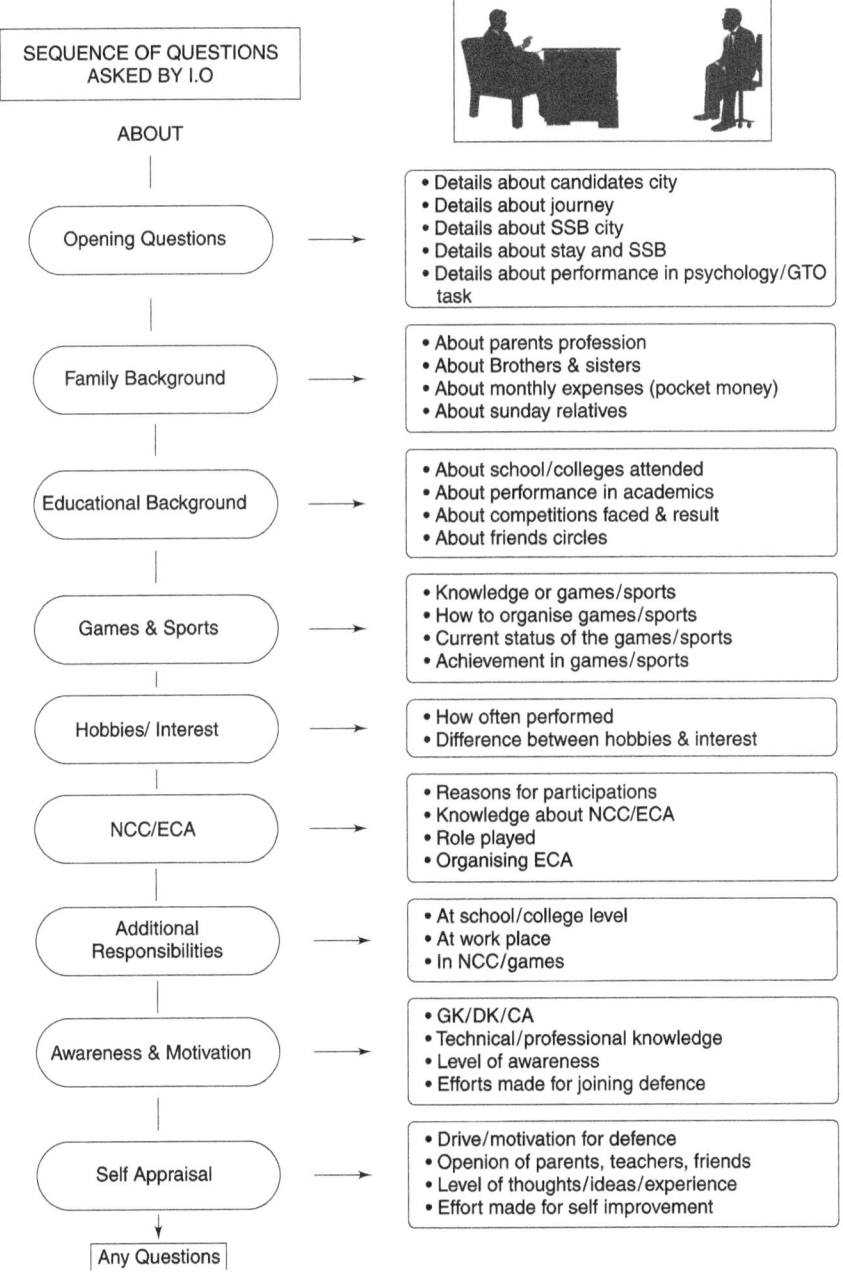

Candidates are put through the following type of questions usually and their qualities are assessed based on their responses:
1. Rapport building questions or feel free questions
2. Rapid fire questions (on family and educational background)
3. Social interactions/Solutions type questions
4. Current affairs and defence awareness
5. Technical questions or practical knowledge questions
6. Self-appraisal questions

Let us discuss in detail about these types of questions and the way of approach to these questions. But before that, let us examine what are purposes of major questions asked from the candidates. As candidate, you should know the purpose as given below:-

INTERVIEW QUESTIONS When you are asked about	PURPOSES The Assessor wants to know
Family background	Environment of personality growth
Educational	Intelligence level
Co-curricular activity	Organizing & Initiation
Friends circle	Social & Extrovertness
Activity planning	Planning & Dynamism
Reasons for joining defence	Motivation for defence forces
Describing personality in terms of strength & weakness	Natural projection of what one is - no masking.

1. Rapport Building Questions or Feel Free Questions

Usually these types of questions are put to the candidates after their entry into the IO room. The IO asks some basic questions which can be easily answered by the candidate so that the candidate feels at ease with the IO. The questions may be as follows:
1. Which place are you coming from and tell me something about that place?
2. Tell something about your name and why named so?
3. Tell five things about your native place and which you like most?
4. How was journey from home city to SSB city?

How to Answer?

For the first question, answer should not be like this: Sir I am from Bangalore.

But the answer is: Sir I am from Bangalore, the IT hub of India, and capital city of Karnataka. The population is about one crore and people are engaged in IT,defence sectors and public sector undertakings which are plenty. The specialty is good weather and quality of life and tourism is high in attracting visitors and the important PSUs and Defence establishments if any etc.

In this manner the answer should cover overall aspects of Bangalore. This gives a broad approach to your answer and it shows your knowledge.

- The answer given to the IO should be crystal clear and optimistic (positive) and truthful. These are about the Introductory Questions. It is easy to answer the introductory Questions with an optimistic view and it plays a vital role.

2. Rapid Fire Questions

The Rapid Fire Questions (RFQ), also called comprehensive introductory questions, is a set of questions which are asked at a stretch to check the grasp/memory. Nearly eight to ten questions will be triggered out by the IO to check how many questions are observed by the candidate and answered well and how truthful he is with his replies.

The RFQs may start from family background, friends including daily routine, educational background, views about teachers, friends' view about you and your view about them; hobbies and interests at free time, checking leadership qualities by asking about extracurricular activities and how the candidate will organize a task or situation, games and sports etc. To be crispy about RPQ, every question will be from the PIQ only. So just prepare possible questions that IO may ask you generally about family background or educational background. Set of questions may be raised from any other part of the PIQ for the rapid fire questions.

From Family Background

> **Example:** I will be interested in knowing about your family background, in that I will like to know what your parents are doing, whom are you close to, mother or father & why, how many brothers and sisters you have & what they are doing, how much pocket money you have been getting & how do you spend it, what type of friends circle you have & the qualities of friends. Who is your best friend & why? What is your Sunday routine from morning till you go to bed at night?

A list of such questions which could be part of RFQ are as below:
- How much pocket money you got in your college days and how did you utilize it.
- How you help your mother during your holidays
- How you help your father

- You are close to father or mother, and why
- How much you like your father and mother
- How you are a responsible person to your family
- Say something about your sister and brother
- Whom you like most and why?
- With whom you play more?
- Which person other than in your family and friends you like more and why?
- What are the qualities in your parents that you do not appreciate much?
- If your family is totally dependent on you tomorrow, how you will help or run the family?

From Friends

- How do you make new friends, male & females?
- Which type of friends you like?
- How many friends you have?
- Out of friends how many are close to you?
- In your friends circle with whom you share the personal things?
- What you like in your best friend and what he likes in you?
- What your friend or friends say about you?
- Which aspect you like in your close friend and why?
- How you will help your friend or helped your friend in any bad moments?
- What you and your friends/friend do in your free time?

> **Example:** Tell me from 10th standard (for Graduates & above) (8th standard for NDA + 10+2 TES), which schools you have studied, what are the marks obtained in major exams, what are your favourite subjects and teachers and why; why did you take up BA/B.Sc/B.Com or Engineering in _____, what are competitive exams you have applied so far and what happened to those and finally tell me why do you want to join army/navy/airforce?

You must speak for a minute as to why you want to join the Defence Forces. A lot of weightage is given to the response of this question, as it highlights about candidate's motivation and commitment for Defence Forces.

A satisfactory reply, for why you want to join Army would be:

Sir, it was desire from the class level of 10th that I serve the nation directly.

After passing my 12th, I wanted to join NDA but my parents were not very sure if I would be able to go through the tough routine or not. Moreover, I was not in a position to convince them either. They thought if I couldn't survive the routine or life in defence, it would be their fault at first place to misjudge me. Now after completing my B. Tech I have convinced them and they support me now as they think I am mature and responsible to take my own decision.

Another reason is that, I would like to initiate this career in my family as there is no one from defence in my family, so that future generations consider defence as their career too. I must also add that, it's a dignified & noblest job to do in the country. It is a job of respect, discipline & one becomes a part of an elite institution.

A list of questions that could be included in your educational background RFQ, are below:

- How much you scored in your tenth, twelfth and graduation?
- Why there is decrease in the mark level and what you did to overcome those difficulties?
- Which subject you like more and why?
- Which subject you don't like and why?
- Achievements in the study?
- Specialty about your school and college?
- Which teacher you like most why?
- Which teacher you don't like and why?
- Why you have chosen to study this branch?
- Whether you chose the particular branch of study by self or by others compulsion (Parents)
- Why there is some gap in studies between inter college and graduation?
- How you improved the percentage from tenth to twelfth and what are the steps you have taken to achieve this?
- If you scored less marks in twelfth than in tenth, the question is: What are the steps you have taken to overcome this decrease in percentage not to continue in graduation?
- What your friends and teachers think about you?

For Working Professionals

> **Example** How did you get selected for this job, what are the roles/responsibility given to you, for how long you have been working & how do you spend the salary you get and where do you see yourself in next two years?

A list of questions that could be asked as RFQ, are as follows:

- What your coworkers say about you?
- What you say about your boss?

- What your boss says about you?
- Tell about your company or organization?
- How do you spend your salary?
- What you like most in your job?
- What you don't like in your job?
- What difficulty you faced in your job and what are the steps you have taken to overcome those difficulties?
- Why are you leaving the present job?

For Service Candidates

Example A combination of the following questions can form RFQ:

- Why did you initially join Army/Navy/Airforce?
- How did you feel during the training period?
- Which units/stations have you served & which was the best unit/station?
- What has been your contribution in department?
- Who was your best CO and why?
- Why do you want to become a Commissioned Officer?
- Which has been the most challenging task that you have performed so far?
- What impression does your superior have about you?
- Have you achieved any commendations from superior authority?
- How will you organize a Barakhana/Picnic for your department?

Note: Candidates should remember all the questions and answer them systematically. Avoid asking IO for repetition of these questions as it will reflect poor memory and grasp on the part of the candidate. The order may be changed while replying to the Rapid Fire Question.

3. Social Interactions/Solutions (Games/Co-curricular Activities)

- Which game you like and why?
- Why you have chosen an indoor game rather than an outdoor game?
- Why you have chosen an outdoor game rather than an indoor game?
- Whom you like more in your team (if we say cricket or football etc.)?
- What is your position in the team, i.e. as a team member or captain?
- Depth of knowledge in the games or sports
- Questions from size of the playground/court size and rules of the game and recent world records in the game etc.

- Which player you like most and why?
- What you want to improve or your suggestion for our team in the game/sports you play?
- What is difference between games and sports?

A good young youth with good physique should play a game in his spare time. So everyone must have a game/sport to play. If you don't have a game to play just join any club of your interest and start to play as it helps you to get more OLQ's.

Also get a thorough knowledge in the game which you used to play.

About Hobbies and Interests

- What is your hobby?
- Why have you chosen this hobby?
- Since when you are pursuing this hobby?
- What are the things you have learnt from your hobby?
- What are the new things you implemented in your hobby?
- What's your childhood hobby and what are you doing now?
- Why did you change the childhood hobby to this (recent one)?

You require vast knowledge in the hobby since everyone will have a hobby, but a candidate with good attitude will get information about their hobbies. Different types of hobbies are music, singing, blogging, reading, philately, photography, trekking etc. Create questions based on your hobby and make responses for that to get thorough knowledge over that.

Interests

What type of news channel, TV shows you see and which periodical you have read and why? How are interests different from hobbies?

Identifying the Leadership and Organizing Ability

Leadership and organizing ability is an important quality of every officer, and this part of the process seems to be important. The officer may give a situation to check your organizing ability; also he may ask questions from the PIQ in the fields of extracurricular and co-curricular activities such as NSS and NCC, drama, debate, workshops, scouts, blood donation etc.

If you play a game or sports, how you will organize that game. Work out in advance the various actions that are required to be taken systematically – starting from putting the details on the notice board till the distribution of prizes if any.

Co-Curricular and Extra-curricular Activities

The co-curricular and extra-curricular activities include those such as NSS, NCC, volunteer for NGO activities.

- When you joined in NCC/NSS and why
- What you achieved in that
- Positions held in that
- Grade of certificates such as A, B, C etc.
- Who motivated to join in NCC

4. Current Affairs & Defence Awareness

In this part the IO may ask questions on world issues, national issues and solution for those issues. Also he checks the depth of knowledge and candidate's approach to the issues.

Example

- Tell five things you recently read in newspaper. Tell your views about a particular news/event. Has Intolerance in India increased many fold?
- What is the role of Army/Navy/Airforce?
- Interviewing Officer may ask the candidate about the views of nation on GST, is it good or bad; if good, why it is good, and if bad why it is bad, then tell your solution like this – Cover the subject, cover pluses & minus (i.e. both aspects) and then conclude based on merits of the facts. IO also asks some questions on Defence awareness and current HOT SPOTS.

5. Technical Questions or Practical Knowledge Questions

If you apply the TGC entry, TES entry Technical Graduation Course and Technical Entry Scheme they may put forward some basic technical questions related to our day to day life.

Example 1: How does a fan or a tube light work? What is the difference between CDMA and GSM phones?

Example 2: If you say that you play cricket, he may ask how you will apply physics to the swing bowling etc. Also, what is the Pythagoras Theorem or how does a ship float or how does an aircraft fly?

In these set of questions, IO finds out the candidate's level of practical knowledge, i.e. application of theoretical knowledge in the physical day to day tasks which is essential for a defence personnel.

6. Self-Appraisal Question

Finally the IO asks the candidate to speak about his good qualities and about not so good qualities. He can also put the same question as - what are the strengths and weaknesses of your personality and how will you improve your weaknesses?

Candidates are advised to include 70% of their strengths and 30% of their weaknesses while speaking on self-appraisal. Do not ever present yourself that you do not have any weakness. Speak for about 45-60 seconds while replying to these questions. Candidates generally end up answering this question in a few sentences (not more than 10-15 sec). This is not considered adequate. Most of the candidates are found to be weak in conversational skills in English, current affairs, defence awareness, and systematic organising skills.

Finally, before the IO closes the interview, he gives a chance to the candidate to ask a question/query. If you feel you are a smart candidate, ask sensible questions of high level. Do not ask low level questions like, how I have done in the interview? will I be selected? or what improvements are required in me? These types of questions reflect poorly about the candidate. Some sensible questions could be:

1. How do you find the present task of being an IO, as compared to your operational task?
2. Why several aircraft accidents taking place in IAF, is it lack of training or otherwise?
3. Why is the aircraft carrier, INS Vikramaditya delayed in joining Indian Navy?
4. Why are not women officers given PC in combat force.

Summary – Facing Interview

Impact creation through interview

Candidates should be now aware, that during three processes i.e Entry, Q/A session, Motivation/Awareness (M/A), they need to create **impact and the level of impact** on interview officer created is important to succeed. The percentage of impact is shown below:

SAMPLE OF QUESTION/ANSWER SESSION BETWEEN I.O. & CANDIDATE

Q. Which is your native place?
Ans: Allahabad.

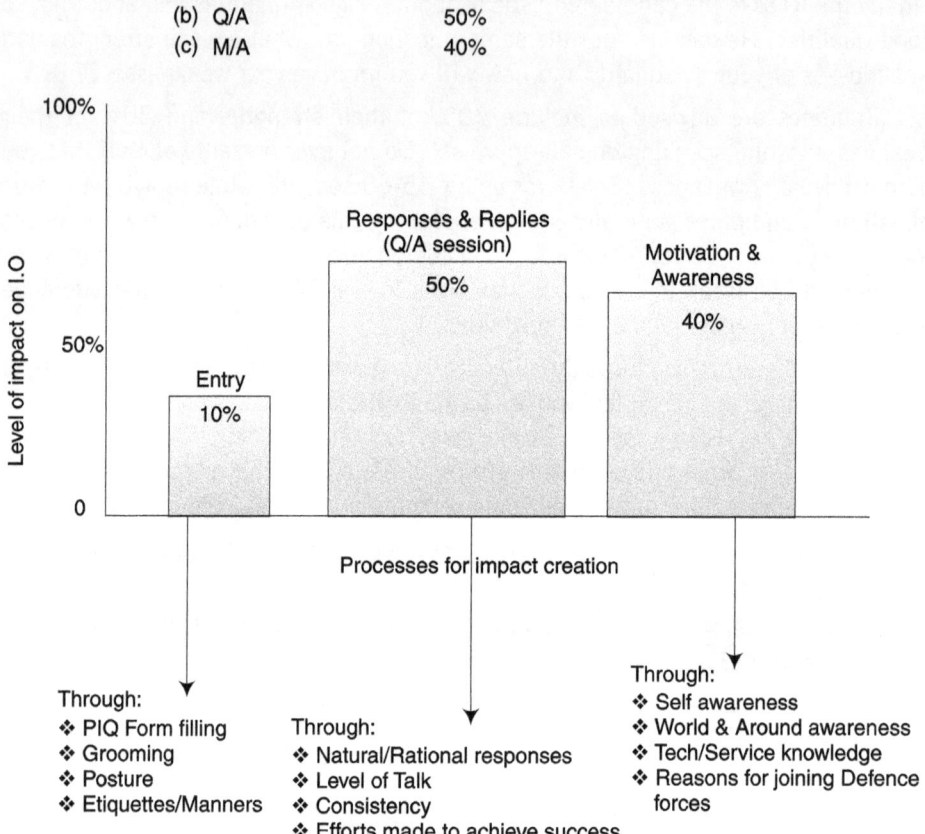

Q. Tell me something about Allahabad?

Ans: It is an historical and cultural city. Now it is the administrative, commercial and educational centre of Uttar Pradesh.

Q. How was your stay at the SSB?

Ans: It was very interesting, enjoyable, I made new friends. Overall, it's a memorable experience.

Q. Tell me about yourself and your family background?

Ans: I'm a young achiever who has captained his team to win the Inter University Football Championship for the first time. I am energetic & social person with a great zeal to be part of armed forces. My parents are presently teachers in high school at Allahabad.

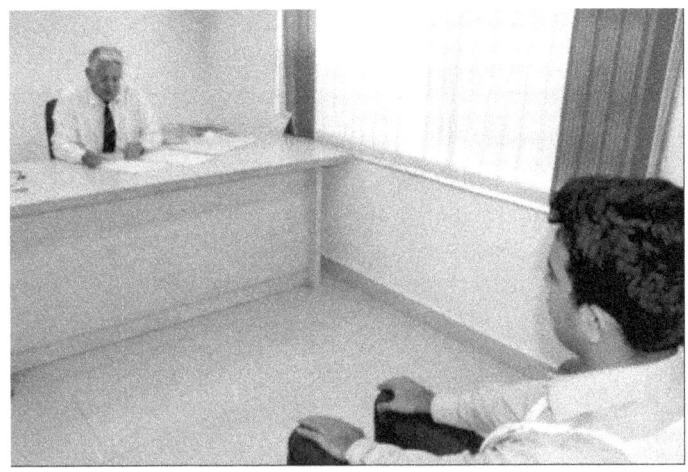

Q. How many brothers and sisters you have? And what they are doing?

Ans: Sir I have one brother and one sister, sister works as a teacher in a government school and brother is preparing for the medical education.

Q. What was the reason behind your low score?

Ans: I was actively involved with football team of my college and much of my time was spent on playing and training. So, I was not able to concentrate much on studies.

Q. How would your friends describe you?

Ans: My friends would probably say that I am a social and daring person/individual. I have never been afraid to keep going back until I get what I want. When I was in the first year of my college, my friends told me that I would never make it to the college's football team, but I worked hard and not only got selected in the team but by the time of final year, I became captain of the team. A lot of people might have given up after the first rejection, but it's just not in my nature. This is appreciated by my friends.

Q. Why do you want to join the armed forces?

Ans: Sir, I want to join the armed forces because it offers me an excellent career at early age that combines in itself a good status or good future prospects, active life and service to the country to live in armed forces.

Q. How playing football is going to help you in the armed forces?

Ans: It makes me become more disciplined and organized person. It's a team game, so it helps me to develop team spirit in me and it also improved my fitness level. I think these qualities are much required to become an Army Officer.

Q. What's the most difficult part of being a captain?

Ans: I think every captain finds it challenging to motivate the team when it's in a losing patch. But that's probably the strongest test of a captain. I feel this is one area where I excel.

Q. Why India is not doing well in football?

Ans: Sir, there are many factors but most important are lack of finance, poor infrastructure, bleak future, lack of modern techniques, favoritism and nepotism and lastly the most important the lack of national spirit.

Q. What do you feel are your greatest strengths & weakness?

Ans: My greatest strength is that I have a lot of initiative. I am always looking for a better way to do things at work. e.g., one time during a tournament, I give chance to some new players and they performed really well. I am very hard on myself. I am always expecting myself to do a little bit more. However, I guess this works out well for me over the year.

Or

I have never been very comfortable with public speaking which at times is a hindrance in the work. But since I have become captain of my team I've given lots of presentations to my team which enable me to overcome my life-long fear.

Q. What are your long range goals?

Ans: I am looking for a position in an institution where I can stay and grow with and I feel in the Armed Forced as an officer, would give me this opportunity.

Q. Do you prefer to work independently or on a team?

Ans: I am equally comfortable working as a member of a team and independently. In college, I enjoyed playing football and performing with the marching band. Each required a different kind of team play, but the overall goal of learning to be a member of a group was invaluable.

Q. What is your greatest failure and what did you learn from it?

Ans: When I was in the last year of college, I didn't take my studies very seriously and assumed that I will be able to get good marks like in previous years. My low marks in the final year showed me otherwise. I learned that no matter what I'm doing, I should strive to do it to the best of my ability. Otherwise, it's not worth doing at all.

Q. What motivates you to join the NDA?

Ans: NDA is a premier defence institution, where integrated training of Army, Navy & Air force is carried out. I want to be an alumnus of this Institution. This institution shapes boys into gentlemen.

Q. Apart from playing football, what are the other hobbies or interest you have?

Ans: Sir I like to read good books.

Q. What good books have you read lately?

Ans: Change your thinking, change your life. Brian Tracy

Q. What's the theme of this book?

Ans: Changing the thinking process and what difference it can make in life.

Q. How do you feel about work environment in the Armed Force?

Ans: I greatly admire it as an institution that hires and promotes on merit alone. That's the best type of work environment you can hope to find.

Q. Why aren't you focusing on earning more money at this stage of your career?

Ans: Making money is very important to me, but throughout my life, what's been more important to me is doing work I really like to do.

Q. Suppose you do not get selected. What will be your further course of action?

Ans: Sir I have done very well in the test and very hopeful for my success but if I am not selected then I will try for another attempt next year with more preparation.

Q. Do you have any question or query?

Ans: No sir.

Q. Thank you Mr. Ravi, wish you all the best

Ans: Thank you sir, have a great day ahead.

SAMPLE OF QUESTION/ANSWER SESSION BETWEEN I.O. & SERVICE CANDIDATE

Q. How are you feeling gentleman?

Ans: Sir, I am feeling quite comfortable.

Q. How is your stay, messing and accommodation?

Ans: Sir, my stay is very comfortable and everything is up to the standard.

Q. Which place are you coming from?

Ans: Sir, I am coming from Dehradun as my unit is located there.

Q. What is the population of your district as well as your city?

Ans: Sir, population is:

(a) District - 12.5 lakhs approximately

(b) City - 5 lakhs approximate (not accurate)

Q. What is the importance of Dehradun from various points of views?

Ans: Sir, Dehradun is the temporary capital city of newly formed state Uttarakhand. This is located at the foothills of the Shivalik closer to Rishikesh, Haridwar and Mussoorie. This is a cosmopolitan city famous for school education. This is big commercial centre. This place has many important Central Government establishments like ONGC Headquarters, Survey of India, Geological Survey of India, Forest Research Institute, Indian Institute of Remote Study, Indian Institute of Petroleum, Indian Institute of Wild Life and Indian Institute of Visually Handicapped etc.

This place is also known for various defence organizations like Indian Military Academy, Naval Hydrographic Centre, HQ 14 RAPID(S).

Q. What is the meaning of Green Hedges and Grey Heads?

Ans: Sir, few decades back, there was govt. rule if anybody wanted to settle down in Dehradun, he has to purchase minimum 5 bighas of land. A huge amount of money was required to construct the boundary wall to cover the area and the people did not have so much money. So people used to cover the area by planting hedges, hence it is called 'the city of green hedges'. Since the city is big cantonment and has many central government establishments, so people, who come to posting in this station, are settling down here after their retirement. Hence it is called 'the city of Grey Heads'.

Q. What would you like to improve in Dehradun?

Ans: Sir, I would like to improve the city on following:-

(a) Unplanned growth - No infrastructure, no facilities

(b) Lack of sewerage system.

(c) Lack of facilities of higher education.

(d) Lack of job opportunities

(e) Increasing population

(f) Lack of cleanliness

Q. Tell me population and history of your home town Jaipur?

Ans: Sir Jaipur (the Pink City) is the capital of the state of Rajasthan. Jaipur has a population of 55 lakhs of the district and 23 lakhs of the city approximately. Jaipur was founded on 18 Nov 1727 by Maharaja Sawai Jai Singh-II and the design of the city was prepared by the famous engineer and vastushastri, Shri Vidyadhar Bhattacharya who was from Bengal. In its time Jaipur was the great monument of engineering & vastushastra and it was the most planned & beautiful city of Asia. The whole city is protected with thick and high walls and has 07 gates in different directions. Jaipur is also famous for handloom work, sculpture, blue pottery, quilts, bed sheets, gems & diamonds and Ivory work.

Q. Tell me about your Service background and locations you have served.

Ans: Sir, I am coming from HQ 116 Inf Bde. It was raised on 01 May 1964 at Thiruvananthapuram under the command of Brigadier S.Y. Munshi. During 1965, Bde participated in OP ABLAZE in Khemkaran Sector. After ceasefire, the bde was moved to Babina under HQ 14 Inf Div. Finally the bde moved to Dehradun along with HQ 14 Inf Div which is now known as HQ 14 RAPID(Strike).

Q. Who is your CO/Cdr and what are your primary duties?

Ans: Sir, Col Rajesh is my CO/Cdr and my duties are as follows:

(a) To take dictation and transcribe it and to do the other typing work as directed by my boss.

(b) To screen visitors and telephone calls tactfully.

(c) To fix up appointments, to keep accurate list of engagements and to remind the boss well in advance.

(d) To submit complete papers required for meeting.

(e) To ensure that the matters to be dealt with by the boss are not lost sight of and brought to his notice promptly.

(f) To maintain proper record of files/papers passed by the boss to other officers.

(g) To destroy the computer records and other classified waste papers by burning.

(h) To maintain his reference books and personal files up to date.

(i) To observe the security instructions in respect of his office.

(j) To ensure the proper handing/taking over the papers, files, boxes, keys etc. in his charge when proceeding on leave/retirement and to submit a report duly signed to the officer concerned.

Q. Which CO/Cdr you have liked the most & why?

Ans: Sir, my CO/Cdr is _____ :-

because he was

(a) Disciplined

(b) Master of his profession

(c) Good Administrator

(d) Solves problems with ease

(e) Hard working

(f) Setting examples for others

(g) Source of encouragement

Q. Well gentleman, tell me about your service, where all you have served?

Ans: Sir, since my enrolment, I served in:

A suggested format to give answer

From	To	Unit	Achievements

From	To	Unit	Achievements

Q. What are your professional achievements?

Ans: Sir, Ministry of Home Affairs had examined that I had done extraordinary, unexpected, better than routine work for the better functioning of the organization.

Q. If you are made the CO tell me one area where you would put maximum attention?

Ans: Sir, I would give maximum stress to improve professional as well as physical training to keep the men fit for fighting.

Q. Tell me about your schooling and percentage of marks obtained starting from 9th Std.

Ans: Sir, I did my schooling in various stations as my father was an army man and he was subject to frequent postings. However from class 9th to 12th I did my schooling in Govt Senior Higher Secondary School, Khatipura, Jaipur and I was the class monitor during the period.

A suggested format to give answer

Class	Division	Marks Obtained	% age	Subjects	Class Teacher

Q. Which friend you wanted to avoid?

Ans: Sir, I would not like to avoid anybody as they all were very co-operative, obedient and good friends.

Q. Why there is a break in your graduation?

Ans: Sir, in _____ I did my BA first year, in _____ I did my BA second year but in _____ I could not appear in BA final year examinations as I was enrolled in the Army in Jan 1996 and I was under training. So I completed my BA final year in _____.

Q. Why did you join the Army without completing graduation?

Ans: Sir, I was fully aware that I would miss the opportunity of completing the graduation but it was the need of hour. I decided to grab this opportunity to become a part of this elite organization and just after the training I completed my graduation accordingly.

Q. Do you have any of your family members in the Defence?

Ans: Sir, my father is an Ex Hav Clerk – Army

My elder uncle an Ex-Chief Mechanical Engineer - Navy

My cousins Mechanical Engineers – Navy

Q. Tell me about your parents.

Ans: Sir, Shri. Ram Kumari is my father. He is intermediate. He is retired from Corps of Signals as Hav/Clk and presently re-employed in Rajasthan Secretariat as UDC.

Smt. Prema Kumari is my mother. Though she is illiterate yet she is managing the home very smoothly.

Q. Tell me about your wife.

Ans: Sir, to be very honest, when I applied for commission in January, I was divorced. During February I have got remarried and adopted a daughter. So in my application my wife's name has not been reflected. Now Mrs. Anita is my wife. She is post graduate in history. She has diploma in basic computer and fashion designing (02 years diploma). She is simple and straightforward lady. She is responsible and caring. Now I have two kids, son Master Nitesh Kiran and daughter Shilpa. Both are six years. They are not twins as my daughter is adopted.

Q. Your wife is having diploma in fashion designing. Is she doing any job?

Ans: Sir, she is very much interested and me also because at least it will boost up our status. Dehradun is a small town and there are few opportunities at low salary. She had applied in 2-3 firms for job but she was not offered appropriate salary, so we are in search; as and when we will get good call, she would definitely join.

Q. How many brothers and sisters do you have and what is their education?

Ans: Sir, I have two younger brothers. They are running their own business. The first one Mr. Chetan Kumar is BA and deals in property. He earns approximately around 20,000/- pm and second one Mr. Mahesh Kumar studying for graduation B.Sc.

Q. How do you spend time during your leave?

Ans: Sir, during leave, I get up at around 0500h, I go for running and after coming back, I read newspapers. I help parents in their work, fulfill household requirements. I spare some time to meet my relatives & friends to carry on our relations further. I also teach my children regularly at fixed time. Rest of the time I read newspaper, watch Ted Talks.

Q. How do you spend your salary?

Ans: Sir, my total monthly income is Rs. 25,800/- pm including all emoluments and I spend it as under:-

Monthly deductions	Expenditure
AFPPF	Children's Fee
AGIF	Grocery
PCA	Phone
PLI	Milk
Total Deductions	Wife, for day to day expense
The salary after deductions	Mother
	For Self use
	Cell Phone - Professional Fees
	Internet - Memberships/Subscriptions - Books
	Total

Q. What are your good and not so good qualities?

Ans: Sir, no human being is perfect and everyone has some merits & demerits. I do also have some:

Good qualities	No so good qualities
I am mature, sensible, intelligent, responsible and cooperative. I remain cool and calm during adverse conditions. I am systematic and professionally very sound	I reasonably can communicate in English but I would like to develop further more. I can work efficiently on computer but I would like to improve my computer knowledge more. I watch cricket and waste lots of time and i want to set rid of this.

Q. How many friends you have and who are your close friends?

Ans: Sir, I have a good team of friends in civil as well as in Army. My close friends are:-

(a) Hav Vijay Singh – Punjab
(b) NB Sub Mathew Kerala
(c) Hav Ahmed – UP
(d) Mr. Deepak Kumawat – Rajastan
(e) Mr. Rajesh - Tamil Nadu
(f) Mr. Dheeraj – Haryana
(g) Hav Ashok Kumar – Maharashtra

Q. What qualities you look for while making friends?
Ans: Sir, I find following qualities while making friends.
   (a) Commitment to each other
   (b) Social & enthusiastic
   (c) Trust on each other
   (d) Honesty to each other
   (e) A good friend wanting to change

Q. What steps have you taken to improve your knowledge?
Ans: Sir, I read newspaper, listen to news, watch CNN. Read periodicals, watch Ted Talks, You Tube debates, watch Discovery Channel etc.

Q. Who is your role model and whom would you like to follow?
Ans: Sir, I have role models for different subjects. I could not find all rolled into one to look up for every answer. I have people like _____, _____, _____.

Q. What are the principles of your life?
Ans: Sir, Honesty and sincerity are the principles of my life. Also changing with circumstances.

Q. What is your aim in life?
Ans: Sir, my aim is to rise high and to be progressive in life. Also to build a personal brand like Apple.

Q. There is lots of absenteeism during PT, your CO has asked you to stop the same, what will you do?
Ans: Sir, first of all I will assure my CO that such incident will never occur in future. I would take the special roll call and pass the instructions very strictly that PT is compulsory for all and if anybody is found absent, disciplinary action would be taken against the absentees. I would personally check the attendance with parade state and also check the lines / mess etc. during PT time and initiate disciplinary action against the absentees. Most importantly, I will educate them the importance of daily exercises for a healthy life in detail. This will do the job without any pressure.

Q. Your CO said PT is not organized properly, what will you do?
Ans: Sir, I shall be physically present in the PT. I shall put all my PT instructors to check and ensure that they are doing PT properly.

Q. You find your driver is going fast crossing the speed limit, what will you do?
Ans: Sir, I would tell the driver to control the speed by lowering the gears and remain under speed limit at all times.

Q. He is not following what you instructed, what would you do?

Ans: Sir, I would immediately get up and take the steering in my hands. Replace him and put him for other duties.

Q. How have you done so far in the SSB?

Ans: Sir, I have done reasonably satisfactory in all the tests but my Group Testing has been the best.

Q. Why it was the best? What about your performance during Psychological tests?

Ans: Because in Group Discussion my topic was accepted. I took active part and gave logical ideas during discussion. My plan was acceptable and with some suggestions it was accepted by the group. In PGT I enjoyed with the group and helping to cross the hurdles. I gave an appealing lecture for 03 minutes. I crossed 10 obstacles. I completed my command task and was called as helper for 04-05 times. So I think my Group Testing was the best. In Psych, I am satisfied. I have written appealing stories based on those pictures. In WAT I have given mature, sensible ideas. In SRT I have reacted in positive, optimistic and responsible manner. In self-description I have written what others have been talking about. So I am satisfied with my Psychtest.

Q. Which test you like the most? What preparation you made to face the SSB?

Ans: Sir, nothing in particular, because I know it is the test of personality and personality can't be changed in short time/period. I met my seniors firstly to know what happens in SSB and in each test my aim has been to show my best performance and present what all I have gained or learnt during the last many years. At the same time I have been regular reader of newspapers/periodicals. I had a lot of practice of Intelligence tests. I have also been collecting material for Lecturette and Group Discussion. I used tools of internet to fill the gap. Google and Ted Talks have created depth in my knowledge level.

Q. What you think about your chances of selection?

Ans: Sir, I am satisfied and hopeful.

Q. What if you are not selected?

Ans: Sir, firstly I am hopeful, if not I shall find out my shortcomings and analyse my performance comparing with those who got recommended from the group. I will improve my points and come again with better preparation.

Q. Have you been to SSB before? Which type of entry you like?

Ans: Sir, I have availed following chances:-

A suggested format to give answer

Ser No.	Type of Preparation	Batch No.	SSB	Chest No.	To	Result

I have analyzed myself and found out that my stories were not appealing. I left many words blank in WAT. I left many SRTs unattended. I was not an active participant in the discussion. I was not active in PGT.

Both the commissions are equal, so what type of commission I am recommended for does not make any difference because my aim is to rise high and to be progressive in life.

Q. What is it that you liked about SSB Testing?

Ans: Sir, I got a chance to prove my abilities and qualities. I enjoyed unique way of testing, systematic way of conduct of tests. I got an opportunity to meet people coming from different parts of the country and developed friendship.

Q. Why do you want to become an officer?

Ans: Sir, every human has a natural desire to rise high in life, so do I. It would be improving my social and economic status and I would able to discharge my duties and responsibilities in a better manner and I have those qualities which a defence officer has. As a far-fetched thought, my children and next generation will be benefited from my efforts.

Q. Why do you think that you are fit to become an officer?

Ans: Sir, it is human desire and I am mature, sensible, confident, loyal and punctual, who works with dedication & devotion and respects others. I am performing my duties in family, profession and in outer environment very well. I never give chance to my elders / friends to feel hurt and embarrassed. I have the potential and qualities which my boss has.

Q. What would you like to do during your leisure time?

Ans: Sir, as and when I find leisure time, I like to teach my children.

Q. What is your hobby? And explain them.

Ans: Sir, my hobby is reading and interest is in teaching.

Reading

Sir, reading changed my life and I am passionate about it. I get valuable information from the highest authority on the subject by reading a book. I can't read all books, so I choose a book which is *New York Times* bestseller. Books give the right kind of tools to steer my life logically, also to educate my dear and near ones. Book is the source of continuous education and I want to read as much as possible in my life.

Interest

    (i) My interest is to teach children

    (ii) 3-4 students from my vicinity who are studying with my children come to me and I help them in completing their homework.

Q. Have you taken any coaching?

Ans: Yes Sir, I have been taking coaching all my life directly or indirectly. Whatever I am today it is the result of various forms of coaching I received. For SSB preparation I have taken coaching from Cavalier India, leveraged from Google, TED Talks, SSB Books, You Tube Videos, friends and seniors. It is my life dream and I want to achieve it and I did put in 100% effort.

Q. What games do you play?

Ans: Sir, I play volleyball. Though I am not a regular player of volleyball as I have to attend office in the evening also, yet I spare some time to play the game.

Q. Tell me the measurement of ball, the court and team size?

Ans: Sir, the ball is made of flexible leather or synthetic leather with a bladder inside made of rubber or similar material. Circumference of the ball (pridhi) is 65 to 67 cms, Weight – 260 to 280 gms, Air Pressure – 0.48 to 0.52 kgs. Ground measures 18 mtrs, 09 mtrs wide. It is marked with 05 cms wide lines. Attack line is 03 mtrs wide from the centre line. Net is placed over the centre line at a height of 2.43 mtrs for men and 2.24 mtrs for women. The net is 01 mtr wide and 9.50 mtrs long made of 10 cms square mesh. Team consists of a maximum of 12 players, one coach, one assistant coach, one trainer and one medical doctor. But only 06 players play at a time whose names have been recorded in the score sheet. The other players, who are part of the team but not playing, sit on their team benches which are located beside the scorer's table.

Q. Give me the organisation details of your unit/department?

Ans: Sir, Centre Comdt of respective regimental training centre performs the duties of IOC records. Col Records performs the duties as CO. CRO performs as 21C. Under him 04 groups function and these are: LA group, CA/RA Group, ER Group and NER Group. Every Group has OIC under whom certain section officers are posted for proper functioning of the section.

    (a) LA Group Local Adm Group is headed by Adm Officer/Adjutant of the rank of Maj/Capt. It functions as Regt HQ and ensures documentation, leave, posting, promotion & discipline of the personnel posted in the Record Office including the civilian employees.

(b) CA/RA Group Corps/Regt Adm Group is headed by OIC CA/RA group of the rank of Lt Col/Maj. It deals in:-
  (i) CA/RA Co ord – Performs as coy office (company commander)
  (ii) Posting/Promotion JCOs/OR
  (iii) ACRs JCOs/OR
  (iv) Courses/Re-mustering
  (v) Honorary Commission
  (vi) Discharge JCOs/OR
  (vii) Stat Section
  (viii) UN Mission/Commission JCOs/OR

  Every section has it shown section officer of the rank of Maj/Capt.

(c) ER GROUP Effective Records Group is headed by OIC ER Group of the rank of Lt Col / Maj. ER Group maintains the sheet rolls of the effective JCOs / OR command wise. Scrutinize the part II orders received from the units and enter them in the sheet rolls. Publish the corps / regt part II orders. It has the following sections:-
  (i) ER Coord – Performs as coy office (company commander)
  (ii) Documentation - 1 (South Comd)
  (iii) Documentation - 2 (East Comd)
  (iv) Documentation - 3 (West Comd)
  (v) Documentation - 4 (Cent Comd)
  (vi) Documentation - 5 (North Comd)
  (vii) Documentation - 6 (South-West Comd)
  (viii) Automation Cell – Maintain the automation record of PBO Rs
  (ix) Liaison Cell – Disposal of statement of A/C and settlement of observations raised by PBO Rs on Statement of A/C

  Every section has its own section officer of the rank of Maj/Capt.

(d) NER Group Non Effective records Group is headed by OIC NER Group of the rank of Lt Col/Maj. NER Group maintains the sheet rolls of the Non Effective JCOs/OR in numerical order up to 50 years of their retirement and has the following sections:-
  (i) NER Coord – Performs as coy office (company commander)
  (ii) NER Libraries
  (iii) AGIF Section

(iv) Pension
(v) Family Pension
(vi) Gratuity
(vii) Death cum Retirement Gratuity
(viii) Final Settlement of account
(ix) Legal Cell

Every section has its own section officer of the rank of Maj / Capt.

Q. I have completed the interview, do you have any query or question to ask?

Ans: No Sir, it was nice talking to you, thanks sir.

FREQUENTLY ASKED QUESTIONS BY THE INTERVIEWING OFFICER AT SSB

Interview is a very important part of your SSB. Your performance in interview mostly is responsible whether you make it or not. IO has different ways of testing whether the person is fit enough for being an officer or not and some questions he asks may confuse the candidates and they generally go with the flow and answer something which dismisses their chances of selection. Here are a few such SSB Interview questions along with their suggested answer.

Question: Why did you fail in previous SSB attempt? (for repeaters)

Suggestion: Tell the truth what you feel, don't blame the SSB that 'I did good and they didn't take me', or 'I don't know', this gives a negative impression about you. You can say that 'I was not prepared well Sir in _____' (say a particular thing) like 'psychological part'. You can add up by saying that 'but Sir, I have prepared well this time'.

Question: Why do you want to join Defence Forces?

Suggestion: Now you may tell the IO the real reason because definitely a defence aspirant has a solid reason behind joining the defense forces. That reason may be patriotism, love for aeroplanes, ships, guns, craze for uniform, wish for an adventurous life or any other. Now one thing to be noted here is that boys, except for those giving interview for an entry after 10+2, should not say things like 'Sir it was my childhood dream' or 'I always wanted to do this only', otherwise IO might ask you 'where were you after class 12th?'

Question: What is your belief of marriage? (Love/Arranged)

Suggestion: Please don't act smart (actually foolish) by giving a childish reply that 'I don't believe in marriage' or 'I have not yet thought about it'. IO expects you to be grown up at this age (graduate people). You can say that you believe in both kinds of marriages but the person you are getting married to should be acceptable to everybody in your family. Hence in case of love marriage your parents should agree to that guy/ girl; in case of arranged marriage you should agree.

Question: Do you have a boyfriend/girlfriend? (And for the obvious answer 'No' - why you do not have).

Suggestion: Well, this is your call guys & girls, but if you say 'yes' for this then be ready for a lot of counter questions and more counter questions IO asks regarding your personal life, more you are likely to reveal yourself and I believe down the line we are not perfect. So to avoid any mishap simply say 'NO'. If he asks why then you can say that I have not yet felt anything like this for anybody yet. This is merely subjective suggestion.

Question: Do you drink/booze/smoke?

Suggestion: Now that's a catchy one, for boys especially if you are going for UES or anything above college level then IO knows that most of you would have done at least once. So tell the truth; if you do then say 'yes sir, I have done it once or twice', and if you don't then say 'I don't'. For girls, well you can be ready for counter questions if you are saying 'yes' or 'sometimes' etc. Saying 'NO' saves you from being asked unnecessary questions.

Question: What if you do not get recommended this time?

Suggestion: You have to sweetly and simply say 'Sir I'll try next time with more preparation'. Now he may counter you by saying that if you do not make it into defense then what? Here you have to show your attachment for defense, you have to say 'Sir I'll work very hard and make it', or 'I have not thought of anything else as yet except defence'.

Clearing Psychological Tests

"A strong, positive self-image is the best possible preparation for success in life."

– Dr. Joyce Brothers, Psychologist

The psychological tests are one of the easiest tests at the SSB, and if you have prepared well success is certain. Follow the guidelines given and practice as many times as possible. Do a post mortem of each assignment that you have done, critically analyze it, correlate with the qualities that the SSB is looking for. The catch again is: demonstrating all the qualities that the SSB is looking for in all your written tests.

For IQ tests, regular practice is required for verbal and non-verbal reasoning tests; a good Officers Intelligence Rating (OIR) is between one and four. You should work hard to score well.

All other tests too require extensive practice and application of thinking tools. At the SSB, for Thematic Apperception Test (TAT) you are required to write 12 stories, so prepare about 50 stories on different pictures. Write more than one story for the same picture and so on. This will help you for an easy going during TAT. For Word Association Test (WAT), you are required to make 60 sentences, so practice writing minimum 600 sentences, write more than one sentence for the same word and choose the best and retain in your mind. Take good sentences from a thesaurus, novels, newspapers and other English literature. These sentences should align with the requirement of SSB. In Situation Reaction Tests (SRT), visualize day to day situations that are similar to what is given in this book and articulate practical answers. Design minimum of 300 situations and create apt and crisp answers for them. Scrutinize your answer and weed out unwanted and meaningless words and sentences so that your answer can be more powerful and with real depth. It will also help you to articulate the answers within the given time. Your ability to complete the tests within time will dramatically improve if you practice enough and go into depth. The ultimate mantra for psychological tests success is: be a master preparer and create high level of responses, projecting your personality traits and officer like qualities (OIQ's)

In Psychological test, candidates should continuously maintain good handwriting and high level responses. Unfortunately these days we do not write letters but send SMS and E-mails. It would be good to improve your handwriting – if your handwriting is illegible you are in for trouble. There are only 26 letters in the English language. If you spend 5 minutes to properly write one letter then you know how much time is required to perfect these 26 letters. It would be worth the homework and practice.

Keep in mind the following:

   (a) **Positivity** (By your attitude and behavior projection)
   (b) **Practicality** (Be natural and not artificial in your responses)
   (c) **Pleasantness** (In your theme & writing)

Overview of the Psychological Tests Comprising TAT, WAT, SRT & SDT

Exploratory Test (TAT+WAT)

TAT	WAT
• Write stories on 11 pictures & one blank picture • Time for seeing picture – 30 sec • Writing story on each – 3 minutes	• 60 words one by one shown • Make sentence on each word within 15 sec • May or may not use the word in sentence
HIGHER LEVEL RESPONSES	
GOOD HANDWRITING	

▷ Foundations of success in Psychological tests

Confirmatory Test (SRT+SDT)

SRT	SDT
• Tackle 60 situations one by one • Time given – 30 seconds for each • Negative guidelines are given more emphasis	• Write opinions of parents, teachers, friends & own opinion • Show insight & motivation • Write in paragraph & not point-wise
HIGHER LEVEL RESPONSES	
GOOD HANDWRITING	

Foundations of success in Psychological tests ◁

What you need to do?

PLAN - PREPARE - PRACTICE - PERFORM

THEMATIC APPERCEPTION TEST (TAT)

General

There are twelve pictures depicting different situations – positive pictures, negative pictures, pictures showing social activities, group activities, adventure, individual based and so on. The twelfth slide is a blank one. As a thinking person what is it that you can do to deal with the blank slide?

The best possible preparation for the twelfth slide is to make a perfect story and retain in your brain; that slide is not going to be a surprise for you at the SSB.

You can do similar preparations for the other eleven pictures too. If you write stories for different kinds of pictures as explained above you will have enough material and ideas in your head. You will be in a position to fish out the best ideas and sentences to be used to construct your story for the picture shown.

Write a story and sleep over it. Next day morning read it again. The time period that you have to write a story must be effectively used. If you critically analyze what you have written, you will see five to six sentences can be compressed into one or two sentences with more powerful meaning and gist.

If there is one picture shown to a group of 100 students there will be one hundred different stories and the reverse is also true. Having sufficient material to design a good logical story is important. If you prepare well, you will be in a position to utilize the entire time period allotted for each slide. If you are short of ideas your story will be too short and you miss the chance to show your full potential. Here I am not talking about clearing the SSB but to come among the top five in the order of merit.

Remember: it would be a better idea to correlate your stories matching your qualifications, experience, family background etc. Do not forget that you are living in the 21st century and a day will come soon where space will be your playground. When you write a story you need not reduce yourself to the ice age. Be current and relevant.

The Theory

Thematic Apperception Test is one of the effective methods of the projective techniques used by the psychologist in order to reveal a great deal of one's personality. The techniques employed are that in the interpretation of an ambiguous situation a person will reveal the innate and hidden aspects of his thoughts. From this interpretation of the individual an appraisal of his personality is measured. The intention of the test is to ask the candidate to give an appreciation of his own qualities without being conscious of it, there being a very short time. But in its broader sense, it means attributing to the external world any quality of the self.

TAT consists of a series of standard pictures which are shown to the candidate for a short time and his thoughts and reactions are connected to this stimulus in the form of the story. From this story an assessment of his personality is drawn by the psychologist.

TAT is a test of imagination. A candidate is required to perceive (observe) the theme (subject) hidden in the scene of the picture. Having understood the theme or the subject, an imagination of Hero or Heroine (central figure) is to be created who will be reflecting the personality of the candidate himself. The imaginative Central Figure (CF) would be shown facing a particular need or a problem as seen in the picture. Subsequently, what actions CF takes which will result into the note of success for the CF, would frame the story.

This test was developed by Prof Murray (USA) in 1941 based upon his theory which is known as "Need cum Press Theory". According to this theory, a human being at any time feels a particular need to achieve something or feels a kind of problem which needs to be solved. After the arousal of need, a kind of press action takes place, meaning the physical and mental pressures are built leading the individual to take certain action so as to fulfill the need or solve the problem successfully. Therefore, while writing a story for this test this concept of Prof Murray may be kept in mind. With the story, between a kind of need or problem and resulting into certain action, finally ends into the success of Central Figure.

Procedure

About 12 picture slides are shown one by one to the candidates in succession. Each slide is kept displayed for 30 seconds and three/four minutes given to form a story on the basis of the picture shown to the candidate. Every picture shown has a situation which gives the base of the story. The story is nothing but the candidate's reaction in the form of thoughts to the environment. Invariably the series of the pictures contains a blank slide where the candidate gets an opportunity to form stories and each story provides valuable clues about the candidate's emotional attitude and temperamental make up.

Rules of the Test

- 01 to 12 pictures are shown to candidates one after the other. 11 pictures + 1 blank slide
- Time – 30 seconds for the projection of picture and 4 minutes for writing the story.

Important Points

- The picture has two elements: background or backdrop and characters. Characters are of two types: One is the main character or hero/heroine of the story, and others are the side characters who play a supportive or helping role. A candidate should identify the hero/heroine by his age and sex and give him a name. There is no name to the side characters.

- Story should have three parts:
    1. What led to the situation (shown in the picture) or the opening part: 2-4 lines
    2. What is happening at the moment or the middle part: 10 lines
    3. What is the final outcome or the end part: 1-2 lines
- In the opening part, a need or problem or challenge is presented and along with the identification of hero, the aims of the hero are given. In this part it is told whether hero is college student, an officer or a businessman and what he has to do. It should be given in 2-4 lines of the story.
- The middle part is the most important part of the story. In this part all the actions of the hero are given. The efforts or steps he takes, the methods he adopts and his journey to achieve his aim, all these are presented in this part. This part reflects the picture. That means, what is shown to the candidates is presented in this part. A candidate must write much more in this part as to what is happening at the moment (what he saw in the picture but he should not describe the picture).
- The end part reflects the final outcome. It shows the result of hero's efforts and the level of his satisfaction.

Length of the Story: Half a page.

Analysis of the Theme

1. Form the following questions in your mind:
    (a) What? This means what action is taking place in the scene of the picture.
    (b) Where? It means the place where the action took place, like village, city, office, market, road, hilly area, river side etc.
    (c) Who? It means two types of characters, i.e. the Central Figure and Side Character.
    (d) Why? It means why was the CF shown in the picture, the need part of Prof Murray's theory.
2. The above four questions and their answers will bring out the theme of the picture very clearly and ultimately a rough sketch of the entire story.

Criterion of Central Figure

1. Identify the CF by matching with your personality age level and sex.
2. Give a short, attractive name. Give the current name not the old name to the CF.
3. Give a suitable status to CF which would be a manager, engineer, doctor, scientist, professor, principal, CEO, Capt. of team, sarpanch of village, CO of the unit or an Army officer etc.

4. The CF should not be shown as a Negative Person with expressions like disappointed, dejected, depressed, injured and dying in the end.
5. Escaping or running away of your CF from a situation never to be reflected.

Criterion of Side Characters

1. No name is to be given to side characters.
2. Classify the side characters as CF's neighbours, friends, colleagues, office bearers, village folk, crowd on the street, team mates etc.
3. No villain is to be created out of side characters.

Technique of Writing Story

1. A story will have three parts, i.e. the opening part, middle part and end part, to be written in a single unified paragraph.

   Opening Part: What led to the situation.

   CF = Central Figure's Name and Status

   N/P = Need / Problem

   A = Aim of the CF

   This part should consume nearly 20% of the length of the story.

Middle Part (70% of the space): What all is happening or happened; meaning all actions taken by the CF to solve the problem or fulfill the need. This part should reflect all the four factors of OLQ in the following ways:

(i) Factor-I: Planning and Organization - This factor will be reflected by the aim taken by the CF showing the planning part and subsequently actions will reflect the organization part.

(ii) Factor-II: Social Adjustment - This factor will be reflected by CF's immediate interaction with other people with the aim to solve the problem in a very friendly and respectful manner so as to create a sense of social adjustment.

(iii) Factor-III: Social Effectiveness - This factor will be reflected by the CF as the leader going forward to solve the problem along with others.

(iv) Factor-IV: Dynamic - This factor will be reflected by the CF's successful achievement of the aim which also forms the last part of the story.

End Part (10%): Result of the story will be shown in concluding sentence of the story by showing CF achieving the target or aim. The CF should not expect any award/reward etc at the end for the good work done.

General Instructions

1. Never show your central figure as an award/reward gainer where he or she receives cash award, appreciation or thanks from others for the good work done.

2. Do not give any heading or title to the story.
3. Write your story in past tense & in third person.
4. Avoid any overwriting and cuttings.
5. Write only one paragraph in half of page including all the parts of the story.
6. Convert a negative scene in picture into a positive theme.
7. Avoid stories based on suicide, drugs, rape, murder, etc.
8. All 12 stories should look consistent in length, depth and qualities, including the blank one.
   (a) Length - 90-100 words
   (b) Qualities - 6-7 qualities in each picture
   (c) Depth of situation - Average.
9. Avoid theme within theme.
10. The story should be like a chain, there should be no missing links. Connect all actions in a logical and systematic way.
11. Do not jump from one theme/plot to another.

Keep in mind:
- Maintain a good handwriting throughout.
- There is no villain in the story.
- Hero should lead the story, side characters are just the good followers of the hero.
- The theme or plot of the story should be within the limitations of a normal human being. Interesting but normal situations should be created and the hero, assisted by the other characters in the story, should be able to tackle the situations and resolve them to the best of his capacity, leading to a logical and happy ending.
- The candidate has to identify himself with the hero or chief character in the story. The qualities of the hero have to conform to the nature of the candidate himself and reflect his own personality.
- Do not write any lessons or morals at the end of the story. Leave it to the reader to think for himself. It should, however, be self-evident.

Some pictures along with a suitable story for each are given below purely as guidance for candidates:

Picture No. 1 A young man is sitting in a room in deep thought/pensive mood

Story: Thomas after completing his graduation with outstanding grade, decided to join civil services after deliberate thinking. Then he started preparation for UPSC examination with the help of experts on his subjects and took guidance from others who had already succeeded in the same field. Internet and Google was extensively used for preparations. Lots of online resources were used for preparations. With his hard work and sincere efforts, he cleared his written exam in his first attempt and started preparing himself for interview with renewed vigour. He was called for interview and was recommended for the IAS Cadre. He worked hard throughout the training and based

on his outstanding merit, he was posted directly as District Magistrate and thus he achieved his goal.

OR

Story: Rajesh was posted as SP (Traffic) of a district after probation period. Soon after taking over, he felt a serious problem of traffic jams due to illegal parking, improper bus stops and encroachments by shopkeepers. He, with help from Municipal Corporation, prepared a broad plan to eradicate the problem in phased manner. Firstly he marked fixed bus stops and diverted heavy vehicles to bypass routes, proper road markings and traffic signals were posted at all needed places. Then, removed encroachments, made available proper places for wheel vendors and penalized heavily the violators with the help of other civil authorities. The traffic problem was removed to a great extent due to the above systematic actions taken by him.

Picture No. 2 A well-dressed man briefing some villagers

Story: Shamim was an Agriculture Development Officer. During his visit to the villages, he found there was a shortage of food grains in some parts of the district and wanted to improve the annual turnover. He carried out the survey, met with the villages' heads, motivated and convinced the people to use hybrid seeds, modern technologies, fertilizers and agriculture insurance etc. He also helped them in getting loan from the bank to purchase machineries and for installation of bore wells. He provided guidance and support to the villagers from time to time. He used lots of videos to educate the farmers about various modern methods of irrigation, germination, use of fertilizers etc. Every week he organized this activity. People gathered to watch this like a movie and all the farmers got charged up and changed the way they did farming. Finally it provided good results and improved the quality and quantity of food grains to a great extent and this brought happiness and prosperity to the villagers.

Picture No. 3 A senior man sitting in his chair and two persons are standing before him

Story: Rohit was a production manager of a company and he was briefed by the CEO about the company's low earnings. He willingly took over the responsibility to improve the annual return of the company. He, by introducing latest technology and meticulous planning, not only cut down the production cost but also improved the quality and quantity of production. Then, he searched new markets for their products with the help of Marketing Manager by adopting healthy advertisement. He briefed and trained his two marketing managers on regular basis to bring out better sales. He used social media marketing, Google Ad words and other internet-based marketing strategies to increase the customer base. Through internet he expanded the business to various parts of the country. Tremendous growth was achieved in a short span of time. By virtue of his foresight, professional skills and sustained efforts, the company was in a position of good earnings at the close of the financial year.

Picture No. 4 **A well-dressed man at the main gate of a house pressing the button of call bell**

Story: Joseph was the son of a businessman and a good student at college. After doing his MBA, he became the Managing Director of his own Finance Company. One day he got a call from one of his friends who was homeless and residing in a rented house. He immediately went to his friend's house and discussed the matter in detail. He paid the whole amount of the cost of a new house on easy repayment EMIs and even without any interest. Meanwhile he gave his friend a flat in his company's premises and very soon he moved to the new house. Thus he was very happy that he could help his friend at the time of crisis. Also he educated his friend about the Airbnb model so that occasionally he could rent out one of his rooms to tourists and get money to pay the loan installments.

Picture No. 5 **A young man and a girl talking to each other in a park or elsewhere**

Story: Captain Rahul, an Army Officer, was on long leave at his hometown. A girl from the neighbourhood who cleared her graduation with good marks came to meet him as she wanted to join the Army through WES. She contacted Capt. Rahul for guidance and general material for preparation. One day he came to know that the girl had cleared her written test. He again provided her useful information about test in SSB interview and made her to practice all the SSB tests under his guidance and by virtue of that she was recommended for WES. Thus he helped this girl to become a commissioned officer. The village was very proud of this first woman officer.

Picture No. 6 **One boy who is swimming and waving both his hands cheerfully**

Story: Alok was an outstanding swimmer. One day when he was enjoying swimming, few known people were passing by in a boat. He wished them by waving both his hands. Some of them had already seen his performance in the past when he crossed the river from one side to the other. Alok motivated the younger ones from his college to learn swimming without any charges and told them to sound more people. Within a short period he trained a good number of swimmers and he sponsored some of them to competitions at various levels. They performed very well in all the competitions. His initiative and enthusiastic action resulted into creation of many good swimmers in his college. The college became the overall champion in the inter college championship of swimming.

Picture No. 7 Two men running with a ladder and a man guiding them

Story: Aslam, a Chief Fire Officer was posted in Bangalore. He always ensured his men are trained to the highest standard and remain physically fit. One night, he got a call from his fire station that fire had broken out in a government building in the nearby area. He swung out of the bed, ordered his firemen on duty to reach the site immediately along with the fire tenders and  other equipments. He, himself, rushed to the site, quickly assessed the situation and launched his operation in a very professional and systematic manner and subsequently controlled the fire. The small portion of the building was damaged but it was still repairable. He also called up the press people/video shooter who could record the whole operation; this video was kept as a training tool for his men to carry out such operations in future plugging all the flaws. By virtue of the professionalism and dynamism, the lives and national property, both were saved.

Picture No. 8 One man is leading a team of two to three persons to a monument

Story: Rajesh, an Executive Engineer in the Department of Tourism, noticed a decreasing strength of foreigners visiting historical monuments in his area and went about finding out the reason for that. He felt a need to beautify these monuments and extend basic facilities there without changing its original look. He along with his counterparts in various departments like CPWD, Transport Department, etc., conducted a visit to these monuments and identified the areas to be improved. Very soon these monuments, which are great cultural heritage of the nation, were given a face-lift. Also he used the internet to advertise about these monuments and other facilities this town offered. All required tourist information was made available at the click of a mouse to people all over the world and these actions attracted more and more foreigners to visit these monuments.

Picture No. 9 One man on a rope bridge and some villagers looking on

Story: Rakesh was posted in the PWD department as an Executive Engineer at Rishikesh. During his visit to his village he found there was a rope bridge which was the lifeline of the villagers, and it was in a very poor condition and the villagers were facing a lot of problems due to that. He immediately apprised the village Sarpanch of the situation, and together they approached the district authorities with the technical data and project map of a new steel and cemented bridge. They projected their demand strongly and got it cleared and got the fund approved for the project. Then he started the work and monitored the ongoing work by paying frequent visits to the village on Sundays/holidays. Very soon there was a new and strong bridge in place of the rope bridge and villagers were happy. Also it became the main link of progress of the village in all respects.

Picture No. 10 A young man is sitting and a doctor is standing

Story: Jackson, the son of a businessman was the eldest among three siblings – a younger brother and sister. Despite his best efforts, he could not save his ailing father, even though the doctor provided best treatment. He immediately took control of himself and pacified his mother, brother and sister. Then he took over all the responsibilities of the family including running of the business set up of his father. He looked after his mother well and also took care of the education of his younger brother and sister. He made his father's business to run efficiently. He changed the way the business was done earlier; he took the business to a different level using all the modern technologies and internal sources. He ensured good education for his brother and sister which enabled both to get good jobs. He also gave jobs to some needy people of society in his company. His company prospered and grew many folds. Finally, he became a role model and great inspiration for the society.

Picture No. 11 Two persons sitting on chairs and talking to each other in a room

Story: Robert was pursuing his MBBS at Calicut Medical College, Kerala. He felt that due to shortage of blood in blood banks, people were losing their lives. He discussed the issue with his roommate and planned to organize a blood donation camp in the Medical College. He met with the Dean and sought his permission. He visited colleges, govt. offices and localities, organized lectures and motivated the youth to donate blood. He used social media network such as whatsapp, face book etc. to get more and more people to donate blood. He explained to them that as there is no other substitute the blood donated by them could save lives. On the D-day the camp was organized more & more people came forward to donate blood. They collected a huge quantity of blood and thus by his efforts several lives could be saved.

Picture No. 12 One man talking to two ladies.

Story: Faizal was the District Medical Officer posted at Jaipur. He felt that there was much gap in male-female sex ratio due to increasing female foeticide. He made a plan to curb this problem with the help of the lady doctors to educate the people on the issue. He and his team of lady doctors visited the villages under his jurisdiction, met with the village heads and with their help organized lectures to make people aware

of the importance of the females in the society as we cannot even dream of this beautiful world without them. He also made them aware of the law that if people were found involved in female foeticide they would be prosecuted. Lots of social media campaign was done to advertise the bad effect in the society due to less number of female. People got educated and it drastically reduced the cases of female foeticide.

Picture No. 13 One person standing with motorcycle and one person repairing the tyre under the tree.

Story: D. D. Singh was an Engineer in a leading automobile company. When he visited his parental village he noticed that most of the youth were wandering and unemployed. He made a plan to give them the training on automobile repairing. He called the youth and motivated them to learn automobile repairing as it is in demand and could provide them lucrative employment. They got inspired; then he met the

village head and got some financial help to purchase necessary tools. He started the training camp under the free VTP Scheme of Ministry of Labour, Govt. of India. The youth took interest and after training they became efficient mechanics of automobiles. Some of them started their own auto repairing shops and some got employment in auto company. Thus D. D. Singh accomplished his aim to curb the unemployment problem in his village to a great extent.

Picture No. 14 One person standing in the bushes among trees.

Story: Ashish a forest officer, when visiting the area under his jurisdiction, felt the problem of deforestation which was leading to shortfall of rain and causing ecological imbalance. He made a plan to protect the forest by growing more & more trees. He visited the villages in the surroundings of the forests, educated the villagers and made them aware of the importance of the forests to live a healthy & prosperous life. He issued the saplings to the villagers free of cost and organized  tree plantation camps. Also introduced drift irrigation and educated people about rain water harvesting. He also organized few films by National Geographic channel to villagers. This hugely motivated the villagers to follow the right thing. After short span of time he noticed the increase in density of trees to great extent in the forests and rain also increased. Thus he protected the forests by virtue of his professionalism and team work.

Picture No. 15 Three persons sitting on chairs, playing cards and XXX Rum bottle is there on the table.

Story: Ashok working in a bank, noticed that most of the youth of his village were involved in alcoholism and wasting time by playing cards. After investigating the matter he found out that they did not get appropriate job and it led them to get discouraged & go astray. He made a plan to rehabilitate them by initiating a "SELF EMPLOYMENT PROGRAMME". He encouraged & motivated them to start small scale ventures close to their residential areas for which he helped them in getting repayable loan from the govt. and provided them training under the skill training program of Govt. of India. Very soon, they were able to learn and develop required skills. After short span of time he noticed that those people had completely settled down and started

encouraging others in the village to lead a progressive life. They were living a happy & prosperous life.

Picture No. 16 One person giving money to another person.

Story: Siraj, a businessman and an active member of an NGO, was doing a noble job for organising group marriages of the girls who belonged to poor economic status. In this regard he met with many people, friends, his fellow businessmen and also publicized the issue in newspapers and on city cable network, internet, WhatsApp to grow the funds. In this way he motivated the people to come forward with financial help for this noble venture. People got inspired and extended the help in the form of cash, articles and other valuables. By his full involvement and wholehearted efforts he managed all the items required for marriages in time. The marriages took place in a very healthy and happy atmosphere; the task was accomplished with tremendous satisfaction.

Picture No. 17 One man climbing on snow covered mountain.

Story: Capt Prakash was posted in 69AR located in Drass Sector of J&K. One day he learnt from reliable source that a group of intruders were planning to capture the small hill. Capt Prakash informed his CO and along with his team left for the post as communication between unit and post was cut off due to heavy snowfall and bad weather. He started climbing the hill with determination but as soon as he reached midway he was tired and exhausted but he took little rest, recollected the courage and started again as it was getting dark. He reached the top, organized the soldiers and kept track of the enemy with the help of night vision to foil the plan of intruders. As soon as the group came within the range Capt Prakash and his team opened fire and foiled the plan of the intruders. His bravery and systematic planning and operation saved his men and the post of paramount importance to the nation.

Picture No. 18 One child drowning in the river, one man looking at him, one man standing behind him.

Story: Ajesh, while he was on his evening walk heard the cry of 'help, help!' He immediately ran towards the area from where the sound was coming along with his friend where they noticed that a boy was drowning in the river and seeking help. Ajesh was an outstanding swimmer so he immediately jumped into the river with the aim to save the life of that boy. He held the boy in his hand and swam across. He gave him first aid and rushed him to hospital; the vehicle was organized by his friend while Ajesh was rescuing the boy from the river. They provided him required medical treatment and informed his parents. The boy recovered soon. His timely action saved the life of that boy. Ajesh and his friend felt happy about it.

Picture No. 19 Accident scene: Car hits a cyclist

Story: Jocob while on his morning walk saw a fast-moving car hit a cyclist thus causing serious injury and running away from the scene. He immediately noted the number of that car and rushed towards the injured person. Many people had gathered there but no one was coming forward to help due to the fear and harassment by the police. Realizing the gravity, he immediately gave him first aid and brought him to hospital with the help of

those people and by taking lift from a passing vehicle. On reaching the hospital he informed the police as well as his family members. Due to his timely action he was able to provide required treatment to the cyclist to avoid further complications. He also wrote to the government authorities regarding the consequences of attending an injured person in an accident; his letter and appeal was well received. Now as per the latest rules there is no police harassment if we attend to an accident victim.

Picture No. 20 One man climbing on hill with the help of rope.

Story: Saju after his schooling joined mountaineering course at Mussoorie. It was a month long course and test of selection was going on. The test was to climb the height of 250 ft in 20 minutes. Saju was the last candidate and started climbing with determination. After climbing 150 ft he got tired and exhausted but this was the golden chance for him. His hands were slipping and not

supporting him but still he gathered all his strength and stamina once again and was able to cover the height in the given time span. He got selected and joined for training. He did extremely well during training and came among the top five in the batch. Now he is an instructor at mountaineering institute.

Picture No. 21 **One man holding a pistol on the door and one man standing inside.**

Story: Joseph a leading scientist in DRDO, decided to invent Laser Guided Glock Pistol for the Commando Forces to replace the old one. He submitted his detailed project paper to the Chairman of DRDO and got permission to go ahead with the project. Then, he formed a team of two fellow scientists, collected technical data and started the research. In considerable period of time, they designed the pistol equipped with laser system, it could be fired in the night, was lighter in weight and had longer range. After constant deep experiments and trials, they found it fit to launch and was proving a boon for the commando operations of our armed forces. DRDO was considering mass production of this and to sell it to other countries to earn precious foreign exchange. It can be effectively used to shoot down drones. Joseph was very proud of his contribution to DRDO and to the Armed Forces.

Blank Stories

Story 1: Dr. Dinesh when visiting his parental village, found some common health problems among villagers. He thought that it might be due to polluted water, therefore, he went to the village pond which was the only source of water to the village. He found that the pond was much polluted. He along with other villagers cleaned the pond and directed the drains towards the wasteland. He also made sure that no one washes clothes on the pond bank. He also advised the villagers about the use of boiled water and chlorine tablets. He organized all the villages to a local auditorium and showed them few YouTube videos and films affecting health due to contaminated water. This was an eye opener for villagers and they became very keen

to follow all the directions. Dr. Dinesh gave them timely help and his efforts led to good health of villagers.

OR

Story 2: Prem, an executive engineer got a posting in Irrigation Department at Bijapur. On taking the charge, he felt that most of the areas were affected by drought due to shortfall of rain and the water level was very low. He made a plan to accumulate the rain water. He visited the villages, met with the villagers and motivated them to accumulate the rain water by making water reservoirs. He also persuaded them to provide physical labour. He took up the case with the department and got financial help sanctioned from the government side. He provided JCB machines for speedy execution of work. In due course the work was finished before monsoon. It rained heavily and the water reservoirs were full. He noticed after a short span of time the problem was reduced to a great extent. He also educated the villagers about proper use of water, drip irrigation, rain water harvesting. The villagers were happy and prosperous due to increase in the agricultural activities.

OR

Story 3: Manoj a young social worker of Meerut city was pained to learn about the increasing dowry harassment cases in the city. He gave a serious thought and after discussing it with like-minded people decided to organize street plays in various localities of the town. Then he along with his team decided to spread awareness of the social stigma using all the media available – Internet, mobile tools, TV commercials, radio channels and posters etc. He had a challenge of organizing the required funds for which he approached various industrial houses and he got sufficient funds to spread the awareness. Finally a day came there was not a single case of dowry harassment in his village.

WORD ASSOCIATION TEST (WAT)

1. WAT is a confirmatory test confirming the behaviour and the qualities shown by the candidate during TAT. In this test a word is shown for 15 seconds and after seeing the word, the candidate has to write a meaningful sentence using that particular word that is shown to him. The spontaneous thoughts and ideas that come to one's mind, directly or indirectly, reflects the personality of the candidate.

2. This is the test of imaginations, thoughts and ideas. It checks candidate's likes, dislikes, feelings, emotions, grooming and various personality traits.

3. The words are positive or negative – merely 70% words are of a positive nature and the remaining are of negative nature. However, there are certain words which can be used for positive or negative sentences, e.g. criticism (healthy criticism or negative criticism).

4. 60 words on the list of the WAT are selected on the basis of 15 words which are chosen from each of the four factors of OLQ. The meaning of the words is very simple and clear.
5. The responses or sentences are categorized as high level (HL) and low level (LL) responses. The HL response is a sentence which is highly meaningful to one of the factors of OLQ from which the word is chosen and other words which are also rich in content. Whereas, an LL response is the one which is meaningless to any factor of OLQ and the other words are also of ordinary nature. Therefore, only the HL sentences are to be used in this test.

Procedure

In this test a series of 60 words is shown to the candidate one by one, and he is asked to form a meaningful sentence. Each word is shown to him and kept exposed for 15 seconds and within this time he has to record his thought in the form of a meaningful sentence. There might be various ideas and feelings in relation to a particular word. But the first spontaneous reaction gives true picture of one's personality which is judged by the psychologist on completion of the test. The time limit to record one's reaction to a specific word is restricted to 15 seconds only so that a candidate is not confused with the subsequent thought, and gives his first natural response only.

The Psychologist's interpretation

Words in WAT are designed and arranged in such a way as to attract spontaneous reaction of candidate's personality traits. Every candidate has different perception of a given word on the basis of which he associates his thoughts with that word. These thoughts are influenced by his environment. The same word may arouse different feelings, thoughts and reaction in different persons. The psychologist interprets this reaction or he estimates from these associations or reactions, the personality traits of the personality of the candidate. With the help of this test, the psychologist understands or gets a fair idea of the candidate's personality: his likes and dislikes, his achievements, his emotional attitude and his temperament.

Personality traits assessed in WAT

The basic purpose to employ the WAT technique by the psychologist the SSB is to have realistic diagnosis of personality of the candidate in the form of sentences which help the psychologist to assess the personality traits. Some of the personality traits, which are revealed by the candidates while forming a sentence of a given word in WAT, are given here:

- Initiative
- Loyalty
- Liveliness
- Leadership
- Adaptability
- Co-operative spirit
- Intelligence
- Courage
- Determination
- Team spirit
- Spirit of adventure
- Hard work
- Organizational ability
- Sociability
- Resourcefulness
- Service to the nation
- Show of duty and responsibility
- Self-confidence
- Fearlessness
- Sense of justice
- Unselfishness

Rules of the Test

1. 60 words – shown one after another.
2. Time – 15 seconds per word (to see the word and to write a sentence)
3. After every 15 seconds there may be a bell to look up for the next word.
4. The page of the answer sheet on which the candidate has to write his reactions has a serial number marked on it. He has to write the reaction to each word against the proper serial numbers.

Technique of Writing Sentences

- Different types of words, inclusive of positive and negative are given to judge candidate's personality.
- Candidates are expected to write a meaningful and qualitative sentence.

Example: Love: An Army officer loves his soldier like his kith and kin.
- ➢ The original word can be used as the starting word of the sentences.

Example: Love: Love binds people, brings unity.
- ➢ The original word can be dropped from the sentence; instead a closely related or synonymous form is used to denote the meaning of the word.

• Negative words are written in one of the following methods:
- ➢ Along with the negative word denial expression is used to deny the existence of the negative words. For this method words like no, does not, did not, never, was not are used in this sentence.

Example: Hate: Hate never pays in a relationship.
- ➢ Instead of the original word, its antonym can be used in the sentence.

Example: Hate: Loving others brings them closer to us.
- ➢ A remedial or curative word can be used as a starting word showing its remedial effect for the negative word.

Example: Fear: Courage removes fear.

Note:
- ➢ A candidate can use the word in one of these four forms of parts of speech – Noun, verb, adjective, adverb. A word like Beauty can be used as Beauty, Beautify, Beautiful, Beautifully and Beautician.

Method for Positive Words

(a) TPSN method

Formula = TPSN + OW + Other words

TPSN   : Third Person Singular Number
OW   : Original Word
Other words : To complete the sentence with meaningful idea.

(i) **TPSN:** He or she, an officer, an army officer, a manager, a director, a scientist, a scholar, a professor, a doctor, a captain, a sarpanch, a businessman, a citizen, a principal etc. Adjective can be used with TPSN as good, honest, intelligent, sincere etc.

(ii) **Original Word (OW):** This can be used as a noun, adjective, verb, adverb. Generally the original word is written in the present tense in the form of verb.

(iii) **Other Words:** Should be meaningful to the factor from which the original word is chosen.

(b) Role play method

Formula = OW + Role Verb + Other Words

Role Verbs are reflects, shows, reveals, demonstrates, symbolizes, projects, leads, creates, builds, depicts etc.

Method for Negative Words

(a) Denial method

Formula = TPSN + Denial Verb (Never, does not, is not) + OW + Other words

(b) Remedial method

Formula = RW (Remedial Word + Overcomes / Removes + Negative Word) General Instructions

1. Do not use the following in your sentences:
   (a) Proverbs, idioms, quotations in which the original word has been used (because it is a borrowed idea).
   (b) Modal verbs like should, can, could, may, might, must, etc (because they are conditional words).
   (c) Imperative sentences (orders, instructions, suggestions like, be this, be that, do this, do that etc.)
   (d) Use of words such as is/am/are/was/were/has/have/do/does/will/shall/always/never/require and need.
   (e) Defence Mechanisms

2. After seeing the word, write the sentence directly but underline the original word. Original word need not be written.
3. Do not escape any word. Write a sentence for each word.
4. Use your sentences in the present tense.
5. Avoid any overwriting/cuttings.

> **KEEP IN MIND**
> - Handwriting should be legible without any cutting or overwriting.
> - Do not write the word before sentence, write the sentence right away.
> - Use present tense in the sentences. Do not use future and past tense as it is always uncertain.
> - If you cannot think of anything on seeing a particular word, leave the space blank against its serial number and pass on to the next word which is shown. Come back and complete the sentence when you get time.
> - Do not use proverbs, idioms, quotations and phrases in the sentences.
> - Do not use the words – can, could, may, might, should, must, ought to.
> - Avoid giving orders, instructions, advice, preaching in your sentences.
> - Try to show and express your positive attitude with the feeling of determination, optimism, dedication and sacrifice.
> - Always remember that your questionnaire already contains a lot of information about you. Hence, do not contradict that while giving your thoughts in this test.
> - Regular practice of forming the sentences can help you a lot in successful completion of this well within the given time.
> - Do not form a sentence showing negative traits like pessimism, anti social feelings.

WORDS AND THEIR MODEL SENTENCE

SAMPLE 1:

Abuse	: ISIS committed human abuse in Iraq.
Accept	: Strong people accept challenges willingly.
Accident	: Implementation of traffic rules avoids accident.
Accomplish	: Perseverance accomplishes success.
Achieve	: Go-getters achieve big things in life.
Active	: Inspiration activates people to do well.
Admire	: Admiring others for good deeds brings them closer.

Adventure	:	Adventurous people enjoy life to the fullest.
Adversity	:	Brings out man's real qualities.
Affection	:	Prevails in the close-knit family.
Afraid	:	Brave people are never afraid of adversity.
Again	:	Practicing again and again improves performance.
Against	:	Government works against the odds to make nation develop.
Agree	:	Agreement is the result of mutual understanding.
	:	Defence agreement with USA shows India's growing status.
Aid	:	The whole world provided aid to Tsunami victims.
All	:	All citizens are responsible for the nation.
Alone	:	When alone, books give good company.
Aloof	:	Company of friends removes aloofness.
Ambassador	:	A peaceful man is an ambassador of peace.
	:	Mother Teresa was an ambassador of charity.
Annoy	:	Mature people keep everyone happy.
Appeal	:	Human rights groups appeal against injustice.
Approach	:	Positive approach always gives positive results.
Argument	:	Reasonable argument promotes good ideas.
	:	Strong arguments convince the opponent.
Army	:	The backbone of nation's security.
	:	Symbol of discipline.
Ask	:	Indian forces always help UNO whenever asked for.
Assist	:	A good leader assists his seniors with due respect.
Atom	:	India uses her atomic energy for peaceful purposes.
	:	Future source of energy.
Attack	:	At the right time with good strategy wins battle.
Attempt	:	Serious attempts ensure good result.
Attract	:	Nice people attract everyone.
Average	:	Average people rise to glory with continuous efforts.
Avoid	:	Proper planning avoids suffering.
Award	:	Hard work is an award itself.
Ballot	:	Plays important role in democracy.
Barrier	:	Large population is barrier in development.
Beat	:	Scientists beat the world in IT.
Beauty	:	Nature is bestowed with beauty.
	:	Nature beauty refreshes mind and body.

Bee	:	Symbol of team work/co-operation/unity.
Beggars	:	Social workers work for upliftment of beggars.
Begin	:	A good beginning entails a good end.
Behave	:	Good behaviour shows maturity.
Best	:	Indian Special Forces are amongst the best in the world.
Betray	:	Loyalty binds people.
	:	Relations are based on loyalty.
Bilateral	:	India is improving bilateral relations with Pak/China.
Blame	:	US blamed Saddam to have WMDs.
Blessing	:	Priceless gifts by elders.
Blood	:	Saves life.
	:	O+ is universal donor.
Bluff	:	Truth always win over bluff.
Blunder	:	Timely precaution averts any blunder in a task.
Bold	:	As Captain he leads his men boldly.
Bomb	:	Bombing on Hiroshima/Nagasaki was inhuman act.
Books	:	Power house of knowledge.
	:	Increase horizons of creativity.
Border	:	Effective border management ensures national security.
Boredom	:	Removed by engaging in sports.
	:	Removed by reading/talking to friends.
Borrow	:	Pak borrowed missiles from China/North Korea.
Boss	:	Boss is a role model/inspiration to juniors.
	:	After hard work, bed gives relief.
Brave	:	Brave men build society.
Break	:	Continuous effort helps to break records.
Bribe	:	Taking and giving bribe is moral crime.
	:	Strict punishment and moral education is answer to it.
Bright	:	Future of India in space science/IT is bright.
Burden	:	Cheerfulness eases the burden.
	:	Good citizens burden their responsibility willingly.
Calamity	:	Effective disaster management minimizes the harm in a Calamity.
Calm	:	Calm and cool mind brings better results.

Candle	:	Even a candle removes darkness.
Cannot	:	Honest people cannot compromise with wrong policies.
Capable	:	Continuous efforts increase capability.
Captain	:	Motivates his men/leads by example.
Care	:	Caring and sharing makes the relations strong.
Careful	:	Careful preparation keeps errors away.
Change	:	Determined people change the fate.
	:	Science fought for a change in the system.
Character	:	Is the pillar of success/personality.
Charity	:	Is the way to help others.
Cheat	:	Cheating does not give long lasting results.
Child	:	Priceless asset of parents.
	:	Future torch bearer of country's progress.
Choice	:	Choosing right path brings goal closer.
Circumstance	:	Brave people are always ready to face any circumstances.
Class	:	Class differences are slowly but surely, fading.
Climb	:	Determined people climbed the ladder of success.
Company	:	Of good people gives good habits.
Compel	:	Compelling reasons win a lot of supports.
Complete	:	Completing work within time gives satisfaction.
Conduct	:	Conducting environmental campaigns increases awareness.
Confidence	:	Knowledge increases confidence.
Congratulation	:	Congratulating others on their success motivates them to do well again.
Conquer	:	Conquering heights gives thrill/satisfactory happiness.
Convince	:	Confident people convince others easily.
Co-operation	:	Improves performances/brings positive results.
	:	Is the strength of team.
Corruption	:	Moral education and strict punishment is answer to it.
Criticize	:	Positive criticism improves performance.
Cry	:	To check growing population is the crying need of the hour.
Culprit	:	Is brought to justice by law.
Danger	:	Depletion of ozone layer is dangerous for environment.
Death	:	The brave soldier died a Martyr's death.
	:	Death of a Martyr inspires young blood.

Decision	:	Deliberate decision shows clarity of mind.
Defeat	:	True sportsman faces defeat cheerfully, wins next time.
Delay	:	Doing work without delay shows sincerity.
Demand	:	Talented people are always in demand.
Desire	:	Indian youth desires to take nation forward.
Deteriorate	:	Illiteracy deteriorates a country's progress.
Determined	:	India is determined to eradicate polio.
Develop	:	Youth plays crucial role in the development of country.
Dialogue	:	Is the only solution of problems like Kashmir.
Dictator	:	Democracy is the answer to dictatorship.
Differ	:	India is a home of different yet unified cultures.
Difficult	:	Strong people face difficulties bravely.
Discipline	:	Strict rules and regulations create discipline.
Discourage	:	Coach encourages team to win the match.
Diversity	:	Crop diversification is necessary for good cultivation.
Doubt	:	Knowledge removes all doubts.
Drink	:	Clean drinking water is essential for public health.
Duty	:	Duty and responsibility go hand in hand.
Earn	:	Honesty earns respect.
	:	Farmers earned respect from countrymen and others as well.
Efficiency	:	Regular practice increases efficiency.
Elder	:	Is the best inspiration.
Encourage	:	Encouragement motivates people and improves performance.
Enemy	:	Lively people have lots of friends.
	:	Troops fight with enemy with full enthusiasm.
Enjoy	:	Friends enjoy each other's company.
Escape	:	Braves don't escape from difficulties.
Examination	:	Good leader examines a problem from all angles.
Excuse	:	Strong people never give lame excuses.
Extraordinary	:	Stephen Hawking is an extraordinary scientist.
Failure	:	It is an event not a person.
	:	Gives chance to mend the shortcomings.
Fair	:	Book fairs draw people from diverse fields.
Faith	:	Is the base of relationship.
Favourite	:	Dr. Abdul Kalam is a favourite of all Indians.

Fear	: Indian army fight with exemplary courage.
	: Enemy is fearful of Indian troops.
Film	: Documentary films educate masses.
Finish	: Finishing work in time gives satisfaction.
First	: Country always comes first for its citizens.
Foe	: Terrorism is the biggest foe for all countries.
Follow	: Good leaders command healthy following.
Forest	: Is a treasure of the country.
	: It's a gift of nature to mankind.
Future	: Future of Indian space research is very bright.
	: Upcoming generation is the future of country.
Gallant	: Gallant mountaineers scaled the peak successfully.
Gold	: Nature provides golden opportunities in life.
Group	: Work produces more creativity.
Guard	: Defence forces guard the border with full devotion.
Guide	: A leader guides his men in right way.
	: Good guidance comes from wise people.
Guts	: High in Indian troops.
Habit	: Good habits go a long way in life
	: Good habits are inculcated by practice.
Hand	: India always gives a helping hand to its neighbour.
	: India joined hand with others to fight terrorism.
Happy	: Meeting friends gives happiness.
	: Having a goal is a state of happiness.
Hard work	: Always pays in life.
	: Persistent hard work in right direction brings positive result.
Haste	: Thinking man take deliberate decisions.
Hate	: Good people love others.
	: Helping others is better than hating
Headmaster	: Takes his institution to great heights.
	: Is the role model for students.
Height	: Conquering heights brings excitement.
Help	: Friends help each other.
	: Helping others gives immense pleasure.
Hesitations	: Knowledge overcomes it.

Home	:	Learning starts from home.
Honest	:	Good citizens show honesty towards their responsibilities.
Humorous	:	People are liked by all.
	:	People create light moments in life.
Identify	:	Man is identified by his deed.
	:	Discipline/courage is the identification of Indian Army.
Illiterate	:	Literacy brings prosperity in society.
Imagination	:	Scientist's imagination brings wonders.
Impossible	:	Persistence made it possible to reach the moon.
	:	Consistent efforts make everything possible.
India	:	Indians are making a mark in the whole world.
Influence	:	He influenced his friends by his intelligence and behaviour.
Initiative	:	Leaders take the initative.
Injury	:	Is a part of sportsman's life.
Injustice	:	Government brings policies to remove injustice from society.
Insist	:	Constitution insists on equal rights to all.
Insult	:	He respects his elders.
Jealous	:	Love overcomes jealousy.
Land	:	Effective use of land and its resources brings prosperity.
Leader	:	Always shows right path to his men.
	:	Good officers lead their men effectively.
Life	:	Of great leaders motivates young generation.
Limit	:	Intelligent people bring good results from limited source.
Lively	:	Characters spread happiness all over.
Lose	:	Strong people bounce back from their loss.
	:	Determined people never lose hope.
Love	:	Is the sweetest and strongest bond.
Loyal	:	Loyalty towards duty/work shows character.
	:	Loyalty makes relations stronger.
Luck	:	Luck favours those who take initiatives.
	:	Great efforts bring good luck.
Lazy	:	Exercise overcomes laziness.
Logic	:	Logical ideas are welcomed by all.
Mad	:	Fanaticism is madness of mankind.
Make	:	Timely decisions help in making the career.

Meet	:	Meeting regularly creates better understanding.
Mend	:	Mending fences improves relations with neighbours.
Merit	:	Recruitment on merit improves organisation.
Method	:	Methodical approach saves efforts.
Mischief	:	Children are generally mischievous.
Money	:	Cannot buy everything in life.
Mood	:	Moody people do not fit well in a company.
Mother	:	Is an embodiment of faith and sacrifice.
Movement	:	High morale gives momentum to the goal.
Necessity	:	Motivates man to work hard.
Newspaper	:	Carries important information.
Notice	:	Great deeds are noticed by everyone.
Obey	:	Proper command and control brings obedience to orders.
Opportunities	:	Wise man always makes proper use of opportunities.
Overcome	:	Self-confidence helps in overcoming difficulties early.
	:	One can overcome the hurdles with determination.
Patriotism	:	Makes a nation great.
Picnic	:	Brings change in the routine.
Plan	:	Planned work helps in overcoming difficulties.
Polite	:	Politeness always pays in life.
Poor	:	Poor need help in achieving big objectives.
Popular	:	Extrovert is always popular among friends.
Prosperity	:	Hard work brings prosperity among friends.
Protect	:	Parents protect the child against all odds.
Puzzle	:	Logical thinking helps in solving puzzle.
Quick	:	Army officers take quick and correct decisions.
Read	:	Reading enhances knowledge.
Recognition	:	Great deeds are always recognized.
Respect	:	Good deed is always respected.
Responsible	:	Rank and responsibility go together.
Rights	:	Rights and duties are co-related.
Rigid	:	People find it difficult to adjust with a rigid person.
Risk	:	Higher the risk, higher the returns.
Rule	:	Enforcement of rules and regulations brings discipline.

Shy	:	Shyness can be avoided by free interactions with others.
Sister	:	Elder sister is a good friend and an advisor.
Sportsman	:	Sportsman spirit helps in winning the match.
Stamina	:	Regular exercise increases stamina.
	:	Sports help in building stamina.
Struggle	:	Struggle makes life a thrilling experience.
System	:	Systematic approach makes work easier.
Teacher	:	Guides and helps in bringing out the best in a child.
Team	:	Team's victory depends on each one's efforts.
Temper	:	Short tempered people create more enemies than friends.
Thank	:	Thanking people brings better result.
Tired	:	Short break after hard work avoids tiredness.
Travel	:	Travelling improves knowledge.
Understand	:	Friendship is based on mutual understanding.
Uniform	:	Gives pride and unity.
Unity	:	Mutual understanding brings unity in a team.
Up-to-date	:	Google provides up-to-date knowledge.
Victory	:	Sincere efforts lead to victory.
War	:	War is not the solution to human problems.
Worry	:	Hurry and worry brings diseases only.
Young	:	Young performers are goal oriented.
Youth	:	Youth can build a strong society.
Zeal	:	He plays with zeal and josh.

SAMPLE 2:

Able	:	Abilities reveal qualities
Accept	:	Acceptance reflects adaptability
Accident	:	Alertness prevents accident
Active	:	Activeness reflects cheerful personality
Actor	:	Good actor teaches the masses by his acting
Administration	:	Reflects qualities of an administrator
Admire	:	Admiration leads to good performance
Aeroplane	:	A power house of technologies
Affection	:	Leads to unity and integrity
	:	Reflects sense of love

Afraid	:	A brave person is never afraid of any challenge
Aggressive	:	A balanced aggression is good to achieve the goals.
Agree	:	A good leader agrees with the positive ideas of others.
Aim	:	Aim motivates one to work hard.
Aloof	:	An aloof person generally remains self-centred.
Annoy	:	Annoying others reflects one's short temper.
Anxious	:	Anxiety motivates to create new ideas.
	:	Anxiety brings new inventions.
Approach	:	Positive and correct approach leads to solution.
Army	:	Army is a strong force to defend the nation.
Arrange	:	A good arrangement shows organizing abilities.
Astrology	:	Astrology is absolute enemy of reason & science.
Attack	:	Sudden attacks give surprise to the enemy.
Avoid	:	A good officer always avoids controversies.
Battle	:	Brave fights the battle with valour and vigour.
Beat	:	Skill beats strength.
Beautiful	:	Beautiful scenery attracts everyone.
Behaviour/Behave	:	Behaviour reflects character.
Boys	:	Responsible boys bring glory to their families by their good deeds.
Blood	:	A soldier never worries of his blood in battlefield.
Bluff	:	An honest person never bluffs to anyone.
Bold	:	Bold action leads to success.
Book	:	Reading of books enhances knowledge.
		Is a treasure of knowledge.
Break	:	A good citizen never breaks laws and social norms.
Bring	:	Dynamic person brings forth constructive ideas.
Calm	:	Bold persons keep themselves calm and cool in stress and strain.
Cannot	:	Brave persons never believe in cannot.
Capability	:	Capability leads to good performance.
Cause	:	Cause helps in resolution.
Certain	:	Certain facts are the realities of life.
Character	:	Character reflects personality.
Childish	:	Maturity removes childishness.

Cinema	:	A source of entertainment and learning.
Clever	:	Cleverness is good quality of a leader.
Co-education	:	Builds healthy cooperation between the two sexes.
College	:	A gateway to higher education.
Command	:	Strict command ensures discipline.
	:	Command over language is the strength of a speaker.
Competition	:	Healthy competition brings up talent.
Confidence	:	Confidence ensures success.
	:	Knowledge gains confidence.
Confuse	:	A bold personality never gets confused while taking decision.
	:	Clear instructions remove confusion.
	:	Confusion comes due to ignorance of facts.
Continuous/ Continue	:	Continuous and constant efforts provide positive results.
Cooperation/ Cooperative	:	Cooperation is a good quality of a leader.
	:	Cooperation strengthens unity.
Country	:	Country gives identity to its citizens.
	:	I love my country.
Courage	:	Courage helps one to face difficulties.
Coward	:	Bravery overcomes cowardice.
Criminal	:	Criminal gets punished in the court of law.
	:	Strict rules restrict crimes.
Criticism	:	Healthy criticism improves any system.
Crowd	:	A good crowd maintains peace and harmony.
Cruel	:	Cruelty shows one's inhuman nature.
Curiosity	:	Curiosity enhances knowledge.
Current	:	Current affairs enhance the general knowledge.
Custom	:	Customs are the mirror of society.
Danger	:	Bold personality removes danger by confidence.
	:	Alertness avoids dangers.
Death	:	A brave soldier is never afraid of death
Deceive	:	A good leader believes in clear perception.
Decision	:	Quick and correct decision leads to success in every field.
Defeat	:	Courage and zeal avoid defeat in battle.

Depression	:	Motivation removes depression.
Desire	:	Desired results come through hard work.
Destroy	:	Destroying forests creates ecological imbalance.
Difficulty/ difficult	:	Confidence removes difficulty.
Discipline	:	Discipline is backbone of Armed Forces.
	:	Strict command maintains discipline.
Discourage	:	Encouragement removes discouragement
Discuss	:	Healthy discussion brings solutions.
Dislike	:	Good leader never dislikes his followers.
Dispute	:	Constant dialogue resolves dispute.
Distance	:	Internet removes distance.
	:	Closeness overcomes distance in relations.
Duty	:	Dutifulness shows one's responsible attitude.
Early	:	An early riser rises to great heights in life.
Education	:	Education imparts knowledge.
Efficiency	:	Efficiency leads to perfection.
Efforts	:	Hard efforts lead to success.
Empty	:	A good leader never commits empty promises.
Enemy	:	Brave soldiers face the enemy with courage and zeal.
Enjoy	:	Enjoyment creates cheerfulness.
Escape	:	Bold personality never believes in escape.
Exam	:	Exam results reflect performance.
Excel	:	Hard work brings excellence.
Excuse	:	Inadvertent mistakes while working are excusable.
Exercise	:	Regular exercise enhances physical stamina.
Experience	:	Experience brings perfectness.
Failure	:	Failure teaches a lesson to succeed.
	:	A pre-requisite for success.
Faith	:	A good leader wins the faith of his followers.
Family	:	A company of love and affection.
Father	:	A source of inspiration.
	:	A role model for the family.
Fatigue	:	Stamina overcomes fatigue.
Favour	:	Favouring the poor shows one's good grooming.

Fear	:	Courage overcomes fearfulness.
	:	Courage removes fear.
Fight	:	Braves fight with vigour and valour.
Firing	:	Firing speeches is the art of leadership.
Follow	:	A good citizen follows social norms in letter and spirit.
Forgive	:	Forgiveness is a good habit.
Fortune	:	Fortune comes through hard work.
Fountain	:	Life is like a fountain.
Friend	:	Friendship inspires.
Future	:	Hard and sincere efforts make the future bright.
Gallant	:	Bold soldiers are gallant and brave.
Game	:	High spirit wins the game.
Give	:	Giving good ideas reflects one's intelligence & helpful nature.
Gloomy	:	Optimism removes gloominess.
Golf	:	Golf courses are full of green grass and fresh air.
Good	:	Good behaviour reflects positive attitude.
Greedy	:	Greed for knowledge is the tendency of a scholar.
Group	:	A group effort always leads to success of goal.
Guide	:	Guiding others is the art of leadership.
Gun	:	Gun is a useful weapon for soldier.
Harmful	:	Precautions avoid harmful effects.
Hate	:	A good captain never hates his teammates.
Heat	:	Heated argument creates difference among people.
Help	:	A good leader always helps his followers.
Helpless	:	Helplessness shows one's weak will power.
Hint	:	Ted talk Hint helps to find a solution.
Hobby	:	Good use of leisure time.
Honest	:	Honesty is liked by all in every field.
Honour	:	Comes through sacrifice.
Hope	:	Hope is a big motivator.
Humour	:	Humorous remark relieves one's tension.
Hunger	:	Hunger for success provides results.
Idea	:	Constructive and positive ideas lead to solution.
Illiteracy	:	Education removes illiteracy.
Illness	:	Medication cures illness.

Imagination	: Imagination creates foresight.
Impossible	: A man of strong will power makes it possible.
Improvement	: Comes through hard work.
Indiscipline	: Strict rules remove indiscipline.
Initiative	: Bold person always takes initiative.
	: Volunteers take initiatives.
Injure	: A good soldier never highlights minor injuries.
Injustice	: True justice removes injustice.
Institute	: A place for professional education, training and entertainment.
Insult	: A good leader never insults his followers.
Integrity	: Integrity leads to unity and patriotism.
Intelligent	: Intelligence always leads to solution.
Joint	: Joint efforts bring desired result.
Jump	: Jumping to great heights reflects glory of success.
Justice	: True justice brings out the truth.
Kidnap	: Kidnapping creates problem in the society.
	: Brain drain is a form of kidnap.
Kill	: Killing instinct wins every battle.
Knife	: A useful instrument for a surgeon.
Knowledge	: Knowledge changes lives.
Late	: Late coming depicts one's irresponsible attitude.
Laughing	: Reflects a happy mind.
Leader	: Good leader motivates his subordinates.
Life	: Life is evolving constantly.
Lonely	: Company removes loneliness.
Loneliness	: Friendship removes loneliness.
Loyalty	: Loyalty creates integrity.
Manage	: Management reflects professionalism.
Map	: Mapping the way to success is the art of leadership.
Marriage	: Marriage brings more responsibilities in life
	: A union of two souls
Merit	: High merits are the index of high achievements/performances.
	: Merit brings up talent.
Moral	: Behaviour reflects moral character.

Morale	:	High morale leads to success.
Mother	:	Is the first teacher of a child.
	:	A source of love and affection.
Move	:	Healthy moves bring desired results in the society.
Murder	:	A civilized person has no murderous intention.
Music	:	Entertainment and a big industry.
Mutual	:	Mutual support strengthens the governing body.
Must	:	One must put in sincere efforts to achieve the goal.
Nation	:	Nation gives one his identity.
Neglect	:	Strict orders and instructions remove negligence.
Never	:	A brave personality never surrenders before a challenge.
	:	One never follows dishonest ways to prove oneself.
Noise	:	Noise disturbs the mental concentration.
Novel	:	Novelty of items attracts the people.
Obedience	:	Obedience shows discipline.
Offer	:	A good leader offers constructive ideas.
Peace	:	Peace creates tranquility and growth.
Persuades	:	Leader persuades with his ideology.
Play	:	Fair play is the symbol of impartiality.
Poison	:	Snake poison is very useful for medicinal purposes.
Precaution	:	Precaution avers any problem later.
Principle	:	A man of principles creates good impression on others.
Problem	:	Knowledge solves problems intelligently.
Progress	:	Progress leads to human development.
Punishment	:	A good judge never punishes innocents in court of law.
Quick	:	Quick and speedy decisions produce results.
Rape	:	Rape depicts social evil.
	:	Rapists get punished in the court;
Regular	:	Regular practice brings perfection.
Reject	:	A good director never rejects positive suggestions.
Responsible	:	Duties and responsibilities go hand in hand.
Rest	:	A dedicated worker never takes rest during working hours.
Reward	:	A reward inspires for better performance.
Rise	:	A rise in life is an index of achievements.
Risk	:	A courageous person never hesitates to take risk.

Rope	:	A rope to success is woven by a bold personality.
Rude	:	Politeness removes rudeness.
Sacrifice	:	A good officer/leader sacrifices his own ease and comfort for his men.
Sad	:	Happiness removes sadness.
Score	:	High scores demonstrate high achievements.
Secret	:	Hard work is the only secret to success.
Sleep	:	A good leader never sleeps over any matter.
Slow	:	Speed overcomes slowness.
Snake	:	Is useful for ecological balance.
Soldier	:	A symbol of bravery and discipline.
Speed	:	Speed in action brings fast result.
Spirit	:	High spirit wins the game.
Sports	:	Instill killer instinct and increase energetic level.
Strong	:	Strong will power leads the way to success.
Struggle	:	Life is to be used to its full potential.
	:	Struggles make a person strong.
Success	:	Hard work leads to success.
	:	Every success leads to higher success in life.
Suicide	:	A courageous man never thinks of committing suicide.
Support	:	Mutual support strengthens the governing body.
Surprise	:	Knowledge and confidence remove surprise.
Sympathy	:	Sympathy shows kindness.
System	:	Systematic working produces positive results.
Table	:	Table manners reflect good behaviour.
Team	:	Team spirits lead to achieve the goals.
Treat	:	Treating people in friendly manner reveals one's cooperative nature.
Temper	:	Balanced personality never loses his temper.
	:	Patience maintains temperament.
Think	:	Positive thinking reflects positive attitude.
Tiredness	:	Good stamina overcomes tiredness.
Training	:	Training brings perfection.
Tree	:	Maintains environmental balance.
Trust	:	A good leader trusts his followers.

Truth	: Prevails forever.
Universal	: Universal laws are respected everywhere.
Upset	: Self confidence and patience overcome it.
Victory	: Comes through dedication and hard work.
War	: War divides the people.
	: War is not a solution.
Watch	: Strict watch ensures security.
Water	: Water is vital for life.
Weapon	: Latest weapons win war.
Weather	: Weather brings different experiences.
Whether	: Bold personality never believes in it.
Wife	: Wife is an equal partner of husband in life.
Woman	: Deserves equal rights in the society.
Work	: Hard work leads to success.
	: Hard work produces positive results.
Zeal	: Brave people work with zeal and enthusiasm.

Note: The above words are not given in the order from the SSB assessment point of view. These are given to generate more ideas and capabilities to create more sentences. At the SSB these words are arranged in such a way that the psychologist can check all the factors of OLQ. Here overall aim is to be able to write good sentences for any word that comes in the SSB. The order in which it is shown at the SSB will be different from the above.

SITUATION REACTION TEST (SRT)

"It is not the situation... It's your reaction to the situation that matters."

–Robert Conklin

This is a confirmatory test given to reconfirm the performance of the candidate displayed during TAT and WAT. In this test each candidate is given a booklet containing 60 day to day routine situations and he is asked to write his REACTIONS if he happens to be in those situations. Reaction is the immediate thought which comes to the mind after facing that situation.

Psychologist is interested to know one's behaviour pattern and intentions. So the andidate should write mature, sensible, responsible reactions considering himself as a good citizen having officer like qualities and of positive and optimistic nature.

In the answer a candidate has to write only a few words which have the solution to the problem given in the situation. A full sentence is not required in the answer; write in point form.

Never assume anything other than what is written in the test. Avoid the use of words will, shall, try; rather use the word "would" or past indefinite tense. Don't leave any situation. Try to attempt all SRTs.

This is largely a test of common sense. In everyday life one comes across certain unforeseen situations and one is called upon to resolve these or has to find a solution for these and to act in an appropriate manner to meet the requirement of the situation.

Nature and scope: SRT measures the individual in action or confronts him with situations related to own life, in response to which he gives expression to his feelings. This way he reveals some of his personality traits through reasoning ability and maturity because one learns to act appropriately to these situations by the virtue of the gains through classroom instructions and social interactions at all events.

Procedure: At the SSB, a candidate is required to answer nearly 60 questions in 30 minutes. The time limit has been purposely reduced to the minimum to ensure that the candidate gives his response without protracted thought and deliberation to attract spontaneous response.

The situations given in the test resemble those confronted by all of us in our day to day life. Therefore, there is no right or wrong answer for these situations. Candidate expresses his choice which matches with his attitude, temperament and other personality features. No special intelligence or knowledge is required to answer these questions.

Sometimes an imaginary character is introduced and he is made to face the situation and asked to find out a solution. Whatever is the name given to this character, in reality he is none other than the candidate himself.

- Write minimum possible words in your response, using action words and punctuation marks.
- Use telegraphic language.
- Don't worry merely on reaction, write sentences full of action.

Example

Just before the starting of a doubles match, he found his partner missing. He.....

Reaction – He took the substitute player, played the match and won.

Keep in Mind
- Candidate has to attempt all situations within the stipulated time. Therefore, candidates should attempt easier questions first and then the situations he or she finds difficult.

- Your response should be for the situations. If you do a realistic analysis of one of these aspects, you will find that the responses being given have relation to reflect qualities like co-operative attitude, positive approach.
- You may find that one situation is repeated in other form. Therefore, you have to be cautious not to contradict an expression of your personality already given in respect of previous situation.

If a candidate is down to earth, alert and has positive approach, quick in uptake, helping nature, co-operative, friendly, courageous, bold and firm to his decision, he can do well in this test.

Model Situations and their Answers

Few model situations with their possible answers are given below. Candidates should read them carefully and try to give suitable answers to the situations. They are given for practice.

Rules

1. 60 situations
2. Time 30 minutes only

General SRTs (Accident)

1. He met with a serious accident while going on a bicycle/motorcycle/scooter resulting into serious injury to pillion rider and serious damage to his vehicle. He.....

    *took the injured to the nearest hospital leaving the vehicle safely behind/ or locked behind, for repairs later.

2. Going on a bicycle he was hit by a speeding car. He.....

    *Balanced his movements, noted down car number and reported to traffic police.

3. While moving on a bicycle towards his village, carrying his brother, he suddenly found the vehicle got punctured and his brother was running high temperature, no public transport was available. He.....

    *Took lift from passer-by vehicle (bullock cart/tractor/truck) to take his brother to the nearest doctor on the way.

Crossing the River

4. While returning from picnic he had to cross the river with his friend, when he found that the temporary bridge has collapsed. He.....

    *Swam across the river or crossed over by boat.

5. While going over the bridge on a river with his friends, he found half of the party had already crossed the bridge when suddenly the bridge collapsed. He.....

   *Arranged boat for the remaining to cross over.

6. Mid-stream of the river, he found his boat overturning. He.....

   *Jumped out and swam across the river, used lifesaving jacket / inflated rubber tube to cross over the river.

7. While going in a boat he found that the boat had developed a leak / or hole when water started coming in. He.....

   *Plugged the leak/hole with cloth, threw the water by filling bucket and continued boating.

8. Due to very heavy rains the river was rising and he had to cross the river. He.....

   *Waited for rain to stop and then crossed over by boat.

Fire Station

9. He saw fire in a village, people were panicking. He.....

   *Pacified the people, used sand and water to put off the fire and called up the fire brigade from city.

10. He saw fire in a city building, people were panicking. He.....

    *Pacified the people, switched off the mains, used the fire extinguisher, sand/water buckets to put off fire, called up fire brigade, rescued people.

Financial Crisis
For self

11. Urgent need. He.....

    *Borrowed money from friend.

12. Need was of long term duration. He.....

    *Took up part time job or tuition and continued with his aim.

13. When his close relations refused to help him financially. He.....

    *Borrowed money from his friends.

For others

*Helped them financially.

*Arranged money from his friends.

Jungle

14. He was passing through a jungle. It was getting dark when he heard some noise in the bushes behind him. He.....

    *Looked back, found nothing suspicious and so carried on.

15. He, accompanied by his younger brother, was going through a thick jungle when he spotted a tiger going ahead of him at some distance. He.....

    *He and his brother ducked quietly behind the bushes, let the tiger pass and carried on after sometime.

16. You're on a patrol or on shikar, found a tiger coming on to you and there is no tree to climb up. What will you do?

    *Use the fire arms and shoot the tiger dead.

17. He was face to face with armed Nagas in the forest. He.....

    *Gave them his identity through body language and was allowed to move on since he was not the target.

Games and Sports

18. While playing hockey match, he twisted his ankle very badly. He.....

    *Took first aid and continued playing.

19. As captain of the team, he found his players rather discouraged while playing a match. He.....

    *Encouraged them, and told them to win the match.

20. Just before the start of a doubles match he found his partner is missing. He.....

    *Took substitute player and played the match.

21. While watching a match he found the supporters of two rival teams started fighting. He.....

    *Urged both sides to show sportsman spirit and controlled the situation.

22. He found his captain was unable to continue due to serious injury. He.....

    *Took over the responsibility of the captain.

Hiking and Mountaineering

23. While going on a mountaineering trip, he found some members of his team were injured and some had got tired because of long route taken by the party. He.....

    *Gave first aid to the injured, consulted route map to take shortest route to continue further movement.

24. Just before reaching the mountain or peak, he found his feet were slipping due to sand/snow underneath his feet. He.....

    *Used the axe to control his body balance, changed steps and moved up to the top.

Journey by Train

25. During a train journey, he found the compartment catching fire and people were trying to jump out. He.....

*Pulled the alarm chain, advised the people not to jump out until train stops.

26. During the journey he found some miscreants or robbers entering the compartment and trying to loot the passengers. He.....

    *Overpowered the miscreants with the help of fellow passengers.

27. While going to a particular destination at the platform, he entered into a wrong train when two minutes were left for the right train to start. He.....

    *Rushed to board the right train.

28. During the journey he found someone pick-pocketing his purse. He.....

    *Caught him red-handed, handed him over to the railway police.

29. He found an old lady was about to fall from the door of the compartment. He.....

    *Rushed to save the lady from falling.

    *Rushed to the lady, helped her to board, asked about her well being and occupied his seat.

30. Conductor came to ask his ticket, but he found that his purse was pick-pocketed containing the ticket and cash. He.....

    *Established his identity, requested cash from a fellow passenger in lieu of cheque and paid his ticket charges.

Journey by Bus

31. While going to a place on urgent mission, he found the only bus left was full and no other public transport was available. He.....

    *Somehow managed his entry into bus and traveled the distance standing.

Natural Calamity

32. Being the eldest of the family, he found his family was uprooted due to cyclone. He.....

    *Rehabilitated the family by arranging necessary things.

Picnic

33. He found a few members were going to back out from joining picnic. He.....

    *Persuaded them to join the picnic.

34. In a picnic towards the late hours of the evening he was served with cold food. He.....

    *Accepted the cold food.

Social Disorder

35. He saw people crowding outside ticket window trying to buy the ticket first resulting into quarrel. He.....

    *Tactfully persuaded them to form a queue.

36. He was working under two officers who were giving conflicting orders. He....

    *Obeyed both tactfully.

37. He found a group of people holding hockey sticks surrounding a lonely individual. He.....

    *Rushed to persuade them not to harm the individual.

38. He saw in his native village two groups of people fighting each other for the post of Sarpanch. He.....

    *Tactfully persuaded both groups to follow electoral rules for the post.

39. In a show he found the main organizer or actor missing. He.....

    *Took the responsibility of the organizer or actor.

Road

40. He was returning from office, after seeing a late night show; at a lonely place he was confronted by some people bearing lathis. He.....

    *Asked them the reason, finding that he was not their target, they let him go. He then informed the police patrol van standing at a distance.

    *He persuaded them tactfully not to commit any violence.

41. At a lonely place, he found a person teasing a girl. He.....

    *Rushed to the place, challenged the person who ran away.

42. His car broke down on a lonely road. It was dark. He.....

    *Used his cell phone, called the helpline and got his car repaired. *Repaired the fault himself and continued driving.

Crowded Place

43. While travelling in the crowded bus he saw a person picking the pocket of a passenger. He.....

    *Caught the man red-handed and handed him over to the police.

44. He was in the picture hall and when the interval was about to be over, he saw a man brushing/teasing the girl sitting by his side. He.....

    *Immediately caught hold of the person, called the staff and the policeman on duty and handed him over to them.

45. He, accompanied by his sister was moving in the market when two persons teased his sister. He.....

    *Asked them to stop and apologize.

46. One of his friends didn't like his arguments and rebuked him. He.....

    *Asked him to calm down and made him to realize his mistake.

47. Due to some misunderstanding a close friend hit him. He.....

    *Coolly removed his misunderstanding and made him to apologize.

48. He was in NCC, during annual camp his team was assigned a difficult task. But his teammates refused to co-operate. He.....

    *Persuaded them to complete the task in time.

Studies and Examination

49. While preparing for his examination his sick father needed a lot of attention. He.....

    *Managed his time by paying adequate attention to both father and studies.

50. All through he got first division but in one exam he failed to get first division. He.....

    *Worked hard to get first division in the next exam.

51. His roommate in the hostel was constantly disturbing him when he wanted to study. He.....

    *Compromised with him so as to concentrate on his studies.

52. His teacher threatened to fail him in the exam. He.....

    *Respectfully inquired the reason and removed teacher's misunderstanding.

53. While going to the exam centre, he was stopped by the police due to curfew in that area. He.....

    *Showed his hall ticket or admit card to police and requested him to proceed further.

54. On the last day of application the clerk refused to accept his application as one testimonial was found unattested. He.....

    *Rushed to get his testimonial attested and re-submitted the application on same day.

55. While discussing a subject with other friends he found he was wrong and others were right. He.....

    *Accepted his mistake gracefully and overcame the mistake.

56. While expressing his view, others were not willing to accept his idea. He.....

    *Convinced them logically.

57. He was called for a job interview and required to appear in his final exam on the same day. He.....

    *Postponed the interview and appeared for the exam.

Sickness

58. Sickness of somebody at home (unconsciousness, heart attack etc). He.....

    *Called doctor at home for checkup & medicine

59. When the sickness is not of serious nature of somebody at home. He.....

    *Took the patient to the nearest hospital for treatment.

Strike and Union

60. He was asked by the union to go on strike. He.....

    *Tactfully persuaded them to call off their strike.

61. He was asked to speak in a debate whether student union should continue. He.....

    *He spoke against the union why these are undesirable.

Miscellaneous Situations

62. He was asked by his instructor to walk a long distance when he was having fever. He.....

    *Took medicine to control his fever and obeyed the instructor.

63. While riding a horse, he saw the horse going amok. He.....

    *Controlled the horse by holding the reins tightly.

64. He suddenly saw a snake creeping towards his foot at his house. He.....

    *Let the snake go the other way; (alternatively, Killed the snake.)

65. The issue of his marriage created a rift between his father and grandfather. He.....

    *Brought about a compromise between the two to settle the issue.

SRT – for Service Candidates

1. His sister's marriage was fixed and his relative refused to give him promised loan. He.....

   *Took advance from AFPP Fund, en-cashed FDs, borrowed from some friends and conducted marriage happily.

2. He was on exercise in a desert. His vehicle had gone for collection of rations and on his way back the driver lost his way. His troops were hungry. He.....

   *Sent a search party with jeep.

3. He quarreled with his neighbour. But later he realized that he needed his help. He.....

   *Compromised with him and got his help.

4. He and his wife were travelling by bus when a miscreant snatched his wife's chain. He.....

   *Overpowered him and handed him over to police.

5. He was assigned the task of capturing terrorists at midnight. They were hiding in a hut in a village nearby. He.....

   *Made a plan, surrounded them along with villagers and captured them.

6. While returning from range practice he found one of his men is in possession of live ammunition. He.....

   *Deposited ammunition in Ammunition Point, informed Senior JCO/Officer, correct SOP so that such a thing does not happen again.

7. His troops were patrolling in a high altitude area when it started snowing heavily. He as a Commander.....

   *Provided/issued warm clothes to them and told them to take precautions.

8. His sister's marriage was fixed. But he was refused leave due to Adm inspection. He.....

   *Organized marriage with the help of parents/friends, sent money and best wishes and joined family after inspection.

9. He was to join his unit after leave when Bharat Bandh was declared. He was stuck. He.....

   *Showed his identity card to Bandh organizers who allowed him to proceed.

10. While travelling by train, he was woken up by a noise. He found some miscreants were trying to break open the window. He.....

    *Overpowered the miscreants with the help of fellow passengers and handed them over to police.

11. He was to attend an important meeting. He was getting late and there was traffic jam on the road. He.....

    *Used mobile phone/STD phone to inform Secretary about his delayed arrival.

12. He was to go for patrolling duty in high altitude area and his driver was running high fever. He.....

    *Admitted him in the nearby hospital and took standby driver instead.

13. He was running high fever and his captain insisted upon him to play football match. He.....

    *Took medicine and played.

14. He was to go for patrolling duty in high altitude area and his coat parka was missing. He.....

    *Got it issued from store.

15. While coming from picture, he found two persons quarreling. He.....

*Enquired the reason and brought about a compromise between them.

16. He and his troops were to dig trenches when his friends denied to cooperate. He.....

    *Tactfully persuaded them to cooperate.

17. As Commander of the Patrol Party he saw some intruders hiding inside the hideout. He.....

    *Immediately re-organized and coordinated patrol party, attacked and nabbed intruders.

18. He could not complete a difficult task in time. He.....

    *Explained the reason for delay, regretted and assured to be more organized in future.

19. While returning from market he faced three persons with knives who asked him to part with his belongings. He.....

    *Tactfully dodged them and came out unharmed.

20. While on duty at the main gate he was hit by bullet in the leg and the terrorist tried to snatch his rifle. He.....

    *Shouted for help and over-powered him.

21. He was on leave when he heard Radio/TV announcement of declaration of war. He.....

    *Sought blessings of parents and rejoined the duty.

22. He was in the Field Area. Already short of manpower he was approached by one of his men for leave on flimsy grounds. He.....

    *Looked into the ground and persuaded him to postpone the leave.

23. He was already late in completing his assignment/task and his colleagues refused to co-operate. He.....

    *Enquired the reason, removed misunderstanding and with the cooperation of his friends completed the task/assignment.

24. He along with his friends was attending a camp in Nagaland. Once they forgot the way to camp and came face to face with Nagas. He.....

    *Used compass and map to locate the camp and tactfully used body language to convince the Nagas not to prevent their movement.

25. He and his friends went to a thick jungle. Suddenly a tiger came in front of them. He.....

    *Quickly climbed the nearest tree, alternatively used fire arms.

26. He was attached with the senior commander. One of his friends came and asked for a favour. He.....

    *Helped him reasonably to the best of his capability within the framework of rules.

27. His boss did not agree with his view. He.....
    *Convinced him logically & explained merits & demerits.
28. He worked hard for achieving his objective, but failed. He.....
    *Made introspection, removed shortcomings and again attempted to succeed.
29. He thought of his promises and realized that his top-most priority was.....
    *Duty first, other things later.
30. He was asked by his CO to undertake a job in his suggested manner. But he realized that his CO's approach was wrong. He.....
    *Did the task, thereafter respectfully put across his suggestions.
31. While travelling in a train he found his pocket picked. He.....
    *Used money kept in inner pocket and informed the TTE/RPF staff.
32. Due to financial difficulties his parents were unable to support him in his studies. He.....
    *Took up part time job and continued his studies.
33. He was waiting for a bus when an accident took place in front of him. He.....
    *Rushed to help the injured.
34. He went for a mountaineering expedition. His friend slipped and died and expedition was called off. He.....
    *Informed next of kin, conducted last rites, again organized the expedition by motivating his party.
35. He felt that he was engaged in useless work. He.....
    *Yet carried on cheerfully and constructively.
36. His friend lost his job and was facing financial problem. He.....
    *Helped him financially and secured another job for him.
37. He realized that his arguments were not finding favour with his friends. He.....
    *Convinced them by giving fresh ideas and new data.
38. His office staff was not working efficiently. He.....
    *Enquired the reason and motivated them.
39. He was given a difficult task. He.....
    *Planned and solved it intelligently.
40. His plan foiled in the very beginning. He.....
    *Had already done contingency planning so tried again with new plan.
41. He was at home when dacoits attacked and started looting his house. He.....

*Called the police and resisted their attempt.
42. He was asked to organize a variety show in his unit. He.....

    *Planned, rehearsed and happily organized the show.
43. His company was camping in a jungle where shooting was prohibited. Just then a leopard appeared. He was on guard duty. He.....

    *Scared the leopard by firing in the air/blowing whistle/lighting fire and informed Guard Commander.
44. Emergency was declared in a city where his unit was located. As CO of the unit, he.....

    *Ordered the unit personnel to follow SOP.
45. When he was required to take a new step. He.....

    *Planned and took the step willingly/boldly.
46. While going to the office, he saw a man climbing up a house with the help of a rope. He.....

    *Enquired the reason and took the best suitable action.
47. He was given the responsibility to take a group for all-India tour. He.....

    *Planned the itinerary and conducted the tour successfully.
48. He heard a cry of 'fire, fire' from the neighbouring house. He.....

    *Informed fire brigade, organized people and took effective steps to extinguish the fire.
49. On way to his office his scooter met with an accident and the scooter got slightly damaged. He.....

    *Went to his office and later repaired the scooter.
50. He lost his way in the jungle. He.....

    *Used compass/GPS/route map to find his way.
51. While travelling in the train he realized that he had lost his ticket. He.....

    *Produced photocopy of ticket/gave PNR number, proved his identity and obtained new ticket.
52. To the growth of population in the country he suggested.....

    *Family planning methods & educating the poor.
53. The light in the neighbour's house went off. He.....

    *Helped him to rectify the fault.
54. He was travelling in a bus when it suddenly caught fire. He.....

    *Evacuated the co-passengers, put off the fire using sand and water and informed fire brigade.
55. He was coming back home after meeting a friend when he was attacked with a lathi from behind. He.....

*Confronted the culprit, over-powered him and handed him over to police.

56. He was passing by a lake where he saw a boy drowning. He did not know swimming. He.....

   *Threw a rope/long cloth tied with stone and saved the boy.

57. He met with an accident and got injured slightly. But he realized that the person who caused this accident was quite seriously injured. He.....

   *Rushed the injured to nearest hospital, informed his family members and police.

58. He had an argument with his neighbour, but at the dead of the night he heard cries from the house of that very neighbour. He.....

   *Rushed to find out the reason and helped him.

59. He found that one of his very close friends was dealing in drugs. He.....

   *Persuaded him to stop the same.

60. The team was tired and ready to surrender. He was trying his best to motivate the members when one of his teammates asked him to keep quiet. He.....

   *Again motivated them not to surrender.

SAMPLE SRT-1

1. He was asked to arrange basketball match by his CO. He.....

   *He organized the basketball match efficiently.

2. The Station HQ assured all facilities at the site for the tree plantation but when he reached with ten men there, no arrangements were seen to have been made. He.....

   *Himself made the arrangements and carried out the tree plantation as scheduled.

3. He was Convoy Commander. On the way he learnt that there was a landslide. He.....

   *Removed the landslide and proceeded further.

4. Although there was a confirmed ticket, the conductor was refusing him entry to the compartment and the train was about to move. He.....

   *Boarded in the General compartment and at the next stop he persuaded the TTE and got the seat.

5. He was going on temporary duty in military vehicle and he suddenly developed fever. He.....

   *Took the medicine and went on temporary duty.

6. He was performing the duties of MES NCO and MES staff refused to attend his complaints. He.....

   *Convinced the staff with the genuineness of work.

7. He was to prepare for military promotion cadre exam but other friends wanted him to attend a private party. He.....

   *He humbly expressed his inability to attend to his friends and prepared for the military promotion cadre exam.

8. While he was returning to his unit location in an auto rickshaw, a car hit his vehicle from rear and he was thrown on the footpath. He.....

   *Got up immediately, ensured the well-being of the auto rickshaw driver, noted down the car number and informed the traffic police.

9. While travelling by train he noticed that he forgot to carry his railway ticket. He.....

   *Got the ticket from the TTE in the train.

10. While he was studying in school his father died leaving behind his brother and sister. He.....

    *Completed his studies and looked after/helped his brother and sister.

11. After firing he wanted to sleep whereas he was asked to accompany a long range patrol with his Sub. Maj. He.....

    *Accompanied long range patrol with his Sub Major.

12. He was appointed team captain of his unit volley ball team whereas other players objected his appointment. He.....

    *Proved his eligibility for captaincy by his performance.

13. He found that his father differs on what he should do. He.....

    *Persuaded his father giving the merits/demerits. *Convinced his father giving the logic.

14. His colleague wanted to borrow some money when he himself needed it most. He.....

    *Arranged money for his friend from other sources.

15. During the social camp, he was assigned the job of getting the drain cleaned but his other group mates showed their reluctance. He.....

    *Persuaded his group mates and got the drain cleaned.

16. All the members of his family wanted him to come on leave for a social party. He.....

    *Proceeded on leave only if situation allowed him.

17. While carrying out his duties in Nagaland he lost his route and he had no supply of food available for 48 hours. He.....

    *Found the route using route map/compass.

18. His family members had fixed his marriage but his commanding officer detained him for an adventure activity. He.....

*Spoke to his parents to postpone the marriage and attended the adventure activity.

19. He was duty NCO and he found that fire had broken due to short-circuiting of electric connection. He.....

    *Switched off the mains and extinguished the fire.

20. While passing through a lane, he saw some persons beating a boy. He.....

    *Saved the boy from the persons.

21. He was asked to give extra time for JCO club on Sunday. He.....

    *He obeyed the order.

22. The very family who borrowed a gas cylinder from him refused to lend theirs when he needed it most. He.....

    *Arranged from elsewhere.

23. His father negotiated his marriage but he had already decided a girl of his choice. He.....

    *He convinced his father and got married to the girl he wished to.

24. While purchasing a ticket at the counter he found his purse missing. He.....

    *Purchased the ticket using the money kept in inner pocket and informed the police of theft of his purse.

25. He is detailed regularly on LRP (Long Route Patrolling) but he has brought his family in station. He.....

    *He obeyed the orders.

26. While going on temp duty he had no reaction time to get his warrant exchanged. He.....

    *Got the warrant exchanged in train from TTE.

27. On reaching home on 60 days Annual Leave he got a signal of his recall from his leave due to military emergency. He.....

    *Sought the blessings of his parents and rejoined the duty.

28. His subordinates call him as an informer of SM. He.....

    *Ignored it.

29. On reaching late on parade his BHM humiliated him. He.....

    *Apologized for the delay and assured to be punctual in future.

30. He was required to go 10 kms more at midnight and his cycle got punctured. He.....

    *Locked the cycle, took the lift from passer–by vehicle and reached at the destination.

31. He wanted to carry extra rum bottle while going on leave but canteen officer refused to give him. He.....

*Carried entitled bottles along with authority letter.

32. His Commanding Officer asked him to give him 4 blankets for his residence. He.....

    *He gave 4 blankets to the CO on loan voucher.

33. He is performing the duties of mess Havildar and there is often a complaint of bad quality of food. He.....

    *Improved the quality of food.

34. While on night duty his colleague fainted. He.....

    *Called the guard commander and provided the first aid.

35. His father wanted him to quit military service but he wanted to continue. He.....

    *Convinced his father and continued in service.

36. His family was staying in peace station and he was asked to go to war front and send his family to his native town. He.....

    *Sent his family to his native town and went to warfront.

37. After reaching his promotion exam centre, he found that he forgot to carry writing material. He.....

    *Arranged from his friend.

38. After his marriage his in-laws were forcing him to leave the service. He.....

    *Persuaded his in-laws and continued his service.

39. His wife often wrote to him about the ill treatment she was getting from his other family members. He.....

    *Spoke to his wife and removed her misunderstanding.

40. While going on military duty on his private scooter, he found that a child met with an accident by his scooter. He.....

    *Stopped the scooter, provided first aid and admitted him in the nearest hospital.

41. While travelling by train he noticed that some civilian passengers started abusing the military persons in general. He.....

    *Ignored

42. Village patwari wanted some bribe for doing a land work for his family. He.....

    *Did not give any bribe.

43. His colleague wanted to go to cinema but he did not like it. He.....

    *Accompanied his friend.

44. He is required to reach for an examination but on the way he noticed curfew and no vehicular movement was permitted. He.....

*Produced his admission card and reached the examination hall.

45. While travelling by train, he noticed that his suitcase is stolen and his identity card has gone. He.....

   *Carried out the search, informed the TTE and lodged the FIR with the RPF/GRP.

46. He had gone to cinema with his friend and he found students chasing a young girl. He.....

   *Challenged and asked them to behave properly.

47. He entered his bathroom and noticed a cobra hanging from the ceiling of bathroom. He.....

   *He let it escape. (Alternatively – he killed it).

48. At railway platform he found a suitcase lying unclaimed. He.....

   *Informed the RPF/GRP immediately.

49. During the discussion he noticed that his colleagues were not paying attention to his talks.

   *He came out with more logic and persuaded them to pay attention.

50. He is asked to write an article about his unit. He.....

   *Wrote

51. He noticed that two persons were fighting with each other at a hotel where he had gone for dinner. He.....

   *Intervened and persuaded them not to do so and took the dinner.

52. His younger brother is an alcoholic and he often goes to take illicit country liquor. He.....

   *Advised him giving suitable examples and convinced him.

53. His wife blames him for all the failures at his home. He.....

   *Spoke to his wife and removed all the misunderstandings.

54. While negotiating a thick jungle he was surrounded by six Nagas carrying lathis in their hands. He.....

   *Proved his identity by body language and was allowed to move as he was not their target.

55. He wanted to bring a point to his friends and they ridiculed his arguments. He.....

   *He came out with more logic and brought point to his friends.

SAMPLE SRT-2

1. When travelling by train he went to toilet and on return he found his briefcase missing. He.....

*Carried out the search, informed the TTE and lodged the FIR with GRP/RPF.
2. He receives conflicting order from his two superior officers. He.....

   *Obeyed them both tactfully.
3. He was appointed team captain of basketball but other players revolted against his appointment. He.....

   *He proved eligibility by his game and won the confidence of the friends.
4. An epidemic has spread in the village due to poor hygiene conditions. He.....

   *He controlled the epidemic with the help of district health officer and improved the hygiene & sanitation conditions in the village.
5. Once he discussed his view points but others did not listen to him carefully. He.....

   *Gave his views more logically with suitable examples.
6. He notices a car running at high speed and runs over a child on the road. He.....

   *Noted down the car number, gave first aid to the child and informed the police.
7. A fellow passenger has fallen from running train. He.....

   *Pulled down the alarm chain and inform the GRP/RPF and guard.
8. His parents want him to marry a wealthy and less educated girl and he has already found a suitable educated girl for himself. He.....

   *He persuaded his parents that education is more valuable than the wealth and got married to the girl he wished to.
9. He made a silly mistake and his friends pointed out. He.....

   *He accepted cheerfully and sorted it out.
10. While walking on the road you find three unknown children are fighting each other. You...

    *Stop the fight and send them to their home.

PRACTICE SRT- 1

1. A fellow passenger pointed out to him that smoking is an offence in train. He.....
2. He reached home from office and saw his house on fire. He.....
3. He was to go to Delhi for interview but realized after one hour that he sat in a wrong train. He.....
4. He was travelling in a lift and the light went off. He.....

5. He took his friends for dinner to a hotel but forgot his wallet at home. He.....
6. His friends came to borrow the book from which he was preparing for his next morning paper. He.....
7. He was appointed to supervise evening games in the college but he was staying far away. He.....
8. He proposed to invite a political leader to preside over the annual day celebration but others were against it. He.....
9. He had to undergo an urgent surgical operation but there was no one to look after him. He.....
10. His father was insisting on his marriage but he wanted to take up a job. He.....
11. Hearing an unusual sound at night he woke up and found a man jumping out of his window. He.....
12. He was going to attend the SSB interview. On reaching the Railway Station he noticed that his suitcase has been stolen with his original certificates needed at SSB. He.....
13. He was travelling on his scooter and at gunpoint someone demanded his purse. He.....
14. He went to college and rowdy students told him to boycott the college class. He.....
15. His father has a dispute with his uncle on land/property. He.....
16. He wanted to borrow money for his sister's marriage. The relation who assured him declined to lend him at the time of marriage. He.....
17. He was going on cycle in thick jungle. It was already dark and his destination was 10 kms more. His cycle got punctured. He.....
18. He was in Nagaland jungle and he saw six Nagas with lathis rushing to him. He.....
19. He went to buy a ticket to travel by train. On getting the ticket he found that his purse was missing. He....
20. He was cookhouse commander. The dal often had stones and there were complaints from the dining members. He.....
21. He didn't do well in written test of SCO commission. His friends advised him not to venture in future. He.....
22. He was travelling in a train on reserved seat; a fellow passenger claimed to have the same seat on his reservation ticket. He...
23. He won a lottery of rupees one lakh. He.....
24. His two school going children frequently miss the classes. He.....

25. He was going to the market and he noticed a car and tonga had collided. He.....
26. He was asked to organize a picnic to nearby historical place. He.....
27. On coming back to his barrack from the firing range he found that his friend had brought 20 rounds of 7.62 mm SLR live ammunition. He.....
28. A helicopter fell in the vicinity of his unit lines. He.....
29. He saw a rifle lying in the football field of his company. He.....
30. A speeding motor truck ran over a man as he happened to pass by. He.....
31. He was called upon to organize a variety entertainment show in aid of Jawans Welfare in his unit. He.....
32. Due to financial difficulties his father could not support him for further studies after he passed his matric. He.....
33. Demand of a loan from his close relative in urgent need whereas he needed the same money for his son's hostel admission. He.....
34. He was going on his cycle and it became dark, he has to cover 10 kms distance to reach his destination and the cycle got punctured. He.....
35. He was watching cinema and he noticed suddenly smoke coming out of cinema hall and the viewers started running causing stampede. He.....
36. He was working in a private firm and his two immediate seniors gave him contradictory orders. He.....
37. While passing a mountainous track he was challenged by two persons with weapons in their hands. He.....
38. He has to appear for an exam but on reaching the city site, he noticed that curfew has been clamped. He.....
39. He was the Captain of basketball team and his team was about to lose in the final. He.....
40. After marriage his in-laws forced him to leave the job. He.....
41. His parents often irritated him with their orthodox ideas about the role of women in the society. He.....
42. At the time of interview he found that his certificates were missing. He.....
43. When he observed that his friend was having some suspicion about him. He.....
44. He had already decided to vote for a particular candidate whereas his friends wanted his commitment for the other candidate. He.....
45. When his colleagues advised him to be tactful with his boss. He.....
46. He happened to be present at a bus stop when a child who was with his mother was hit by a speeding motorbike and was injured seriously. He.....

PRACTICE SRT– 2

1. He and his friend are standing on a bridge over a river. His friend suddenly falls down. He does not know swimming. He.....
2. He and his brother have gone to a forest, they lost their way and it is becoming dark. He.....
3. While going to attend an important meeting, he saw a ghastly accident between an auto rickshaw and a tonga. He.....
4. His father has fixed his marriage with a rich girl but he is in love with his classmate. He has never disobeyed his father. His girl friend on the other hand says that if he does not marry her, she will commit suicide. He.....
5. His exams are starting next week and he is not fully prepared. His father's best friend suddenly comes to the house and there is no one else to look after him. He...
6. His parents have gone to their relatives leaving him behind with his younger brother. After midnight his younger brother develops very high fever and there is no medicine in the house. It is raining very heavily. He.....
7. He was studying late in the night and at 2 a.m. he finds a man's shadow entering neighbour's house through the ventilator. His exam is starting next day. He.....
8. Two groups are quarreling over a religious problem and he belongs to the minority group. He.....
9. Fire broke in the village due to short circuiting of electricity at night. He is the only electrician in the village. He.....
10. While studying he is giving tuition side by side. But his parents and friends are advising him to leave the tuition as he is not getting sufficient time for examinations. His financial condition is quite weak. He.....
11. While going in boat in the river Ganga, he falls down in the river having very fast current. He does not know swimming. He.....
12. When he gets up in the morning, he finds two cobras under his cot on either side. He.....
13. He is about to take bath in the bathroom and has removed his clothes, put on the hook in distant corner (6 feet away) and suddenly one black cobra comes through the drain and stands in front of him. He.....
14. He finds that his girlfriend is moving with his opponent. He.....
15. While going for his exam, he finds that a person has a stepmother who does not want to open the door of the house. He.....
16. He returns late at night from NCC camp and his stepmother does not want to open the door of the house. He.....

17. There is a flood in the river and many houses of his village have been destroyed. His house is about to collapse, it is late at night. He.....
18. Some persons are climbing the mountain but one of them loses the grip on the rope and falls down. He.....
19. He has gone to the coastal area with a group of friends for sight-seeing. Suddenly, the storm starts approaching. The tide is rising. He.....
20. He is working in an organization and one of his close friends, in the same office, is being harassed by his boss. He.....
21. His final degree exams are starting tomorrow and he also got a job call tomorrow. He is in great need of the job. He.....
22. He has arranged a party in his lawn and suddenly it has started raining very heavily. He has a large number of guests, who have already arrived. He.....
23. He has arranged a party to please his boss for his promotion; party is half-way through, someone close to him gives him bad news. He.....
24. In a party thrown by him for his promotion his boss gets annoyed due to the sarcastic remarks of his elder brother and he leaves the party without taking meals. He.....
25. While going to college, he finds that a cyclist has been knocked down by a fast moving car and he could not note down the number of the car. He.....
26. In the marriage of his friend, his friend and his father got annoyed due to non-receipt of dowry. They both went away even after lot of request by all including the bride and her father. Bride has become unconscious. He.....
27. He was taking his father, who is in a wheelchair, for treatment. While getting out of the house, he slipped on a banana peel and got hip joint fracture. It is raining heavily and no conveyance is available nearby. He.....
28. In the cinema hall, where he is seeing the picture in last row, some bad elements are teasing a girl in front row. He.....
29. He is going in a taxi to catch a train. The vehicle moving ahead of him throws out a person and speeds away. He.....
30. He goes with his friends to play a hockey match in the city. His friend does not turn up and both tyres of his scooter are flat. He.....
31. He finds ten people quarreling over a purse fallen from the bus. The police have approached and they have run away and he is found with purse by the police. Police takes him to police station. He.....
32. While going to attend the SSB, he lost all his belongings including ticket and SSB papers in the train, when he went to toilet. The destination is just 5 km away. He.....
33. While returning from a late show, he finds that two boys armed with knife are molesting a girl and she is crying. The road is quite lonely. He.....

34. He has to deposit his exam fee after two days but his friend demanded money due to urgency today only. He is very poor. He.....
35. While climbing the mountain, he finds that one of his team-mate has sprained his ankle and cannot move. He.....
36. While going on a picnic on a cycle, his cycle got punctured in a jungle and no help is readily available. All other cycles are already overloaded. He.....
37. His exams are drawing near and he has to cover a large syllabus but his friend, who is weak in studies, comes to him for help. He.....
38. His parents are not in a position to bear his studies expenditure but he still wants to continue studies. He.....
39. His mother and his wife are not pulling on well and quarrel takes place every day and hence there is tension. He.....
40. His father wants him to join his profession (property dealing) but he is interested in joining Defence Forces. He.....
41. His parents are quite old and he is their eldest son. The economic condition of parents is quite weak. They want him to continue his studies. He.....
42. His friend is extremely poor but good in studies. He can't pay his fees. His own financial condition is also not very sound but he wants to help his friend. He.....
43. His marriage has been fixed but just one week prior to the marriage the girl meets with an accident and loses one eye. He.....
44. He is to catch a train but the coolie has disappeared with the baggage. The train is about to leave. He.....
45. He lends some money to his friend. Now he needs the money badly but the friend is not in position to pay. He.....
46. Your sister's marriage is fixed. Your relative refused to give loan/money. You.....
47. You are in a desert on an exercise. Your vehicle goes for collection of ration but has lost its way. Your troops are getting hungry. You.....
48. You had a quarrel with your neighbour yesterday. Today you need his help. You.....
49. You along with your wife are travelling by a bus. A person from behind is snatching chain of your wife. You.....
50. You are the Commander of a section. You are assigning a task to capture terrorists at midnight. The terrorists are hiding in a hut in the village. You.....
51. After returning from the range, you found that one of your colleagues is having live ammunition with him. You.....
52. You are patrolling in high altitude area. Heavy snowfall starts. You are the patrol commander. You.....

53. Marriage of your sister is fixed. You are not granted leave due to unit nspection. You.....
54. Bharat Bandh is likely to be declared while you are on leave. Your leave is to be finished after two days and commencement of Bandh. You.....
55. In your train journey, at midnight certain noise is disturbing your sleep. On waking up, you find someone trying to break open the window. You.....
56. You are going to attend an important meeting and you are already getting late. Suddenly the road is blocked due to traffic jam. You.....
57. You have to go on patrolling duty in field. Your driver is having high fever. You.....
58. You as a player of football team required to play the match. Suddenly, on the day of match you have high fever, but your team captain does not allow you to leave the game. You.....
59. You are required to go for patrolling at night in high altitude area. You do not have coat parka. You.....
60. While returning home after watching cinema at midnight, you found two persons quarreling on the way. You.....

PRACTICE SRT-3

1. He has gone on the cycle expedition with six persons but two cycles have got punctured in a deserted/isolated place. He.....
2. His call for the SSB has come for 10th of this month but on the same day he has interview in an MNC. His best friend is also getting married the same day. He.....
3. In the SSB he finds that no one is talking to him. Today is the first day. He.....
4. He has been kidnapped and taken to a jungle. Kidnappers have asked him to sign a note for his father to send Rs. 10 lakhs as ransom. He.....
5. Two of his best friends are quarreling with each other. He.....
6. In the train two dacoits are looting everybody. They demanded their belongings also. He.....
7. In NCC camp, on guard duty he finds two strangers approaching the camp at night. He....
8. He, as in charge of picnic, has gone halfway with the picnic party and finds that food packets and music system had been left behind. He.....
9. He has gone to the marriage of his friend. Before the final ceremony a scuffle took place between the bride and bridegroom's parties. The matter is likely to be reported to the police. He.....

10. He is staying in a rented accommodation with six other students. House lady is quite rude to him only and he has been issued ultimatum to vacate her accommodation. He.....
11. In the circus show two lions go out of control and jump on the crowd. He.....
12. In an exhibition a fake company is attracting crowd by false propaganda. He knows the reality. He.....
13. His father has decided to change his will in the name of his younger brother. He.....
14. He has won Rs. 25 lakhs in KBC, his mother wants to donate Rs. 10 lakhs to a temple, and his father wants to give Rs. 5 lakhs to an ashram. His friends need some money. He has yet to complete his own education and has three younger sisters and one brother. He.....
15. He and his girlfriend have gone to see a new movie. It is houseful. Tickets are available in black. His girlfriend insists to see the movie. He.....
16. He returns from a picnic and comes to know that his mother had been insulted by his neighbour's son. He.....
17. There are two good looking girls who are attracted towards him but his father wants to marry him to a wealthy girl, who is not very good looking. He.....
18. There is dispute amongst two of his friends and they want him as mediator, he has to go out for an urgent work of his father. He.....
19. He has gone to a religious place and he finds beggars harassing a young foreign girl. He.....
20. His father and uncle are not on good terms. His uncle has no child and he treats him like his own child. His father wants to finish all relation with his uncle. He.....
21. A function is to be organized in his school. On the last day the organizer has fallen sick. The principal asks him to take the charge. He is not in the picture of anything. He.....
22. His neighbour's son has fallen into the river, flowing nearby. He is not on talking terms with him. No adults are available to save the child. He.....
23. A girls hostel located in remote corner, noise of fire heard. His house is also located nearby. Chowkidaar does not allow gents to go in. He.....
24. He is returning from college on scooter, an old man asks for lift but his rear tyre has very less air. He.....
25. His mother has to go on a lonely road to a temple which is quite famous, and he has to go for exam. There is no one in the house and other conveyance is not available on the lonely road. He.....

26. He has to go to attend the SSB after two days at Bangalore from Delhi but there is train strike. He.....
27. He has gone for a picnic with boys and girls in two buses. After the picnic was over at 3 a.m., he found that one of the buses had all four tyres punctured and the other bus driver was missing. He.....
28. After shikar, he with his friends reached the circuit house to spend the night but found that the chowkidar was absent. He.....
29. In a debate when his turn came all spectators walked away. He.....
30. In the marriage party of his close friends he found that the food was delicious but ran short. He.....
31. In the train he found that some bad elements have stabbed another lady and she is in critical condition, at the same time another lady is about to deliver a child and crying with pain. He.....
32. At the railway station he found a beggar shivering with cold. He is going to meet his relative and he is wearing a pant and pullover only. He.....
33. He had gone to receive his friend but the train is two hours late. He decides to come back and then would like to go back again. He got caught in the jam and can go neither forward nor back. The jam is likely to take about 2-3 hours. He.....
34. He wanted to organize a cricket match of his college but his opponent has approached the authorities for hockey match. He.....
35. At his college gate he found a nice unclaimed bag and found the bag containing explosive and bomb but before he could take any action people saw him. They are suspecting him and hence want to take him to police station. He.....
36. There is a murder in the village and the opposition party blames his party for it. He....
37. He is coming with his family members from a hill station and while coming down the brake of the vehicle fails. He was driving the vehicle. He.....
38. While delivering a lecture he finds the audience is not showing interest. He.....
39. His friend informed him writing about his visit to his location but he being away from town did not come to know. He went back without meeting him and his friend is quite upset and annoyed with him. He.....
40. He is not finding any job due to massive unemployment. But still he is keen to do job only. His father offers him to join his business, which he has refused many times earlier. He.....
41. You are required to dig trenches, but your colleagues are not co-operating with you. You.....

42. While working in the kitchen garden, it starts raining. You.....
43. You are assigned a difficult task which you have not done earlier. You.....
44. While returning from a market, three persons with knife ask you to hand over everything. You.....
45. While patrolling at unit main gate, a terrorist fired at your leg and it started bleeding badly and he is snatching your rifle. You.....
46. While on leave, you heard radio announcement about outbreak of war. You.....
47. In field area, you are short of manpower, one of your jawans asks for leave on important financial issues which you know. You.....
48. You are already late to complete your task. Your colleagues refused to co-operate in your task. You.....
49. You are attending a camp in J & K and forget the way to camp. You and your friends are surrounded by few people. You.....
50. You are with your friend in a jungle on a picnic. Suddenly a tiger comes in front of you. You.....
51. While returning from picnic, it starts getting dark and you have lost your way. You.....
52. When your boss does not agree with your views. You.....
53. You work hard because.....
54. You consider that the most important thing in the world is.....
55. You received an order from your boss to do certain work, but you feel that the boss's approach is wrong. You.....
56. While travelling in a train, you came to know that someone has picked your pocket. You.....
57. Due to financial difficulties, your parents find it difficult to give you further education. You.....
58. While you are waiting for a bus, an accident took place in front of you. You.....
59. You went on a mountain expedition which was a failure and one of your friends died in the attempt. You.....
60. You feel the work you are presently engaged in is useless. You...

PRACTICE SRT-4

1. During the examination days he had studied till late night and he was just about to doze off when cries of 'fire', 'help' reached his ears. He....
2. He happened to visit his uncle in the forward areas. When the war started his uncle's bunker was bombed. He....

3. Though his joke was well-meant, his friend became angry and so he....
4. He was rather young, when his father was killed in the war and his mother kidnapped by anti–group. He....
5. In a free period he wanted to study but his friends were continuously disturbing him. He....
6. Once after the girls from his class had wrongly reported against him to the college principal for using abusive language. He....
7. The last day for the submission of application forms came but one of his testimonials was yet unattested and the clerk refused to accept his application. He....
8. He was required in Varanasi at the earliest but when he reached the railway station the train was over-crowded and he had a forty-eight hour journey to cover. He....
9. It was 2 o'clock in the early morning when he was started to find a big cobra near his brother's cot. He....
10. They were travelling by train and one of the compartments caught fire. He saw people trying to jump off from doors as well as windows. He....
11. In group discussion some of the people were not agreeing with him. So he....
12. He fell seriously ill just before his examination, and he....
13. There was rush at the platform and the train was about to start but the coolie carrying his luggage could not be traced. He....
14. He had gone for mountaineering with his friends and their leader chose a rather steep track which was very slippery. It was extremely cold and one of the party slipped right into a crevice. He....
15. Whenever his opinion differs from others, he....
16. He had to go to the city from his village to take his examination but due to unexpected floods, the train service had been suspended. He....
17. The money which his father used to send him every month was not sufficient to meet his needs. Therefore, he....
18. He was not getting along well with his new classmates, therefore, he....
19. He and his friend were to put up a variety show that evening for the visiting Minister of State. Unexpectedly, his father's father, who was already ailing became serious. He....
20. Being the last year's Champion of the state Table Tennis he was too confident of victory in this year's matches. But when he lost the first game to his opponent he....
21. Once he was steering a boat in the sea, when all of sudden a storm came. He....

22. He was idly watching the river flowing past, under the bridge, when he suddenly noticed a man desperately fighting with the current. He....
23. His elder brother wanted to celebrate the death of their very old father but he felt otherwise. He....
24. It was midnight when he was awakened by a man's shrieks. He found one poor farmer was being beaten by four fellows with lathis. He....
25. He woke up in a running train to find all his luggage missing. He....
26. He was returning alone from a midnight show, when he spotted behind a group of trees, two goondas blind-folding a lady. He....
27. He was made captain of the tug of war team and the match was to be held the very next day. He....
28. He and his friend were going for an afternoon walk on a cold, windy day. Suddenly two men surrounded his friend and started asking for his wrist watch. He....
29. During the examination, he felt that some of the questions were too difficult for him to answer. He....
30. One night when his parents were away at their village, his younger brother developed high fever and became unconscious. He.....
31. He was out on a picnic with his friends when one of the boys stole some mangoes from the garden and the gardener came out with his stick. He....
32. He was on board a ship for training when a telegram arrived informing him of his father's serious condition. He....
33. He urgently had to accompany his friend on cycle at night to the latter's house which was five miles out of the city area. They hardly reached halfway when a gang of robbers surrounded them. He....
34. He was beaten by some of his class fellows as he was trying to dissuade them from joining the strike. He....
35. It was during the match that one of his team mates hit the referee in anger and the situation became more tense as the spectators grew agitated. As the captain of team he....
36. While playing a hockey match, he twisted his ankle badly. He....
37. The subject of the debate was hot one: whether the students union in colleges should be allowed to continue. He....
38. He had reached Jamnagar that very day during the Pak Aggression 1965 when the bomb was dropped by the enemy in his locality. He....
39. He was serving two officers who were always against each other and they used to give conflicting orders. He....
40. Late one night while he was running on his cycle to get medicine for his seriously ailing mother, he was stopped by a man with a knife. He....

PRACTICE SRT-5

1. A speeding car hit against a bullock cart, seriously injuring its driver. The car driver escaped unhurt and took the injured man to the hospital. However, the hospital staff was on strike. He....

2. On account of a land dispute, his uncle was threatening to shoot his brother. Both were armed. He....

3. The friendly discussion took a heated turn and he....

4. He did not know swimming. His friends who knew how to swim insisted on his jumping into the pond and promised to help him. He....

5. He was swimming in a pool when he saw a boy about to get drowned. He....

6. Early in the day he had set out with his younger brother for hunting in the forest. They got a deer and a few birds but lost their way as it had grown very dark. He....

7. He was appointed monitor of the class. He....

8. He was returning alone from the cinema late one night. It started raining heavily and there was no shelter on the way. He....

9. His father needed special treatment in the capital and they were already short of money. He....

10. A live wire was lying in a flooded street and he saw a labourer stepping on it and falling unconscious. He...

11. He had boarded a wrong train and came to know of it only when he was asked to pay more money. He....

12. His father required a lot of attention as he was ailing but his examination was also drawing near. He....

13. They had gone to the outskirts of the town for the firing practice. On their way back, they had to cross a river which had become over flooded. It was winter time and night had fallen. He....

14. He returned home to find his father dead, his mother fainting and his brothers and sisters weeping helplessly. He....

15. He had gone to buy stamp from the post office but he saw a lot of people already crowding at the window and quarrelling with each other to get first place. He....

16. His parents burst into tears just as he was about to leave for his SSB interview. He....

17. He had hardly stepped in the express train when it started moving. His luggage was still to come. He....

18. He was idly walking in the canal side where the small boy was swimming with the help of an inflated tube. Suddenly he noticed the tube becoming flat. He....
19. When he comes in conflict with others, he....
20. He was serving in the medical unit which was attached to an engineering company detailed to clear the mines. The foot of one havildar was blasted by a mine and the others were afraid of entering the area. So he....
21. Money was needed to meet the expenses of the sister's marriage and relatives had refused to help. He....
22. He picked up a quarrel with one of his colleagues the previous day at work and he needs his help. He....
23. A terrorist hideout was to be nabbed at midnight. As a leader of the group he....
24. On returning back from trekking they lost their way and it was getting dark. He....
25. He had to reach urgently his HQ but there was a traffic jam. He....
26. On returning to the barracks from the firing range, he learnt that one of his colleagues had brought some live ammunition with him. He....
27. He was made in-charge of looking after the unit of garden but he found that the other members were not fully cooperating. He....
28. He was going with one patrolling party in border area but due to heavy snowfall tracks were not visible. He...
29. He saw a boy being swept away in the water current and he did not know swimming. He....
30. While his annual leave was coming to an end he came to know that trains were cancelled due to Bharat Bandh. He....
31. He had some dispute with his uncle on property matters. He therefore....
32. He was unwell when his senior turned down his request for exemption from playing inter sub unit volley ball match. He....
33. He was given a task by his commanding officer, he had not done similar task earlier. He....
34. One of his officer's sons was suddenly bitten by a snake in the night. He....
35. While returning from the movie late at night he saw two young men were fighting. He....
36. An unusual sound at night woke him up in the train. He saw a man trying to enter the compartment by breaking open the window. He....
37. Everybody was hungry in his unit as the vehicle carrying ration for them, lost track in desert area. He....

Clearing Psychological Tests 183

38. While travelling in the train he found one unclaimed suitcase lying in the compartment. He....
39. Most of the personnel under his command showed irritation as the time was less to complete the assigned task. He....
40. By travelling by bus with his newly-wed wife, he saw a man snatching his wife's necklace. He....
41. He was made in-charge for bunkers urgently but manpower was not sufficient with him. He....
42. Due to administrative inspection at the unit, he was not getting leave to attend his sister's marriage. He....
43. It was decided to form a youth club in his village but many were opposing it. He....
44. During heavy snowfall he was to go along with the other colleagues for recovery of a vehicle at midnight. He was not having sufficient winter clothing. He.....
45. While he was sleeping at the railway platform he found his pocket picked. He....
46. He was in great hurry when he saw a car accident on the way. He....
47. While travelling he found some unauthorized passengers had already occupied his reserved seat and they refused to vacate. He....
48. While going on a cycle he was knocked down by a car and no one was around. He....
49. He was on leave in his hometown when fire broke out in his neighborhood. He....
50. His friend approached him for some money on loan when he himself needed it urgently. He....
51. He wanted to give financial help to his parents but his wife was not in favour. He....
52. While returning to the unit in an auto rickshaw at night two strangers stopped him and forced him to hand over all his belongings. He....
53. While on duty at the observation post, he heard firing across the line of control. He....
54. He used to give all the possible help to his friends but they did not reciprocate. He....
55. One of the sons wanted to join the Army but his family members were not in favour. He....
56. While on guard duty one unidentified person came and attacked him with the knife to snatch his rifle. He....

57. He was requested to take army vehicles loaded with ammunition and stores to the field area when he found two of his drivers running high temperature. He....
58. He saw a man tripping from the compartment while getting into the train. He....
59. While travelling in a bus he asked a co-passenger to stop smoking but he refused. He....
60. They had to swim across the river and the water level was rising fast. Many of them were scared. He....
61. He was asked to organize a cycle expedition in a hilly terrain. He....
62. He wanted to go for some personal work but his friends wanted him to accompany them for a movie. He....
63. He wanted to send his brother to the town for higher studies but his brother declined and wished to remain in the village. He....
64. While travelling in a bus he saw a person indulging in eve-teasing. He....
65. He was to reach his destination by morning but suddenly his vehicle was off the road and the required spare parts were not there with him. He....
66. He was attached with commanding officer when one of his friends approached him for some favour with his boss. He....
67. In a train his friend started arguing with a ticket collector. He....
68. He was walking near the river side, suddenly he saw a man drowning and shouting for help. He....
69. While returning from annual leave he slept in the train and missed his station. He....
70. In the football match he had an argument with the referee and he was warned. He....
71. While he was supervising the work he found that some misunderstanding had taken place among the group members. He....
72. It was snowing heavily and he was to reach a picket urgently with some ammunitions. He....
73. He wanted to get his son admitted in a college but there was no college in his village. He....
74. He was asked to do instructional duties in the evening in addition to his normal duties. He....
75. He had a difference of opinion with his colleague on some issues. He....
76. He was asked by a criminal of his village to give a statement in his favour in a court. He....

77. As a result of flood in his village his crops got damaged and he was having a lot of financial commitments in the family. He....
78. While on sentry duty at night he found a bag containing currency notes. He....
79. When he came to know that his younger brother wanted to live separately, he....
80. In forward areas a fire broke out in one of the tents where stores and equipment were kept. He....

PRACTICE SRT-6

1. Your friend owes you money but again he asked money from you for an urgent need. He....
2. He saw his sister talking to one of his known persons who is not a good person. He....
3. Your dad had an argument with your neighbour. He....
4. His motor cycle hit a pedestrian. He....
5. He was stopped by the police and asked a bribe of Rs. 200 else pay a fine of Rs. 1500. He....
6. While shopping in a grocery store he saw a person shop-lifting. He....
7. He finds his younger brother smoking. He....
8. He finds his neighbours throwing garbage in front of his house. He....
9. He finds his teacher is not taking the classes properly. He....
10. He finds his mother is becoming overweight. He....
11. He is going for an urgent work and there is a traffic jam due to lack of traffic personnel. He....
12. He saw his friend's family torturing the domesticated bull. He....
13. He finds his friend is losing faith in him. He....
14. His superior is ill treating him. He....
15. He wants to join the Army because he....
16. He finds others are not fair with him. He....
17. He lost his cell phone which has all his personal and confidential information. He....
18. He found out that his friend has hacked into his E-mail account and sent out mails. He....
19. He likes a girl but she is from a poor background. His family is against this friendship. He....
20. He finds his parents cannot afford his further education. He....

21. He is desperately looking for a job but he got rejected everywhere. He....
22. He took his girl friend for a dinner, when the bill came he found that his purse is missing. He....
23. He finds his family is not doing well as compared to his neighbours. He....
24. His boss is not happy with the work he has done. He....
25. While walking he slipped and fell on the body of a girl and she slapped him. He....
26. He and his friend had dinner in a restaurant and next day both of them got stomach problem. He....
27. His neighbour comes drunk every night and creates nuisance in his home. He....
28. While going to attend the interview he missed the train. He...
29. His friend started smoking and drinking. He....
30. He is not getting the respect he deserves. He....

Note: As highlighted in the earlier pages, your success depends on how much effort you put in. Homework and self-preparations will go a long way in deciding your fate. You should be in a position to create your own SRTs, say about 200 of them and design its possible answers. Do not ignore the latest technologies that are available, e.g. Internet, cell phone, social media etc.

(For Female Candidates)

SITUATION REACTION TEST: I

Instructions:-

- There are 60 situations given in this booklet. You have to put yourself into the situation and response accordingly.
- Answer all the 60 situations in 30 minutes in the space provided in the answer sheet.
- If you have stuck up in a particular situation proceed further without wasting time at one particular situation as each situation is allotted 30 seconds time approx.
- There is no right or wrong answers to these situations. It depends how individual approaches to them.
- While travelling in bus few goondas were teasing her friend continuously. She would ....
....
- While returning to home a group of boys were commenting over her. She would ....
....
- While watching movie in cinema hall with your friends, a boy was teasing her friend. She would ....
....
- She wanted to be a doctor but her father wanted to send her in teaching career. She would..
- She got selected in defence and now her father forbid her to join defence. She would ....
....
- She loved a boy but her father wanted to do her marriage in other family. She would ....
....
- She wanted to go in computer career but her father was not in favour of her because of high fees. She would ....
....
- She had a misconception with her sister-in-law. She would ....
....
....
- She had quarreled with her husband. She would ....
....
....

- She was working on a good post but her would be husband told her to quit the job. She..
....
- There was an urgent need of money in her in laws house. She ....
....
....
- On her wedding ceremony the next party was demanding for dowry. She ....
....
- While going to college few boys were chasing her. She ....
....
....
- While going on auto rickshaw. Suddenly she saw that she had missed her purse. She ....
....
- While returning to home in the evening her scooty got punctured. She ......
....
....
- In a train journey at a midnight certain sound disturbed her sleep. On waking up, she found someone trying to open the window. She ....
....
....
- She had quarreled with her neighbour yesterday. Today she needs his help. She ....
....
- Two of her best friends were quarrelling with each other. She ....
....
....
- While travelling in a auto-rickshaw a boy next to her teased her. She ......
....
....
- There was her exam next day and today her father had a heart attack. She ....
....
- While going to exam she saw a serious accident on the road. She ....
....
....
- While going to the college she got stuck in heavy traffic jam. She ....
....
....

- While going to market a boy snatched her purse. She ....
  ....
  ....
- There was a misconception between her and her brother. She ....
  ....
  ....
- She had a quarrel with her friends. She ....
  ....
  ....
- Her friend circle boycotted her. She..
  ....
- While going to college she met with an accident. She ....
  ....
  ....
- While going on scooty a car pushed her scooty. She ....
  ....
  ....
- There was an urgent need of money in her family. She ....
  ....
  ....
- Tomorrow was her exam and today she missed her admit card. She ....
  ....
  ....
- While enjoying on picnic spot she saw a snake next to her friend. She ......
  ....
  ....
- In her sister's marriage her friend, her relative refused to give money. She
  ....
  ....
- In the train two dacoits were looting everybody. They demanded her belongings also. She ....
  ....
- In NCC Camp, on guard duty she found two strangers approaching the camp at night. She..
  ....
- She returned from a picnic and came to know that her mother had been injured by her neighbour's son. She ....
  ....
  ....

- In a debate when her turn came all spectators walked away. She ....
- In the marriage party of her close friends she found that the food was delicious but short. She ....
- At the railway station she found a beggar shivering with cold. She was waiting to meet her relative and was wearing a pant and pullover only. She ....
- There was dispute between two of her friends and they wanted her as mediator. She had to go out for an urgent work of her father. She ....
- In the circus show two lions went out of control and jumped into the crowd. She ....
- Her father decided to change his will in the name of her younger brother. She ....
- She returned from a picnic and came to know that her mother had been insulted by her neighbour's son. She ....
- When her Boss did not agree with her views. She ....
- She worked hard because ....
- She considered that the most important thing in the world is ....
- She felt that the work in which she was presently engaged was useless for her. She ....
- She went on a mountain expedition which was a failure and one of her friend died in the attempt. She ....

- While she was waiting for bus, an accident took place in front of her. She ....
- Due to financial difficulties, her parents found it difficult to give her further education. She ....
-
- While travelling in train, she came to know that someone picked her pocket ....
- She received an order from her Boss to do certain work, but she felt that the Boss's approach was wrong. She ....
- While working in the kitchen garden rain started. She ....
- She was assigned a difficult task which she had not done earlier. She ....
- She was required to a field project, but her colleagues were not co-operating to her. She ....
- While returning from market, three persons with knife asked her to hand over everything. She ....
- While on leave, she heard an announcement that all trains were cancelled, the day she was to travel. She ....
- In an outdoor project, she was short of manpower, one of her team members asked for leave on wrong excuse which she knew. She ....
- She was already late to complete her task her colleagues refused to co-operate in her task. She ....
- Her friend loved a boy. She knew about his flirting nature. She would ....
- There was a misconception between her and her manager. She would ....

"You need to see yourself as already being and achieving your objective."
"Everyone has a social mask."

SELF DESCRIPTION TEST (SDT)

The self-description technique, also known as self-appraisal, is another effective and powerful tool in the hands of the psychologist to obtain confirmation on the findings already recorded regarding candidate's personality traits – his merits, demerits and what his friends and others may think about him.

Every one of us has some strong and weak points, good qualities, shortcomings and even vices. Most of these qualities are exhibited in one's normal behaviour and, therefore, exposed to others. Sometimes, we try to suppress or conceal these from the public eyes. We generally do not try to admit or accept our weaknesses and rectify or correct them. If we know ourselves or know our weakness, we can try to get rid of these and improve our personality. In this test a candidate is given full opportunity to highlight all of his personality traits.

The Aim

The basic intention to employ this technique is to give a chance to the candidate to reveal his own personality or character to the psychologist. Secondly, it shows whether the candidate has fair insight into himself. If he knows himself and is conscious of his weaknesses, he will overcome and get rid of some of these and improve his personality. But if he does not have a fair insight into his own character, how can he be expected to improve upon his personality?

Procedure

The self-story writing or self-appraisal exercise, as a task proper, is generally given to the candidate as the last item in the psychological test. The time given is about 15 minutes. Here an opportunity is given to the candidate to write anything he wishes to write without being questioned. He can mention his strength, achievements and other special qualities to give a high profile and projection of his personality. Besides the normal method of writing one's own assessment of oneself, the SSBs also adopt another method of giving the test. They ask the candidates to write about opinions of parents, teachers and their friends.

Importance of the Test

The importance of self-appraisal cannot be over emphasized. The psychologist will confirm his observations about the candidate. His self-appraisal is re-confirmatory test for his traits. Everyone has some strong and weak points and there is no restriction in even highlighting his weakness along with his good quality, it will give a true picture of his personality. The best way to describe himself is to be truthful and faithful to himself. Therefore, he should not overestimate or under estimate his personality. It helps in finding out insight & motivation of a candidate. Trainability of the candidate is based on this test.

Keep in mind

- Do not waste time in describing your place of birth, home, school etc. at length. The emphasis should be on such factors which will provide details regarding your personality traits.
- Give your strong and weak points; do not refer to your likes and dislikes. There is no need for you to write about your likes and dislikes at some length.
- Give correct and accurate information. Be careful – avoid contradictions with what you might have written in the PIQ Form.
- Prepare in advance and get sufficient practice of writing again and again several times. Since the question, in some form or the other, is invariably asked, the candidate should be ready for it. He must write it down several times and see that it does not exceed the time limit.
- It confirms the psychologist's findings. But your self-description should be a correct estimate of your own qualities so that it may help the psychologist assessing your character and personality. Again, since he has drawn a pen picture about your personality as a result of other tests like TAT, WAT and SRT, your self-description, if truly drawn up, should help to confirm his findings.
- Your self-description is sometimes asked by the interviewing officer also. His question is based on the performance of the candidate during interview process. From the answer he can not only confirm his own findings but also obtain a fair estimate of the candidate's insight.

Model Self-Description

A model self-description is given below. Candidates should read it carefully:

1. **Parent's opinion:** My parents think that I am a bright child who is also an obedient and responsible son. They have strong faith in me and the amount of trust they have in me, makes me more responsible and dutiful. They believe that I am bound to succeed in my desired field. They believe that I will bring good name and fame to my family. They love me a lot and I respect them from the core of my heart. At times they say that I spend more time with my friends but I manage time effectively and convince them.

2. **Teacher's Opinion:** My teachers believe that I am an inquisitive but simple and average student who is punctual in his work and respectful in dealings. They never hesitate in giving me the responsibilities to organize a function or a show. They appreciate me for taking part in extra-curricular activities. They are generally satisfied with my performance and with my behaviour

with my seniors and juniors. At times they ask me to be more attentive and concentrate fully in the class.

3. **Friend's Opinion:** I have a wide circle of friends. They feel I carry a good head over my shoulders. We enjoy each other's company and social evenings together. We discuss all the matters under the sun and there is no secret among us. They have full faith in me and they know that I will be there in their thick and thin and vice-versa. At times if there is any difference among us, we solve it meticulously. We know the value of friendship.

4. **Self-Opinion:** I am a simple individual with all possible emotions present in different degrees. I believe that I am a sincere and good citizen of my country and above all I am a confident person who never lets any stone remain unturned to achieve goal. I live to the expectations of my parents. I like to visit new places and meet new people. I am a self-motivator and want to increase my knowledge as much as possible. I want to be a learner all my life and bring out the best in me in all given situations.

5. **Qualities for future:** I would like to learn from the experiences of wise people. I would like to improve upon my reading habits as reading helps to have different edges to one's personality. I would like to be more careful in approach to everything. I want to improve my endurance, perseverance and patience. I want to keep myself very fit, eat healthy and keep pace with the changing world. I want to be an all-rounder and be able to contribute to my society any which way possible. Overall I want to be a good and worthy person.

For working professionals: Write your strong and weak points as per opinion of the following:

Parents: As per opinion of my parents I am mature, sensible, intelligent, systematic, responsible and duty-conscious. I am respectful, obedient and take active part in household discussions and come out with sensible ideas. I give a helping hand to my parents and look after my younger sister and brothers very well. They are well satisfied with my attitude and my best efforts for their ease and comfort despite my being in the Army. Sometimes, they complain whenever there is a delay in making call to them; however, it rarely happens. I humbly pay my apology to them about the delay.

Employer: My employer has the opinion about me that I am disciplined, regular and punctual. I am professionally well qualified and perform my duties to the utmost satisfaction of my superiors in time. I maintain good relations with my seniors and colleagues. I take additional responsibilities cheerfully and keen to learn more. I remain cool and calm during adverse situation. As in charge I am capable of organizing various activities properly. My employer knows that I keep updating my professional knowledge and I go into details of the work I do. I also take out time to improve my professional skill by availing the facilities that internet offers.

Colleagues: I have a good circle of colleagues and this is what they feel about me – that I am a social, cooperative, trustworthy and cheerful person who believes in friendly atmosphere and helps others in official as well as personal matters. According to them, I have give and take attitude and provide impartial and justifiable advice and legitimate solution to any problem/difficulty. They want me to be more spontaneous as I need encouragement at times to face unknown challenges and I value their feelings & sentiments. My friends know that I am a good motivator and my knowledge level is high and up to date. They look at me for guidance for difficult situations.

My Own Opinion: I am an above average, simple, straightforward person. I am optimistic, practical, painstaking, loyal and punctual who works with dedication & devotion and respects others. I am performing my duties in family, profession and in outer environment very well. I never give chance to my elders/friends to feel hurt and embarrassed. I am impartial in my dealings. I am a little bit emotional and get excited at times but know how to control. I am a good friend and enthusiastic person. I am accountable for my everyday actions and I work adding value to my life and social network including family.

Qualities you would like to develop: No human being is perfect because everyone has certain shortcomings, I am no exception. I too have certain areas which need further development. These are physical stamina, spontaneity and communication skills in English which have been not up to the mark due to lack of exposure, limited facilities and opportunities. I have already taken remedial steps which are giving desired results to some extent. I too will like to enhance my general awareness and general knowledge. I want to hear more of Ted Talks and read more books and also study as much as possible.

5

Cracking GTO Tasks / Tests

"When you learn how to set one goal, you will know how to set all goals".

CONCEPTS OF GROUP TESTING

GTO Series

It is a series of tests where the GTO uses a chain of tests mostly practical and verbal to assess the same qualities. The tool psychologist uses is basically in written form. Here the mode of test changes; however, qualities being checked remain the same. Here too the responsibility of demonstrating these qualities lies with you.

All the tests under these series are very simple and easy. If you prepare well these tests become a highly fun-oriented and enjoyable one.

Group and its Implication

Man is a social being, therefore the social 'field' influences and determines the human personality and behaviour. The effect of a man's group membership, his experiences with other men, of his past and present interpersonal relationship is reflected in each of his activities. There is therefore, a need to study not only the static pattern of an individual but to analyse and interpret man as a member of a group.

"Group is a collection of individuals who accept a common task, become interdependent in their performance with one another to promote its accomplishment". A collection of individuals forming themselves into a 'group' would have some characteristics such as:
(a) An individual's acceptance of own goals as a common goal of the group in which each of them is equally involved.
(b) Accomplishment of the group task involves interaction which will have communication – a specific type of interaction.

These characteristics are applicable to a GTO group too and he looks into these Traits.

A group must be considered in its dynamic aspect – in terms of growing, developing and progressing set of relationship. It is in this context that the development of a group through its well-defined stages helps in building a group.

Nature and Function of a Group

Every society consists of inter related social groups. No matter how short-lived or ongoing, how simple or complicated, such groups influence the needs, beliefs, attitudes and actions of people in it. The structure and functions of such groups are, in turn, determined by the dynamic interactions of their constituent members.

To understand one's behaviour we must understand the tensions and relationships and the various forces working within a group. Understanding an individual would not suffice. The members of a group are in dynamic relationship with one another. The behaviour of each one affects all the others. These effects rebound on the original member, who in turn influences others and this complex effect is taking place simultaneously amongst all members. These adjustive changes occurring in the group structure on the whole as produced by changes in any part of the group constitute "Group Dynamics".

Structure of the Group

To study structural characteristics of a group we must consider the size of the group, individual roles within the group and intra group relations.

Size – Minimum of six and maximum of ten candidates form a GTO group.

Introduction to Group Testing

The purpose of selection is to determine the suitability of a candidate for the job. For example, the main requirement in the Armed Forces is combatant personality. The job of selection therefore involves personality appraisal with specific reference to 'officer like qualities'. Group Testing Technique is one of the three techniques employed at the Selection Boards.

Rationale of the Group Testing Technique

Man is gregarious by nature. All his activities are group oriented. Group is his most natural environment. His behaviour in a group will be his natural behaviour. Therefore the basic characteristics of an individual can best be observed when he is in a group. In a group, where there is social interaction, behaviour patterns will emerge revealing the personality traits. In this process, a person's group effectiveness can easily be evaluated by the candidate displaying the following:

(a) Ability to contribute towards the functional aspect of the task (effective level).

(b) Ability of the members to relate emotionally to each other and to the task – to bind the group (group cohesiveness)

(c) Ability to stand up to resistance and frustration (stress bearing).

In the Group Testing Technique, the GTO observes a candidate in a group to determine his group effectiveness.

The Nature of Group Task

The tasks in the series are leaderless, situational, action-oriented, role-playing and stressful. They are simulated to job performance in service life.

The Concept of Group Development

The process of transformation from a collection of individuals to a well-formed and fully developed group passes through certain definite, though overlapping stages of development.

These stages are:

(a) Formation

(b) Exploration

(c) Competition

(d) Co-operation

(e) Discipline

Formation is a process of collecting individuals in an area for some purpose. Exploration takes place when each individual in the group tries to know the other in relation to his own standing in the group. Competition arises when each member shows his need for recognition. Compromise, reconciliation and co-operation come in when individuals realize the need for collective efforts in accomplishing a common task. Finally, the discipline stage is reached when individual interests are submerged for the larger good of the group.

The tasks in Phase-1, the Basic Series are designed and conducted in a definite order to promote a smooth development of the group.

Three-Phase Group Testing

The Group Testing battery is divided into three phases namely, the Basic Series, the Confirmatory Series and the Final Series. The Basic Series enables the GTO to get a general view of the effectiveness of the candidate in the leaderless group. The Confirmatory series allows the GTO to shift his observation from a distant point to a 'close up'. This is selective differentiation, as the GTO concentrates on less clear aspects, and also delves deeper. The final series allow the GTO to refer back to 'whole' group, so as to re-orientate the perspective and correct any overemphasis.

Rationale of Three Phase Testing

The three-phase testing is based on the concept of Gestalt. Gestalt means a pattern or form. A pattern is not a summation of its parts but an integration of its components where each part is interlinked, intertwined and interdependent with other parts and with the whole that one perceives as a diversified whole. The process of perception has three stages:

Integration – perceiving the thing as a whole.

Differentiation – attention on parts.

Reintegration – relating part to each other and to the whole.

Basic Series represent integration stage, Confirmatory Series the differentiation stage and the Final Series the reintegration stage.

Need for Stress

An individual's social contact is dependent on his basic attitude in relation to others. This basic attitude is the product of social experience of the individual. Upon the basic 'set' are imposed superficial attitudes because of convention, social norms, compensatory behaviour or maybe even conceit. These facades, worn by an individual, mask his true self. Stress causes the facade to tear off and reveals one's basic set.

Essential Features of GTO Battery of Tests

Phase 1

Integration Phase – General Impression of Candidate's Group Effectiveness

Purpose

To enable the GTO to get a balanced sample of each candidate's group effectiveness. It has three components, viz.

(a) Functional ability
(b) Group cohesiveness, and
(c) Stability

Basic series

(1) Group Discussion
   'Exploration Stage' (45 minutes)
(2) Group Planning (45-60 minutes)
   'Competition Stage'
(3) Progressive Group Task (45 minutes)
   'Co-operation Stage'
(4) Group Obstacle Race Type
   'Discipline stage' Leaderless Group Tests

Note: The 'Formation' stage takes place on arrival and batching of candidates at the Selection Board.

Phase 2

Differentiation Phase – Differentiation of candidate's behaviour into components parts.

Confirmatory series

To enable the GTO to concentrate on individual's abilities outside the group.

(a) Half Group Task (15-20 minutes each) – smaller group or individual tests.
(b) Individual Obstacles (3 minutes each)
(c) Lecturette (3 minutes each)
(d) Command Task (15 minutes each)

Phase 3	Purpose
Re-integration phase – return to the general impression	To resolve the GTO's residual queries from phase 2 and confirm – or, if necessary, rebut – provisional findings on the candidates.

Final series

Final Group Task (20 minutes) – Leaderless Group Test of a "wide entry" type, with in-built frustration with a large total area, so that candidates are spread out, easily observed and all can participate. It is a series of tests where the GTO uses a chain of tests mostly practical and verbal to assess the same qualities. The tool psychologist uses is basically in written form. Here the mode of test changes; however, qualities being checked remains the same. Here too the responsibility of demonstrating these qualities lies with you. All the tests under these series are simple and easy. If one prepares well these tests become fun-oriented and enjoyable.

GTO tasks are held during day 3&4

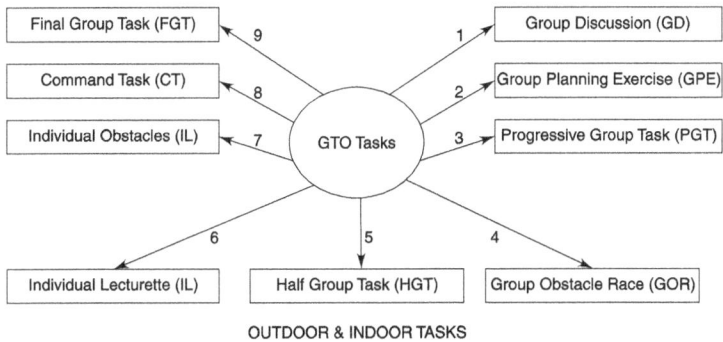

OUTDOOR & INDOOR TASKS

1. GROUP DISCUSSION

"A goal properly set is halfway reached."

– Zig Ziglar

What is Group Discussion?

Group Discussion (GD) is a discussion between a group of persons about a topic which usually ends with a solution. GD can be done well in advance. If you do not have a team, make use of your friend circle. Explain the requirement and conduct few discussions and master your way to perfection.

Group Discussion at SSB

In the SSB, the GD is the first basic and important test of the Group Testing process as it shows many of the OLQs to the group testing officer. This is the stage of exploration where the GTO is trying to find out group as well as individual performance. In the first discussion GTO gives two topics and the group is asked to select one out of those two after little discussion. Generally one topic is simple and routine where everyone can take part without much preparation. The other topic is generally difficult, demanding and controversial, and where material is required to take active part in discussion. The purpose of giving two topics is to check the level of each candidate as well as of the group. So if the material is available, go for the difficult topic because that will create a better image. For the second discussion the topic is given by the GTO himself after seeing the performance of the candidates.

Rules followed at the SSB in a GD

Usually two GDs are held at a stretch with a little time gap. The topics given for the first GD will have two options to select from and topic given for the second GD is a compulsory one.

The group is divided into 8 or 10 candidates based on the order of the chest numbers.

Two options are given for the first GD and candidates have to choose one. In this scenario the candidates have to discuss within themselves to choose the topic which most of them agree on. After informing the chosen topic to the Group Testing Officer, he gives the group time to think about the topic for few minutes (usually 3 to 4 minutes) and thereafter that he orders the candidates to start the discussion. (The war begins).

After the first GD is finished, the GTO gives 2 minutes gap and gives the second topic which is of his choice. The time given to think about this topic is only 3 to 4 minutes and he starts to observe the group.

The duration of both the GDs will be 10 or 15 minutes.

What the GTO expects in a GD?

First, as a good human being a candidate with good qualities, should be able to put his points in front of others or in a group. This is what is expected from defence officers also, since he should command his men at normal time or at the time of war. So he should be clear in expressing his thoughts and give good points at discussion even under pressure. For this reason, GD is conducted.

The GTO expects qualities such as
- Communication skills
- Listening to the group members point
- Leadership and coordination with the group members (heart)
- Express oneself truthfully in the group

- Depth of knowledge in the given topic
- Sharing of knowledge with the group members
- Running the group parallel to the given point
- Let us discuss in depth about each expectation.

Communication Skills

This is the most important aspect at GD since the heart of the GD is effective communication. To be an active member of the group, the candidate should be able to put his points before the group and should preferably make the group accept or agree with his/her points. For this the candidate's communication should be effective (able to influence the group.)

Effective communication results in getting the attention of the group members. If you communicate well, then your point will be given weightage and everyone will discuss around your point. So you are becoming the centre of attention. After you have gained their attention, and the group seems to conclude your point, try to give a new point with relevance to the previous one so that the group tries to hold to that point and start to discuss. Make the GD as a GD – a 'group discussion', and not as a debate; i.e. don't argue with anyone.

If someone puts forward a negative point, never say that he is wrong. Even though wrong you can overcome the negative view with a positive point. It will give a better impression of you.

After giving your point, listen to the group member who is speaking, and if you get a chance you can give a point supporting your previous point (merge your previous point and the current point being made by the group member).

Now let us see how to put forward your point to the group when someone is talking. That is, how to interrupt?

While others are talking, the ways we can put forward our points are:

- Excuse me gentleman, I have something to say.
- Excuse me gentleman, I agree with your point but also wish to add one more point.
- Excuse me gentleman, my solution for this issue is _____ (while two members are debating try to give a solution. This gives you credit, since a real leader is the one who finds solution to the problem).
- Excuse me, wait please, let's give a chance to chest number _____. He is also having some point to discuss. (This shows your helping attitude and broad-minded mentality, i.e. giving chance to the weak ones). It should be as a natural process and not as a tactic to show to the GTO, to gain an advantage.

Listening to the Group Members Point

As explained earlier, the importance of communication, is patient listening. A patient listener gives more quality points than a continuous speaker. It is easier for a person to make good points when he is an active listener rather than when he is speaking continuously. In the SSB quality is what matters and not the quantity. How much we speak does not matter, but how much depth in what we speak on the subject matters.

Example

If we give a good quality point by listening to the group members, the group members will rally around point, and then you draw attention and become the centre for further discussion, hence try to be the initiator, if not give a strong point (the point should be strong enough with examples), or your point with the initiator so that the group sticks to your point. Also try to give examples for your point.

Leadership and Coordination with the Group Members (Heart)

In the OLQ factory, this is the heart for an Defence officer since he has to lead a group. He should have good leadership qualities, and able to coordinate with the group.

During a GD leadership quality is analyzed by a GTO by noticing

- Initiator in the group
- Good Listener in the group
- Helping the weak member to participate
- Supporting the good points from the members
- Able to analyze and prioritize good point from the members

- Explaining others' point by giving addition example
- Able to overcome an equally competent candidate, with his depth of knowledge and communication skills.

The coordination of the group is not a separate quality. If we follow the above guidelines, then coordination of the group comes naturally.

Who is the real leader?

A real leader is need not be the person initiating first by fighting with others (i.e. starting the discussion with an argument).

A real leader is the person who is cool, and he starts when nobody from the group has knowledge about the topic or has the guts to initiate. He volunteers himself to start the discussion by giving valuable points. The SSB appreciates this type of leaders.

Expressing Oneself Truthfully in the Group

The success mantra of recommended candidates is "Be Yourself". This is not a corporate interview where one has to put on an act and behave like some character that he is not. In a corporate interview it is a known fact – if we are good in communication with basic technical skills, we will get a job for Rs.25000 per month. But the defence service is not just a job – it is a devoted service. So it wants the person who is geniue and truthful and doesn't like a person who acts.

Defence Services is not a desk job where one has to act and keep a smiling face at the office from morning to evening and then gets home. This is service with field work, so be truthful to yourself by taking responsibility of your men and materials around you. At the SSB, it's not possible to bluff or act as someone you are not. Be yourself and show project your positive qualities fully. If you have all the OLQs then the officers surely recommend you.

How SSB find out the fake/bluffing/acting persons at the SSB

On the very first day while you are filling the PIQ, the psychologist checks your responses as a psychological test with the PIQ and prepares a map representation of every candidate. (That is why psychological tests are held on the second day of the interview before the personal interview and GTO tasks.) The representation is given to the personal interviewer. So if we act as someone other than who we really are, then we ourselves are opening a door return from the SSB. Therefore "Be Yourself" – this is the key for success.

Depth of Knowledge in a Given Topic

While talking during a discussion, as I mentioned earlier, the quality is what matters and not quantity. To be a good participant in GD you should have depth and sound knowledge on the given topic. You can increase your depth and knowledge of topics by listening to various discussions on the news channels such as NDTV, CNN, BBC, IBN, etc. Also read the national newspapers such as the *Hindu*, *Hindustan Times*, *The Times of India*, etc. View sites Google to increase your depth on any given topic. Take time out to listen to Ted Talks and YouTube videos on various important topics. Ted Talks is a powerhouse of knowledge which is freely available at the click of a mouse. This will help you to gain more knowledge day by day. It is a long term process and the results will be good in a GD. Also put your points across with clarity of thought and brevity.

Sharing of Knowledge with the Group Members

In a GD, to have a smooth flow of discussion, sharing knowledge is an important role. Since every candidate gives a valid point and expects the group to stick to his point, it will lead to a non-cooperative discussion. So to make it fruitful, with supportive points by motivating them in sharing knowledge, with citing examples to their point. These acts help being an active member of the group, supportive and helping nature, with our depth of knowledge and making the discussion interesting.

Running the Group Parallel to the Given Point

If you are among the first three to take part in the discussion, give a good point with an example. Also if any of the group members agree with your point and talk, it means at that time you should run parallel to that person by giving more supportive points to him. So if both of you are in the same stream the weak members will automatically stick to both of you. In this scenario all are contributing around your point, hence it is also important to support them.

IMPORTANT PARTS OF THE GD

- Initialization
- Conclusion

Initialization

Initialization during a GD gives either of two things; either wear a King's Crown if you start/initiate the GD well; i.e. everyone agrees to your initialization or Else it will be an indelible remark on you, if you stammer at the start of GD. If you know very well about the topic just start the discussion confidently, otherwise just listen to others, summarize your point and trigger it to the group.

Initiation in Group Discussion Techniques

There are several techniques in the initiation of a group discussion. These are
- Real time example initiation technique
- Defining the Topic technique
- Interrogatory type technique

- Starting with hot issues and sailing over that, technique
- Using phrases or quotes at the start.

Let us discuss in detail the various Techniques.

'Real time example initiation' technique

This is a common initiation technique followed by many in the GD; i.e. if the topic given by the GTO is about "Bribes in India", then the candidate may start the discussion by giving real time examples such as CBI enquiry for various scams etc. This is merging the theme of the topic with the real time.

'Defining about the topic' technique

This is a basic initiation technique followed by most persons in GD; i.e. if the topic given by the GTO is about "Bribes in India", then the candidate may start the discussion defining the root cause for bribes, various topics related to bribes, and pros and cons of the topic. So he is defining about the topic by giving a Theme so that the team members can latch up on the point and discuss.

'Interrogatory type' technique

This is an interesting technique followed by few bold candidates during a GD; i.e. asking interrogatory type questions such as what, when, who and how about the given topic. Since this may give a good or bad image to the GTO, the technique should be used at the appropriate time; and if used wrongly, it may convey an impression of a negative thinker.

Example

Let us take a topic on "Nuclear Reactor in India". In this topic if the candidate starts the discussion with why India wants a nuclear reactor rather than choosing an alternative source for power, after saying this he should be able to support his point by giving positive points such as, what has happened to Japan due to nuclear reactor incident. Even though the starting seems to be negative he finishes the topic by giving a strong positive point, i.e. importance to the people of India rather than power production. Also he is not leaving the discussion on power production; he also makes a point on finding an alternative solution. So this is a good initialization.

Example of a

Bad Initialization in Interrogatory type

Let us take the topic "Nuclear Reactor in India". In this topic if the candidate starts the discussion with "What happened in Japan? A large number of lives lost and devastation. So Nuclear Reactor should be abolished from India and it should be closed". This is also the same question type initialization but the point is he didn't give a supportive positive point to the question type initialization and the starting seems to be negative. So avoid this type of initialization.

These are the pros and cons of the interrogatory initialization technique.

'Starting with hot issues and sailing over that' technique

This is an interesting technique, given a hot topic on social welfare, such that everyone will get more interested to discuss.

Example

Let the topic be "Tiger Preservation in India". Start the discussion by giving an accurate statement that the number of Tigers is decreasing rapidly. If this continues what will be the count after five years. Be sure that the hot issues you are initiating should not be negative ones. That is, when talking about depletion in Tiger counts, don't blame the reason as forest officer, or government etc. Give the point positively to sail over that point throughout the discussion. In this scenario if you want to give the number of Tigers in India, be clear about the count, i.e. be accurate in your statistics.

Using Phrases or Quotes at the start

Conclusion

In the SSB group discussion they don't expect you to conclude the GD. The conclusion is expected only in MPE, i.e. Military Planning Exercises/GPE. So to conclude the GD don't hang on or stick to your points till the end, instead try to summarize all the important points of others by mentioning their chest numbers and also add your view with that Also try to add your own solution for the issues which you discussed in the group discussion session. This shows your leadership qualities (since the person who finds a solution for the problem is the real leader).

Briefing by the GTO

- GD is an informal discussion on a current topic.
- Discussion is of a type that one has in a cafeteria or at home or on a picnic or during bus or train travel.
- It is not a debate, therefore, there is no chairman or moderator and there is no sequence in which you are required to speak.
- You can speak whenever you want, whatever you want and whatsoever level you want.
- You can speak for the subject or against the subject or choose to speak in between the two.
- You are required to speak in English, however, if you get stuck for word or expression you can switch over to Hindi but get back to English as quickly as possible.

- For the discussion GTO will give two subjects. Both the subjects will be average in nature, current in context and will have three sub points so that different views are available and hence a discussion is possible.
- The first task for the group is to select one of the two topics. For this GTO will give you a minute or two; within that time either by consensus or majority, the group is to decide the subject.
- Once the topic or subject is decided by the group, GTO will read out the topic once again so that everyone is clear as to what topic is to be discussed.
- Discussion will be for 10 to 15 minutes only. Once that is over, GTO will stop the discussion. Within this period each candidate puts across his views on the subject.
- When the first discussion is over, GTO will give another topic to discuss.
- This topic will also be current and will have three sub points, however, the level of topic will be decided by the GTO based on your performance in the first discussion. He may raise the level, lower it, or keep at the same level.
- The second topic will be discussed for 10 to 15 minutes and when that is over, it will be considered that your first task, GD is over.

Seating Plan

- Candidates are required to be seated in a circle.
- Senior-most candidate by chest No. can sit on any chair. Others will sit in sequence in a clockwise manner.
- GTO will be seated outside the circle and observing you all. In GD 1, the GTO sits in a manner that he can observe the body language of half the group members. In GD 2 his chair is so positioned to observe the balance half of the group.

What to Do?

- Help the group in deciding the Topic by giving few points in favour of topic which you wish to discuss.
- These points must contain ideas, knowledge, facts, figures, data, information, etc.
- Take part early in the discussion; preferably be among the first 3-4 candidates.
- There should be enough participation in the discussion; that means at least 3-4 times you must speak.
- Every time you speak, take one point and elaborate it clearly in 6 to 8 sentences or 30 to 45 seconds.
- Your voice should be loud and clear.
- Sit upright on the chair.

- While speaking look at all the members of the group.
- When somebody is speaking you should look towards the speaker.
- There should be no awkward body actions. Do not touch each other to make a point.
- No consensus is required.
- No conclusion is required.
- Do not regulate or monitor the discussion.
- Do not point out or ask others to speak.
- Do not concentrate on the past; discuss present situations, future trends and possible solutions.
- You may cover the topic from all aspects but have a firm and fixed views.
- Listen attentively.
- GD is an exchange of views, opinions and thoughts.
- Avoid chaos; remain alert and keep a cool head

Important Tips for Group Discussion

- First listen to the GTO's instructions keenly and patiently.
- If you have enough knowledge about the topic and good effective communication then start the discussion, else be patient and wait for the sequential chance to summarize your point in your mind and then trigger it into the discussion. Why I am saying this is: if you are weak in communication and start stammering in the initialization, it may give a bad impression.
- Keep proper eye contact with the group member who is talking and don't ever look at the GTO.
- Have sound and thorough knowledge of basic topics and national issues as it will be easy for you to cross the group discussion stage.
- Don't ever start a debate in the discussion by joining hands with two or three candidates within the group itself, then all may lose their chances of getting selected.
- To be well prepared, read newspapers, view discussions on national news channels, also discuss with your classmates / friends in English to avoid stammering and to get good flow of points, in your mind even under pressure.
- Listen to Ted Talks, watch 'You Tube' videos etc. on important current issues.

Common Group Discussion Topics in SSB

1. India in Olympics
2. Global Warming
3. Naxalism
4. India's Nuclear Deal
5. Education in India
6. Should military training be made compulsory for all able-bodied youth
7. Even after 69 years of independence poverty, illiteracy & communalism exist in India. Is it due to lack of vision of our leaders, wrong policies, or is it due to our conservative thinking?
8. Corruption is rampant in our society. Is it due to lack of good governance or lack of moral values?
9. Terrorism has grown out of proportion & getting out of control. What are the reasons for the same and how do you think we can contain it?
10. Casteism, communalism, untouchability still exist in our society. What do you think is the reason & how do you think we can overcome them?
11. There is slow growth in rural areas in terms of development, infrastructure and basic amenities. Is it due to lack of vision by our administrators or is it due to lack of resources? How can we improve the situation?
12. Should dress code be followed in the colleges?
13. India's economic growth is very slow. How do you think we can revive it? Can good government policies, corporate assistance and think tanks help to revive it?
14. Internal security is threatened by terrorism. What do you think is the cause? How do you think we can overcome the problem?
15. Our relationship with our neighbours is not congenial & friendly. Do you think there is a requirement to change our stance and be more proactive, friendly and helpful to improve our relation with our neighbours?
16. Should we strengthen our relationship with USA or remain neutral?
17. Should reservations be continued for the deprived, underdeveloped communities or should it be based on economic conditions?
18. Who is a greater threat to India – is it Pakistan or China?
19. Are we civilized? If yes, how do you justify? If no, what are the reasons and how can we improve?
20. Should retiring age go and minimum education be specified to politicians?

21. Has globalization helped India or has it affected our culture?
22. Role of MNCs in India. Should we encourage or discourage?
23. Who is a greater culprit – a person who gives bribe or takes bribe?
24. How do you think violence against women can be controlled?
25. Should schools in India have common syllabus?
26. Has globalization affected Indian culture?
27. Parliamentary/presidential system of governance. Which is better suited to our country?
28. Should criminals be allowed to contest elections?
29. Should divorce and remarriage be encouraged in our country?
30. Are we compromising our environment for development?
31. Federal structure or union structure is good for our country
32. Is media a responsible media?
33. What are the effective ways to check brain drain?
34. How do you think youth of nation can contribute towards national development?
35. Should mercy killing be encouraged?

2. GROUP PLANNING EXERCISE (GPE)

"You cannot tailor-make the situations in life, but you can tailor-make attitudes to fit those situations".

–Zig Ziglar

GPE is a combination of various SRTs; if you club few SRTs together it forms the GPE. Create your own Group Planning Exercise and practice besides what has been given in this book. If you can prepare for 30 different types of GPE then this test becomes a cakewalk for you. You can demonstrate an outstanding performance.

1. This is the second basic test of Group Testing. This is the stage of competition where a candidate tries to emerge as the winner. In this, there are two types of tests:

    (a) Individual Plan and a

    (b) Group Discussion to make a Common Group Plan

2. Group Planning Exercise or Military Planning Exercise (GPE or MPE) Group Planning or Military Planning Exercise is followed after the Group Discussion on the third day of the SSB testing.

What is GPE or MPE in the SSB?

It is a set of problems or critical situations in which a candidate has to put himself in, engage his team or group of friends to find the solution for those problems. He along with his team should succeed in solving their own problem.

It is a situation where the candidate has to think for himself as leader and has to allocate tasks extract work from the men and materials around him. He should give priority to the situations and analyze which should be solved first and which should be solved last. He should also be able to allocate the manpower based on the complexity of the problems.

Rules for the GPE or MPE

The candidates will be seated in a semi-circle based on the chest numbers and the GTO will give a narrative with a set of problems like a short story, on a wooden model sketch before the group; In that map, fields are painted as green, river (water bodies) are painted in blue, tar roads are painted in black and mud roads in pale yellow colour, houses marked

After narrating the set of problems, while the GTO asks the group any doubts. He also tells them about the time and direction from which they have to start the wooden model sketch is also marked with directions.

Each candidate will be given a writing pad; in that a narrative as "stories with set of problems" will be indicated and the candidate has to read it quickly place it that by the side.

Next, the candidates are given time to write down their individual solutions for the set of problems indicated. The candidates are given ten minutes to discuss the set of problems indicated and arrive at a solution to all situations.

Type of problems faced by the candidate in the GPE

- Rescuing a person from snake bite
- Rescuing persons from a train accident
- Diffusing or giving information about a bomb
- Natural calamities such as earthquake, tsunami etc.
- Saving the weak people from dacoits
- Giving information to the police station about terrorists/dacoits hiding out of town
- Informing the railway authorities about broken rails

Besides the above many such day to day situations can be given.

Expectation from the GTO in MPE

In the MPE, a series of tough situations are where posed candidate is putting himself and his team in action i.e. extracting work from his team by allocating jobs based on priority of the problem to be solved. He is expected to show his OLQ in this test.

The GTO will observe some basic things like:
- Whether the candidate has observed and analysed the problem well
- Whether the candidate allocates work properly to his team mates
- Whether the candidate is able to prioritize the problems
- Whether the candidate is able to resolve all the situations in the given set of problems.
- Whether he is forceful in putting across his point to the group etc.
- Whether he is able to influence the group

How to Approach GPE in the SSB

- Listen keenly to the GTO's instructions.
- Note down every situation carefully and try to use the resources in that, e.g. using a telephone at the railway crossing, cell phone and all other resources that are available etc.
- Narrate the solution by giving a prioritized approach
- At the discussion, put your points in a convincing manner with ideal solutions to the problems
- If you find your solution is better and time then never give up your point to others. Also if you find your solution has comparatively low weightage than others, then it is better its accept their points.

How to prioritize the problems

Problems are prioritized based on threat to life and things. For example, priority should be given to a train accident rather than in closing the dripping drinking water pipe.

Briefing

- In this task a story will be given to you which has 3-4 problems.
- It will have minor problems.
- The requirement is to solve all the problems.

Summary of Conducting a GPE

- GTO will explain the Area in which the story is taking place with the help of a board/sketch/model.
- The GTO will read out the story from a story card, pointing out relevant features of the story on the story board so that the story is better understood.
- In the next part GTO will give candidate a story card to read, understand and assimilate the story. Time given is five minutes only, and after that the story card is withdrawn.
- Next you are given 10 minutes along with a sheet of paper and writing material. You are required to write individual solution to the various problems which you may have perceived. After 10 minutes your written solution and the writing material will be withdrawn from you.
- You are required to discuss your solutions in 10 minutes with an Aim and to arrive at a group solution, acceptable to most of the members of the group if not all. Once the group solution is ready, any one of the group member nominated by the group has to get up, and explain the group solution on the board.

- In each exercise there will be one or two distractions diverting the candidate's thoughts from the real issues to the fake problems like are, wild elephants, mad dog, tiger, cattle not returning home in the evening after grazing; Pujari's daughter eloped with somebody, and construction bridges etc. To handle such problems never run after them, rather take the help of trained, qualified and experienced persons who are more suitable and capable, such artificially created issues are called red herrings.

Note:
1. Credit is given to the Candidate giving the group solution, in case he gives it out well.
2. When a candidate is giving out the Groups solution, nobody else is permitted to speak, prompt or add on to the solution.
3. You are required to give the group solution on which majority have to.

Procedure to a solution

1. Identifying No. of problems.
2. Priority of solving
3. Resources. There are two types of resources :-
   (a) Open Resources

   These are the resources which are clearly outlined; written or shown in the model or in the text.

   (b) Hidden Resources

   These are the resources which are not clearly obvious written or shown, but one has to assume. Always assume resources in a positive and practical manner. Assumptions are of three types:

   (i) Positive (ii) Negative (iii) Desired/ Wishful.

4. Solution – How many? How to go? Distance/Time? What to do?
5. Aim

The Plan

We were on our way to/returning from _____ when we reached the _____ we faced _____ problems. I will divide my group into smaller teams and solve all the problems simultaneously.

PROBLEM-1
(Save human life)
↓
PROBLEM-2
(Prevent mass/Natural disaster)
↓
PROBLEM-3
(Any other problem)
↓
Never forget your AIM

Individual Written Solution Key Issues

The GTO gives marks for the following issues in the individual written solution:

1. Grasp of the Narative
2. Aim
3. Priorities
4. Utilisation of Resources
5. Timings
6. Solution to all the problems

Situation (as shown below)

You are travelling with in a marriage party with the bridegroom to the marriage which would take place at the village 5 kms away from the highway. When you reached here ( ),

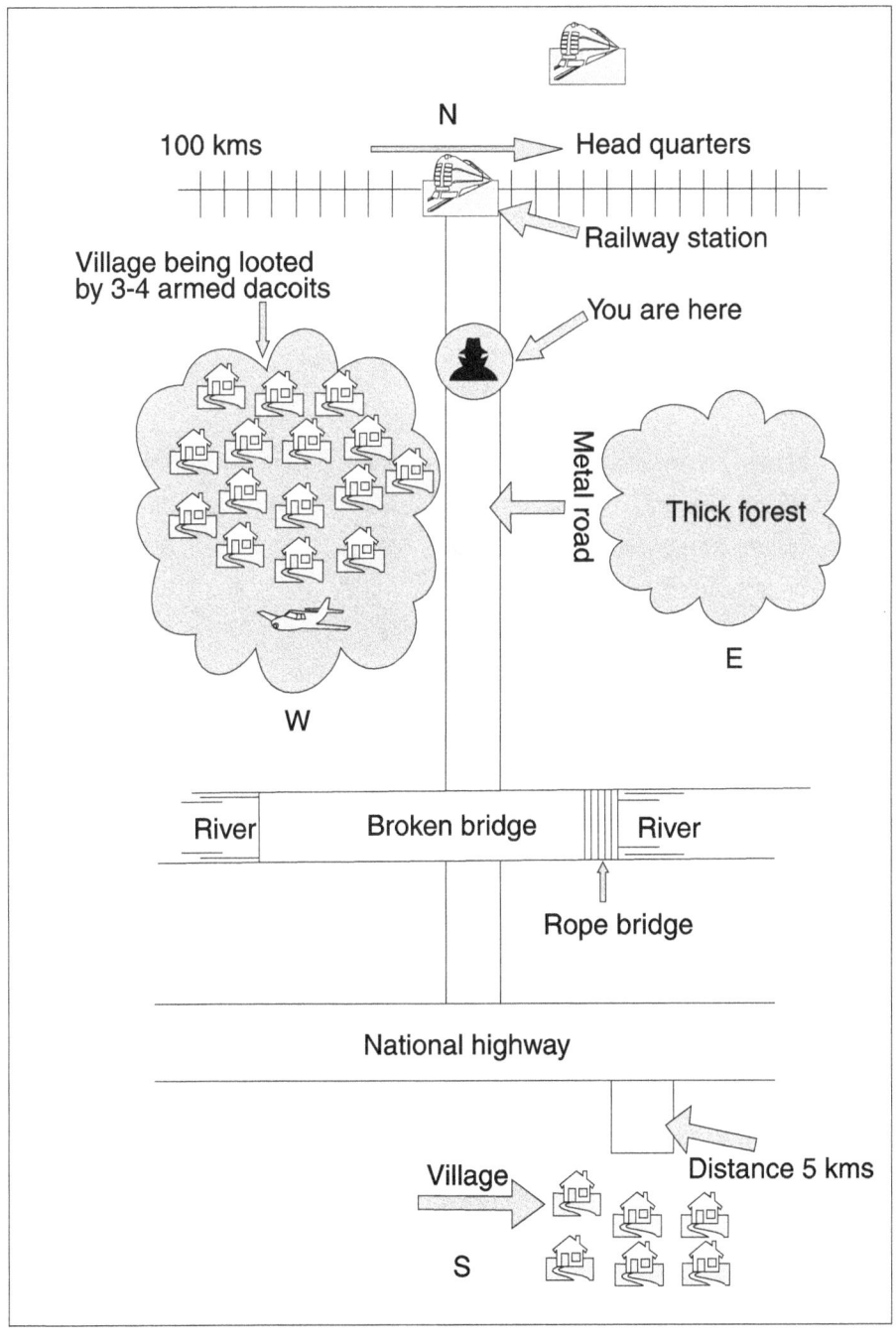

you saw a helicopter crashing in the forest to the west. You immediately reached there with two persons by small vehicle. The pilot of the helicopter tells you that there are documents to be handed over at the HQ approximately 100 kms away from the railway station in the east before 1915h and then the pilot faints. There is a train at the railway station going towards the east at 1630h. In the meantime a man from the village in the forest comes and asks for help as his village was being looted by 3-4 armed dacoits. Now the time is 1600h. How will you handle all these problems?

Priority

1. To provide first aid and required medical treatment to the pilot.
2. To hand over the documents at the HQ's.
3. To stop dacoits going on in the village.
4. To reach the village for the marriage ceremony.

Resources

1. Normally marriage party has vehicles and manpower.
2. Generally railway station has a RPF railway staff and telephone.
3. A police station in that area.
4. Forest security guards.
5. Some permissive weapons in the village.
6. Train leaving railway station at 1630h.
7. These days cell phones and internet which can come of use at specific locations.

Plan

We were on our way to attend a marriage, on the way we faced the problems as mentioned in _____.

The priorities

1. I will divide my group into smaller teams and solve all the problems simultaneously.
2. I immediately would provide first aid to the fainted pilot and send him along with two persons with the documents by a small vehicle to the railway station. They would reach there within 20 minutes or so as the distance is only 15-16 kms. They would board the train leaving the railway station at 1630h.
3. The driver of the vehicle would inform the HQ using the telephone available at the railway station; also use cell phones if network is available about the accident of the helicopter and would request them to send an ambulance

and an authority letter to receive both the documents and the fainted pilot. The driver would also inform the police station of that area about the accident as well the dacoity which is taking place in the village. While coming back he would collect RPF personnel who are not on duty, enroute collect forest Security guards and marriage party male members and come direct to the village where I, with that villager would reach the village and collect all physically fit persons with whatever weapons they can manage and keep an eye on the dacoits' activities. After some time the police and other security personnel would reach and handle the situation. The marriage party would be allowed to move ahead and after crossing the rope bridge they would proceed to the village for the marriage functions by taking lift from other set of vehicles planned and positioned by me earlier. In this way, I, along with the help of my friends and other agencies would handle all these problems successfully.

SALIENT FEATURES OF GPE (GROUP PLANNING EXERCISE)

1. Understanding/grasping power.
2. Planning must be workable.
3. Resources – minimum appropriate use.
4. Convincing/influencing ability.
5. ractical and scientific knowledge.

To view some of the live demo, visit the following websites:

www.theexcel.com, www.cavalierindia.com

GPE Example 1 - Bani

1. You are a group of friends as many of you are there who belong to RATNAGIRI wanted to visit BANI wild life sanctuary at 7 p.m. On your way in a van you stopped as your vehicle got punctured near the bridge. You heard a boy shouting and requesting for help to save his friend who is drowning and does not know swimming. A cyclist came from the tea shop side and told you that a bulldozer got stuck at the railway crossing at MLC-1.
2. At the same time a cyclist from BIRPUR comes and tells you that he saw a helicopter catching fire and falling in the forest. While you were contemplating what to do, tea shop keeper's brother came and told that while he was grazing the cattle near rocky area he heard some noise, he hid himself and heard that some anti-social elements are going to abduct the nuclear scientist who was on his way to helipad along with an important nuclear device. They wanted to take the scientist to the BALI temple area. They were also wanting to hand over the device to a foreign agent who is likely to meet them near the temple at 6.30 p.m.

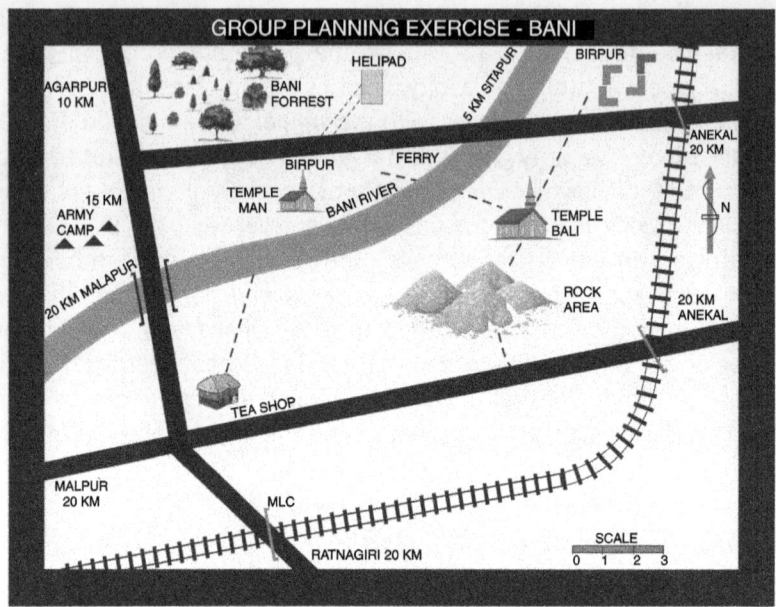

3. A lady who claimed to be a film actress requested you to find her jewel bag which was misplaced at the guest house and also to drop her at MALPUR as she has to attend a film premier at 5 p.m.

4. You have the following information :

   (a) An Army camp is established at Kilometer 15 on road RATNAGIRI-AGARPUR.

   (b) An hourly bus service is available from ANEKAL to MALPUR and MALPUR to ANEKAL.

   (c) A train from Malpur is crossing MLC 1 at 5 p.m.

   (d) No telephone/mobile communication is available in this general area except at MLC 1.

5. Time now is 4 p.m.

6. As a bold young man what action will you take?

Possible Solution

1. **Aim:** To visit wild life sanctuary at 7 p.m.
2. **Time now:** 4 p.m.
3. **Resources:** Van, Cycle, Telephone at MLC. Ferry.
4. **Priorities:** 1. Drowning boy 2. Stopping the train. 3. Nuclear scientist 4. Helicopter catching fire. 5. Helping the lady.

5. **Priority 1:** Immediately jump and save the child, give first aid. If not Ok take him to the hospital at AGARPUR. Inform police regarding train accident, nuclear scientist, helicopter fire.
6. **Priority 2:** Move by the cycle or the vehicle on road, go to MLC-1, inform railway station master to stop train. Ask for crane. Tie ropes and pull with the help of trucks. Alternatively use red flag 500 meters away to stop train.
7. **Priority 3:** Go to MLC and inform police. Move by van to the temple area through AGARPUR road. Take help of Army personnel. Hide and keep a track of antisocial elements till police arrives. Distance 10 KM, 15 min. Alternatively, inform police through station master. Go via Army camp, inform them and take their help, go via BIRUR- ANEKAL road. Go to temple area hide and keep a track of antisocial elements till police arrives. If army help is available ambush and capture them.
8. **Priority 4:** Go by van, take the help of Army and forest official and put off the fire. Ask for fire brigade – ring up from MLC-1. Alternatively, ring up AGARPUR for fire brigade and forest officials and take their help to put off fire.
9. **Priority 5:** It is a red herring. If time permits help her.

GPE Example 2 - Nandi Hills

1. You are group of young college students who wanted to visit NANDI HILLS by 7 p.m. to attend a musical concert organized by a famous musician. On your two wheelers you reached the rest house at 4.30 p.m. The rest house in charge told you that while he was crossing the rocky area he saw some suspicious looking antisocial people and he hid himself behind a rock and heard them talking that they belong to RAJAN smuggler group, who is an international smuggler and they are going to receive a consignment of weapons from the fishermen who are landing at BAGI beach at 5.30 p.m., who in turn will hand over the same to a BALA international smuggler for exchange of huge amount near Khajji area at 5.45 p.m., who then will be taking it to an unknown destination at 6 p.m.
2. A cyclist came to the rest house and told you that a train accident has occurred between passenger train and goods train at MLC-1, at 4.30 p.m.
3. Meanwhile a lady staying at the guest house requested you to help her find her jewel bag which she lost on way to the guest house when she was coming from the beach.
4. You were thinking what to do when you heard a big bang. On enquiring you found out that a school bus met with an accident at the RANIPUR road junction.

5. You have the following information:
   (a) A train from RAJPUR is likely to start at 6 p.m.
   (b) No communication including mobile is available except at MLC.

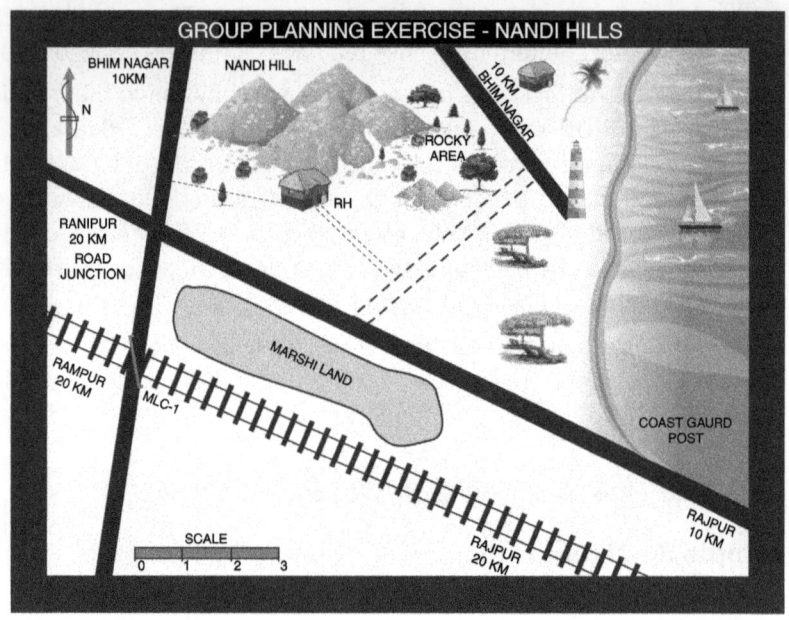

   (c) An hourly bus service is available from RAJPUR TO RANIPUR AND RANIPUR TO RAJPUR.
6. Time now is 4 p.m.
7. As bold, young, responsible people what action you will take?

Possible Solution

1. **Aim:** is to visit NANDI HILLS to enjoy musical concert.
2. **Time now:** 4.30 p.m.
3. **Resources:** Two wheelers, cycle, Telephone at MLC. Hourly bus service, Boats.
4. **Priorities:** 1. Train accident 2. School bus accident 3. Smuggling of weapons 4. Helping the lady. 5. Divide the group in to three (three, two & five).
5. **Priority 1:** Go by two wheelers – Dist 10 KM, 10 min, give first aid to Passengers. Use MLC telephone, ask for ambulance & relief and help from the civil administration. Mobilise the people and use available vehicles and take them to RAMPUR hospital. Alternatively inform RAJPURA railway station master to send relief.

6. **Priority 2:** Go to the accident spot by two wheelers. Distance 6 KM. Time taken is 6 mins. Give first aid. Stop the vehicle on the road and take the injured to the hospital at BHIMNAGAR. Inform police. Alternatively give first aid and take them to the RAJPUR HOSPITAL.
7. **Priority 3:** Two persons on two wheelers to go to beach, hide and keep track of smugglers. Distance 8 Km. & time 15 min. Other two persons to go to BHIMNAGAR, inform Police. Alternatively, go to the coast guard post and inform about the smuggling and help them.
8. **Priority 4:** It is a red herring. If time permits help her.
9. After completion assemble at rest house at 6 p.m. and go for the concert.

GPE Example 3 – Pani

1. You are group of college friends from MANIPUR on your way in a van to visit the RAJ Ruins which is famous for its historical monuments. You have to reach by 11 a.m. You parked your vehicle at the parking lot which is one kilometer away from the PANI lake. After enjoying the boating at PANI lake, while you were having a cup of tea at the tea shop, a milk vendor who came to deliver milk to the tea shop told you that a school bus has met with an accident with a truck at kilometer 10 on MANIPUR-RAJPUR road.
2. The shopkeeper's brother who happened to be the boatman told you that due to flash floods the railway bridge near MLC -1 has developed a crack and is likely to fall any time.

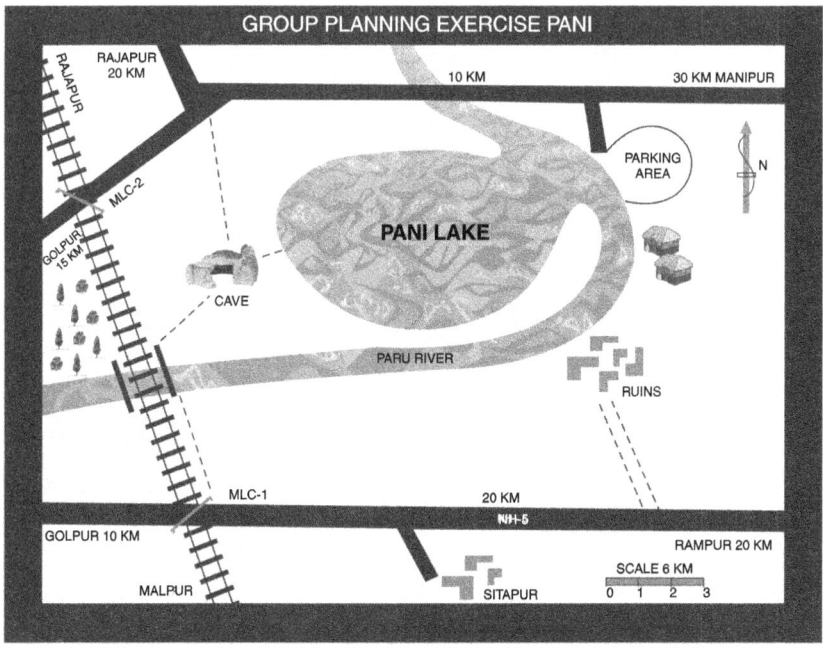

3. He also informed that he overheard some antisocial elements who happened to travel in his boat discussing that an improvised explosive device has been placed on road RAMPUR—GOLPUR at kilometer 20. They are likely to explode the device when a state minister is going to travel back to GOLPUR at 10.30 a.m.
4. As you were thinking what to do you see the neighbouring tea shop has caught fire and is burning rapidly.
5. You have the following additional information:
   (a) Train from RAJAPUR to MALPUR starts at 10 a.m.
   (b) There is an hourly bus service from RAMPUR to GOLPUR and GOLPUR to RAMPUR.
   (c) Telephone and mobile communication is disrupted due to heavy rains except at MLC-1.
6. Time now is 9 a.m.
7. As bold young men what action will you take?

Possible Solution

1. **AIM:** To visit RAJ ruins by 11 a.m.
2. **Time now:** 9 a.m.
3. **Resources:** Van, cycle, telephone at MLC-1, ferry.
4. **Priorities:** 1. School bus accident. 2. Railway bridge 3. Explosive device 4. Tea shop fire.
5. **Divide group into three (three, two and five)**

   Priority 1: Three students to proceed to car parking, take the vehicle and go to accident spot. Give first aid. Take the children to the hospital at GOLPUR. Inform railway station master and police regarding crack of bridge, explosive device, Distance 15 km. time 20 min. Alternatively, take the children to MANIPUR after giving first aid.

   Priority 2: Go with same van, get down at MLC2. Inform RAJAPURA railway station master to stop the train and send repair teams. Inform police. Alternatively take the vehicle from the highway and go to the bridge area; put red flag 500 meters away to stop train. Distance 22 km. Time 30 min.

   Priority 3: One person to go with van along with group and inform police through MLC; rest four to go by ferry to the highway with the help of highway vehicle, alert the minister and keep a watch on the antisocial elements. Distance 12 km, time 45 mins. Alternatively go to RAMPUR, inform police to further inform minister.

   Priority 4: It is a red herring. Help if time permits.

GPE Example 4 – Green Resort

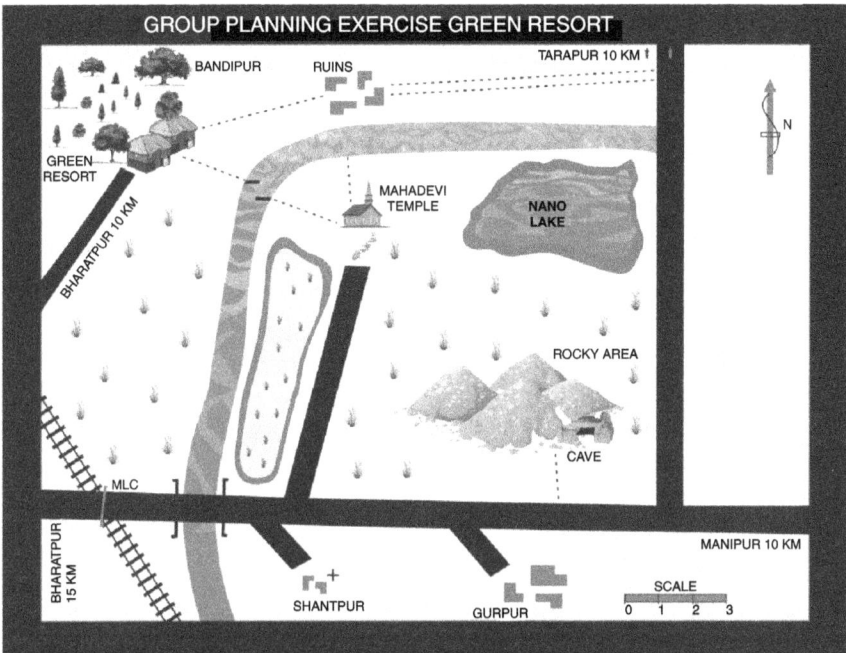

1. You are a group of friends who belong to BHARATPUR travelling in a van. After visiting the BANDIPUR Wild Life Sanctuary you halted at the GREEN resort for the night. Next morning at 8 a.m. when you were about to proceed for RAJ RUINS a middle aged person who was bleeding profusely and gasping came to you and told that he belongs to the famous BIJU dacoit group. Sardar of BIJU dacoit group wanted to abduct the bride who belongs to GURPUR village and loot their jewels and other belongings at 9 a.m. when she comes to visit the Mahadevi temple to take blessings before her marriage which is likely to take place at her village at 10 a.m. 'Since I am an ardent believer of goddess MAHADEVI I refuse to loot the bride, Sardar shot me on my leg. I managed to escape and came here.'

2. Bridegroom along with the marriage party from TARAPUR will be coming in a bus for the wedding. Members of the same group of BIJU dacoits will be looting the bridegroom's party when they are crossing at kilometer 10 of NH-5 near the caves at 9.30 a.m.

3. A cyclist who was the brother of guest house chowkidar came and told you that a school bus met with an accident with another truck at MLC and lying on the track blocking the traffic.

4. You were thinking what to do, when an old man came running to you and said that when he got up this morning he did not find his buffalo and it was missing. He also told you that he has a large family to look after, by selling the milk he was able to take care of them. One of his friends told him that he saw the buffalo going towards the forest.
   1. You have following additional information with you.
      (a) There is a hourly bus service that runs from MANIPUR to BHARATPUR and BHARATPUR TO MANIPUR.
      (b) A train is leaving BHARATPUR at 10 a.m.
      (c) There is no communication including mobile available in this area except at the MLC.
   2. Time now is 8 a.m. As bold young dynamic responsible citizens what action you are going to take?

Possible Solution

1. **Aim:** is to visit the ruins by 11 a.m.
2. **Time now:** is 8 a.m.
3. **Resources:** Van, Telephone at MLC, Ferry, Bus, highway vehicles.
4. **Priorities:** 1. First aid to the dacoit 2. School bus accident. 3. Bride 4. Bridegroom's party. 5. Helping old man
5. **Divide the group in 3 sub-groups (three, six and one).**

   Priority 1: Give first aid to dacoit, take him in the van to the BHARATPUR hospital and admit. Ask for ambulance. Inform Police regarding accident, abducting and looting. Inform Railway station master to stop train. Alternative: Take him to SHANTIPUR.

   Priority 2: Go by van via BHARATPUR to MLC-1. Give first aid to children. Take them to BHARATPUR Hospital. 15 KM, 15 min. Tie rope, pull school bus, clear the track. Alternative: Use red flag 500 mtrs away.

   Priority 3: Go to the ruins by running, use ferry to cross, hide and send one person towards SHANTIPUR to inform bride's party about dacoits. Alternatively cross the river by using logs, hide and keep track of dacoits till police comes.

   Priority 4: Go to BHARATPUR in van, inform police to further inform TARAPUR and MANIPUR police to intercept bridegroom's party. Police can disguise as barat party and catch dacoits. Alternatively use ferry by TARAPUR crossing, intercept barat party, disguise and capture the dacoits.

   Priority 5: It is a red herring. Not important. If time permits help him. Get together at temple by 10.30 a.m. and go to visit RAJ ruins.

GPE Example 5 – Rana Firing Range

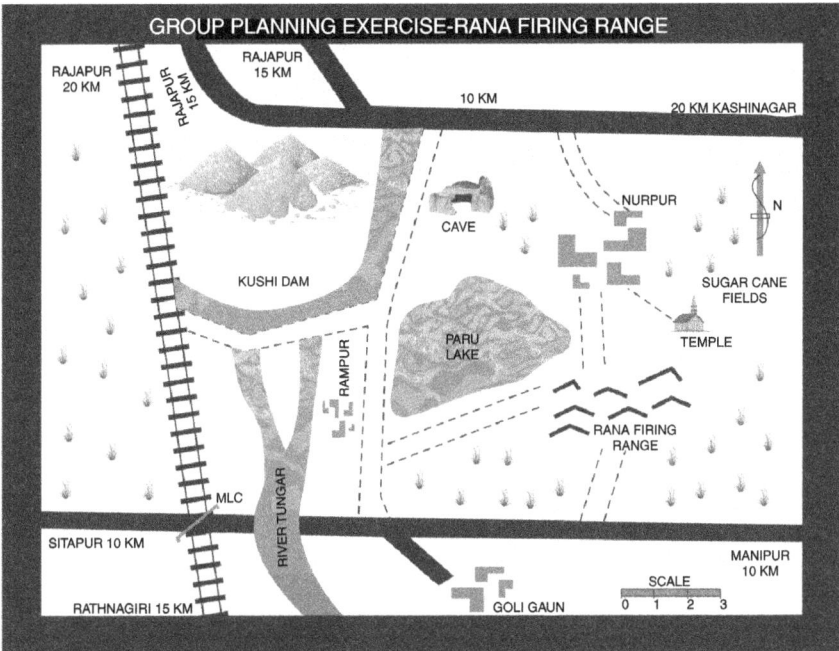

1. You are a group of college NCC cadets from KASHINAGAR who came in a bus to practice for rifle firing competition at RANA firing range. At 4 p.m., when you were about to finish the firing practice you saw a man come running towards you. He told you that he and his friend were grazing sheep at the temple area, when a stray bullet splinter hit his friend's right leg and he is bleeding profusely and lying near the temple.

2. At the same time a man on a cycle from NURPUR came to you and told you that while he was coming on the KASHINAGAR – RAJAPUR road at kilometer 10, he saw a man lying on the road and bleeding from his head. On further enquiring he said that he was the driver of the scientist and he was taking them to the chemical factory at KASHINAGAR. Scientists were carrying an important part of a container at the chemical factory which was to be fitted to stop the leakage of poisonous gas by 6 p.m., failing which heavy leakage can occur, explode the container and can cause danger to the civil population. He heard a group talking that one of their gang members planted a bomb at the TUNGA DAM which will blow off at 5.30 p.m. If bomb explodes whole of RAMPUR will get submerged. Then antisocial elements kidnapped the scientist and moved in a jeep towards the cave which is near the TUNGA DAM. They were likely to blackmail and demand 1 crore rupees from the owner of the chemical factory to release

the scientist. They hit him on his head, after that he fell unconscious. He then gave him first aid and put him in a bus and sent him to KASHINAGAR.

3. A security personnel who belongs to RAMPUR village who came to attend duty at PARU lake told you that his brother told him that fishplates of the railway track were missing at 500 meters towards TUNGA DAM from the MLC 1.
4. You were thinking what to do when a lady came crying requesting you to help her to trace her daughter who went on a boat ride an hour back and had not returned and missing for the last one hour.
5. You have the following additional information:
    (a) An hourly bus service is available from KUSHINAGAR to RAJAPUR and RAJAPUR to KUSHINAGAR. Similarly from MANIPUR and SITAPUR.
    (b) A train from RAJAPUR to RATHNAGIRI at 6.30 p.m.
    (c) No telephones/mobiles are functional in this general area except at MLC-1.
6. Time now is 4 p.m.
7. As bold and responsible young men what action are you going to take?

Possible Solution

1. **Aim:** After the firing practice get back to KASHINAGAR.
2. **Time now:** 4 p.m.
3. **Resources:** Van, cycle, telephone, MLC, hourly bus service, jeep at km10, boats.
4. **Priorities 1:** First aid to the bullet injured persons. 2. Scientists 3. Dam 4. Fish plates of railway track. 5. Helping the lady.
5. **Priority 1:** Give first aid to the injured person at the hospital at MANIPUR.
6. **Priority 2:** Take the bus, pick up the injured person from km10 and proceed towards RAJAPUR, admit him in hospital, inform railway station master, police regarding fishplate, dam and scientist. On the way drop two members near cave crossing so that they can keep a watch on anti-social elements. Distance 15 km, Time 30 mins.
7. **Priority 3:** We use the cycle to proceed towards RAMPUR and DAM. Inform headman of RAMPUR village and security personnel of dam. Mobilise the people to move to higher areas. Keep a watch till police help comes, help them to catch the culprits. Distance 12 km, Time 30 mins.

8. **Priority 4:** The person who proceeded to RAJAPUR can inform the station master. Alternatively two persons to go to the spot and put red flag. Early warning to the driver of train to stop.
9. **Priority 5:** It is a red herring, if time permits help the lady.
10. Lastly get together at km 10 on RAJPURA road at 6.30 p.m. and proceed for KASHINAGAR.

Group Planning Exercise – 6

You (as many as in the group) are a group of students from Govt. College Lalitpur, going by train to Bapu Dham, to take part in the Basket Ball Tournament which was starting at 8 a.m. At 3:30 a.m. you suddenly woke-up on hearing the screeching sound of the train stopping. On inquiring from the fellow passengers, you were told that it was due to chain pulling. You saw that the train had stopped near the unmanned level crossing and four men, who were travelling with you, had got down and sped away in a jeep towards Iiam Nagar. Meanwhile, the train started again. When you got back to your seats, one of you found a diary left behind by these men. While going through the diary, you found that they were antisocial elements and had planned to poison the milk in the milk-truck which leaves Ram Nagar for Bapu Dham, at 4.15 a.m. to be distributed further. They had also planned to place a suitcase bomb in a bus at Ram Nagar Bus Stop. The bus will depart from Ram Nagar for Lalit Puri at 4.15 a.m. The suitcase-bomb is timed to blow off at 5.30 a.m. The other members of the gang had kidnapped the village headman's daughter and planned to use her for their escape, in case their friends were caught. They had taken the girl to the ruined fort and will wait for their friends. As you were planning what to do, you hear your friend shouting that his bag containing his digital camera is missing. At present, the train is passing over the rail bridge on River Cauvery. As bold young persons, what do you intend doing in such a situation?

Reasonable assumption can be made.

Solution - GPE-6

Problems

(a) To stop milk van and distribution of milk
(b) To inform police and diffuse the bomb at Ramnagar
(c) To save the life of the girl
(d) To search for the camera
(e) To attend the tournament at Bapu Dham.

Divide the group: 3 + 3 + 2 + 2

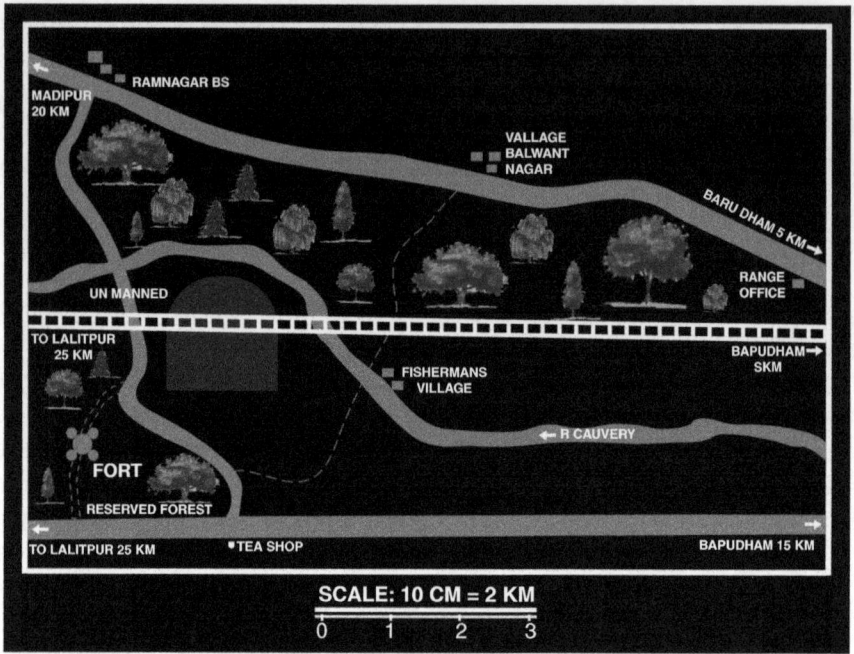

Solution No. 1

Stop the train at Fisherman's village

Three students go by car to Balwant Nagar and further to Ramnagar to stop milk van.

Total distance 15 Km. Time taken approx 45 min Task - To stop the milk van and distribution of milk

Solution No. 2

3 students move to Ramnagar by motorcycle

Total distance - 16 km – time taken – approx 45 min

Task – inform police about the bomb & help to diffuse the bomb

Solution No. 3

(a) 3 students move to Fisherman village
(b) They cross river by boat
(c) Total distance – 10 kms, time taken approx 35 min
(d) Task – collect few arms from Fisherman village with few men, save the girl

Solution No. 4

(a) Two students remain in train and pull the chain to stop train near range office
(b) Search for the camera
(c) Reach Ramnagar distance – 10 km, time taken 25 min
(d) Inform police at Ramnagar about the bomb in the bus, about the position of milk van. At last all get together at Bapu Dham for the tournament.

Group Planning Exercise – 7

You (as many as in the group) are a group of students from Bharatpur, who have come on a picnic to Maharaja Forest. You plan to get food from Gondia by 7 p.m. before the shops close and then go to the Forest Rest House. While proceeding to Gondia by your jeep, you stopped to have tea at tea shop. You suddenly noticed a man coming out of the shop and getting into a van to go. As he started his van, you heard loud noise of accident; you saw that a truck had hit the van, badly damaged the van and sped away. On reaching the van, you found that the man had fractured his leg. He asks for your help and tells you that he is from CBI and was going to Gondia to inform Police that some anti-social elements have planned to loot the State Bank at Bharatpur at 4.30 p.m. To divert the attention of police, they have also planted a suitcase-bomb in first-class compartment of train leaving Gondia for Bharatpur at 3.15 p.m. The bomb will blow-off at 4.15 p.m. He also told you that the gang, on its way to Bharatpur, shall be picking their member up Raj from Rupa Village. As you were planning your course of action, an elderly lady approaches you and tells you that her goat had slipped on the side of the river. She pleads with you to save the goat, as it is the only source of livelihood for her.

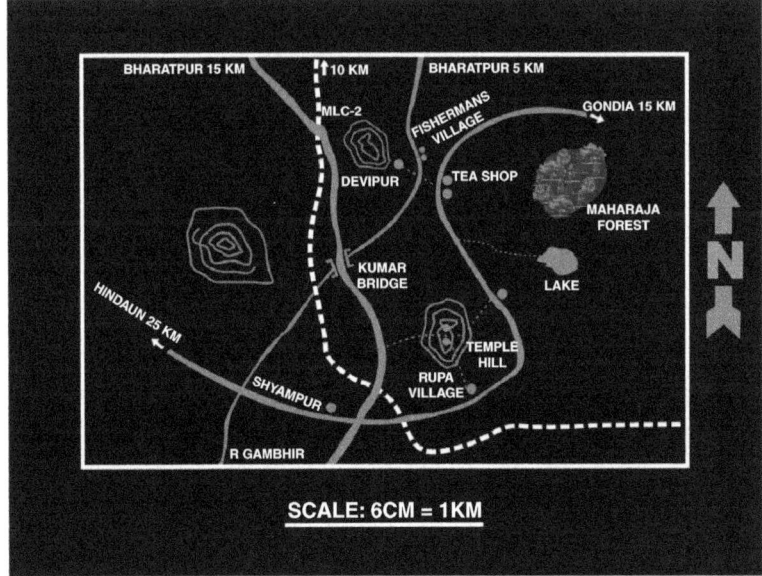

The CBI officer also informs you that due to P&T strike, all the telephone lines in the area are out of order. There is a one hourly bus service between Gondia and Bharatpur. Under these circumstances what actions will you take?

Time now is 3:15 p.m.

Reasonable assumptions can be made.

3. PROGRESSIVE GROUP TASK (PGT)

"The biggest failure of all is the person that never tries".

– Dr Larry Kimsey

Progressive Group Task is conducted after the GPE. This task is about a set of obstacles on ground in a specified area. In this task you and your team members should cross each obstacle defined by set of rules. Also while crossing the obstacles you should carry a load. To cross these obstacles, some helping materials are given by the GTO, i.e. balli (wooden log), plank, and a rope to tie.

The time given for this is usually 40 to 45 minutes depending on the GTO and also based on the difficulty level of the task. If one task is finished the group has to move to the next PGT. So the group has to finish all the tasks in one stretch. Also the difficulty of the tasks increases from one task to another.

No leader is nominated and the whole group is allowed to participate in this. The person who is having better analyzing capability, and is able to apply his basic physics (such as fulcrum, cantilever) in real life, will find it easy to finish these tasks. Also he will be noted as a leader.

Example

Scenario about the PGT.

The obstacles are painted in three colours namely

(a) White

(b) Blue/Green/Yellow

(c) Red

Each colour describes one Rule.

White: Both the candidate and the helping materials can touch the obstacle at this region.

Blue/Green: Only the candidate can touch the obstacle in this region and not the helping material.

Red: Both the candidate and helping material should not touch the obstacles.

Out of Bound Areas

The areas in the PGT which should not be touched are called out of bound Areas. These areas include the mud surfaces inside the task area and some colour codes as described above.

Helping materials and its usage

The helping materials given are wooden plank (6 feet in length), balli (wooden log), and a rope. Along with this they will give a load to carry from the start point to another end. With these helping materials you can implement several techniques such as cantilever, fulcrum etc. to cross over the obstacles along with the Group. Use the existing structures on the ground and with the helping material make simple bridges, cantilever, fulcrum and swing. Try to do some homework as to how to create such structures. Few methods are given in this book also; you can take useful ideas from various pictures shown in this book.

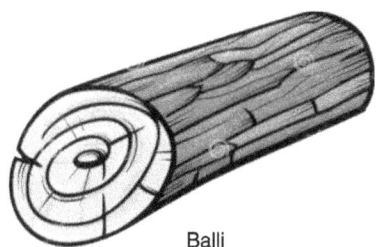
Balli

Rope

Plank

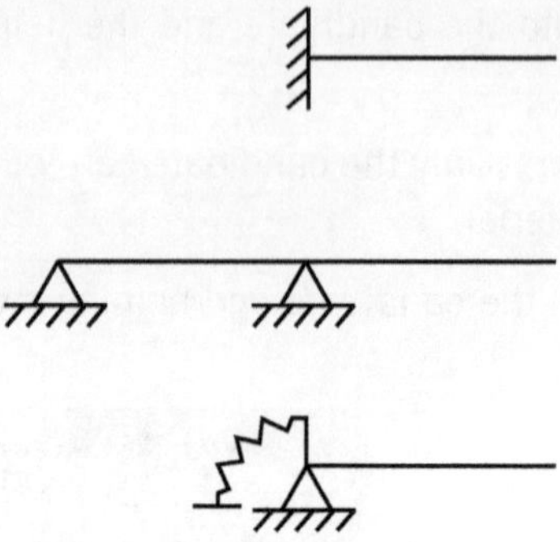

Centilever

Swing

Bridge — Start line / Finish line

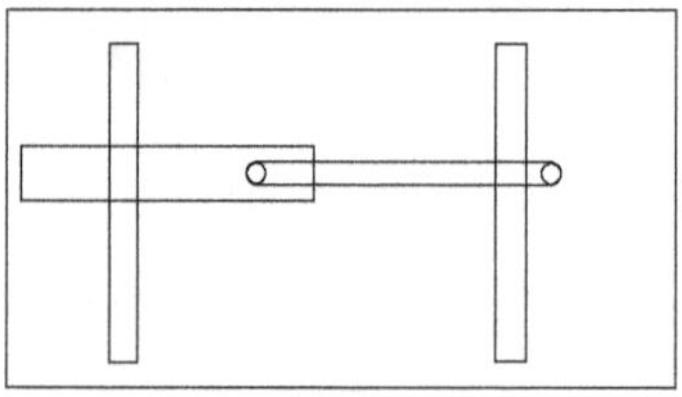

Force / Fulcrum / Load

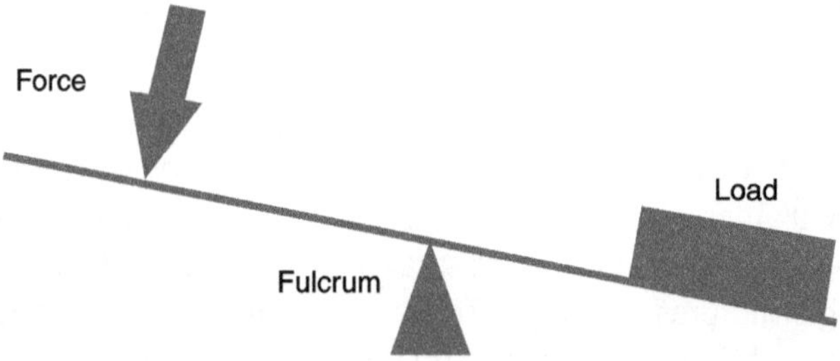

Guidelines to follow at the PGT

- Never look at the GTO while doing the given tasks.
- Be yourself as stated earlier in the GD itself.
- Give good ideas to the group and if you don't have any ideas just help the idea givers honestly.
- Never violate the Rules, it is the basic of GTO tasks, and in case you do violate the rule, you go back to the structure from where you violated the rule.

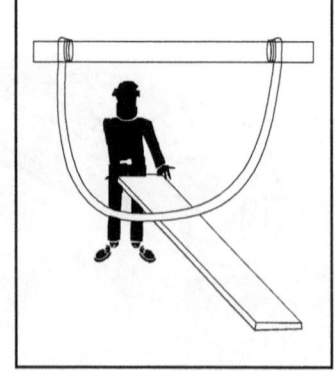

- Be an active participant in the team by giving your full cooperation.
- Be positive in your views and give due consideration to other member's ideas if it they better than yours.

This being the third Basic Test and this is the stage of co-operation a group is required to cross certain obstacles laid in FOUR STAGES by carrying a load and using helping material. The PGT test is based on 'Funnel Theory'.

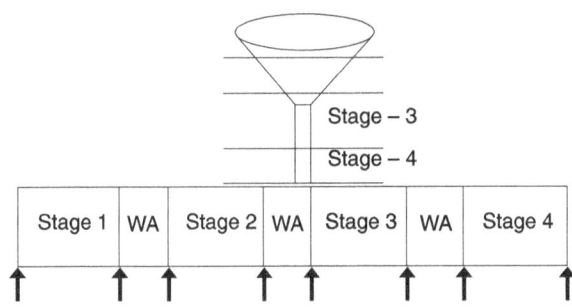

SL = Start Line
FL = Finish Line
WA = Waiting Area

(a) **Stage No.1:** Wide open stage. Simple and small obstacles, easy to cross, 4-6 persons can work at a time. Time required 4-6 minutes. In this stage GTO checks the co-ordination of group so act as a 'CO-ORDINATOR' and encourage the group to move ahead as early as possible. Simple planking/

making bridges would be sufficient to cross this stage. All can get space to operate.

(b) **Stage No. 2:** Head and Tail Stage. Difficult hurdles, not easy to cross, 2-3 persons only can work at a time. Time required 8-12 minutes. In this stage GTO checks the role which each candidate would like to take up. So try to act as a 'LEADER'. Lead the group by setting examples with your full involvement. Here simple planking will not work, you have to look for other high level ideas. Since limited place to operate try to be in the action point as a positive contributor.

(c) **Stage No. 3:** Impasse Stage. Very difficult hurdles, not easy to cross. One or two persons can work at a time. Time required 12-15 minutes. In this stage GTO checks the 'MENTAL LEVEL' of each candidate and finds out whether the group or the individual following 'scientific' methods or 'hit & try' methods. Always use 'scientific methods'. No use of muscles power or guess work.

(d) **Stage No. 4:** Frustration Stage. Very difficult hurdles; by appearance they look simple but execution almost impossible. One or two persons can work at a time. Time required more than 15 minutes. When the execution is almost impossible in that case no shouting, no passing of remarks etc., rather keep cool and keep on trying. The name of the test indicates that the difficulty level of obstacles keep on increasing from stage to stage progressively. When the task is difficult and not easy to reach a final solution, find all combination of swing, fulcrum, cantilever, bridging etc., carefully study the structure on ground. Focus on those areas where candidates and helping material have access. The catch is: do not lose the ability to think and observe. Always ensure you are not just a passive onlooker but a contributor, very active and eager to try and help the team.

Group Task and Command Task

Try to understand the basics and visualize them on ground. Create your own structure and practice. Use all the home resources to create basic model at your home practice. It would be a better idea to join Cavalier India/The Excel to undergo training. This will give you real exposure to these obstacles. More details can be seen at www.cavalierindia.com and www.theexcel.com.

Your home–work plus few days of training at these academies will ensure that you come out with flying colours at the SSB. A little bit of homework and few days of training will make it a reality for you.

The GTO will address the Candidates as follow:

1. So far as you were working indoors on a non-physical task, you will now be working outdoors on a physical task. The task is called PGT.
2. The task is called Progressive as it is divided in four parts progressively from first to fourth part task becomes more and more interesting.
3. Task also requires more time, more physical and more mental efforts in incremental order from first to fourth stage of the task.
4. We will bring out as if we are playing a four stage obstacle course game.
5. Since there are no natural obstacles like river, canal, nalah etc. at the SSB, we will create the obstacles by embedding bricks in ground and making lines thereof.
6. A Start Line (SL) and Finish Line (FL) will be marked and the area between them considered as an obstacle, which will be placed out of bounds.

7. These lines will be painted white to stand out on the ground.
8. To help you with the task some structures made up of balli, plank, rope, drum and brick etc. may also be found embedded in ground. You can make use of them.
9. To help you even more some helping material in the form of balli, plank, rope, small wooden blocks etc. may also be given to complete the task.
10. To make the task little more interesting a load (black box) and a drum may also be provided and if required to be carried along with you to the FL of fourth stage of the task.
11. So, now the task is that all the candidates along with the load and making use of helping material and the structures embedded in the ground are to cross obstacle after obstacle and finally reach beyond the FL of the fourth stage of the task.
12. Like all games this four stage obstacle game also has some rules.
13. These rules will be explained to you by the GTO with fair amount of details.
14. Please pay very close attention when these rules are being explained to you.
15. These rules are explained only once before the task commences thereafter no clarifications are given.
16. The same rules will be applicable for all subsequent tasks carried out on the same day and the next day and these rules are not explained again. Therefore, it is more important that you understand these rules thoroughly.

Rules for PGT

17. **Group Rule:** All candidates along with helping material and the load are to cross the finish line of the first stage of task before they can proceed to the next stage of the task.
18. **Distance Rule:** Any distance which is more than four feet (vertically, horizontally or diagonally) you are not permitted to jump and go across it.

Note: Everyone must have a very good idea as to how much is four feet distance.

19. **Rules of Infinity:** SL and FL are white painted embedded brick lines extending for 12 to 15 feet, however, they will be considered to be extending to infinity on either side.
20. **Rules for Helping Material:** There are two types of helping material provided to you. Solid like balli, plank, wooden blocks etc. and soft rope or ropes.
    (a) Two single solid helping material (SSHM) cannot be tied together.
    (b) One SSHM can be placed or supported on another SSHM.
    (c) A SSHM can be tied to any structure embedded in ground.

(d) Rope can be tied to any SSHM and/or to any structure embedded in ground.
(e) Two ropes if given, can be tied together to form a longer rope.
(f) Rope can be bundled or coiled together and can be placed on any structure or helping material.
(g) While carrying a rope, it will be carried in a bundle or coiled form in your hand or on your shoulder.
(h) Under no circumstances whatsoever, a rope will be carried around your neck.

21. **Rules for Load:** Load wherever provided will be treated like baby/will be handled like baby.

Note: Do not get too much attached with the load. It is basically provided for the working satisfaction of a candidate who is physically strong but mentally weak in ideas.

22. **Rules for Colours:** There are basically four colours seen at SSB. White, Red, Blue / Yellow / Green and Black.
    (a) **White:** This is universally considered colour of peace therefore, anything which is painted white will be considered in bounds for all.
    (b) **Red:** Red is universally considered to be colour of danger, therefore, anything which is painted red will be considered out of bounds for all.
    (c) **Blue/Yellow/Green:** One of the colours Blue, Yellow or Green may also be found on some of the structures. This colour will be considered in bounds for the candidate but out of bounds for the helping material and the load.

(d) **Black:** This colour is generally found close to the ground. It does not have any significance of its own. It will be considered of the same colour which is painted just above it. It actually is anti-termite paint.

23. **Rules for OTMD (One Time Mobile Drum):** A white painted drum with a red stripe called OTMD may also be provided in the task.

    (a) OTMD may or may not be provided.

    (b) If it is provided it is only for that stage of the task.

    (c) It may be provided at SL, FL or in out of bounds area.

    (d) Whenever it is provided its location will clearly be explained by the GTO while he is explaining the task.

    (e) As per the rule and the name (OTMD) (One Time Mobile Drum) it can be picked up and placed anywhere in the out of bounds area only once and that too following all other rules.

    (f) Once it is placed it is considered a fixed structure and cannot be moved thereafter.

    (g) Leave the OTMD wherever it was placed by you and carry on further with the task.

24. **Penalty:** Like all games this four stage obstacle course game also has a penalty. The penalty is that whosoever or whatsoever breaks the rule is to take the penalty of going back to the structure of that stage of task and commence again.

Demonstration

25. GTO will then take you around and show you all the obstacles.
26. He will explain SL, FL, Out of Bounds Area, Colours, Helping Materials, Load, OTMD etc.
27. He will not hide anything from you.
28. He may revise rules with you.

Conduct

29. When you reach the FL of the 4th stage of the task during demonstration, GTO will then ask you as to how much time do you need. Please remain quiet unless he asks you specially, then you may say 'as you wish, Sir'. If he insists on time frame you may say, '40 to 45 minutes, Sir'.
30. He will then give you time, ask you to run to the SL of 1st stage of task and commence the tasks.
31. He will then quietly sit down and start observing you.
32. He will continuously note down your performance in his folder.

33. He will not speak to you at all unless somebody is likely to be injured or you are breaking rules persistently.
34. The moment exercise starts, be Number 1 or 2 and enter the area after little planning and explaining the same to the group and try 'tactfully' to occupy the hurdle which is very crucial from where one can contribute maximum for the group. If not, no fighting, be comfortable at second or third best positions and cross at No. 7-8-9 or the last. This would prove that your contribution for the group has been maximum.
35. Do not look towards the GTO during the task. Concentrate on the task. Speak only to your colleagues in the group.
36. Come forward for the task and demonstrate your ideas.
37. Be a gentleman all the time.

SALIENT FEATURES OF OLQ IN GT

1. **Practical Intelligence:** Uses common sense to cross the hurdle.
2. **Planning:** Plan before entering the field.
3. **Resources:** Use maximum resources and appropriately.
4. **Knowledge:** Use scientific methods. No Hit & Trial, No Muscle Power.
5. **Co-operation:** Work as a team.
6. **Group:** Involve maximum candidates and shoulder additional responsibilities.
7. **Impression:** Super active, (Effective participation).
   No dusting of clothes.
   No use of handkerchief
   Ignore if slightly hurt
   No laughing, no snide remarks.
   Show lots of enthusiasm and commitment
   One day effort – life long comfort
   Be a contributor/ participant

T-METHODS TO CROSS THE HURDLES

1. **"T" Method:** This method is applicable when there are three structures in triangle shape, vertically all of the same height, that is 1½-3½ feet. Then send first person by common sense method; i.e. Hold the balli or plank in your hands, increase its length as desired and follow it with "T" Method.
2. **Coil Method:** This method is applicable if one structure is comparatively short by few inches and the given balli or plank is falling short. Then send one person to the structure which is short by common sense method. Let him carry the rope like a **Cross Belt** and neither around his neck nor on his shoulders and then follow it with "T" Method or Bridging Method.

3. **Bridging Method:** When some distance is to be bridged with the plank or a slide of sufficient length. Never throw it, rather tie the rope with one end of the plank or balli, keep it vertically straight. Let other candidate hold the rope so that it doesn't fall on the ground and lower the plank slowly. These three methods are applicable only at short height i.e. up to 3½ feet. The last man comes in the reverse order of the first.

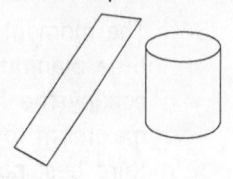

4. **Lasso Method (Rope Bridge – Monkey Crawl):** This method is applicable when there are two structures vertically 4-5½ feet tall and distance between two is more by few inches than the length of balli. First send one person to the other structure by common sense method and then follow it with LASSO Method.

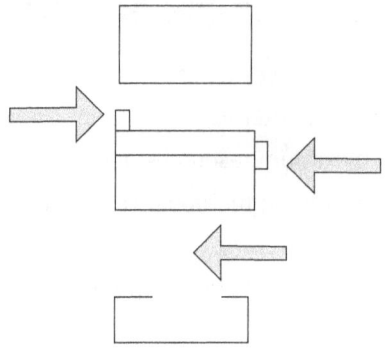

After going, make a loop with the help of given rope and fix that loop in the extended wooden portion "Upwards" or "Sideways".

5. **Cantilever Method:** This method is applicable when there are two parallel bars, two regular bars, square, rectangle, round handle like structures and the given balli generally is conical design. Insert the balli through those bars and squares etc. Balli will get fixed, distance will be reduced and cross over 4-5½ feet.

6. **Half Swing Method:** This method is applicable when there is a goal post like structure 6-7 feet tall "Jhoola" or "Tyre" already fixed which moves even with a slight touch to control its movement.

7. **Swing Method (Small Rope Hanging):** Rest everything same. Take the rope like a cross belt, and place the plank on the loop. Tie the rope firmly, throw it downwards, move it little bit, let the rope be held by other person one by one and cross over. Chances of crossing the hurdles are there.

Hanging rope

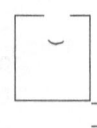

8. **Jhoola Method:** Rest everything same, carry the rope which is a long one and tie it like a "Jhoola".

   Move it little bit, let other candidate hold it one by one and then swing across. Chances of crossing the hurdles are there.

9. **See-saw Method.** Applicable while picking up bomb/ diamond during Command Task. Rope is tied and made tight rolling with balli.

   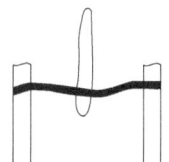

   These methods are further elaborated below by way of diagrams; carefully study them and understand. You can also refer various pictures shown in this book.

FEW OTHER USEFUL METHODS

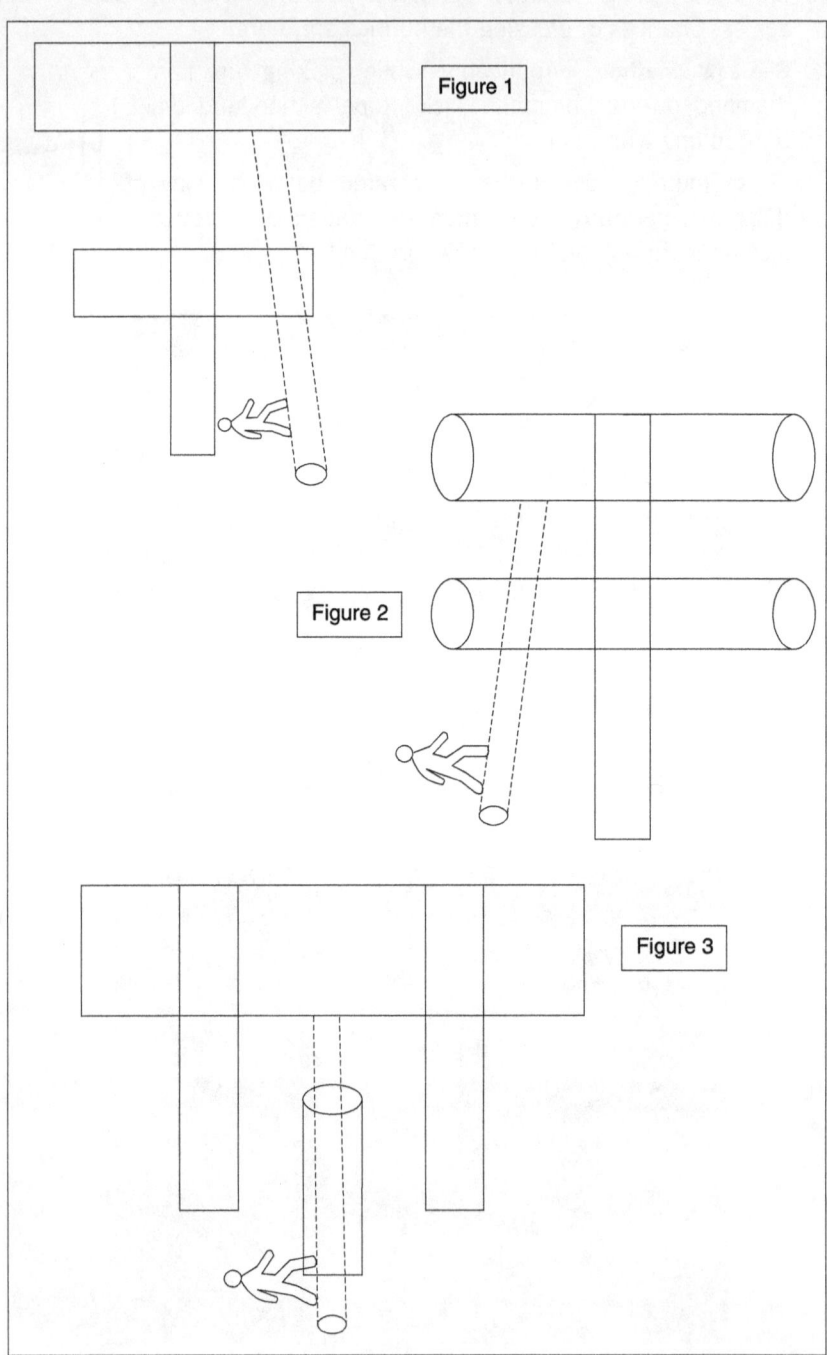

Cracking GTO Tasks / Tests 247

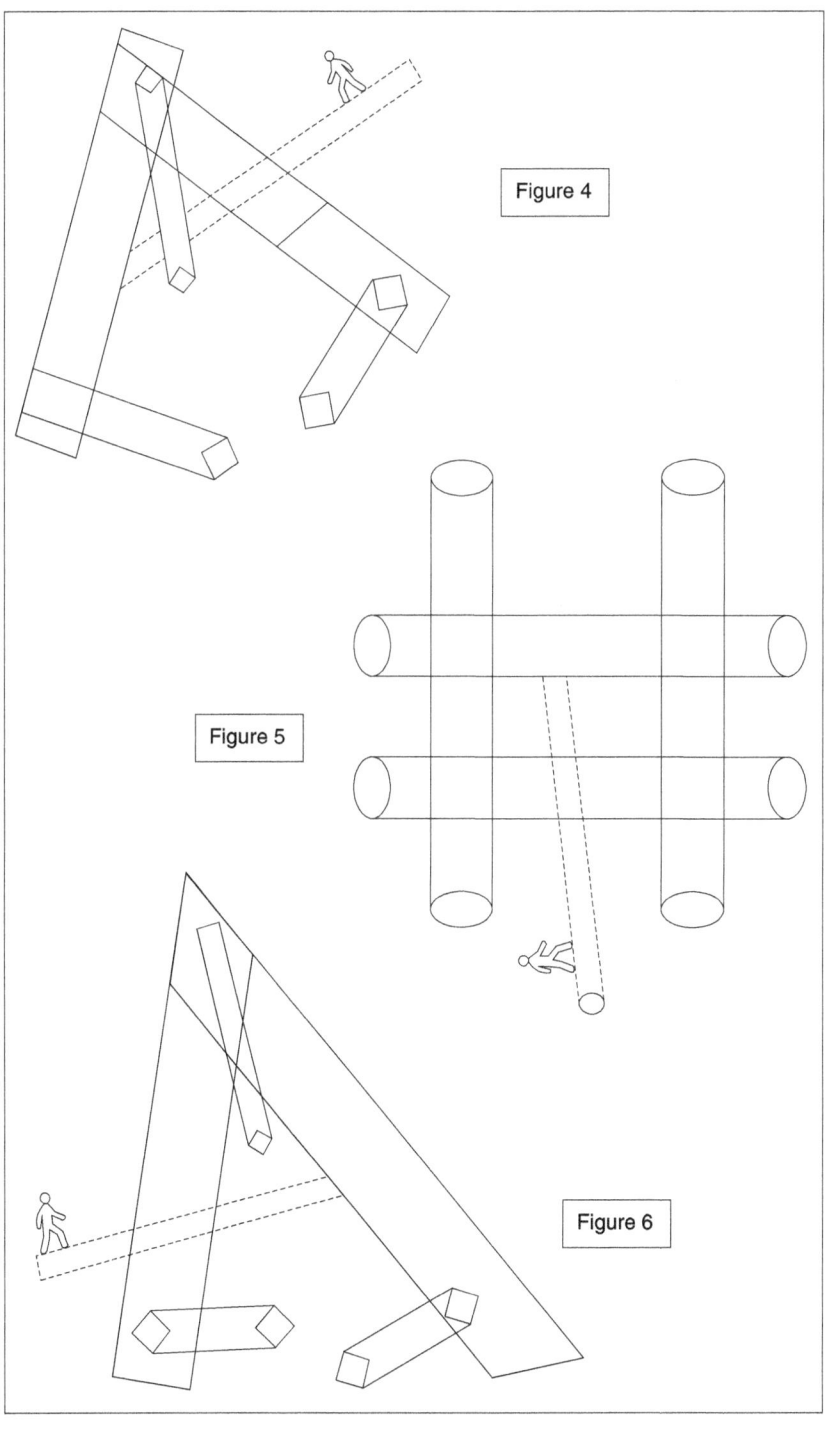

Figure 4

Figure 5

Figure 6

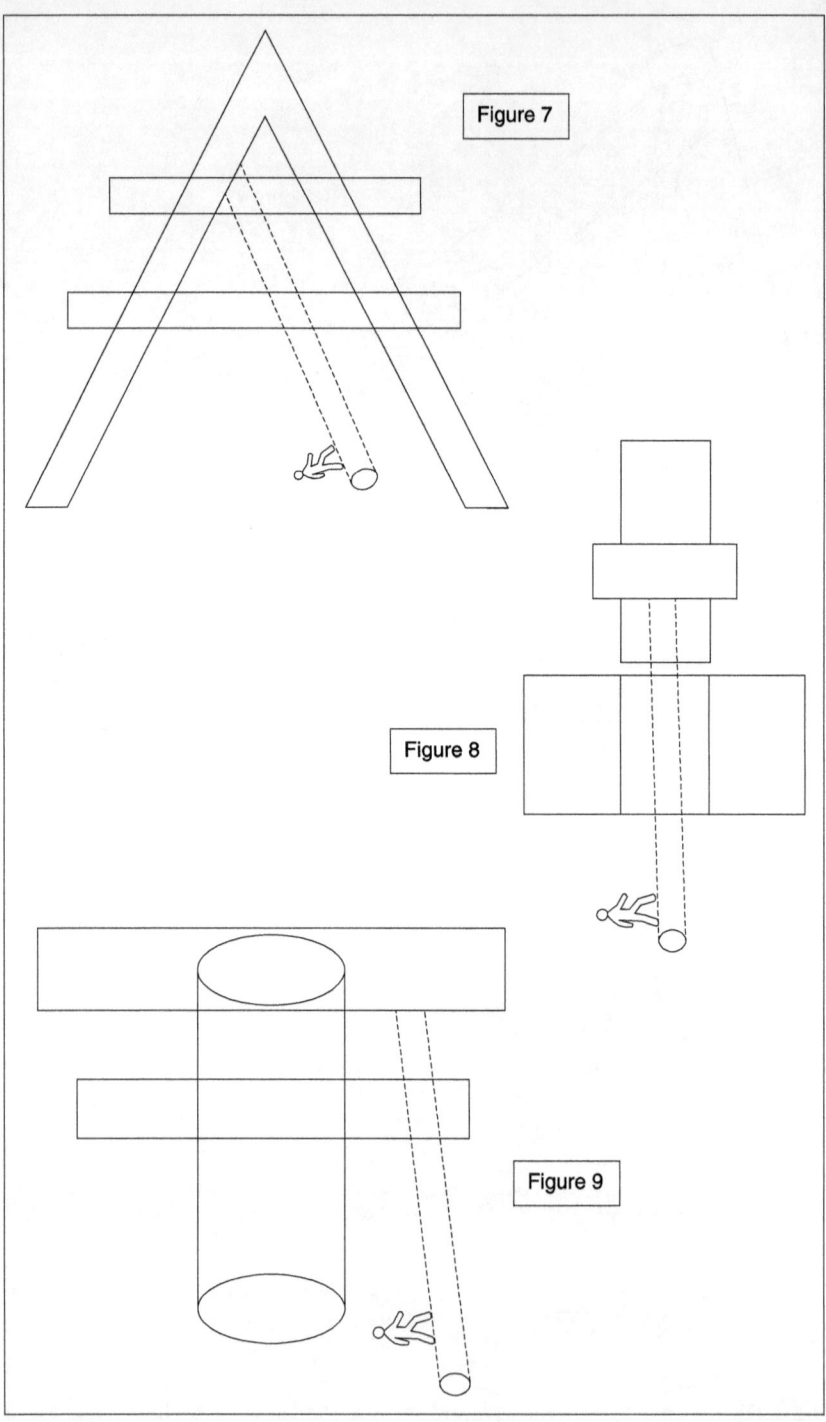

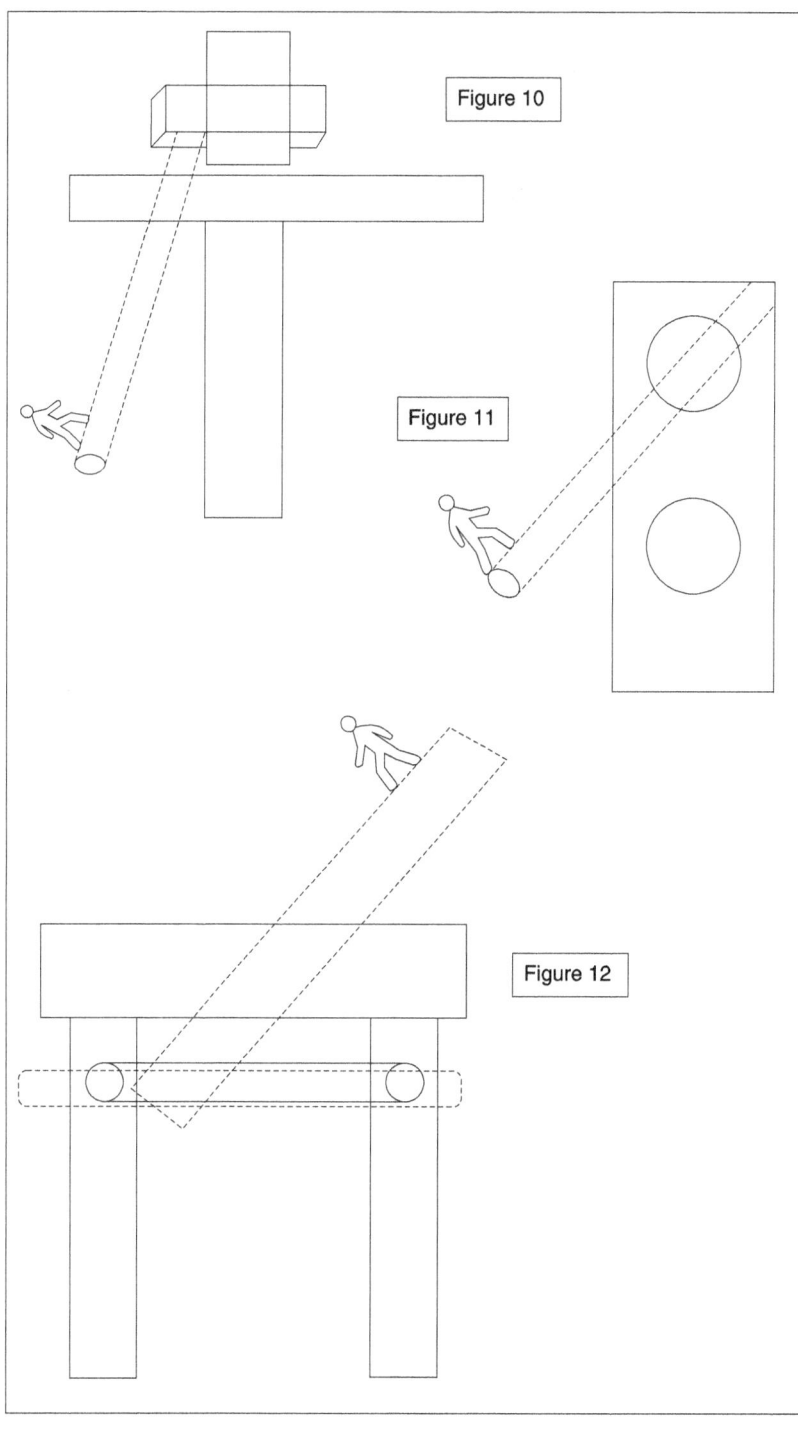

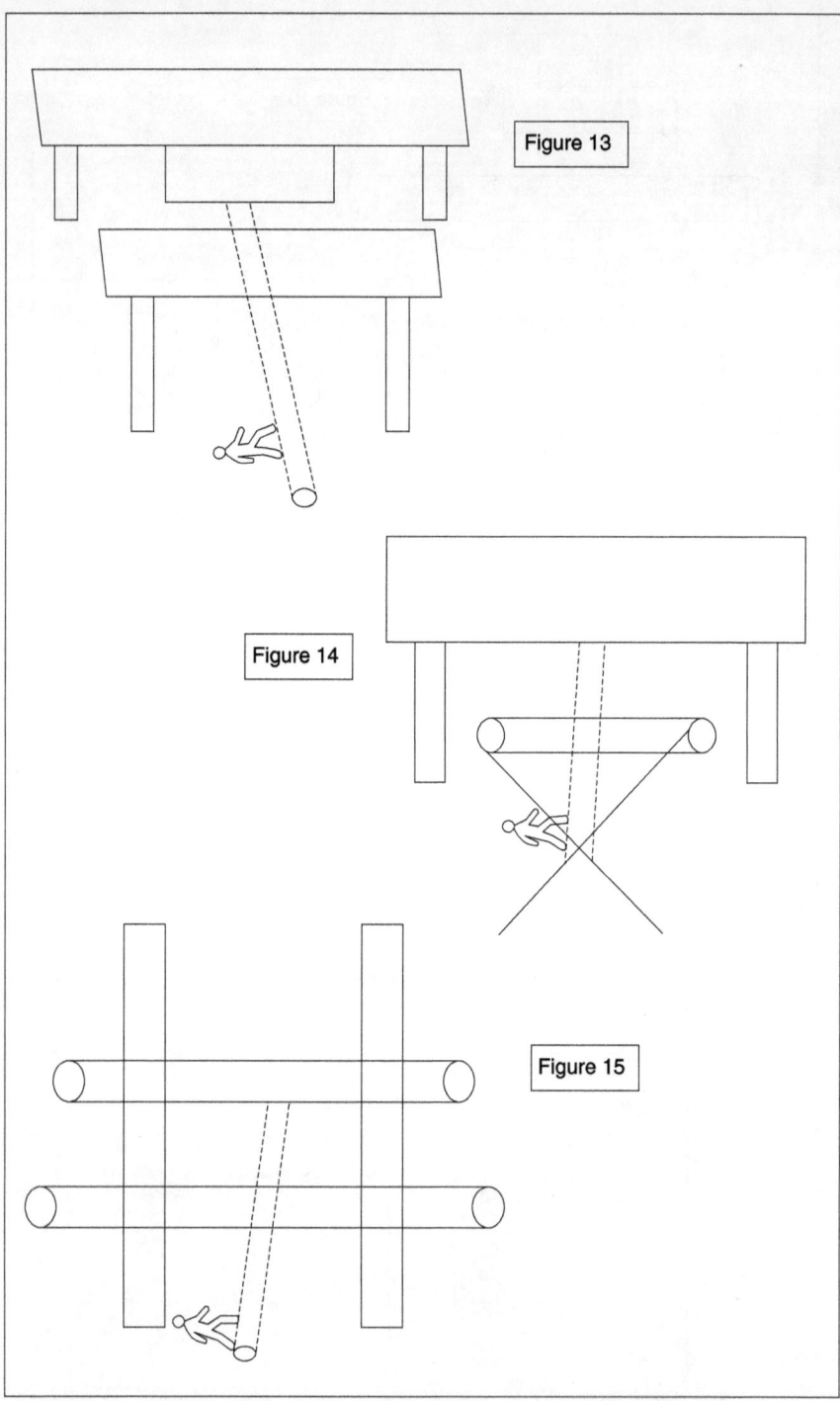

Cracking GTO Tasks/Tests 251

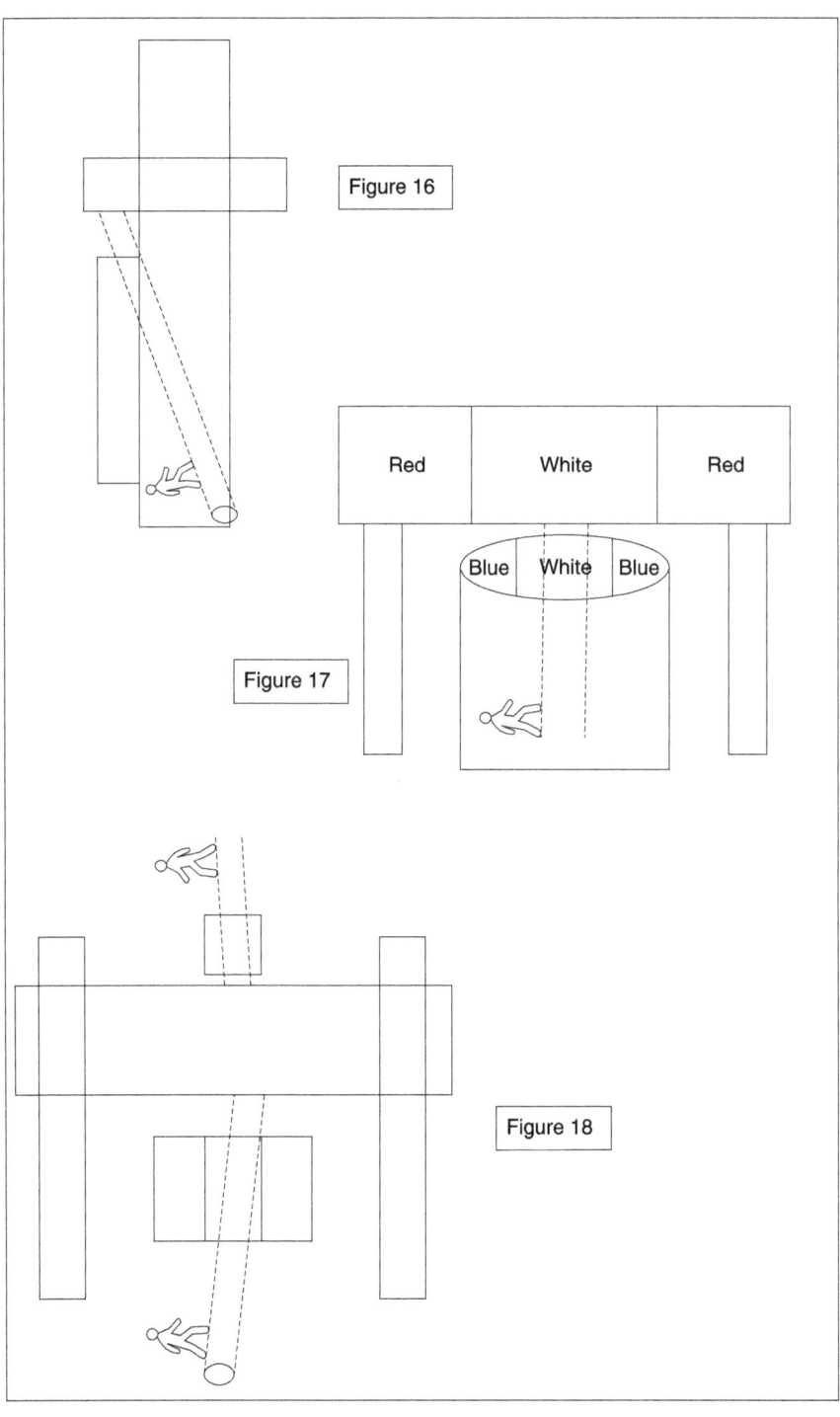

Figure 16

Figure 17

Figure 18

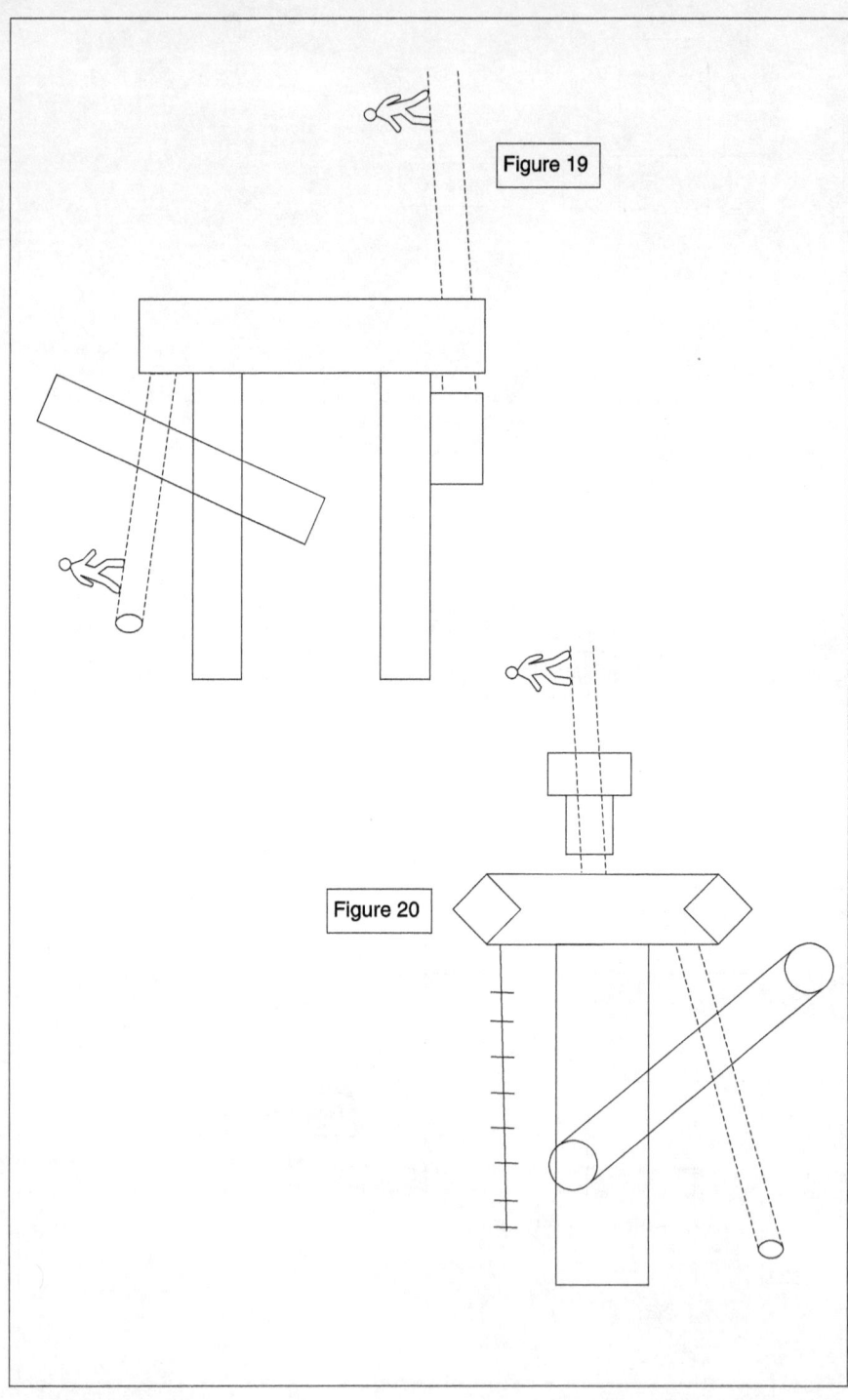

Cracking GTO Tasks / Tests

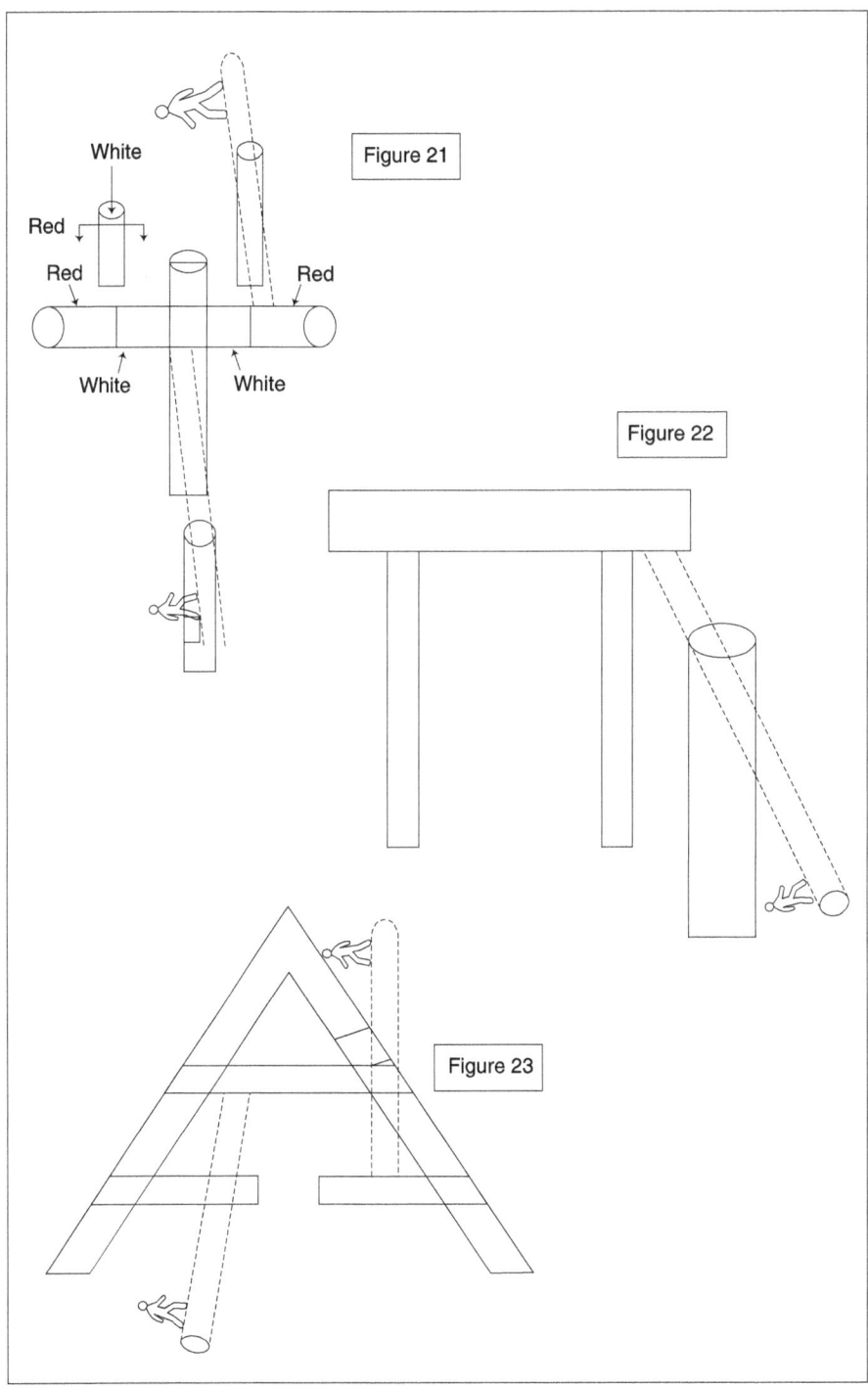

Figure 21

Figure 22

Figure 23

254 SSB Interviews

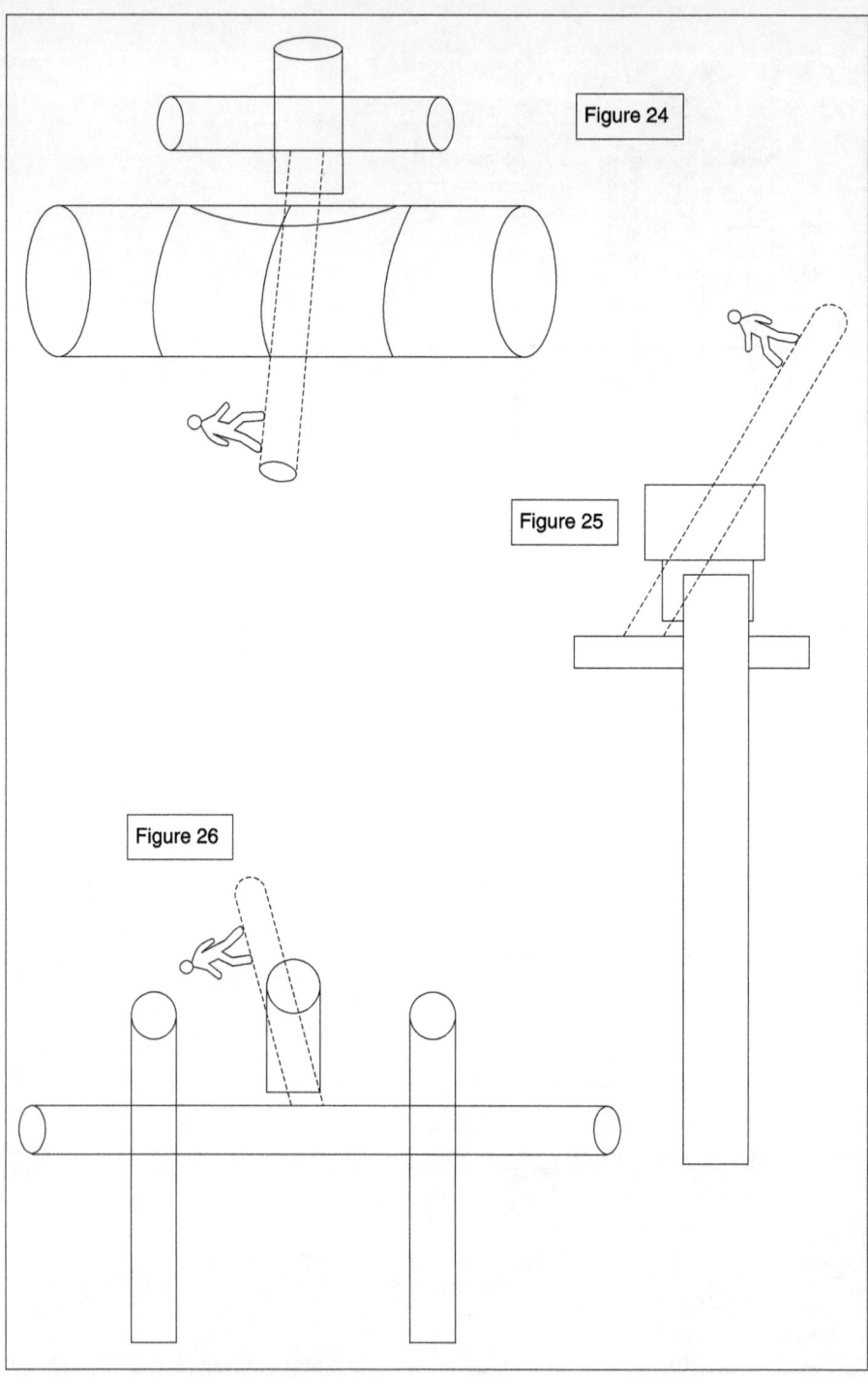

Figure 24

Figure 25

Figure 26

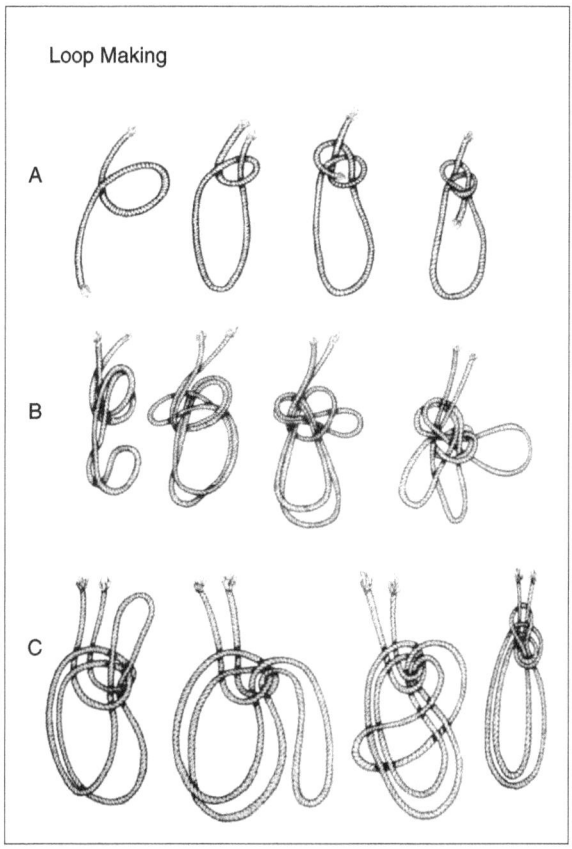

Loop Making

A

B

C

4. GROUP OBSTACLE RACE / SNAKE RACE

1. In this task your group will be competing against other groups over a set of six obstacles. These are Single Ramp, Figure 8, Spider Web, Double Wall, Double Slide, Single Wall.

Snake race or group obstacle race is held after the progressive group task. In this the group is given a material called as snake made up of thick jute cloth which usually has some weight. The snake is 6-8 feet in length.

Rules for Holding the Snake

The whole group has to hold the snake throughout the race. Also there is some exclusion such as while crossing the obstacle, minimum three candidates should hold the snake.

Also, if the group starts to hold the snake at hip region, then throughout the race it should hold the snake at hip region only. Else if the group starts to hold the snake on their shoulder at the starting then it should hold it on the shoulder only till the end of the race. (This rule varies from board to board).

The snake should never be kept or put down on the ground. The snake will follow the same course over the obstacles which the candidate takes.

There are also some out of bound areas in the obstacles such as: some region in the obstacle is painted with red colour. While doing the task the candidate should not touch the out of bound region.

Also the group should not move from one obstacle to another without leaving a single member of the group behind. The group should wait with the snake until all the candidates arrive to hold the snake.

War Cry

The GTO gives option to the candidates to choose a 'War cry'. A War cry is a short encourager quote used at the time of a goal oriented missions/ tasks.

E.g:- 'VANDE MATARAM', 'JAI HIND', 'BHARAT MATHA KI JAI' etc.

Expectation of the GTO from the candidate during a snaker race
1. The candidate should not violate the Rules.
2. He should help his team members.

3. He should give a helping hand for the weak to climb the high wall.
4. He should not worry about his white clothes getting muddy.
5. He should keep his group alone of him rather than putting himself first.
6. He should be able to keep an eye over every individual to ensure that they are not violating rules so that the group moves ahead without any minus marks.
7. Be a contributor whichever way possible.

Obstacles in Group Race or Snake Race:—
1. Spider web
2. Parallel big size iron pipe painted with white, red alternatively, the candidate has to cross it without touching the red lines and bend his body such that making the letter 'S'.
3. 10 feet wall.
4. Crossing parallel walls – In between these walls, a pipe is laid to cross.
5. In this task the obstacles are placed in a length of 200 metres.
6. These obstacles are divided into channels.
7. Your group will be running alone 1st/2nd/3rd or A/B/C channel.
8. In this task you will be carrying a long bundle resembling a snake. Therefore, the task is also called 'Snake Race'.
9. GTO will then tell you that whenever he got this task done, his group has always won the race. Today, also he wants you all to win the race.
10. He will then ask you loudly, "Are you going to win the race?", answer loudly "Yes Sir!"

   (See www.cavalierindia.com)

Rules of the Race

1. Once you pick up the snake, all of you must hold the snake as a team
2. Snake will remain straight and parallel to the ground while running from one obstacle to another.
3. Snake cannot be reduced in its length.
4. Snake will follow the same path which you all are required to go through.
5. Group rule is applicable.
6. Colour rule is applicable.
7. It may not be possible for all of you to hold the snake while crossing an obstacle; at this time minimum three of you are to hold the snake and rest can leave it.

Demonstration and Conduct

1. GTO will then take you around and show all the obstacles.
2. He will explain each obstacle and what is required to be done on that obstacle.
3. He will then show you the finish line and explain the procedure.
4. He will ask you to choose a war cry.
5. He will then ask you to run to start line, pick up the snake and get ready for the race.
6. Senior GTO will then blow the whistle and then give you a countdown ready, 3, 2, 1, GO.
7. The moment the race begins the senior GTO will take out a small sheet of paper, run along with you and start recording your performance. The other GTOs will carry out recordings of their respective groups accordingly.

What to Do?

8. Hold the snake as much as possible.
9. Help each other.
10. Remain very active
11. Remain ahead.
12. Leave an impression that but for your efforts your group would not have won the race.
13. Do not highlight minor injuries.
14. (For live demo visit www.cavalierindia.com or www.theexcel.com)
15. Motivate your group by being enthusiastic & lively.

5. HALF GROUP TASK

Introduction

This is a confirmatory test confirming the candidate's performance shown in PGT. In this test, the group is divided into two and each group is given one stage of obstacles of an average level. They are to follow the rules told to them earlier in PGT. So for the candidate it is very important to put up the best possible efforts and shoulder additional responsibilities as he is now under close observation.

The Half Group Tasks are conducted after the PGT since some of the candidates, even though had ideas to solve the PGT but were not able to express their ideas due to communication problem or shy nature. For this reason, the HGT is conducted.

Example

If there are 10 members, then the group may get divided into 5 members each. So in this situation the candidate is able to analyze different views to solve the task.

The rules and helping materials are same like PGT only. But the difference is the number of persons.

Example

Scenario about HGT

The obstacles are painted in three colours namely,

(a) White
(b) Green/Yellow/Blue
(c) Red

Each one describes one rule.

White: Both the candidate and the helping materials can touch the obstacle in this region.

Green/Yellow/Blue: Only the candidate can touch the obstacle in this region and not the helping materials.

Red: Both the candidate and helping material should not touch the obstacles.

As mentioned earlier in this book different SSBs will have different colour codes, therefore give proper attention when the GTO briefs you about the rules at the beginning.

Out of bound areas

The areas in the HGT which should not be touched are called as out of bound areas. These areas include the mud surfaces inside the task area and some colour codes as described above.

Briefing

1. Working in PGT some of you may have felt that you have the ideas but could not do the task in the exact manner in which you wanted to do it.

2. Keeping this in mind your group will be divided into two so that with lesser number of members in the group you may be able to do the task the way you wanted to do it.
3. The task is known as HGT.
4. A single stage task will be given to you.
5. Time will be ten minutes to do the task.
6. To keep the datum of selection, same task will be given to both the half groups.
7. GTO may ask you as to how should he divide the group – please remain quiet. If he asks you specifically, you may say 'As you wish, Sir'.
8. GTO will then divide the groups into two halves.
9. Take one group to the task area, brief them on the task and make them do the task.
10. Whereas, the other half group will be sent to waiting room, so that they cannot observe what method the first group is using to do the task, task being the same.
11. When the first half group finishes the task, they will be sent to waiting room and the waiting room group will be brought out, explained the task and will be made to do the task.

Note: You would have got enough ideas how to negotiate various structures while doing PGT. Keep those ideas in mind while doing HGT; however, structures will not be the same. Using all the helping materials in various combinations explained in this book will enable you to complete the task. The overall principle for negotiating the entire outdoor tasks remains the same.

6. LECTURETTE

Lecturette is the confirmatory test given to confirm the performance shown by the candidate during Group Discussion GTO tasks in this test. A Candidate gets a list of four topics and he has to select one out of those four and deliver a lecture on the chosen

topic in three minutes time. Candidate gets three minutes to prepare the topic. These four topics are of different level of difficulty. Some are simple while others difficult and demanding. So if the material is available on all the topics, go for the difficult topic because that will create a good impression.

Individual Lecturette or Extempore

In Defence life, an officer is to lead his men with good convincing power. Speaking is an art, and great people in history such as Adolf Hitler, John F. Kennedy ruled their region successfully because they were excellent orators. A lecture given by an officer in Service should give confidence to the team members, so that team members whole-heartedly and confidently follow the leader to complete a given task. Therefore it is also an important task in the GTO series. The duration, a candidate has to talk, is 3 minutes.

Expectation from Candidate in a Lecture

In the lecturette the GTO notices about the candidate's clarity of thought, power of expression, depth of knowledge, confidence level & mental stamina.

Rules of the Lecture

The candidates are instructed to sit in a semi-circle. The GTO will sit behind the candidates (i.e. behind the semi-circular arch).

(a) GTO will place a stack of cards in front of the candidates.

(b) The students are ordered to take one card from the bunch and given three minutes to prepare the topic.

(c) While the first chest number (in ascending order) is speaking, the next candidate is given time to prepare for his topic. (He is allowed to choose his card and topic).

(d) At the end of 2½ minutes out of 3 minutes, the GTO will give a warning bell for the candidate speaking to sum up his points.

(e) Also the bell is an indication to the 'preparing candidate' to muster his points since time is less.

Points to note during lecturette

The important aspects to note while giving a lecture are Body Language and delivery of the topic to the audience.

Body Language

- Keep hands behind – this helps to avoid unwanted mannerisms through hands.
- Look at the audience, and not the GTO.
- Smile naturally and don't make fake one, else, better give the lecture normally.

- Don't shake legs while speaking; also donot stand in a stiff manner. Be at ease and remain cool.

How to choose the Topic for Lecturette

There will be four topics in the lecture card of varying levels of difficulty. One will be a tough topic, the next two of average level, and the last will be a very easy one. If you choose a topic you should be able to sum up your points within those three minutes. Select the topic based on the depth of knowledge that you have about the topic.

Delivering the Lecture

The time given is of three minutes, divided as follows

Intimation of the topic – First 30 seconds.

Getting into the topic – 2 minutes.

Conclusion of the topic (summing up the points) – last 30 seconds.

Preparation for Individual Lecture

No extra preparation is needed for a lecture if one prepares well for the GD as stated earlier. Choose any topic and try to give valuable points with pros and cons in a short period of time (3 minutes). Also stand before a mirror and practice to avoid stammering while speaking.

The lecture should be divided into three parts:

(a) *Introduction* – Here introduce the topic, explain and define it as "Respected GTO sir and friends. I have selected _____ topic for my lecturette."

(b) *Body* – Go in detail and depth, give factual information. Avoid repetition. Include references and examples.

(c) *Conclusion* – Conclude the topic somewhere between the Ist & 2nd bell ring. Avoid abrupt ending. Close the topic in the way it is being built up. You must speak for full 3 minutes and not less.

Conduct of the lecturette

(a) Candidates are seated in a line or a hollow square in front of an unoccupied chair or a lecture stand.

(b) Candidates are seated in sequence and will be called in sequence.

(c) GTO is seated close behind with the cards and a bell.

(d) When called, first candidate will walk up, go to GTO, take up a card, and go away for preparation.

(e) When 2½ minutes are over a single bell be indicated by GTO. Hearing this bell No. 2 candidate gets up, reports to the GTO, picks up a card and goes for preparation.

(f) On hearing the bell, No. 1 candidate will report back to the GTO, returns the card, indicates the chosen subject, proceed to the lecture stand and commences his talk.

(g) When 2½ minutes are over, the GTO will give another single bell at which No.3 candidate will go for the card, No. 2 will return the card to the GTO and No.1 made to realize that he has 30 seconds left to conclude his talk.

(h) When 3 minutes are over GTO will ring two bells, at which No. 1 will sit settle down.

(i) In case candidate finishes talking in less than 3 minutes he may sit down. The next candidate will get his full 3 minutes' preparation time.

(j) During the first candidate's preparation time GTO may ask the other candidates to come upto the lecture stand and introduce themselves one by one.

How to prepare?

- Read topics carefully.
- Select the topic on which you can speak for 3 minutes. Cover the topic with respect to the points 1 to 6 highlighted below:

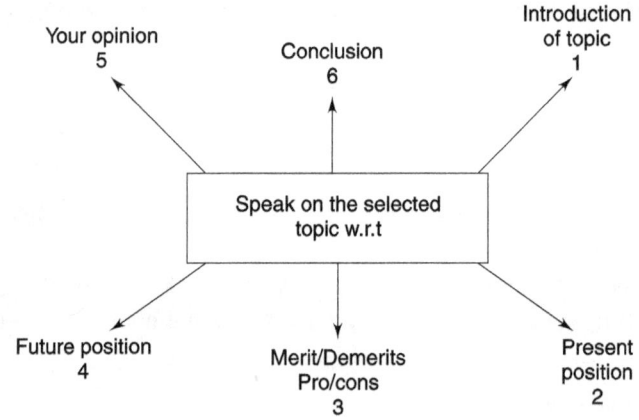

- Collect your thoughts on the topic.
- Structure them in a sequence.

Speak with confidence

(a) Stand smartly
(b) Face the group squarely
(c) Speak in a loud and clear voice
(d) Speak with confidence on the subject,

(e) Control stress, anxiety or tension: Take a deep breath, balance on both feet and keep eye contact with the audience.

SAMPLES OF LECTURETTE TOPICS

Women in Indian Armed Forces

In the modern world, there is no domain of work that women haven't delved into. Words such as chairman and cameraman have been rephrased as chairperson and cameraperson, to accommodate women. Many a male dominated work place has crumbled under the power of woman – her indomitable spirit and energy. The Indian Armed Forces, which for long was considered a male dominated workplace, now has confident, bold women, moulding into every role and setting examples for everyone. Lieutenant General Puneeta Arora, a lady officer from the Army Medical Corps, headed the prestigious Defense institution, the Armed Forces Medical College (AFMC), in Pune. In the land of Razia Sultana and Rani of Jhansi, it comes as no surprise that women make their mark in the Armed Forces.

The role of women in the armed forces for a long time was limited to the medical profession i.e. doctors and nurses. In 1992, the doors were thrown open for women entry as regular officers in aviation, logistics, law, engineering and executive cadres. Thousands of spirited young women applied against advertisements and it was a turning point in the history of time. These women chose a new field where they had to painstakingly pave a path for others to follow.

The initial adjustment problems weren't as much for the women as it was for the men. Wrapped in their tradition of chivalry and respect to women, most gentlemen officers could not treat their female counterparts at par with themselves. Their subordinates too, were men who came from conservative families where they saw women playing only traditional roles. The emergence of these women into totally male dominated bastions did initially create embarrassing moments for both. Men hushed their talks and behaved courteously, while women had to do with makeshift arrangements to suit their needs within units. Over the years and having come a long way now, men have realized that these women in uniform are their efficient and able co-workers. The time is not far when we may use the term 'sisters-in-arms' as equivalent to 'brothers-in-arms'.

Currently, women in the non-medical cadre serve as Short Service Commissioned (SSC) officers. Under this commission, they can serve in the armed forces for a period ranging from 5-14 years. On release they can pursue a career in the civil sector. SSC officers are released with gratuity and can avail some benefits as ex-serviceperson, but they do not get pension. Women in the medical branch i.e. doctors and nurses can serve as Permanent Commissioned (PC) officers and are eligible for pension after retirement. They also have the option to serve as Short Service Commissioned officers.

Eligible women, who qualify various tests successfully, serve as Short Service Commissioned officers in the following branches of the Armed Forces.

ARMY: EME, Signals, Engineers, Army Education Corps, Army Ordnance Corps, Army Service Corps, Intelligence corps and the Judge Advocate General's branch. (JAG)

NAVY: All branches of the Navy (except strips, submariners and divers).

AIR FORCE: Flying (transport aircraft and helicopters), Technical and Administration branches.

COAST GUARD: All branches of the Coast Guard.

TERRITORAL ARMY (TA) Medical branch only

Women Officers in Defence Forces

(a) ARMY	(b) NAVY	(c) AIR FORCE
4% (1300)	5% (358)	8-10% (1300)

In the modern day of electronic warfare, it's more about overcoming stress in warfare than physical combat. It has been proven scientifically that women handle stress better and are also mentally tougher. This is not to undermine a woman's physical capability. Women have done extremely well in physical training as well. In the first few batches at the armed forces training academies women displayed more endurance and some even outran their male counterparts in cross-country runs and long distance marches. They carry on this tradition and keep setting new records.

As Commissioned officers at the age of 22-23 years, they may often have subordinates older than their parents. Hence, from day one, it is a challenge and leadership qualities are under test. The colour of their crisp uniforms and the stars/stripes they adorn differentiate them from each other. Despite the good quality of life, they may sometimes undergo hardships due to the nature of work. An officer may have to work in tough terrains or difficult circumstances. Most women however, who undergo training as cadets in various military academies, cope up with various difficult situations, easily. Being a transferable job, transfers and movements are seen as unique opportunities to travel to remotest locations in the country. Every unit is a mini-India with people and cultures as diverse.

As most lady officers are married to gentlemen officers in the armed forces, as per government policies, they are transferred together. Women officers can also avail of maternity leave; furlough and annual leave in succession, to cater to pre- and post-natal care. On retirement too, they enjoy medical facilities and coveted club memberships. They can afford to maintain the same quality of life due to the various benefits they can avail of. Their experience and qualities imbibed while in service make them much in demand in the private sector. Although the path these women have chosen is tough, they have proved that they have the spirit, the courage and the will to carry on. Presently, women do not serve in combat arms nor do they fly fighter aircrafts, but it won't be long before these forbidden avenues are thrown open to them.

Types of Commission for Women

	Permanent Commission	Short Service Commission
ARMY	Education, Medical & Law(JAG)	Only in SERVICES (Supply, Ordnance, Engineers, Signals & AAD)
NAVY	Medical & Law(JAG)	Only in SHORE DUTY
		ATC
		Logistics
		Engineering
		Electrical
		Architecture
		Education
IAF	Medical, Law & Education	Tpt A/C
		Helicopter
		Admin
		Logistics
		Accounts/Meteorology

India and CTBT

Peaceful relations with neighbours, freedom from colonialism, racial equality and non-alignment with nuclear powers were the main objectives of the foreign policy of Independent India. India preferred to keep away from the power politics of groups which had led to two world wars in the past, Proliferation and a total ban on nuclear arsenal, way back in 1954. But in the sixties, India's relations with the neighbouring countries strained and the need to review India's foreign policy was felt.

With a view to strengthen the country by enhancing its defence arsenal, because of its strategic location, India declined to sign the NPT in spite of its opposition to nuclear proliferation. India held the treaty discriminatory because it was binding on only NNWS (Non Nuclear Weapon States) while the NWS (Nuclear Weapon States) were permitted to retain their nuclear arsenal with a mere mention of disarmament in phased manner which did not take place anywhere even till today. However, this treaty has been signed by all the UN member countries except India, Pakistan and Israel. Accordingly, IAEA came into effect to ensure safeguards and verifications of all peaceful purposes initiated by NNWS.

In May 1974, India conducted its first nuclear test at Pokhran, in Rajasthan to generate power for peaceful purposes. At the NPT review conferences held in 1975, 1980, 1985, 1990, India was asked to sign but India emphasized its concern for a nuclear free world at the UN General Assembly, The UN Security Council and the IAEA. Last review conference was held in 1995, the permanent and indefinite extension of the NPT was signed and allowed all the NWS – USA, France, Britain, Russia and China – to retain their nuclear arsenal by giving the logic of balance the world.

After the NPT was signed, the NWS were pushing towards Comprehensive Test Ban Treaty (CTBT) and as the delegates of 61 countries gathered for the final stage negotiations on the CTBT in Geneva on July 29, 1996, China conducted a nuclear test. The west believed that then CTBT would sustain the viability of NPT and will be a step towards nuclear disarmament. India opposed it, held it biased and asked the NWS to accept a time bound programme of nuclear disarmament. Despite that it was approved on September 10, 1996 by 158 votes to three with five abstained. India, Bhutan and Libya went against the treaty. With its strategic frontiers and a vulnerable sea coast, India could not surrender its sovereignty and freedom. China had already acquired the status of NWS and was openly assisting Pakistan with its nuclear programme. The overall security imperative in the Indian sub continent was totally overlooked by the NWS.

In May 1998, India successfully conducted five nuclear tests at the same venue, Pokhran. These tests were of paramount importance to the national security, which was under threat, because of nuclear imbalance in the region. India reiterated its stand that the tests were conducted for peaceful purposes and it is not intended to mount threats to any country. The tests were intended to act as a deterrent to our neighbours who were openly expanding their nuclear arsenals. Many countries condemned the tests. Pakistan responded by conducting its own tests which proved its nuclear capability.

Now question arises, "Should India sign the CTBT"? The CTBT in its present form would neither eliminate nuclear weapons nor reduce the nuclear arms proliferation. It also does not prevent the NWS from transferring ready to use weapons to their non-nuclear friends and allies. Imposing a test ban, without a corresponding check on nuclear proliferation can swing the strategic and military balance in favour of China and towards Pakistan as a direct implication. So, India's decision in refusing to sign the treaty in its present form is very much justified and is being supported by all the political parties as well as the public because it is a question of Nation's security and integrity.

Internet – The Super Highway of Information

What is Internet
Internet is inter connection between several types of computers belonging to various networks all over the globe. It is an information super highway that has compressed the world into one cyber colony. It is an ocean of information that can be accessed by various people across the globe any time.

Birth of Internet
In 1969, the Department of Defence of US started a network called the ARPA net (Advanced Research Projects Administration network). This network was set up by the military to ensure that the communication did not break down in the event of war. The Department of Defence (DOD) wanted to maintain contacts with the military research contractors and universities doing military funding research. DOD also wanted these agencies to share software and hardware resources that they could not afford. Later, the military allowed other universities to join the network ARPA.

Services Provided by Internet
Internet throws open a World Wide Web market and helps us in making Electronic Commerce and Online shopping. It provides a powerful platform to do the business. Website technology gives information and reach without boundaries and time. From last few decades, ways of accessing information are growing rapidly. Internet is proving to be a major link between people across the world. There are essential services which we are getting through internet.

Every coin has two sides, in the same way some vulgar websites are also there on internet yet we should avoid the negative side of the coin. The internet provides us global reach and access and can definitely be defined as a boon of science.

Indian Missile Program
- With potential threats from Pakistan & China and importance of military power in mind, Integrated Missile Development Program was conceived under the stewardship of Professor A.P.J. Abdul Kalam in 1983. Since then India has developed its own Ballistic as well as Cruise Missiles and Interim Testing Range (ITR, Chandipur, Orissa).
- The Agni Missile System is a series of three Intermediate-Range Ballistic Missile (IRBM) ranging between 700 – 3500 km.
- The Prithvi Missile System is also a series of three Short-Range Ballistic Missile (SRBM) ranging between 150-350km.
- With the help of Russia, India has also developed Brahmos, which is a supersonic cruise missile.
- Akash is a medium range Surface to Air Missile (SAM) ranging 25 km.

- Nag is an Anti-Tank Guided Missile (ATGM) undergoing user trials.
- Trishul is a short range Surface to Air Missile (SAM) ranging 5-9 km.
- There is a large scope of improvement in specialized missiles. As long as India progresses in this direction, pressure will go on mounting. Therefore, a balanced strategy will be needed so that economic interests are taken care.

Global Warming

A rise in global temperature causes other changes like rise in sea level which could mean inundation of low lying coastal belts, and could even lead to many of the smaller islands being totally submerged. Global warming is also said to have contributed to more frequent incidence of extreme weather events like flood, heat waves, droughts, hurricanes and so on.

A majority of greenhouse gases are emitted from fuel combustion, power stations, industrial process and transportation etc.

It is now officially accepted that human activities are the major reason for global warming as opposed to some earlier arguments that the warming was part of natural process and due to non-human causes like solar activities, volcanic emission and so on.

Kyoto Protocol

It has been suggested that countries ought to adopt strategies to mitigate global warming such as energy conservation, shifting to renewable energy rather than carbon fuels. It is the result of such concern that the Kyoto Protocol was drawn up. The protocol is an agreement made under the United Nation Framework Convention of Climate Change (UNFCC). Countries that ratified the protocol are bound to make effort to reduce their emission of greenhouse gases.

The protocol was drawn up in Dec. 1997 and came into force in Feb. 2005 after Russia ratified the protocol in Nov. 2004. By Dec. 2006, 169 countries responsible for 61.6% of emission had ratified the protocol.

The bulk of global emission of greenhouse gases both current and historical comes from the developed world. In developing countries per capita emission is still rather low, hence developing countries have argued that there should be no cap on their emission level because of social and developmental needs. By this logic India and China have been exempted from restrictions. But in developing countries China, which is second to the US in emission, is expected to overtake the US very soon. The biggest polluter, US, has yet to ratify the protocol; Australia too has refused to ratify the protocol. However the European countries that account for 22% of global greenhouse gases emission have ratified the protocol and have agreed to cut emission by an average 8% from 1090 emission level. India too ratified the protocol in Aug. 2002. The protocol exempted India from emission among the world. Kyoto protocol expired in 2012.

Brain Drain

Brain Drain is the loss to a country when skilled and clever people leave their country and work in other countries. It is the depletion of intellectual or professional resources of the country through emigration. Brain Drain is a common problem in developing countries. The problem is more acute in India.

According to the United Nations Report, thousands of professionals and scientists migrate from under developed countries to high developed countries like UK, USA, Japan and European countries. They utilize their skills and serve the new country. This is a direct loss to the native country who trains them at great cost and then loses them to the other countries.

There are number of factors responsible for brain drain in India. Firstly, India lacks job opportunities after completion of professional courses and training. They do not get proper employment in India. The developed countries offer job opportunities with attractive salaries. Secondly, there are no adequate lab facilities required for research. Advanced countries offer attractive lab facilities. They offer a high standard of living as well as high wages. Thirdly, we do not recognize or reward talent in our people. India has vast natural resources like oil, gas, coal ore, minerals, precious stones, etc. These resources have to be fully developed for use. These resources get neglected as there are only few experts in India. In this way brain drain is a big hindrance to India's technological development. India should frame a national policy to prevent brain drain. It should create employment opportunities. It should also arrange well equipped lab facilities. It should offer scope to non-resident Indians so that they return to their motherland and work for its prosperity and advancement. In no time India would become a developed country by 2020.

India's Population Explosion

The current rate of population growth in India is 1.58% and the total fertility rate is 3.11. Although the total fertility rate has decreased, due to the increase in the total number of women between the ages of 15 and 44 (reproductive ages), the total number of births has increased. This has led to the current enormous population size of approximately 125 crores. This has greatly hampered the development of the Indian economy. The amount of resources that could have been available to one person a few years ago now need to be shared between two people, which is not sufficient for either of them. The population increase has led to air and water pollution, unemployment, poverty, lack of educational resources, and even malnourished women and children.

Unemployment and Illiteracy

Suppose we forget about the environment, and only worry about ourselves. Nonetheless, with the increasing population, even that is not possible because with the increasing number of people, we have to share our resources with even more people. Resources of all types are limited, even employment, especially in India.

India, being a developing country, has a limited number of jobs available. Due to the increasing number of people, the competition for the most menial jobs is also tremendous. With the increasing population, unemployment rates are bound to rise even further. Several highly educated people with Bachelors and Masters degrees in India sit at home, because they cannot find jobs. This is the major reason for Indians to migrate to developed countries like the US.

Such unemployment and under-employment leads to corruption and exploitation of people by the richer classes of the society. This lack of resources further leads to lack of educational resources. Due to the non-availability of resources, parents cannot afford to educate their children to higher levels. Some parents simply cannot afford to teach their children further, and in some families, children need to work along with their parents in order to bring food to the table. Also, basic education has become a commodity that acts on the basis of supply and demand.

Basic education has become too expensive in India for a commoner to afford for his/her children. Lack of education further leads to even more unemployment. Due to these reasons, a major part of the population is either illiterate or has the most minimum education leading them to accept minimal work in which they cannot even support themselves.

Unemployment, or underemployment, further leads to poverty. This again starts the vicious cycle of poverty and population explosion discussed above. Poverty leads to an increase in the population, because poverty leads people to produce more children to increase the earning members of the family. This increases the population size of India, which further increases the unemployment rate and lack of educational facilities leading to poverty that started this whole cycle.

Food Resources

Resources are always limited. And in a developing and highly populous country like India, resources are even scarcer. Population explosion results in the shortage of even the most basic resources like food. According to an article by World Bank Group, more than half of all children under the age of four are malnourished, 30 percent of newborns are significantly underweight, and 60 percent of women are anemic. Resources are limited everywhere. Survival of the fittest finds its true meaning on the streets of the urban cities of India. Something like food that most of us consider as a basic necessity, is a privilege for most of the children of India who are homeless because their parents cannot give them the basic necessities of life.

Problems with implementing measures to control population: The success of family planning greatly depends on women and their status. Thus, it is imperative for the women to be educated so that they can decide on the number of children they want and be aware of the available birth control measures. Also, in a country like India, it is important for the women to have equal rights in the decision about the number of children to be produced. Women also need to get educated about the impacts of having so many children on their own bodies and the impacts on their children. In addition, not only the young ones, but also the older women need to be educated so that they can teach the right family planning to their own daughters. However, in India, almost no importance is given to the education of women because of the financial conditions in some families and the religious and social norms in some. In such a case, educating women about family planning becomes an even more difficult task.

In India, most of the population lives in the rural areas. However, family planning is not widely advertised in rural areas. Also, in rural areas, social and religious norms are more strictly followed. As a result, all the above-mentioned problems are even more intense in rural areas with the addition of the lack of family planning facilities in those areas. Family planning is considered a sin in most of the tribal and rural communities.

Rising Intolerance in India

India as a nation has had its instances of religious intolerance for as long as it has existed as a historic and political entity. Right from the Direct Action Day that turned Calcutta into a stage of bloodbath and gore before the Independence, Indira Gandhi being murdered by her own bodyguards for religious reasons and the resultant backlash that Sikhs suffered afterwards, the Bombay Riots of 1993, the Godhra genocide of 2001 to the recent events at Muzaffarnagar, there are instances aplenty where India's secular identity has been faced with embarrassing questions. The situation has only been aggravated by the recent gunning down of rationalist and Kannada writer M.M. Kalburgi and lynching of a man in Dadri for allegedly consuming beef, preceded by the governments of Maharashtra and Gujarat banning consumption of beef.

Speaking on the matter, noted economist Bibek Debroy reasoned that such levels of intolerance have always existed and it would be foolish on our parts if we do not acknowledge it. He believes that if quantitative parameters like communal violence, religious intolerance, caste and gender discrimination, freedom of expression and the like are taken into consideration, it will become clear that such instances have been prevalent. It is not on the rise now, but has always been an intrinsic part of the intellectual circuit.

Looking back, ever since CPI leader Govind Pansare was shot in February 2015 for his autobiography on Shivaji titled "Shivaji Kaun Hota", there has been latent discontent among the thinking population of the nation. When Kalburgi, who is known for his progressive ideas on caste and communalism was shot in August, the intellectuals retaliated to growing intolerance and rise of unwarranted fringe religious groups by returning their awards.

Some of the prominent names in this regard have been literary figures like Uday Prakash, Nayantara Sahgal, C.R. Prasad, K.S. Ravikumar, E.V. Ramakrishnan, Surjit Patar, Baldev Singh Sadaknama, Hardev Chauhan, Rajesh Joshi, Manglesh Dabral, Ghulam Nabi Khayal, and G.N. Ranganatha Rao, poets Mandakranta Sen, Darshan

Buttar, and Jaswinder, and a famed translator named Chaman Lal. They have been joined by Maya Rao, a noted danseuse and theatre performer, Bengali actor Sudipta Chakraborty, and nationally-reputed filmmaker Dibakar Banerjee. They have also been supported by Shabana Azmi.

All of them have cited the issue of growing intolerance – as well as restrictions being imposed on freedom of expression – as the main reason for such actions. Author and activist Arundhati Roy feels that these nuances of violence are an attack on the 'collective IQ' of the people and one needs to stand up to it. Shah Rukh Khan, too, is of a similar opinion which has given a new dimension to this intellectual movement.

However, it would be wrong to assume that the creative figures met with no opposition from the members of their own fraternity. Celebrated musician Zubin Mehta openly stated that he does not understand the logic behind all the artists returning their awards. Vidya Balan, and interestingly enough Shah Rukh Khan as well, said that they will not be returning their awards. However, the most pertinent criticism has come from Kamal Haasan, who has found the gesture to be pointless, and has said that it is insulting the government and the people who have conferred the honour on them. He has asked them – whom he has termed talented and capable – to keep their national awards and instead fight against the intolerance of the government.

The varying opinion

The debate on intolerance has been taken over by many personalities. Recently veteran actress Shabana Azmi expressed her support to those who are raising their voice against rising intolerance in the country. A debate brewed up when actor Aamir Khan said that his wife Kiran Rao wishes for the family and children to leave the country due to increasing intolerance. Many people have lent him support for his statement while the other lot has criticised him for his remark.

The debate

The main question that needs to be asked in this context is that is it right to return the awards. Before we come to the answer, it needs to be taken into consideration that India has seen more gruesome instances of violation of communal harmony time and again in its history. What makes the recent spate of incidents so different? Is it the fact that certain states are banning consumption of beef? In that case it needs to be taken into consideration that Gujarat – one of the two states to have banned consumption of beef – also bans alcohol consumption. Do the incidents at the Pune Film and Television Institute have anything to do with all this?

The next issue that we need to consider is why the protests are happening now, or are they being unnecessarily highlighted now!? Among the people returning the awards some had been conferred with the honour when the previous NDA was in power. What has changed in the past few years that has led them to take such a drastic step? Is it an expression of no confidence in Modi during whose term as a Chief Minister the Godhra Riots had taken place?

It needs to be remembered that in his own way the PM is attempting to set things right by way of programmes such as Make in India and financial facilities for the rural poor. Can these attempts be viewed as efforts to undermine that and be interpreted as an effort to hark back to his less-than-palatable past? Is it an attempt to build up public consensus against a political force which they perceive to be growing in influence with every passing day, or is this an attempt to garner some publicity and relevance as has been alleged by the administrations and its faithful? The main question is: Will these gestures just be limited to being symbolic ones or go ahead and change the attitude of people who bring shame time and again to the country with their irresponsible and reckless behaviour?

Important Lecturette Topics, Candidates should prepare in advance

Human Rights Violation	Natural Resources
Traditions V/s Modernity	Alternative Medicine
Coalition Government	Reservations
Peaceful Uses Of Atomic Energy	Youth In Nation Building
Information Technology	Ocean Wealth
Scams & Scandals	Indian Space Programme
Make In India	Population Explosion
Biodegradable Materials	Censorship Of Media
Mobile Phone Revolution	Space Exploration
Medical Tourism	Film Festivals
Nuclear Family V/s Joint Family	Bureaucracy In India
Non Resident Indian	Traffic Management
Interlinking Of Rivers	Godman Or Fraudman
Internet	Importance Of Monsoons in India
UN Peace Keeping Force	Software Piracy
Doping In Sports & Games	Indian Railways
Family Planning	Human Rights Violation
Pollution	India's Internal Security
Look Before You Leap	Fundamental Rights
Indo-US Relations	Global Warming
Indian Cinema	Yoga & Meditation
Centre State Relations	Cyber Crime
Corruption	Alternative Source Of Energy
My Most Interesting Experience In Life	English As Medium Of Education
Unity In Diversity	India's Nuclear Developement
Sino Indian Relation	Criminalisation Of Politics
Rapid Mass Transportation System	The Most Interesting Book I Read

Panchayati Raj	Natural Calamities
Knowledge Is Power	Special Economic Zones
Energy Scene In India	Role Of Media In National Development
Green Revolution	Drug Addiction
Luxury Goods	India's Economic Status
My Favourite Hero	Festival Is National Waste
Unipolar World	Empowerment Of Women
Superstitions	Sports In India
Dowry System	Old Age Homes
Financial Institutions In India	Advertisements
Is UNO Redundant?	Is Generation Gap Widening
Reservation for Women	Computers In Everyday Life
Increase In Crime Rate	Necessity Is The Mother Of Invention
Right To Information Act	Small Scale Industry
Disaster Management	Child Labour
Distance Education	Consumer Courts
Military As Career Option	National Cadet Corps
Women Empowerment	Experience Is The Best School
Health & Hygiene	Centre State Relations
India's Foreign Policy	Sportsmanship
Multinational Corporation	Deforrestation
Judiciary In India	Whistle Blowers
Vigilance Commission	Cross Border Smuggling
Election Commission In India	An Interesting Experience
Teaching Profession	Swachh Bharat
Social Security	Privatisation Of Railways
Sports Authority Of India	Social Media
Inflation	Conservation Of Natural Resources
Tourism In India	Reserve Bank Of India

The above topics are extremely useful to deal with GD and interview questions related to current affairs. One can get enough information about these topics from Google and TED Talks, current affairs magazines, Radio/TV and Newspapers.

7. INDIVIDUAL OBSTACLES

The individual obstacles follow the HGT. The aim of the individual obstacles is to assess the candidates' stamina level, endurance, boldness, courage and several others factors under the OLQ list.

Cracking GTO Tasks/Tests

There are several obstacles with different difficulty level, each allocated with marks. The number painted near the obstacles denotes the marks allocated for the obstacles.

The total number of obstacles is 10 and the time limit to cross these obstacles is 3 minutes. Total marks are 55.

i.e. $1 + 2 + 3 + 4 + 5 + 6 + 7 + 8 + 9 + 10 = 55$

The obstacle with highest level of difficulty scores the maximum of 10. Also the obstacle with lowest level of difficulty scores a minimum of 1.

Explanation by GTO and Scenario of Individual Obstacles

In this the GTO takes his group of candidates to all the obstacles and tells the rules to be followed in each one. By this time the candidate should think from his mind, i.e. which task should be done first to last, based on their location and their difficulty level. Also don't violate the rules in the individual obstacles; (in case you violate just repeat the task.)

Candidates are advised to sit on a bench and not to face the individual obstacle on the ground.

Rules for Individual Obstacles

The GTO calls the first candidate (based on chest numbers) and instructs him to get ready for the task. When he blows the whistle the first candidate starts the task. At 2½ minutes out of his 3 minutes, he gives a short whistle which is a sign for the candidate doing the obstacle that his time is going to end, also for the next person to come and stand ready for the task. If you complete all the ten obstacles within the time (3 minutes), you are allowed to re-do the process, but you are not allowed to repeat the same, individual tasks again.

Types of Obstacles

(a) Commando walk
(b) Double ditch jump
(c) Tarzan swing
(d) Balanced walk
(e) Jumping over drums winded with barbed wires
(f) Step by step jump
(g) Jumping over the screen (high jump)
(h) Burma bridge
(i) Hang by the rope after jumping off the ladder
(j) Rope climbing

Commando walk

Commando walk is to walk on a lean wooden block which will be at a height of over 10 ft. (See the picture for clarification). You have to walk on this by shouting out a favourite name or any War cry (based on GTO's advice). Usually the plank shakes when you start to walk over it; if you walk with patience and concentration then you can easily complete the task.

Double ditch jump

Double ditch jump is where you have to run fast and hang on to the rope tightly to cross the first ditch which is 6 ft long and land on the ground; after that you should leave the rope and cross another ditch by jumping over 4 ft in length.

For more clarifications and pictures visit www.cavalierindia.com or www.theexcel.com.

Tarzan swing

The candidate should go to some height (8 to 10 ft) with the help of a ladder. Then the helpers will give the rope to him and he should swing from the height to the soft ground (sand). There is one red line and the candidate should not land his body within that red line while swinging from that height. See the picture for clarification. Visit www.theexcel.com or www.cavalierindia.com

Balanced walk

Balanced walk is on two planks which look shiny with varnish having little wooden scrapings for grip. This looks like a zigzag structure. The candidates should cross over this without touching his leg on the ground. See pictures and live demo at www.cavalierindia.com to get a clear idea how it is done.

Jumping over drum winded with barbed wires

This consists of a red painted horizontal drum which is usually 6 ft in length for boys and 3 ft in length for ladies. A candidate has to run and jump over this drum without touching it. The surface of the drum is usually covered with a limbed. See website for clarification.

Step by step jump

This is a platform at a height of nearly 8 feet. A candidate has to climb to the platform with the help of a ladder and jump to another platform which is at a height of 4 feet. After this he should jump on to a soft surface (sand). (See the website for clarification.)

Jumping over a Screen (high jump)

This looks difficult but do not get tense. A Screen over a stand is placed, and the candidate has to run on the inclined plank and jump over without touching the screen. (See picture for clarification).

Burma bridge

The Burma bridge and rope climbing is used in various selection processes. These are parallel ropes tied between two iron pillars. A candidate has to climb up on a ladder to reach the top of the bridge. The best thing is don't look down while crossing, concentrate and cross the bridge by holding on to the ropes with both hands. (See www.cavalierindia.com for clarification).

Hanging by the rope after jumping from the ladder

This is similar to the Tarzan swing, but the difference is that in Tarzan swing after reaching the platform by climbing the ladder, the helper will give the rope to swing. Here, we have to climb up the ladder to reach the platform and jump over (3-4 ft) to hold the rope and then climb down. (See the picture for clarification.)

Rope climbing

This is the usual Rope Climbing. We have to climb up a thick rope and then get down. See the website for more clarification www.cavalierindia.com.

Cracking GTO Tasks/Tests   285

NB: Visit the websites www.cavalierindia.com and www.theexcel.com to view live demo of crossing all the obstacles. Spending some time visiting these sites will go a long way in your preparations. You can see all the structures as seen at the SSB.

Briefing

- An individual obstacle test consists of a set of 10 obstacles which a candidate is required to cross in 3 minutes.
- These obstacles are placed in an area of 50 metres by 75 metres.
- These obstacles are numbered 1 to 10 and carry the same number of marks as the obstacle number as indicated.
- These obstacles are not placed in any sequential order. Therefore, you can do this in any sequence you wish to do.
- This is the only task in which you can score more than 100% marks. That means repeating of obstacles is permitted. However, the rule for repeating is that you should have completed all 10 obstacles successfully once before you repeat any obstacle.
- Whatever obstacle you repeat extra marks will be given.
- If you do all the ten obstacles successfully will get 55 marks.
- In case after one or two attempts you are unable to do an obstacle, leave it and attempt the others. If time permits you can come back and do it.

Demonstration

- After GTO will the briefing take you around show all the obstacles.
- He will explain each and every obstacle to the candidates.
- He will also brief you what constitutes successful completion of each obstacle.
- He will leave the candidates in that area for about a minute or two during which you can orient yourself and plan the sequence in which you would like to do these obstacles.

Note:
(a) Make a strong plan
(b) What is being checked at the SSB is how you reason out in your mind and exercise your body to complete these 10 obstacles successfully within the time frame.

Conduct

- You are all seated facing away from obstacle.
- GTO is seated facing the obstacle.
- He has a whistle and a stop watch.
- You are seated in sequence and will be called in sequence.
- When called, first candidate will get up, run, go and stand next to the obstacle from where he wishes to start.

- You are to start when GTO starts the stop watch and blows the whistle.
- Hearing the whistle No.1 candidate will commence doing the obstacle.
- When 2½ minutes are over GTO will shout 'next' loud enough. Then No. 1 candidate will understand that he has 30 seconds more to complete or repeat the obstacle.
- Hearing 'next', No. 2 candidate will get up, go and stand next to the obstacle from where he wishes to start.
- When three minutes are over, GTO will blow the whistle.
- Hearing the whistle No. 1 candidate will stop and No. 2 will commence doing the obstacles.
- This way, GTO will keep shouting 'next', keep blowing the whistle and complete the task by all candidates without wasting time.

What to Do?
- Get your dress ready in advance and get used to it.
- Make a good plan.
- Plan should be such that the maximum time to be spent in doing the obstacles and minimum time is spent in running from one obstacle to other.
- Run fast between the obstacles.
- Obstacle No.5 as far as possible is to be attempted last as it takes the most time.
- Do obstacle Nos. 9 and 10 boldly
- Repeat obstacles intelligently
- Get yourself medically examined.

Layout of obstacles

Salient features of individual obstacles

1. Planning – Start crossing hurdles the way these are laid.
2. Physical Stamina & Agility – These two qualities are checked as per score one has secured.
3. Determination – Try to cross the hurdles in the first attempt. If not, attempt others and when time permits come back to it and complete.

Note: It is better to take training from Cavalier India Bangalore or Cavalier India Chandigarh which has complete outdoor obstacles as per the SSB.

8. COMMAND TASK (CT)

"Every job is a self-portrait of the person who did it."

This is a confirmatory test given to the candidate to check the commander-like qualities. This is a great opportunity which the candidate gets to prove his qualities.

In this test each candidate is given a task individually to prove his qualities. There are different types of tasks. Some are simple, some are average and some are difficult. The task is decided by the GTO before and after seeing the candidate's performance in the earlier tests. The candidate may or may not be called as per the serial order. If one is not called, remember his tension or pressure level is being checked. In that case remain cool and calm. Whenever you are called, report to the GTO by jogging. No running or casual walking. While jogging, keep looking at the GTO. Never look up, down or sideways. Look cheerful and confident. Stand in front and wish the GTO as per the time of day.

The GTO will place his hand on your shoulders and would walk towards the task which has been planned for you. While walking he would be asking few questions of motivation and insight.

Every army officer should be commanding his troops in peace and war, order and action. For this the Command Task is conducted in SSB. Here the candidate is the leader and he should choose two/three candidates from his group as sub-ordinates.

Rules in Command Task

(a) The GTO will call the candidates in a random manner, then he will have a small pep talk.
(b) Then he will take the candidate to the task area and explain about rules and ask the candidate as to which persons he would be choosing.

What the GTO expects from the candidate

(a) Whether the candidate is good in his command by giving proper ideas to solve the problem.
(b) Whether he is extracting the work well from his sub-ordinates.
(c) While choosing the sub-ordinates, whether the candidate is choosing the weak member or strong member of the group (i.e. he finds out if the candidate has the ability to analyze about the group)
(d) Whether the candidate finds out multiple solutions for the task.

(e) Whether he is speedy in his decision and ideas.
(f) Whether he is having any other solutions in executing his plan after deciding it already.

Important Points for Command Task

Listen carefully and understand the instructions given by the GTO. This is a very important point throughout the GTO tasks. Choose the correct individuals as sub-ordinates, since you have to cross the obstacle with heavy load means you will require a person in your group who will be able to carry the load easily, and another person who is small, i.e. is able to tie ropes, planks easily.

Try to avoid asking ideas from the sub-ordinates, since in this scenario you are the leader and commander. Also if you were in a position of sub-ordinate don't talk or give ideas to the commander unless the GTO tells to do so.

Briefing

1. While working in PGT/HGT some of you may have felt that you have ideas but could not do the task in exact manner in which you wanted to do it.
2. Keeping this in mind each one of you in turn will be made Commander of a task.
3. The task is known as Command Task (CT)
4. A single stage task will be given to you
5. Time given to do the task will be 10 minutes.
6. All the rules except the Group Rule will be applicable.
7. By virtue of being commander it will be your privilege to select any two of your colleagues as your helpers to assist you to do the task.
8. This is one task in which you may not be called in sequence.
9. This is also one of the tasks in which you will be alone with GTO. He may ask you few questions; reply to them intelligently.

Note:
   (a) CT is pre-selected for each candidate based on his performance in earlier task.
   (b) Each candidate is given a different CT.
   (c) A candidate whom the GTO is going to pass will get more interesting CT. GTO will also spend more time with him and will ask more and more ideas.
10. You must stage manage to come as helper with at least two commanders.
11. In this task you have two roles to play. The main role is that of commander and the other role is that of helper or sub-ordinate.

Role as Commander

12. As commander listen to GTO carefully when he is briefing on the task.
13. Select two/three helpers quickly.
14. These should be those candidates who were doing well earlier in the task and would also meet your task requirements.
15. Do not bother about caste, colour, creed, religion, province, language or any other affinity.
16. Preferably, one of the candidates should be tall, slim, active and agile and other should be strong and of little heavy built.
17. When the helpers come, do a short briefing. "Friends, task given to us is this. This is the SL and that is the FL. No. of structures available are _____ (point out), helping materials available are _____ (point out), time given to do the task is 10 minutes. Rules you already know. Have you got any doubt _____, if not let us start".
18. As commander give clear instructions.
19. As commander give workable ideas.
20. As commander enter the task first from the middle approach and remain in a position so that you can exercise total control over the task as well as your helpers.
21. Do not ask for suggestions or ideas from your sub-ordinates. If anybody speaks, politely ask him to keep quiet and speak only when spoken to.
22. Thank the helpers when the task is over.

Role as Subordinate or Helper

23. As subordinate you are also under observation.
24. Obey all the orders of the commander.
25. Do not speak to the commander unless he asks you to.
26. Do not help the commander with ideas directly or indirectly.
27. If the commander asks for any suggestion or an idea and the GTO remains quiet you may give an idea verbally. Do not start implementing it yourself.

SALIENT FEATURES OF COMMAND TASK

1. **Briefing** – First listen to the briefing carefully, never ask any doubt nor seek any clarification. Give the same briefing word by word in the same sequence to your helpers.
2. **Planning** – When helpers are being called, show by movement and action that you are planning your line of action.

3. Resources – There is no task which requires more than 4-6 minutes time and more than two/three helpers.
4. Knowledge and Practical Intelligence – To cross the hurdles follow common sense and scientific methods (10 methods of PGT).
5. Execution – This is the only task where, at least once, the candidate should execute the task which is not a difficult one.
6. Confidence – Confidence is checked by the way you walk, talk, and act. Show maximum josh, speak loudly and demonstrate lot of keenness and motivation.
7. Stress – Once the task is completed, GTO may withdraw some material or manpower or may create certain areas that are out of bounds. In such situation candidate should then try to give him alternative solutions. GTO may ask the candidate to give out alternate solution than already shown while completing the task.

   Visit the websites www.cavalierindia.com and www.theexcel.com for a live demo of command task being performed by a trainee candidate.
8. Command and Control – All three (you + 2 helpers) should work as a team. The so called, risky and difficult work should be undertaken by you. No shouting, no remarks. Rather encourage.

Note: Once the task is over, arrange the items systematically. Take GTO's permission, wish him and go back the way you came.

Sociometry Method

With the help of this method, GTO checks who are the candidates well accepted by the group. Generally such candidates overall get recommended finally.

Various pictures are shown in this book. If you study carefully you can get enough ideas how to cross even difficult tasks.

9. FINAL GROUP TASK (FGT)

This is the last task at the SSB. Already before this task the GTO will narrow down and choose candidates based on their performance in their previous tasks. So it is also a last chance for the candidates to show up their qualities. Even some candidates may get a few chances to prove in PGT. So those candidates should use this to prove their leadership qualities. It is also a PGT, but in PGT the group has to cross four obstacles. Here in the FGT we have to cross only one. So all should be fast in their decisions to work out their plans.

Other rules such as rules for helping materials, out of bound areas are same as PGT and HGT.

Since this type of tasks are known to us by working with PGT and HGT, each candidate should give more ideas in executing the task. Also there should be good team coordination between them as you people were working together for two days.

These are the expectations of GTO in FGT. Others things are same as PGT and it is given below once again:-

Example Scenario about FGT

The obstacles are painted in three colours namely

(a) White
(b) Black
(c) Red

Each one describes one rule.

White: Both the candidate and the helping materials can touch the obstacle at this region.

Black: Only the candidate can touch the obstacle in this region and not the helping materials.

Red: Both the candidate and helping material should not touch the obstacles.

Out of bound areas

The areas in the FGT which should not be touched are called as out of bound areas. These areas include the mud surfaces inside the task area and some colour codes as described above.

Helping materials and its usage

The helping materials given are wooden plank (6 feet length), balli (wooden log), and rope. Along with this they will have load to carry from one end to another end. With these helping material we implement several techniques such as cantilever, fulcrum etc to cross over the obstacles along with the group. See the pictures given in this book and you will get an idea about fulcrum, cantilever and FGT structures.

Rules and colour codes etc were mentioned already in the previous pages.

Please remember different SSB's will have different colour codes.

For various ideas how to connect between points study the pictures given in this book. Also you can have a look at www.cavalierindia.com or www.theexcel.com where you can clearly see how these structures are laid out and live negotiation of obstacles by the candidates.

Things to follow at FGT

(a) Never look at the GTO while doing the tasks.

(b) Be yourself as stated earlier in the GD itself.

(c) Give workable and practical ideas to the group. If you don't have any idea just help the idea givers truthfully.

(d) Never violate the rules; it is the basics of GTO tasks. In case you violate the rule, just repeat the task.

(e) Be an active participant in the team by giving your full cooperation.

(f) Be positive in your view i.e. take consideration about other members' ideas if it is finer than yours.

Note: Be a contributor and a well-meaning member. If you help others to get what they want you will get what you want.

Briefing

1. So far you were working individually. In this last task for the final group task you will be brought together once again in your original big group.
2. A single stage task will be given to you. However, the dimensions of the task and the number of structures may be larger.
3. Time given to you for the task will be 15 minutes.
4. All rules except group rule will be applicable.
5. TO will then explain the task and make you to do one task.

What to Do?

6. Help each other
7. Use workable ideas
8. Do not use the ideas which had not worked earlier.
9. Do not show that you are tired.
10. This is the last look GTO is giving towards you. He is particularly looking at candidate(s) whom he is going to pass. You may be that candidate, therefore, continue to work hard and bring out the best that is in you.

DETENSE STAGE

This is the last test of Group Testing. Once all the tests are over, the group relaxes and the GTO tries to detense the whole situation by being a bit informal with them. At this stage he asks complaints, suggestions, comments etc, if any on testing, food & accommodation.

No suggestions, No complaints, No comments on testing, food & accommodation; rather, express thanks and gratitude. No personal questions. No questions on service.

Pilot Aptitude Battery Test (PABT)

"Success occurs when opportunity meets preparation".

- Zig Ziglar

In addition to normal SSB, candidates who have opted for the Flying Branch have to compulsorily undergo Pilot Aptitude Battery Test. This test is conducted at the Selection Boards at Mysore, Dehradun and Varanasi. A candidate is allowed only one chance in his lifetime to appear for this test. Once a candidate is rejected he is deemed to be permanently unfit for selection into the Air Force in the Flying Branch. Likewise, a candidate who passes PABT but fails in SSB need not appear again for PABT when he appears for SSB next time.

The purpose of conducting this test is to ascertain whether the candidate has the requisite aptitude to become a Service Pilot. A pilot's job is very demanding and it is very vital for him to possess the basic qualities like concentration, ability to undergo stress, ability to monitor and carry out various tasks at the same time and also possess an analytical mind, good reflexes and coordination of limbs.

PABT is carried out in two phases – Written tests known as INS-B, and the Machine Test. We shall first deal with the written tests.

The written part of PABT consists of interpretation of cockpit instruments. You must understand that a pilot flies an aircraft basically by looking outside and taking reference from the visible horizon (the horizontal line separating the sky and the earth) to ascertain whether the aircraft's flying level, climbing, descending or turning left or right is correct. But during night, due to poor visibility conditions or while flying through clouds, the ground and the horizon may not be visible to the pilot. In these conditions the pilot has to look inside and interpret the cockpit instruments to determine the aircraft's flying level, climbing, descending or turning to either side. The written test (INS-B) is designed to determine whether the candidate has the ability to monitor a number of instruments at one time and quickly interpret and extract the required information. It is conducted in two phases.

PHASE – I OF THE WRITTEN TEST

You are shown pictures of six cockpit instruments, below which five statements are given. You are required to tick the correct statements which agree with the readings of all the six instruments. There are 15 questions of this type, to be solved in 12 minutes.

Let us now learn about the six instruments.
- (a) Altimeter
- (b) Artificial Horizon
- (c) Compass
- (d) Air Speed Indicator (Speedometer)
- (e) Rate of Gain or Loss of Altitude / Height – Indicator
- (f) Rate of Turn and Bank Indicator

(a) Altimeter

Altimeter is an instrument which indicates height or altitude of an aircraft. For purpose of this test, height and altitude means the same.

- (a) The dial of this instrument has ten (10) main divisions marked zero (0) to nine (9) as shown in the picture. Each main division is further subdivided into five (5) equal parts.
- (b) There are two pointers in the instrument; one is larger and other smaller.
    - (i) The bigger pointer reads in terms of hundreds (100's) of feet.
    - (ii) The smaller pointer reads in terms of thousand (1000's) of feet.
    - (iii) Each sub-division is equal to twenty (20) feet.

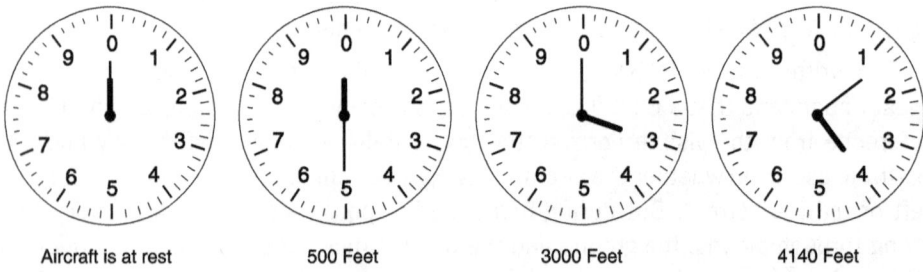

Aircraft is at rest   500 Feet   3000 Feet   4140 Feet

(b) Artificial horizon

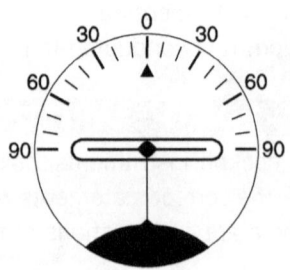

(a) Altitude of the aircraft

   (i) Whether aircraft is climbing/gaining altitude or height/ascending.
   (ii) Whether aircraft is maintaining level/neither gaining nor losing height.
   (iii) Whether aircraft is descending/diving/losing height or altitude.

(b) Bank Indicator

   (i) Whether aircraft is banked to left or right
   (ii) How many degrees of bank to left or right?

   If you see the instrument carefully, you will find:-
   (c) There is one model aircraft which is fixed to the instrument body.
   (d) There is one horizon-bar which moves up or down and rotates left or right.
   (e) There is a scale calibrated in degrees from zero to ninety (90) degree on either side. The scale is marked 0, 30, 60 and 90 against main divisions. Each main division is further sub-divided into three equal to ten (10) degree.
   (f) There is a triangular pointer which moves along with scale and always remains perpendicularly above the horizon bar.
   (g) This pointer reads the bank of the aircraft in terms of degree from zero to ninety against the scale.

Note:
   (a) Pointer doesn't indicate the direction of the bank.
   (b) As a thumb rule, pointer always moves in the opposite direction of the bank of the aircraft.
   (c) Instrument can't read in terms of less than five (5) degrees.

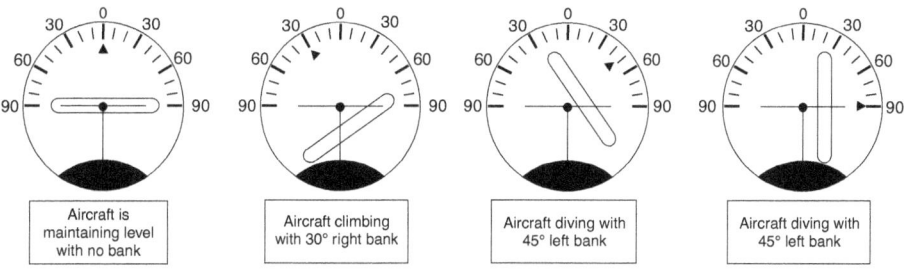

(c) Compass

This instrument indicates the direction of the aircraft into which its nose is pointing or it is flying.

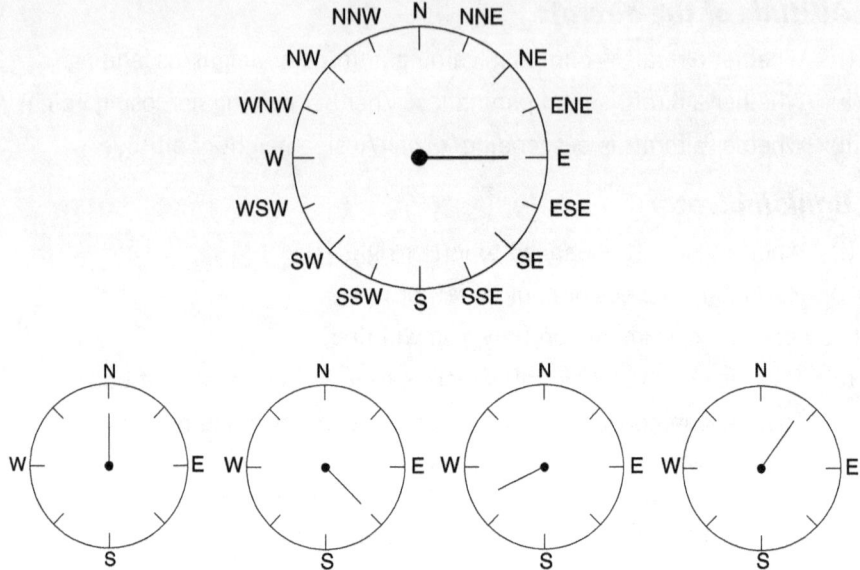

(d) Air speed indicator (speedometer)

Air speed indicator indicates the speed of the aircraft in terms of miles per hour. There is only one pointer which reads the speed against a circular dial which is marked from zero (0) to 440 miles per hour, in steps of 40 miles per hour. Each step is further sub-divided into four (4) equal parts. Each sub-division is equal to 10 miles per hour. The instrument can't read in terms of less than five miles per hour.

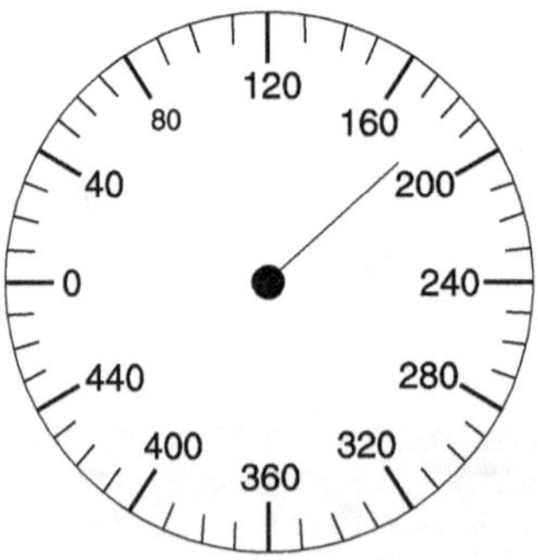

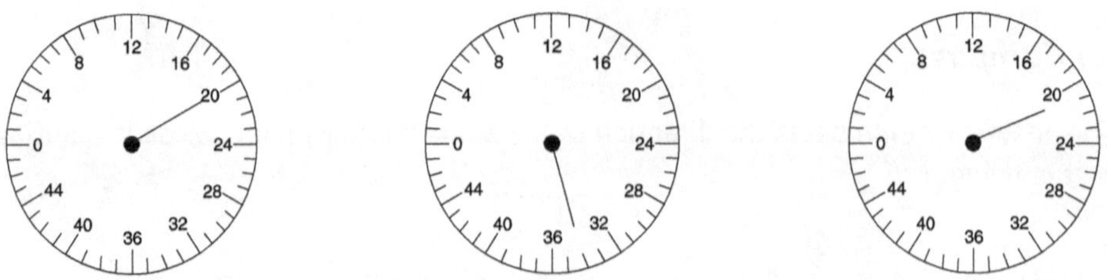

(e) Rate of gain or loss of altitude/height – indicator

1. This instrument indicates the rate at which an aircraft is gaining or losing altitude/height.
2. If you watch this instrument, you will find only one pointer which indicates the rate against a semi-circular scale marked by a thin line. There is a small black mark dividing this thin scale in two equal parts. There is one thick area with arrow heads at both the ends.

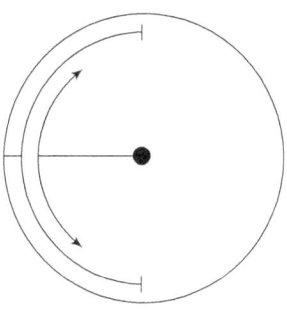

3. Let us see how this instrument indicates the rate of gain or loss of altitudes/height of an aircraft:-
   (a) If the pointer is against the black mark – we say aircraft is maintaining level or the aircraft is neither gaining nor losing altitude/height.
   (b) If the pointer is between the black mark and the top head of thick scale – we say the aircraft is climbing or gaining altitude/height.
   (c) If the pointer is between the top arrow head of the thick arc and the top end of the thin semi-circular scale – we say aircraft is climbing/ascending/gaining altitude/height rapidly.
   (d) If the pointer is between the black arc and bottom arrow head we say the aircraft is descending/losing altitude/height gradually.
   (e) If the pointer is between the bottom arrow head and the bottom end of the thin scale - we say the aircraft is diving/descending/losing altitude or height rapidly.

Practice Exercise - 1

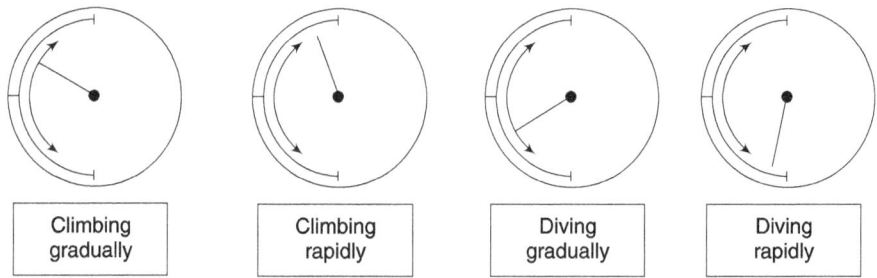

| Climbing gradually | Climbing rapidly | Diving gradually | Diving rapidly |

(f) Rate of turn and bank indicator

1. This instrument has two pointers. Lower pointer indicates the direction and rate of turn against the lower scale while the other upper pointer indicates the amount of bank for the turn is correct *more* or *less*.

2. Take first the lower part of this instrument. There is a thick scale. The scale has one black mark. There are two capital letters written 'L' meaning Left and 'R' meaning Right.

   (a) If the pointer is against black mark, the aircraft is flying straight/maintaining direction or aircraft is neither turning left nor right.

   (b) If the pointer is between black mark and up to first half of the scale towards left, it indicates aircraft is turning left normally or normal left turn.

   (c) If the pointer is anywhere on the second part of the scale towards left, it indicates sharp left turn or the aircraft is turning left sharply.

   (d) If the pointer is between the black mark and first half of the scale to the right, it indicates normal right turn or turning right normally.

   (e) If the pointer is anywhere on the second part of the scale to right, it indicates right sharp turn or turning right sharply.

Practice Exercise - 2

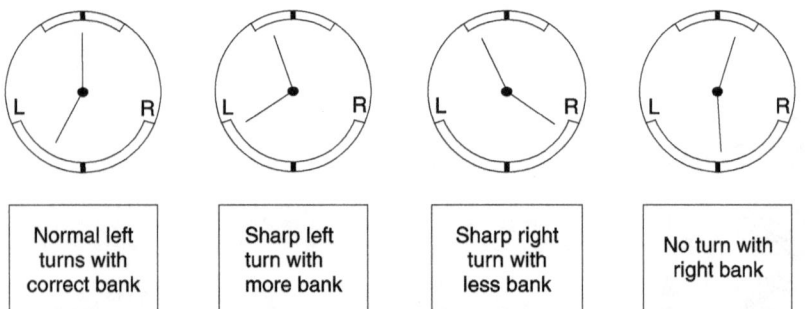

| Normal left turns with correct bank | Sharp left turn with more bank | Sharp right turn with less bank | No turn with right bank |

PHASE – II OF THE WRITTEN TEST

This phase will have only two cockpit instruments (Artificial Horizon and the Magnetic Compass) and, instead of five statements, five three-dimensional pictures will be displayed. The candidate is required to tick the correct picture which agrees with both the instruments. While solving this, the candidates are advised to first compare the pictures with magnetic compass and eliminate the ones that do not agree with the direction indicated by the compass. After short-listing the pictures that agree with the magnetic compass, he must now compare them with the Artificial Horizon and tick the correct answer. Candidate must never try to first compare the pictures with the Artificial Horizon as it will be more time consuming. There will be 60 questions of this type which have to be answered in 20 minutes.

There is no reason for a candidate to feel under-confident or confused with respect to PABT. The examiner conducting the test will first explain all the instruments thoroughly and also give practice by solving examples before conducting the written tests.

Practical Tests or Machine Tests

These tests are designed to ascertain whether a candidate has the qualities like concentration, good anticipation and reflexes, co-ordination of limbs and ability to carry out various tasks at the same time. These tests are also conducted in two phases.

Phase-I: A candidate is made to sit in a cockpit like compartment with a computer screen in front of him. Screen has one inch square marked at the centre of the screen.

When test starts a moving spot light will appear on the screen. The candidate has to control the vertical and horizontal movement of this spot light with the help of the foot pedals and the stick provided to him. When the left foot pedal is pushed forward, the spot light will move to the left, and when the right pedal is pushed forward, the spot light will move to the right. Likewise, when the stick is pushed forward, the spot will move 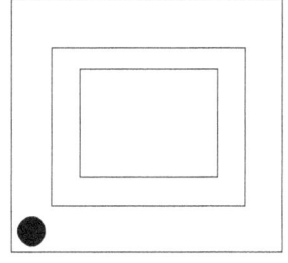 down and when the stick is pulled backwards the spot light will move up.

When the test starts, the spot light will start moving on the screen. The candidate has to control the movement of the spot light with the foot pedal and the stick and bring it inside the one inch square marked on the screen. The spot light will try to move out of the square, but the candidate must anticipate the movement and keep the spot light within the square as long as possible with the help of the controls. Marks scored by the candidate will be proportional to the time he is able to keep the spot light within the square. It is like a computer game and the score obtained by the candidate will be indicated by the computer at the end of the test. The duration of each test is about three minutes or so.

While controlling the spot light, the candidate is also expected to monitor and take appropriate action on other happenings around him. Below the screen in front of him, there are two lights which will come on at intervals. Whenever any of the light comes on, the candidate is expected to put it off with the help of handle provided on the left side. The left light can be put off by moving the handle forward and then bringing it to the original position. Likewise, the light on the right side can be put off by moving the handle backward and then bringing it to the original position. The candidate will be penalized in terms of marks for any delay in putting off the lights.

While doing the test, candidate will be wearing ear phones and through these, a faint sound will be transmitted at frequent intervals. Whenever the audio is detected, the candidate has to cancel (put off) the same by pressing the button provided on the stick.

It can be seen that the tests are meant to ascertain whether a candidate has reflexes and can concentrate on various activities at the same time. The main objective for the candidate must be to keep the spot light within the square as long as possible. Putting off the light and cancelling the audio are only meant to divert the attention of the candidate from the main screen. Therefore the candidate's priority must be to keep his eyes focused on the computer screen and concentrate on controlling the spot light, and to switch off the lights and audio without removing the eyes from the main screen.

The duration of the test is for about three minutes. A candidate is given three chances and only his best score is considered.

PHASE – III INSTRUMENT TEST TWO

The second test is a simple test to determine whether a candidate has anticipation and co-ordination of limbs.

The candidate is made to sit in a chamber as before and there will be a computer screen in front of him. On the screen there will be a round ball. Pink dots will be projected on the screen at random interval. With the help of controls candidate has to overlap the round ball on pink dots. More time the round ball is overlapped on pink dots, more marks the candidate will score.

The duration of the test is 90 seconds. Three chances are given. The best result will be counted.

Conference Procedure

"If you learn from a defeat, you haven't really lost."
"Failure is an event – not a person."

- Zig Ziglar

Final board conference

Aiming at comprehensive assessment of personality traits of the individual, the Psychologist, the GTO and the Interviewing Officer look at the candidate independently. As three techniques are supplementary as well complementary to each other, sharing of information collected by three assessors acquires increased significance in the process of reaching a final decision with respect to suitability of the candidate. Most importantly, Final Board Conference provides a forum to assessors, where they can share important information obtained during the course of their assessments of a candidate. This forum is fruitfully utilized by assessors to highlight both favourable as well as unfavourable inputs received by them. Board conference also enables the assessors to have a 1st look at the candidate. Thus, in the entire process of selection, this occasion assumes vital significance.

There are some important reasons for justifying holding a final board conference. These reasons are listed below:

(a) It provides an opportunity to all assessors to have a final joint look at the candidate.
(b) It gives an opportunity to discuss salient points about the candidate's personality.
(c) It acts as a forum to resolve any doubts about personality profile of the candidate.
(d) It provides an opportunity to probe into any grey areas, if needed.
(e) It assists in reaching a consensus regarding candidate's suitability by the Board.
(f) It is the occasion to award conference marks to the candidate based on his performance.

Procedure for board conference

1. Prior to the day of the conference, candidates are adequately briefed about the procedure that is followed during a Board Conference. A general layout of the conference room is shown below.
2. To provide an order to the proceedings of the conference, candidates are called in the conference hall in an ascending order of the sequence of chest numbers allotted to them.
3. To commence the process of conference, the President of the Board calls out the chest number of the candidate that needs to be discussed. Thereafter, the three assessors announce their respective initial marks. Two assessors total these marks manually, as well as with the help of a calculator to avoid occurrence of any error in totaling. On announcement of initial marks, various situations could develop which may require different kind of handling in the Board Conference. These situations are discussed below.

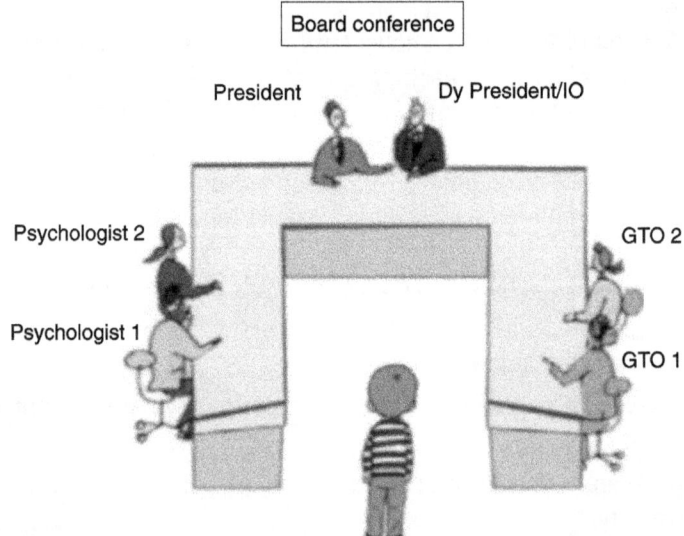

All Three Assessors Recommend or Do Not Recommend the Candidate

4. In case the three assessors have a unanimous opinion about the candidate, i.e., either all three have recommended the candidate or all three have not recommended him, the candidate is called in by the president and a few routine questions are put to him by a designated interviewing officer. Since there is no difference of opinion about the candidate, he is asked to leave the conference room. Soon after the candidate leaves, the three assessors

announce their conference marks. Once again, the conference marks are added to the earlier total by two assessors manually as well as with the help of a calculator and final marks are arrived at. The same process is repeated in respect of all candidates who have been either cleared or not cleared by all three assessors and there is no difference of opinion.

Three Assessors Have a Difference of Opinion

5. It may so happen that the assessors might have a split opinion about the candidate, i.e., some assessor/assessors might not have recommended the candidate. In such situations, consequent to announcement of initial marks, total of initial marks is arrived at in a similar fashion as explained earlier. However, decision to discuss the candidate further would depend upon the quantum of initial marks that are awarded to the candidate by the three assessors. The quantum of marks which make a candidate eligible for discussion in the Board Conference have been spelt out by Army/Navy/Air Headquarters in respect to their candidates. If the candidate has obtained marks equal to or more than the specified figure, only then he would be discussed further in the Board Conference. Otherwise, a similar procedure as explained above will be followed and candidate will be allowed to withdraw after he is asked some routine questions by the designated interviewing officer.

6. If a candidate secures the quantum of initial marks as required, then further discussion about the candidate takes place. In that case, the President may ask the three assessors to give their ticks to find out the specific areas where assessors have a split opinion. In a large number of cases, the three assessors may reach a consensus either to clear/reject the candidate after discussions are held about the strengths and weak areas of the candidate's personality. In such cases also, the candidate is called in, the designated interviewing officer asks routine questions and candidate is asked to leave. Conference marks are thereafter announced and similar procedure as discussed above is followed.

7. There could still be a situation, where despite their discussion, the assessors do not reach a consensus and need further clarifications/additional inputs on some aspects of candidate's personality. In such rare situations, the designated interviewing officer is asked to probe the candidate to bring out that additional information for the benefit of the three assessors. Subsequent to such probing, the candidate leaves and afterwards assessors discuss and reach a consensus either to clear/reject the candidate. Thereafter, conference marks are allotted and similar procedure followed as for other candidates. In such situations the candidate is asked questions during the conference to clear the doubts that the assessors have.

Procedure for Sick/Injured Candidates

8. Many a times, candidates sustain injuries while performing group tasks or fall sick due to any other reason during the process of testing at SSBs/AFSBs. If such injuries/sickness are of serious nature, the candidate may not be in a fit condition to appear before the final Board Conference. In such cases, the following procedure needs to be followed.

   (a) If the three assessors have made the same recommendations, the conference is held in absentia.

   (b) If the three assessors have a split opinion about the candidate, in that rare case, the Board Conference is held at the sick bed to decide about the suitability of the candidate.

Award of Conference Marks

9. As discussed earlier, one of the important functions of holding a conference is to award conference marks to all candidates. Initial marks allotted to each assessor is 225. However, quantum of conference marks allotted to three assessors is somewhat different as shown in the table below. It will be seen that pass marks out of a total of 900 will be 360 i.e., 40% of the total marks allotted.

INITIAL/CONFERENCE MARKS – ARMY/NAVY/GROUND DUTY AIR FORCE OFFICERS

Member	Initial Marks	Conference Marks	Total
Interviewing Officer	225	113	338
GTO	225	56	281
Psychologists	225	56	281
Total	675	225	900

10. In case of Air Force pilots, quantum of 300 marks are earmarked for PABT (Pilot Aptitude Battery Test), therefore initial marks allotted to each assessor are 150. Conference marks as shown in the table below are earmarked for the three assessors.

INITIAL/CONFERENCE MARKS – AIR FORCE PILOTS

Member	Initial Marks	Conference Marks
Interviewing Officer	150	74
GTO	150	38
Psychologists	150	38

PABT	−450	–
Total		150

Some Important Aspects of Board Conference

11. There are a few salient features of final Board Conference. These features are discussed below:

    (a) Initial marks, which are called out before the candidate enters the conference room, are not changed either during the discussion about the candidate or even later.

    (b) The assessors call out conference marks in a planned sequence, soon after discussion about the candidate gets over and a consensus is reached.

    (c) If an assessor had passed the candidate, he would reflect the same in his report, even if the Board had failed the candidate after discussions.

Similarly if the assessor had failed the candidate, he would reflect the candidate as having failed, even if the Board had decided to pass him after discussions.

Sharing of Information during Board Conference

The assessors display their professionalism and broad outlook while discussing a candidate in the conference and not get stuck to their own assessments. A balanced and mature attitude on the part of all the assessors ensures that final decision is arrived at, after careful thought is given to all relevant inputs collected by the three assessors. This is one platform where assessors essentially display their sense of respect for other techniques and supplement their inputs with those obtained by other assessors. Interviewing officers, generally being senior among the three assessors, take a lead in displaying their maturity in respecting other techniques and thereby contributing positively towards reaching a balanced judgment with regard to suitability of the candidate.

1. This is the final stage of SSB and an opportunity is given to each candidate for approximately 3-4 minutes time. During this time/period he is asked few general questions concerning "PIQ" and "Interview" in general. This stage is very crucial for the candidate who is a borderline, which means a candidate who has cleared two techniques and in 3rd is missing the target by few marks.

2. Conference Marks:

GTO	- 56
Psychologist	- 56
Interviewing Officer	- 113
TOTAL	- 225
Total Marks	- 675 (GTO, Psych & IO)

Required Marks - 270 (40%) out of 675
Conference Marks Required - 90 (40%) out of 675

Total minimum marks required for getting through – 90 × 3 = 360 marks

Points to Remember

- It is a formal interview / occasion
- Be smartly dressed up
- Polish the shoes
- Wear a tie if possible
- Do not be unnecessarily tensed
- Walk in confidently
- Wish the board appropriately
- Give mature answers to the questions being asked
- Service candidates will be in uniform
- Salute the board and wish
- While coming out do not look back

Medical Examination Procedure of the Recommended Candidates

Candidates who clear the SSB are asked to stay the back at SSB centre for 5 more days for their medical examination. Medical is conducted in this order over next 4/5 days–

Day 1 – Blood test, Urine test, Chest x-ray, Ultrasound Day 2 – Ear, Nose & Throat (ENT) Day

3 – Surgical Examination

Day 4 – Eye & Dental

Day 5 – General Medical (height, weight, blood pressure, heart beat) & Medical Conference

Recommended candidates appear before the medical board for carrying out their medical board after the SSB results. It takes 4 to 5 days' time for the concerned Military Hospital to complete the medical board and after that the candidates are dispersed. NDA candidates are examined both for Army and Navy unless otherwise instructed and endorsement of fitness status will be made accordingly. President of the medical board will guide the candidates for Appeal/Review Medical Board procedures. Candidates may seek the advice of President Special Medical Board for review/appeal in case they have been declared unfit or temporarily rejected (TR)

Procedure of appeal medical board

The Appeal Medical Board will be held at one of the following hospitals :-

- Base Hospital, Delhi Cantt.
- Command Hospital, Southern Command, Pune.
- Command Hospital, Eastern Command, Kolkata.
- Command Hospital, Central Command, Lucknow.
- Command Hospital, Western Command, Chandimandir.
- Command Hospital, Air Force, Bangalore.
- Command Hospital, Northern Command, C/o 56 APO.
- INHS, Ashvini, Mumbai.

The candidates will report for medical examination within the stipulated period i.e., 42 days from the date last examined by the Special Medical Board for re-examination along with the receipted copy of the MRO/TR as directed by the President Medical Board. The endeavour will be to complete the Medical Board in one day.

Review medical board

In case of candidate being declared unfit by the Appeal Medical Board, he/she may challenge the proceedings and may be granted review of medical proceedings based on the merit of the case. Any candidate desiring for a review should address the request to Recruiting Directorate (Personnel & Coord), Army Headquarters, West Block III, RK Puram, New Delhi with a copy to the President of Appeal Medical Board within one day of the holding of Appeal Medical Board. The application for RMB is routed through DG AFMS. The decision for grant of RMB is with DG AFMS, and is not a matter of right. RMBs are conducted at R&R Hospital Delhi Cantt and AFMC, Pune.

Stay During the Medical Examination

The recommended candidates after the declaration of SSB results will stay in the Selection Centres earmarked for the recommended candidates for their medical examination by the Military Hospital. The candidates will be allotted fresh chest numbers for the purpose.

Candidates who go for Appeal Medical Board or have to get their medical examination done at a later date due to unavoidable reasons will do so under their own arrangements.

Discipline During Medical Examination

It is of utmost importance that recommended candidates maintain proper discipline during their stay in Selection Centres during their conduct of medical examination. The candidates are required to put on their medical chest number (with Red Cross) whenever they are present in the campus of Selection Centres.

Candidates are advised to build themselves up by physical training, sports, running, swimming etc, so that they meet the training goals successfully.

Ideal Age, Height and Weight for Male:

It should be within permissible limits (+ or –10%) of the ideal weight as per correlation table between age, height and average weight given below. Recording fraction lower than 0.5 kg will be noted and above 0.5 kg will be recorded as 1kg.

Height and Weight Standards for Men:-

Height in cm	Weight in KG (Age range in Years)			
	Age 15-17	18-22	23-27	28-32
152 – 158	46 – 49	47 – 50	50 – 54	54 – 58
159 – 165	50 – 53	51 – 55	55 – 59	59 – 63
166 – 171	54 – 56	56 – 59	60 – 64	63 – 66
172 – 178	57 – 60	59 – 63	64 – 69	67 – 71
179 – 183	61 – 63	64 – 66	69 – 72	72 – 74
184 – 185	64	67 – 68	73 – 74	75

Height and Weight Standards for Women

Height in cm	Weight in KG (Age range in Years)	
	Age 20-25	26-30
148 – 151	43 – 45	46 – 48
152 – 155	46 – 48	49 – 51
156 – 160	49 – 51	52 – 55
161 – 165	52 – 54	55 – 58
166 – 171	55 – 58	59 – 62
172 – 176	59 – 61	63 – 66
177 – 178	62 – 63	

Note: A 10% variation on either side of average is acceptable.

Medical Standards

- The candidate should be free from wax (in ears), DNS, Hyrocele/Phimosis. Defective Colour Vision, LASIK Surgery, Over/Under Weight, Under Chest,
- Piles, Gynecomastia, Tonsillitis, Veri-Cocele and AIDS.
- You should be able to read 6/6 in a Distant Vision Chart
- Colour Vision Standard should be CP-III
- Minimum 14 Dental Points With Sound Teeth

Physical standards	Minimum Height	Minimum Weight
Women	152 CM	42 KG
NDA & 10+2 TES (Under Graduate Entry Men)	152 CM	43 KG
CDSE, TGC, UES, NCC SPL AMC, RVC ETC. (Graduate Entry Men)	157 CM	45 KG

Indian Air Force Vision Medical Standards

- One must have 6/6 in one eye and 6/9 in other, which can be correctable to 6/6 only for hypermetropia.
- **Vision Defects**
  - Manifest hypermetropia must not exceed +2.0D Sphere.
  - No Myopia.
  - Astigmatism must be +0.75 D Cyl with +2.0 D maximum

Near Vision must be N-5 each eye.

- Near vision is determined using "Times Roman" type and is assessed at reading distance (30-50 cm) and at 100 cm. The 100-cm distance is important in the aircraft cockpit and similar environments and for users of

CRT displays. When two values are shown, such as N5 and N14, the first value refers to the reading distance (30-50 cm) and the second value to the 100-cm distance.

- Color Vision must be CP-1(ML T). **Color Perception-1:** The correct recognition of coloured lights shown through the paired apertures on the Holmes-Wright lantern at LOW BRIGHTNESS at 6 metres (20 feet) distance in complete darkness.

Lasik surgery

LASIK Surgery for correction of vision is admissible in Transport and Helicopter streams of Short Service Commission (Flying Branch) if the following conditions are fulfilled at the time of Air Force medical examination:

- LASIK surgery should not have been carried out before the age of 20 years.
- The axial length of the eye should not be more than 25.5 mm as measured by IOL master.
- At least twelve months should have lapsed post uncomplicated stable LASIK. No history or evidence of any complication.
- The post LASIK corneal thickness as measured by a corneal pachymeter should not be less than 450 microns.
- Individuals with high refractive errors (>6D) prior to LASIK are to be excluded.
- Candidates must not suffer from colour or night blindness.

Ocular Muscle Balance: Eyes should be well aligned and should have normal binocular vision. No manifest squint permissible. Convergence must be adequate.

Ocular movements: Full and free ocular muscle balance can be tested with the cover test, the Maddox rod or an approved vision tester.

- At 6 meters
  - Exophoria 6 prism Diopters
  - Esophoria 6 prism Diopters
  - Hyperphoria 1 prism Diopters
  - Hypophoria 1 prism Diopters
- At 33 cm
  - Exophoria 16 prism Diopters
  - Esophoria 6 prism Diopters
  - Hyperphoria 1 prism Diopters
  - Hypophoria 1 prism Diopters

Candidates are suggested to apply for all eligible branches, so if you get rejected for flying branch due to high medical standards, you may get a chance to join other branch of Indian Air Force like Technical, GDOC etc.

Candidates are addressed medical checkup before going for SSB interview or Medical tests, so that if you find any problem which is curable, you could start working on it at the earliest.

Most of the terms used above are medical, and many of you might not be able to understand, you can consult an ophthalmologist accordingly.

Dental Inspection

Medical test (Dental Points) is conducted for recommended candidates after SSB interviews. It is a very crucial part of selection procedure. Generally, in each batch the medically unfit rate goes up to 45% – 55%. Candidate can be declared unfit medically for one or various health issues. Aspirants must go for proper body check up before proceeding towards interview, also a regular monthly check is mandatory. 14 dental points is one of the must-haves during medicals.

Treatment for Flat Feet (also known as flat foot)

You can follow some exercise to reduce flat feet by increasing arch.

- Wear shoes which support arch.
- Keep your heels on tennis ball with the big toes touching the ground.
- Lift your toes by keeping heels on ground, hold it for 10-15 seconds, repeat 4-5 times.
- Sit and lift your right foot and touch the last toe of the left foot.
- Consult a physician also.

Knock Knees Problem

Knock knees can be one of the reasons to be unfit for Indian army or Indian defence forces. If you have knock knees then you will be declared as unfit during SSB medical examination. This medical condition is very rare, but few candidates may have knock knees.

Knock knees are a deformity of the knee, in which knees of a standing person touch each other but not the ankles. In other words, in a normal standing position, a person with knock knees has a gap between the ankles but not between the knees.

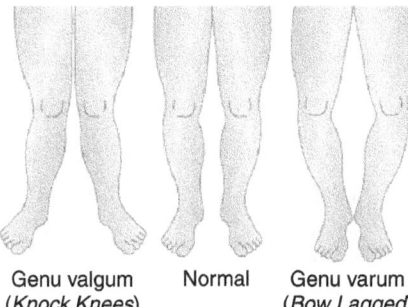

Genu valgum   Normal   Genu varum
(*Knock Knees*)   (*Bow Lagged*)

Treatment and Exercise for Knock Knees

Knock knees problem basically starts from childhood and gets cured on its own as we start growing, but some of us do not get the proper development of bones which leads to knock-knees. This problem prevents us from walking or running freely, which makes it a reason to be declared unfit for Indian armed forces. Candidates with little knock knees can start exercising and doing yoga to cure this problem. Few of the exercise and treatments for knock knees are:

- Take vitamin D and calcium supplements, vitamin C supplements.
- Virasana, or hero pose, is effective in treating flat feet and knock knees.
- Keep a block between thighs and try to move your legs as close as you can, hold it for 3 mins, keep repeating.
- In a standing position, bring the legs 4 feet apart and stretch the arms out to the side. Turn the right toes to the right and deeply bend the right knee. Activate the arches and keep the right knee touching the wall. Hold for 30 seconds and repeat on the other side.
- Do not underestimate this problem. Consult a physician for proper care and treatment and to clear any doubts.

Sweaty Palms

Sweaty palms may create a problem for you in medical examination. A Medical officer checks palms to make sure the candidate is not suffering from Hyperhidrosis. Hyperhidrosis is a condition in which you may suffer from excessive sweating of the hands, feet and armpits etc.

The above conditions affects your overall health therefore it is a good idea to consult a doctor and take appropriate treatment. Majority cases be rectified by corrective exercises.

If you prepare for the SSB interview very well your selection is one hundred percent sure. It is better to clear the medical test at the first attempt than going for an appeal medical.

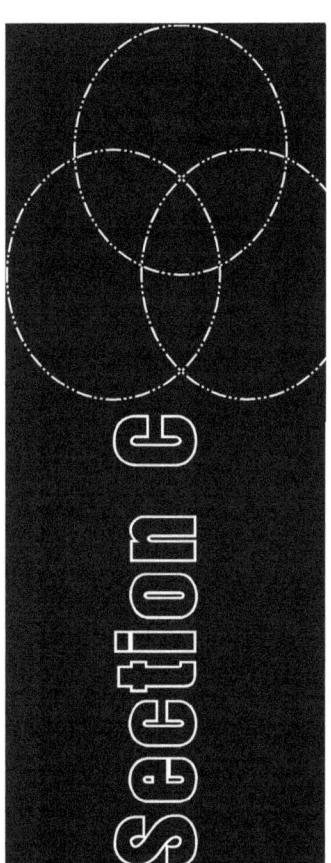

Section C

Defence Awareness

Chapter 1: India's Foreign Policy - From Nehru to Modi
Chapter 2: Indo – China Relations (Past, Present and Future)
Chapter 3: Indo-US Relations & India's Takeaways
Chapter 4: Indian Ocean–Hub of Political & Economic Activities
Chapter 5: Digital India Project
Chapter 6: Smart Cities Mission and Amrut
Chapter 7: India Building Relationship - PM Modi's Visits Abroad
Chapter 8: ISIS – Terror Tentacles
Chapter 9: Nuclear Treaties & Disarmament
Chapter 10: Military Awards
Chapter 11: Defence Organisation - Army/Navy/Air Force
Chapter 12: Types of Entry & Eligibility for Armed Forces
Chapter 13: Call up letter/Certificate
Chapter 14: SSB Interview Training & Development
Chapter 15: SSB Preparation By Services Candidates: ACC/SL/SCO
Chapter 16: If you got rejected at the SSB then there is some thing Special about you.
Chapter 17: Why SSB selection is not perfect
Chapter 18: SSB Interview Training & Development

India's Foreign Policy From Nehru to Modi

Background

Definition: Foreign Policy can be defined in a broad sense as the sum total of the Principles, Aims and Objectives which a country evolves in conducting its relations with other countries.

Foreign Policy during Cold War: India's first Prime Minister, Mr. Jawaharlal Nehru laid down the broad parameters of India's foreign policy. These were based on the twin concept of Non-Alignment and Panch-Sheel. This policy was followed by India during the Cold War period.

Non-Aligned Policy: India's non-alignment policy was designed to not only stay out of the blocs system but also to try and bring the blocs together on various issues as far as possible.

Transformation of India's Foreign Policy Objectives in the Nineties:

a. National Security and economic interest gained a prominent place in foreign policy thinking.
b. The CTBT became a crucial test of India's assertion of an autonomous security policy.
c. The 'look East policy' signaled India's awareness of economic imperatives in an increasingly globalizing world.
d. With the establishment of the WTO, India had to work out a new strategy to facilitate economic growth. There was better understanding about the inevitability of marketing and expanding global financial markets.

Gujral Doctrine: Named after the former Prime Minister, Mr. I.K. Gujral, it was based on the compelling vision for regional cooperation and India's readiness to go the extra mile in achieving it.

Challenges on the Foreign Policy Front: According to the late J.N.B. Dixit, former National Security Adviser, the challenges that face India's foreign policy are as follows:

a. Safeguarding Unity of the Country - The highest priority should be to ensure the contiguity, unity and territorial integrity of India. The foreign policy would have to create a regional atmosphere and equations with important powers of the world to prevent external encouragement to the centrifugal forces affecting the country.

b. Peace and stability - India's foreign policy should ensure an atmosphere of peace and stability in which India can focus on its economic development. Along with an appropriate domestic economic policy a foreign economic policy should also be formulated to ensure the necessary financial, technological and foreign trade inputs to meet India's developmental requirements.

c. National Defence Capacities - India's unity and territorial integrity can be protected by creating national defence capacities. These capacities should primarily rely on indigenous resources and technologies based on a balanced and sufficiently diversified pattern of external inputs.

d. Strengthen Regional Cooperation - Strengthening regional cooperation and working for mutually beneficial equations between South Asian and other regional groups will ensure peace and stability and long-term security and economic well-being.

e. Strengthen the UN - The UN, its organs and its specialized agencies should be strengthened keeping in mind two goals:
- To enable the UN to truly reflect the interests and aspirations of the majority of its members.
- To restrict to the extent possible the UN's becoming an instrumentality of super power policies.

Five Key Aspects of the Government's Foreign Policy

In the foreign policy priorities listed by the President Pranab Mukherjee in his address to the first joint sitting of both houses of parliament on June 09, 2014, five key aspects can be deduced as follows:

Foreign Policy of Enlightened National Interest:
- A strong, self-reliant and self-confident India would pursue a foreign policy of enlightened national interest.
- The enlightened national interest would lead to the possibilities of creating cooperative outcomes including ensuring peace with one, while not letting down the other.

Focus on Neighborhood:
- The foreign policy would focus on neighborhood where India would help in building a democratic, peaceful, stable and economically interlinked neighborhood.
- The Prime Minister Narendra Modi's invitation to the SAARC leaders to attend his swearing-in ceremony clearly sent a message to the region and beyond, including China, that the new government in India intends to proactively engage the region.

- The Indian Prime Minister's invitation was accepted by the SAARC leaders and beyond including the Prime Minister of Mauritius Navin Ramgoolam, boosting India's centrality to the region.
- Prime Minister Narendra Modi's invitation to SAARC leaders has raised huge expectations in South Asia regarding his foreign policy.
- Prime Minister Narendra Modi also held bilateral talks with the SAARC leaders during their visit to India for the swearing-in ceremony.
- In late June 2014, the government convened a meeting of envoys of South Asian countries, China, Central Asian Republics, Iran and Myanmar as part of Prime Minister Narendra Modi's policy of increasing engagement with immediate neighbours and extended neighbourhood.
- Prime Minister Narendra Modi's visit to Bhutan on June 15-16, 2014, and External Affairs Minister Sushma Swaraj's visit to Bangladesh on June 25-27, 2014, pointed to the emphasis on neighbourhood in the new government's foreign policy.

Emphasis on Soft Power, 5Ts - Trade, Tourism, Talent, Technology and Tradition:
- The incumbent government's foreign policy also lays emphasis on soft power – to persuade others based on the attractiveness of their technology, politics, culture, idea or ideals.
- India would offer the world 5 Ts – Trade, Tourism, Talent, Technology and Tradition.

Multi-Alignment Policy:
- The new government's foreign policy indicated that it would adopt a 'multi-alignment' policy with all major powers.
- The government would work with China to develop a strategic and cooperative partnership.
- The government would work with Japan to build modern infrastructure.
- The government would build on the firm relations with Russia.
- The government would bring renewed vigour in India's engagement with the US and to operationalise the civil nuclear agreement.
- It would make efforts to achieve progress in key areas with European Union and its leading members.

Willing to Raise Issues of Concern at a Bilateral Level:
- The key element of the new foreign policy is the willingness to raise issues of concern at the bilateral level.
- Prime Minister Narendra Modi raised all issues of concern in his bilateral meetings with the SAARC leaders after his swearing-in ceremony.
- India has made it clear that stability can be built in the region only if there is an end to the export of terrorism.

Foreign Policy Initiatives Undertaken by the Modi Government

- The External Affairs Minister, Sushma Swaraj said that the Narendra Modi government's diplomatic initiatives have been "strong, proactive, and sensitive".
- The primary focus of the government's foreign policy has been the neighbourhood followed by the 'look East policy' or act East policy of reaching out to ASEAN countries and beyond.
- The strength of the government's diplomacy was seen from its tough stands:
- It was made very clear to China that while India accepts 'One China' policy, China must adopt a 'One India' policy and be aware of the Indian sensitivities in relation to its claim over Arunachal Pradesh.
- The US was told that friendship and surveillance cannot go together.
- Pakistan was told that if they talk to separatists, they cannot be talking to India.
- India's sensitive diplomacy was demonstrated from the evacuation of Indian students from Ukraine and workers from Iraq and Libya.
- The Modi Government has been proactive from the first day with bold initiatives like inviting the SAARC leaders to its swearing-in.
- The focus on neighbourhood continued with the Prime Minister Narendra Modi choosing to visit Bhutan and Nepal in his first and second foreign visits.
- The second focus of the government has been the 'Look East policy' now renamed 'Act East Policy' with Prime Minister's visits to Japan, Myanmar and Australia and the visit of other dignitaries to Singapore, Vietnam and China.
- The third focus of the Government's foreign policy has been the Persian Gulf where seven million Indians work.
- Latin America and Africa also remained in focus of Indian diplomacy with the next Indo-African summit scheduled to have all 54 African nations participating in it.
- The government has moved with rare speed and alacrity to rebuild India's partnerships across the world, setting new milestones.
- The external affairs minister told the Lok Sabha that Prime Minister Narendra Modi's foreign visits had advanced the pursuit of a secure and stable environment that India needed to accomplish its development goals.
- Mr. Modi's visits would contribute in a significant measure to the mission of accelerating economic growth, boosting investment, creating jobs and transforming the quality of life of the people of India.

- The Prime Minister had laid out a clear vision of India's role and place in the world, signaled willingness to assume leadership expected from the world's largest democracy; and demonstrated ability to turn commitments into action and convert opportunities into outcomes.
- The External Affairs Minister told the Lok Sabha that at the heart of the Prime Minister's engagement abroad had been efforts to promote cooperation on skill development, advanced medical research for diseases, like the agreement on research for malaria and TB with the US, food security, such as India's work with Australia on farm research, education, such as the agreement to collaborate with the US on a new generation Indian Institute of Technology.

Prime Minister Narendra Modi's Address to the Indians:
- On February 07, 2015, Prime Minister Narendra Modi addressed more than 110 Indian heads of missions from around the world at their annual conference in New Delhi.
- The Prime Minister asked the Indian envoys to use the current global environment to position India in a leading role and to adapt to global changes.
- The theme of the conference was 'Diplomacy with Development' which included the development agenda of the Government as well as helping Indians worldwide on consular issues, preparing for the international Yoga Day in June 2015, 'Swachch Bharat' and the clean Ganga initiatives.
- Mr. Modi emphasized on the fight against climate change, pointing out that India must lead that fight. He stressed that a love for nature, or *prakriti-prem* was part of Indian culture.

2

Indo – China Relations (Past, Present and Future)

Background

1949 – Diplomatic Recognition: India accorded diplomatic recognition to the People's Republic of China on December 30, 1949. The People's Liberation Army (PLA) made China independent through a revolution in 1949.

1954 – Two Accords Signed: The relations between India and China in the 1950's were very cordial and peaceful. In 1954, the Chinese Premier, Mr. Zou En Lai visited India which led to the signing of two accords as follows:

A. First Accord - India recognized Tibet as an integral part of China and considered it to be an autonomous region of China.

B. Second Accord - The declaration of Panchsheel in the joint communique. The Panchsheel enshrines the five principles of co-existence as follows:
- Respect for sovereignty and territorial integrity of all states
- Non-interference in territorial affairs
- Equality and mutuality
- Peaceful co-existence
- Mutual non-aggression

1962 – War: In the late 1950's China occupied small portions of territory along the Indo-Tibet Frontier. In 1962, India and China fought a war which resulted in China occupying sizeable portions of the India territory in the West (Ladakh) and in the East (Arunachal Pradesh).

1962 – Parliamentary Resolution on recovery of Indian Territory from China: The Indian parliament passed a resolution in 1962, pledging to wage an unending struggle till the complete recovery of Indian territory from China and it also forbade cessation of any occupied territory to China as part of any border settlement.

Normalisation of Relations – 1988 – path-breaking visit by Rajiv Gandhi to China: In the 1980's more efforts were made to normalize the relations. The real breakthrough in the relations between the two countries came during the path-breaking visit undertaken by Mr. Rajiv Gandhi in 1988.

1990 – Détente: The 1990's saw the beginning of the 'détente' in the context of changing equations in the global scenario. China's president, Mr. Jiang Zemin visited India in November 1997. This was the first ever visit by a Chinese Head of State to India. Four agreements were signed during the visit.

Deterioration in Relations After India conducted the Nuclear Tests in 1998: There had been deterioration in Sino-Indian relations after the conduct of nuclear tests by India. China adopted a brazenly partisan attitude by terming India's nuclear tests as "outrageous" but describing Pakistan's nuclear tests as only "regrettable". Senior officials in the government of India articulated the "China threat".

1999 – Normalization of Relations: In April 1999, China restarted an official dialogue with India. The Joint Working Group (JWG) was convened in Beijing after 11 months delay because of China's refusal to set dates. The visit by the external affairs minister of India, Mr. Jaswant Singh, to China in June 1999, followed by the President, Mr. Narayanan's visit in early 2000, helped in the normalization of bilateral relations.

2000 – Indian President's visit to China: The Indian President Mr. K.R. Narayanan visited China from May 28 – June 3, 2000. Mr. Narayanan had visited China in 1994 as the Vice-President of India. The Indian President held talks with his Chinese counterpart Mr. Jiang Zemin and other political leaders of China.

Irritants in Sino-Indian Relations:

- Sino-Pak Defence Relations - The overt and covert military assistance provided by China to Pakistan is the biggest impediment in improving Sino-Indian relations. The Sino-Pakistan collusion in the nuclear field is seen as China's long term strategy in gaining supremacy in Asia.
- Boundary Disputes - The non-resolution of Aksai Chin and other boundary disputes. China has laid claim to 90,000 square kms of Arunachal Pradesh. Analysts feel that by not resolving the boundary disputes China wants to keep India under strategic pressure.
- Military bases in Tibet and Myanmar - China has built military bases in Tibet and Myanmar which are seen by India as a threat to its national security.

Indian Prime Minister Atal Behari Vajpayee's Visit to China (June 22-27, 2003)

Declaration on Principles for Relations and Comprehensive Cooperation between India and China: It formulates core principles that should govern the Sino-Indian relations and rolls out a road map for friendship and cooperation. The key areas are as follows:

- Friendship and cooperation
- High-level exchanges
- Bilateral trade
- Joint study group: To examine the potential complementarities between the two countries in expanded trade and economic cooperation.

- Boundary issue: The two sides agreed to each appoint a special representative to explore from the political perspective of the overall bilateral relationship the framework of a boundary settlement.
- Tibet: The Indian side recognizes that Tibet autonomous region is part of the territory of the People's Republic of China and reiterates that it does not allow Tibetans to engage in anti-China political activities.
- Memorandum between India and China on expanding border trade: The Indian side agreed to designate Changgu of Sikkim State as the venue for border trade market; the Chinese side agreed to designate Renquinggang of the Tibet autonomous region as the venue for border trade market.

Significance of Prime Minister's Visit to China
- New phase of relations
- Breaking the impasse over the boundary dispute
- Movement on linked issues of Tibet and Sikkim
- Anchoring bilateral relations to economics

Chinese Premier Wen Jiabao's Visit to India (April 9-12, 2005):

A. **Resolving the Sikkim Dispute:** China recognizes Sikkim as part of India

B. **Benefits of resolving the Sikkim dispute:**
- Demilitarizing the border between Sikkim and Tibet - resulting in the restoration of trade, tourism and consular links.
- Economic revitalization - of the entire region including India's north-east and southern China.
- Will contribute to bring the two countries together.

C. **Border Agreement:**

(i) Three-phase agreement: India and China agreed to a three-phase settlement of the border dispute:
- **Phase I:** The agreement on the guiding principles to settle the border dispute.
- **Phase II:** It involves the two special representatives of the two sides to construct a framework based on the guiding principles contained in Articles 4-7.
- **Phase III:** Will be to apply this framework on the ground in a single package deal involving give and take, which will be worked on a political basis by the special representatives.

(ii) **Guiding principles to settle the border dispute:** India and China agreed to set up 11 political parameters and guiding principles to resolve the boundary dispute.

D. **Strategic Partnership:** A joint statement declared that India and China agree that their relations had now acquired a "global and strategic" character. The leaders of the two countries have, therefore, agreed to establish an India-China strategic and cooperative partnership for peace and prosperity.

E. **Cooperation in the Energy Security:** The two countries agreed to cooperate in the field of energy security and conservation including, among other things, encouraging relevant departments and units of the two countries to engage in the survey and exploration of petroleum and natural gas resources in third countries.

F. **Trade Ties:**
- Increasing two-way trade
- Joint feasibility study for a free trade agreement (FTA)
- Benefits of an FTA with China:
  - Will boost investments
  - Lower costs of products and services and competitiveness of industry

Reopening of the Nathu La Pass (July 6, 2006):

A. **Nathu La Pass:**
- **Altitude:** 4,545 meters
- **Location:** Indo-China border in Sikkim. Equidistant from Kolkata and Lhasa, Tibet's Capital.

B. **Background:**
- **Part of the Ancient Silk Route:** The Nathu La Pass used to be part of the ancient Silk Route, a vital trade link between India and China, prior to its closure in 1962.
- **2003 – China recognized Sikkim and signed MOU to resume trade:** During the visit of the former Prime Minister Atal Bihari Vajpayee in 2003 China recognized Sikkim as a constituent of India and signed a MOU to resume trade.

C. **Nathu La Pass Re-opened after 44 years:** On July 6, 2006 India and China formally inaugurated trade through the Nathu La Pass, linking Sikkim and the Tibet Autonomous Region (TAR). The pass was closed for 44 years after the 1962 conflict between India and China. Sikkim Chief Minister Pawar Kumar Chamling and TAR Chairman Qiangba Phuntsog jointly inaugurated the reopening of the pass.

D. **Export List restricted:** At present the border trade will be limited to the border zone and the export list is restricted to 29 items of export for India and 15 items of export for China. The list includes livestock products and chemicals from India and wool and herbs from China.

E. **Significance of Reopening the Nathu La Pass:**
   - Firmly establishes China's recognition of Sikkim as part of India
   - An addition to the confidence building measures between the two countries
   - An important step forward in advancing friendly relations
   - Will also help in resolving the border issue
   - Boost to trade
   - Could pave the way for a major trade route between China and South Asia

Chinese President Hu Jintao's visit to India (November 20-23, 2006):
   A. **Second visit by a Chinese head of state to India:** The Chinese president Hu Jintao accompanied by a 40-member delegation including the Foreign Minister Li Zhaoxing, Commerce Minister Bo Xilai, Minister of National Development Ma Kai and Head of the General office of the communist party of China, Wang Gang, visited India in November 2006. This was the second visit by a Chinese head of state to India (the first was by President Jiang Zemin in 1996).
   B. **Significance of the Chinese President's visit to India:**
   - Important step forward in the process at developing a comprehensive framework of engagement with China
   - Adding substance to the strategic relations
   - Visit sent a strong message to the international community that India and China are partners not rivals
   - Both countries committed to future development and diversification of relations
   - Continued engagement with China at the highest level would speed up the process of resolution of outstanding differences
   - Early resolution of the boundary question would further strengthen the strategic partnership
   - Initiatives to consolidate institutional linkages between the two governments
   - China endorsed the Indo-US Nuclear deal

Indian Prime Minister Manmohan Singh's visit to China (January 13-15, 2008):
   A. **Joint Document – "A Shared Vision for the 21st Century:**
   - Boundary solution on the basis of the guiding principles announced in 2005
   - Pledge to promote bilateral cooperation in civil nuclear energy consistent with their respective international commitments

- China supports India's aspirations to play a greater role in the UN
- Global and regional dimensions of bilateral ties – common positions on WTO talks and climate change
- Joint military training exercises
- Bilateral trade target of $60 billion
- Agreement to explore commencing discussions on the RTA through a joint economic group

B. **Significance of the Visit:**
- Successful visit would contribute to the improvement in Sino-Indian relations
- Defining theme of the visit – Sino-Indian relationship would have a significant regional and global influence
- Political Gains – China's pledge to promote civil nuclear cooperation and support for India's aspirations for a greater UN role
- High level political exchanges and the bilateral agreements signed point to the maturation and diversification of bilateral relations
- Plans to hold the second joint military exercises point to the strategically cordial ties
- Growing bilateral trade point to economics as the principal driver of bilateral relations

Outstanding Territorial issues between India and China:

A. **Background:**

Shimla Conference: The 4060 km long Sino-Indian border has been the bone of contention between the two countries. The border dispute dates back to the Shimla conference of 1914 when the representatives of British India, Tibet and China met. It was decided in the conference that:
- Tibet was an autonomous country.
- The McMahon Line would be the boundary between India and Tibet.
- Chinese sovereignty of some sort would extend over Tibet.

McMahon Line: The Indo-China-Tibet boundary or the McMahon line in the East and the boundary (Aksai Chin) along Ladakh in the West remained a boundary by usage and understanding. The result was that the precise boundary was not demarcated, leading to border skirmishes in 1962 and the Chinese penetration into the Sumdurung Chu Valley of Arunachal Pradesh in 1986.

The Main Areas of the Border Dispute:
- The McMahon Line is not recognized by China.
- The integration of Arunachal Pradesh into India is also not recognized by China.

India's position:
- The border in the west should remain at the 1959 position thereby implying that it does not recognize China's claim over Aksai Chin. The northern borders of Arunachal Pradesh and Sikkim correspond to the McMahon Line and hence the boundary.
- India also holds that China is in possession of Indian territory which it occupied during the 1962 conflict.
- The territory west of Karakoram within Pakistan Occupied Kashmir (POK) belongs to India and has been illegally ceded by Pakistan to China.

China's position:
- China claims 90,000 sq. km, which is almost the entire state of Arunachal Pradesh.
- Occupies 38,000 sq. km which is Aksai Chin in Kashmir.
- Occupies 5,000 sq. km of Shaksgam valley ceded to it by Pakistan in June 1963.
- Does not recognize the McMahon Line.

B. **Three Main Territorial disputes:**
- Arunachal Pradesh
- Aksai Chin Region
- Trans-Karakoram

Arunachal Pradesh:
- In 1972 Arunachal Pradesh became a Union Territory and gained full statehood in 1986.
- China refuses to recognize Arunachal Pradesh as part of India.
- China claims 90,000 square kilometers as their territory – almost the whole of Arunachal Pradesh – calling it "South Tibet".
- The border dispute is the legacy of the British colonial rule.
- The 1914 British demarcated boundary called the McMahon Line is not recognized by China. The boundary is now known in both India and China as the Line of Actual Control (LAC).

Aksai Chin:
- India accuses China of occupying 38,000 sq. km in Jammu and Kashmir, in the Aksai Chin region, north-east of Ladakh.
- Aksai Chin, also called the Soda Plain, is almost uninhabited and desert-like.

Trans-Karakoram Tract:
- Under the Sino-Pakistan Boundary agreement of 1963, Pakistan illegally ceded 5,180 sq. km of Indian territory (Trans-Karakoram tract, Saksham valley) to China.

- The transfer is disputed by India as it is part of Jammu and Kashmir.

China's policy of issuing stapled visas to Indian citizens domiciled in Kashmir and Arunachal Pradesh:

A. **India's stand:**
   - **October 2009 – Chinese Embassy issued stapled visas to Indian Passport holders from J&K:** In October 2009, it came to light that the Chinese embassy in New Delhi had begun issuing visas to Indian passport holders from Jammu and Kashmir on a separate sheet of paper rather than stamping them in their passports as is the case with other Indian citizens.
   - Since 2007, China has issued "stapled visas" to the handful of Indian passport holders from Arunachal Pradesh.
   - **Stapled Visas to Indian Citizens of J&K an attempt by China to question the status of Jammu and Kashmir:** The separate sheet visas for Kashmiris was seen by the Ministry of External Affairs (MEA) as an attempt by China to question the status of Jammu and Kashmir.
   - The immigration authorities were told to treat any visa that was not stamped on a passport as invalid for the purpose of travel.
   - India asked China not to discriminate against visa applications filed by its nationals on grounds of domicile and ethnicity.
   - In January 2011, China again issued stapled visas to two Indian sportsmen domiciled in Arunachal Pradesh. The MEA conveyed that a uniform practice on issuance of visas to Indian nationals must be followed regardless of the applicant's ethnicity or place of domicile.
   - India would not accept anything that questions the status of Jammu and Kashmir and Arunachal Pradesh which were an integral part of India.

B. **China's stand:**
   - China claimed that it viewed the visa policy as an administrative issue and not a political statement.
   - China's position was consistent and clear about the China-India border issue, including the disputed area of eastern section. The position had remained unchanged, according to the Chinese Foreign Ministry authorities.

China's attempt to question India's sovereignty in Kashmir:
- China's policy of issuing stapled visas to Kashmiri-domicile Indian citizens
- China's denial of a proper visa to an Indian General from Kashmir
- China's development activity in Pakistan occupied Kashmir (POK)

A. **India's Objections to China's Development Activity in Pakistan occupied Kashmir:**
   - On October 14, 2009, India called upon China to stop developmental activities in areas illegally occupied by Pakistan.
   - India was reacting to China's assurance to Pakistan of help in upgrading the Karakoram highway and building the Neelam-Jhelum hydro-electric project in Pakistan occupied Kashmir.
   - India noted that Pakistan had been illegally occupying parts of Jammu and Kashmir since 1947, and China was fully aware of India's position and concerns about Chinese activities in POK.
   - India hoped that China would take a long-term view of India-China relations and cease such activities in areas illegally occupied by Pakistan.

B. **China's stand:**
   - China said that it was a matter for India and Pakistan to resolve and that China had no reason to change its policies on Kashmir.
   - China's presence in POK had grown in recent years and it was currently involved in several infrastructure projects in the disputed region.

C. **Kashmir is to India what Tibet and Taiwan are to China:**
   - First time India drew a parallel directly between Kashmir and Tibet and Taiwan: During the Russia-India-China Trilateral Summit in November 2010, Indian Foreign Minister S.M. Krishna told his Chinese counterpart Yang Jiechi that just as India had been sensitive to its concerns over Tibet Autonomous Region and Taiwan, China too should be mindful of Indian sensitivities on Jammu and Kashmir. This was the first time India had drawn this parallel directly.
   - The comparison was intended to emphasize the depth of India's concerns over recent Chinese attempts to question the country's sovereignty in Kashmir.

D. **For the first time India refrained from reiterating its "One China" policy during the Chinese Premier's visit to India:** During the Chinese Premier Wen Jiabao's visit to India in December 2010, India, for the first time refrained from reiterating its "One China policy" under which the Autonomous Region of Tibet is an integral part of China.

E. **No change in China's Policy - the problem of Jammu and Kashmir could only be resolved through dialogue and negotiations between India and Pakistan:** The Chinese foreign minister Yang Jiechi said that China always believed that the problem of Jammu and Kashmir could only be resolved through dialogue and negotiations between India and Pakistan and that there had been no change in its policy.

Construction of a Dam on Brahmaputra River by China:
A. **India raises concern over the construction of the Brahmaputra Dam:**
   - During the fourth round of the strategic dialogue held in Beijing on November 16, 2010, India's foreign secretary Nirupama Rao raised concern over China starting construction of a dam on the Brahmaputra River.
   - India was concerned about the possible downstream impact of the project.
B. **China's Response:**
   - China assured India that the 510 MW hydropower project in Zangmu was not a project designed to divert water and would not affect the welfare and availability of water to the population in the lower reaches of the Brahmaputra.
   - China also expressed its willingness to continue exchanging hydrological data and cooperation on flood management through the joint expert-level mechanism set up by India and China in 2003.

   India Suspended Defence Ties with China in August 2010 which resumed in June 2011: In August 2010, India suspended defence exchanges with China after an Indian General from Kashmir was denied a proper visa to travel to China on an official visit. On June 25, 2011, India and China concluded a week-long defence talks. The eight-member Indian delegation was led by Major-General Gurmeet Singh.

Chinese premier Li Keqiang's visit to India (May 19-21, 2013):
   a. India was the first country of the Chinese premier's maiden overseas visit; discussions were held on various issues such as border issue, Tibet issue, trans border rivers including trade and commerce.

Chinese President Xi Jinping's Visit to India (September 17-19, 2014):
   a. **First Chinese President to visit India in 8 years:**
      - Chinese President Xi Jinping visited India from September 17-19, 2014.
      - He was the first Chinese President to visit India in 8 years.
      - Mr. Xi began his visit to India with Ahmadabad where he was received by Prime Minister Narendra Modi.
      - India and China signed two agreements and one Memorandum of Understanding (MOU) in Ahmadabad.
   b. **India and China signed 13 Agreements:**
      - Five-year trade and economic development plan – Enhances economic ties and reduces trade imbalance.

- Modernizing Railways – Study feasibility of partnership in high-speed railways and redevelopment of railway stations.
- Tie-up in Railways – Prepare plan for cooperation on specific projects.
- Trade Balance – Enhancing market access to Indian products.
- New Pilgrimage Route – Kailash Mansarovar Yatra to be routed through Nathula Pass in Sikkim.
- Outer Space – Exploration of outer space for peaceful purposes.
- Customs Administration-Sharing information to fight trans-border economic crimes.
- Drug Administration – Cooperation in drug standards and traditional medicine
- Pact for sister city – Exchanges between Mumbai and Shanghai
- Industrial Park near Pune – 1,250 acre park to provide cluster-type development
- Promotion of Literature
- Cultural exchanges – Collaboration between cultural institutions
- Audio Visual Co-production – Help producers to pool resources to co-produce films

c. **India raised concerns over the Chinese incursions in Ladakh:**
   - India raised concerns over the repeated Chinese incursions in Ladakh following the latest incidents in Chumar and Demchok along the Line of Actual Control (LAC).
   - According to media reports, hundreds of Chinese troops and civilians had gathered at Chumar and Demchok along the LAC in Ladakh forcing a stand-off with Indian forces, and were refusing to vacate the area despite flag meetings to discuss the situation.
   - Prime Minister Narendra Modi said that respect for each other's sensitivities and concerns, and peace and stability in bilateral relations and along the borders were essential for both countries to realize the enormous potentials in their relations.
   - Mr. Modi urged for the clarification or demarcation of the LAC and an early settlement of the boundary question.
   - Chinese President Xi Jinping hoped that the boundary resolution could be resolved quickly and stressed that India and China had to come together for Asia to progress. He pointed out that when India and Asia speak in one voice, the world has to pay attention.
   - Mr. Xi said that while India and China had made some progress on the boundary resolution, some incidents were there because the boundaries had not been demarcated.

- India and China were both committed to maintenance of peace and tranquility at their borders and both countries would like to ensure that the dialogue mechanisms that they had created for this purpose were error-proof, according to India's President Pranab Mukherjee.
- It was important for both countries to improve the dialogue and cooperative engagement between the two militaries to constantly strive to enhance the communication at all levels, according to Mr. Mukherjee.

d. **India raised the issue of China's stapled Visa policy and trans-border rivers:** India's Prime Minister Narendra Modi said that he had raised issues like China's dual stapled visa policy and trans-border rivers with the Chinese President Xi Jinping in the spirit of candour and friendship.

e. **Chinese President announced investments of $20 billion in Indian projects:**
- Chinese President Xi Jinping announced investments in two industrial cities in Gujarat and Maharashtra as well as $20 billion investments in projects in India.
- Although the Chinese investments in India were well short of the expected figure of $100 billion, they were nearly 40 times the present Chinese investments in India of $500 million.
- Mr. Xi said that China would commit another $30 billion in the region for additional projects in the next few years.

f. **China ready to strengthen cooperation with India in multilateral fora:**
- China supports India's aspiration for a bigger role in the UN Security Council (UNSC), according to the Chinese President Xi Jinping.
- Mr. Xi said that China was ready to strengthen strategic cooperation with India in multilateral for a BRICs, UNSC and on the issue of climate change, food, energy, cyber security where both countries have shared common interests.
- China welcomed and supported India's full membership in the Shanghai Cooperation Organisation (SCO) as it expected India to support China in building relations with SAARC so that the two countries could work together to contribute their due share to regional stability and development, according to the Chinese President.
- India has applied for the membership of the SCO and was ready to step up engagement with the security grouping.

g. **Significance of the Chinese President Xi Jinping's visit to India:**
- Chinese President Xi Jinping's visit to India was a marked shift in India's diplomatic handling of the bilateral relations. Prime Minister Narendra Modi's public statement on the repeated incidents of Chinese incursions on the border and his special meeting with Mr. Xi

in Ahmadabad against protocol and conventions were indications of India's diplomatic shift in handling affairs with China.
- Both sides also showed that the strategic ties would be separate from the economic ties as India welcomed China's investments of around $20 billion in Indian projects, although the figure was lower than expected.
- China agreed to address India's concerns on the imbalance in bilateral trade.
- President Xi Jinping and Prime Minister Narendra Modi found common ground to resolve the border row as part of a roadmap that would steer India-China relations in future, according to the Chinese Foreign Ministry.
- The Chinese President invited India to be part of a new inclusive security architecture in the Asia-Pacific which was significant in view of the US China-centric pivot to Asia.
- India did not endorse China's Maritime Silk Route.
- The Bangladesh-India-China-Myanmar (BICM) corridor was accepted by
- India on the condition that it ensures peaceful, stable and cooperative environment.
- India did not receive the expected $100 billion investments from China.
- Both leaders expressed strong views on territorial disputes, economic and other issues.
- The India-China Summit had led to an agreement that 'cooperation would remain the main theme' of India-China relations, according to the Chinese Foreign Ministry spokesperson. It was pointed out that the relations had entered a new age, but implied continued engagement.

h. **India-China Stand-off on the LAC in Ladakh:**
- On September 10, China's People's Liberation Army (PLA) reportedly moved 500 soldiers to Chumar village on the Indian side of the line of actual control (LAC), 300 km south-east of Leh in Jammu and Kashmir.
- Chinese nomads known as Rebos put up tents at Demchok, 500 meters into Indian territory.
- India's Prime Minister Narendra Modi raised the issue with the Chinese President Xi Jinping during his visit to India.
- On September 26, 2014, India's External Affairs Minister Sushma Swaraj met her Chinese counterpart Wang Yi in New York on the sidelines of the UN General Assembly to resolve the issue.

- Ms. Swaraj said that the stand-off at Chumar had been resolved and the withdrawal of troops would be completed.
- China said that with the resolution of the stand-off in Ladakh, the two sides could now maintain peace and tranquility in the border area and implement the consensus reached by the leaders to build a closer development partnership.
- On September 30, 2014, India's external affairs ministry announced that both sides carried out disengagement and redeployment of border troops on September 26 and 27, 2014.
- The status quo as on September 01, 2014 had been re-established after the 20 day stand-off between the troops of India and China in eastern Ladakh.
- The two sides also agreed that a meeting of the working Mechanism for the Consultation and Coordination on India China Border Affairs (WMCC) would be convened to discuss various issues pertaining to the maintenance of peace and tranquility in the border areas, according to the external affairs ministry statement.

3

Indo-US Relations & India's Takeaways

INDO–US RELATIONSHIP ...RECENT VISIT BY PRIME MINISTER NARENDRA MODI TO THE USA

The Indo-USA relationship has been a 'roller coaster one' since the time of US President Ronald Reagan and subsequent Congress and NDA Governments trying to catch up, on strategic and economic agreements.

With several changes in High-Tech Sectors, Industrialization requirements, Climate change issues, Immigration policy, re-alignment of Nations, rise of the ISIS/terrorism, Fossil fuel consumptions and politics and economic issues confronting India, there was a need to strengthen Indo-us ties with the visit by the Prime Minister of India recently.

There were several crucial outcomes of the three day visit to the U.S, in addition to the establishment of a personal equation with the U.S. President Donald Trump; which resulted in perfect meeting of minds between the two leaders. Some of the highlights are:

- **Investment in India:-** Top American CEOs of global giants including Apple, Microsoft, Walmart, and Google discussed investment, visa issue and 'Make in India projects and job creation.

- **Sale of Guardian unmanned aerial systems** (drones) to India worth $ 2-3 billion, approval.
- **Focus on Indo-Pacific region** respecting freedom of Navigation, over flight, Territorial and maritime issues and partnership in commerce.
- **Maritime Security talks and implementation** of the 'White shipping 'data sharing including Maritime traffic and domain awareness and the Naval Exercise 'MALABAR 2017'
- **Liquefied Natural Gas (LNG)** flow to India, worth nearly $40 billion.
- **On Pakistan-** a Joint statement to call on Pakistan's belligerent approach in providing territory to launch terrorist attacks on other countries and expeditiously take action on cross border terrorist activities including 26/11 Mumbai and Pathankot attack.
- **Stress on fighting Terrorism** in every part of the world by rooting out terrorist safe havens and commitment to strengthening cooperation against terrorist threats from groups including al-Qaeda, ISIS etc and in support of the United States efforts to end terror in all its forms.
- **North Korea-** North Korea's continued provocations were condemned and a pledge to work together to counter DPRK's weapons of mass destruction programs including accountability of other nations, that support these programmes.

The meeting between Prime Minister Narendra Modi and US President Donald Trump is on a positive run and in their determination to continue relationship in shared objectives between two of the world's greatest democracies!

Introduction

New Level of Maturity in Indo-US Ties: India's relations with the US have reached a new level of maturity where both sides can live with their differences without their fundamental friendly good relations being affected adversely.

Basic Shift in US Policy towards India:
- **Offer for Cooperation in Civilian Nuclear Technology:** The Indo-US Civil Nuclear Agreement gives India access to civilian nuclear technology which was denied to India for three decades. It is pointed out that this goes well beyond what was being considered under the Next Steps in Strategic Partnership (NSSP).
- **Defence Cooperation Agreement:** The US has also offered a defence cooperation agreement with India that includes joint production. Such a provision is provided only to close allies of the US like South Korea and Turkey. This is seen as unprecedented in Indo-US ties.
- **Institutional Means to Convert Aspects of NSSP into Tangible Projects:** The US has also offered India the institutional means to convert aspects of the

NSSP, including economic cooperation and provision of space technology, into tangible projects.

- **Defence Cooperation and Nuclear Energy were centre-pieces of Indo-US ties:** According to US officials, defence cooperation and nuclear energy were the centre-pieces of Indo-US ties in the current context.

Broader Indo-US Strategic Relationship – Cooperation on a Global strategy for Peace, Defence, Energy and Economic Growth: Indo-US relationship is being transformed from a bilateral one to a strategic partnership, according to the then US Ambassador to India, David C Mulford. The US is in favour of a decisively broader strategic relationship to help India achieve its goals as one of the world's great multi-ethnic democracies. The vision embraces cooperation on a global strategy for peace, defence, energy and economic growth.

Background

Relations during the Cold War: India and the US differed in their strategic perception during the Cold-war. The former Soviet Union was always a factor in the Indo-US relations in the past.

Pro-Pakistan Policy of the US: Apart from the Cold War compulsions, the US always saw India through the prism of Pakistan factor. According to the geo-political considerations at that time the US was always keen to sustain its relations with Pakistan and in the process ignored India's concerns and sensitivities.

1948-54: The Indo-US relations were not upbeat due to the US stand on Kashmir and Cold-War, India's neutrality on Korea and support for China.

1954-60: India's stand on Hungary and anti-US speeches angered the US. The military balance tilted in favour of Pakistan due to US arms supply.

1965-70: Military aid was cut off after the Indo-Pak war in 1965. The US got involved in Vietnam; it ignored the region and economic aid thinned.

1971-80: The US opposed India in the 1971 war and the relations plunged to their lowest level. The 1974 nuclear test at Pokhran and the Emergency did not help in improving the relations.

1980-84: The US resumed arms supply to Pakistan but India tried to improve relations and signed a science MOU.

1985-92: The US agreed to aid LCA (Light Combat Aircraft) project and stepped up high-tech exports. It also encouraged India to play a larger role in the region.

1993-95: The relations again hit a low after the US Assistant Secretary of State, Ms Robin Raphel's remarks on Kashmir. US began pressurizing India to abandon missile programmes and its nuclear option.

1995-98: The relations remained indifferent despite talks of periodic ups wings and strategic dialogue. India's nuclear tests led to the relations hitting rock bottom.

Sanctions: The US imposed unilateral sanctions on India for conducting the nuclear tests. The US also pressurized India through international forums. It got the P-5 (permanent members of the Security Council) to condemn the nuclear tests by India and Pakistan and demand they sign the NPT and non-nuclear weapons states.

Indo-US Talks: In the aftermath of the nuclear tests, India and the US decided to engage in a major political dialogue. The two principal interlocutors in the Indo-US dialogue, were the Prime Minister's Special envoy, Mr. Jaswant Singh and then US Deputy Secretary of State, Mr. Strobe Talbott.

US President Bill Clinton's visit to India: March 21, 2000, Fourth US President visited India.

Indian Prime Minister's visit to the US: India's Prime Minister, Mr. Atal Behari Vajpayee, visited the US from September 13-19, 2000. It was a historic visit in terms of upgrading the Indo-US relations.

Transformation of Indo-US Relations

A. **Transformation in Relations after September 11, 2001:**
   - Indo-US relations have been transformed in many ways since the September 11, 2001, attacks in the US, according to the US Ambassador to India, Mr. Robert Blackwill.
   - There was increased intensity, frequency and transparency of exchanges between the two governments at the diplomatic, intelligence and military levels.
   - India has extended full support to the US in its operations in Afghanistan.
   - The transformation in relations can be traced to the US's changed perception of stability in South Asia in the totality of America's own sense of urgency to insulate itself from the politics of terror.

B. **US Lifts Sanctions Against India:**
   - **On September 23, 2001,** the US President, Mr. George W Bush, lifted sanctions imposed on India after the 1998 nuclear tests. Mr. Bush emphasized that maintaining the embargoes would not be in the national security interests of the US.
   - **Gains for India:** Increase in military-to-military cooperation; resumption of cooperation in the LCA (light combat aircraft) programme; access to high-end computers and routers for faster internet access; improved overall climate of Indo-US cooperation.

C. **Recognizing India as a Global Power:** The Bush administration emphasized that India has earned its place at the table of global powers. This is a shift from the earlier view that perceived India in the narrow prism of the subcontinent. The US is now ready to engage India within the larger framework of a global balance of power.

D. **Converging Interests between India and the US:** For a meaningful engagement there should be a set of political interests between the two powers. The following are the converging interest between India and US:
- Common threat of terrorism emanating from Pakistan. A moderate Pakistan will be in the interests of both India and the US.
- Intensive cooperation in counter-terrorism.
- Maintenance of peace in the Indian Ocean.
- Ensuring free flow of oil from the Persian Gulf at reasonable prices.
- Safeguarding of sea lanes in the region.
- Prevention of proliferation of weapons of mass destruction.
- Preservation of a stable balance of power in Asia.

E. **Next steps in Strategic Partnership (NSSP):** On January 13, 2004, the US President, George W. Bush announced the next steps in the strategic partnership with India. Some of the highlights of the US proposals are as follows:
- **Stepping up cooperation in the quartet areas:** The US proposal will see the two countries stepping up cooperation in the so called quartet areas of non-military nuclear activities, civilian space programmes, trade in high technology and an expanded dialogue on missile defence.
- **Proposed cooperation would progress through a series of reciprocal steps:** According to Mr. Bush, the proposed cooperation would progress through a series of reciprocal steps that would build on each other.
- **Strengthening relevant laws to combat proliferation of WMD:** Mr. Bush emphasized that in order to combat the proliferation of weapons of mass destruction (WMD), relevant laws, regulations and procedures will be strengthened and measures to increase bilateral and international cooperation in this area will be employed.

F. **Broadening the Bilateral Economic Dialogue:** India and the US have agreed to broaden the bilateral economic dialogue and extend cooperation to energy, environment, health, and biotechnology and information technology. The cooperation will also be extended to space programmes and civilian nuclear safety projects.

G. **Strengthening Defence Ties:** Defence experts feel that Indo-US defence ties have been strengthened after September 11, 2001. The defence ties have a long-term perspective. There is a growing consensus in India on supporting the US on two major foreign policy issues – countering terrorism and National Missile Defence.

The US President Barack Obama's Visit to India (November 6-8, 2010)

A. Sixth US Presidential visit to India – The US stands in solidarity with all of India in Eradicating Terrorism
B. **Focus of the visit:**
   - Stalled entry of US nuclear companies
   - Elimination of US curbs on export of hi-tech and dual use items of India
   - Formulation of an action plan on cooperation in counter-terrorism
   - Energy – nuclear and renewable
   - Health care
   - Education and infrastructure
   - Tie-ups in space sector
   - Economic and trade cooperation
   - Military and security cooperation
C. US announced the export control reform package that would remove India's defence and space-related entities from the US entity list
D. **The US backs India's membership of NSG, MTCR and other hi-tech regimes:**
   - The US announced its decision to support India's membership in the
   - Nuclear Suppliers Group (NSG), the Missile Technology Control Regime (MTCR), the Australian Group and the Wassernaar Arrangement.
   - India has to fully adopt the regime's export control requirements to reflect its prospective membership, according to the US Deputy National
   - Security Adviser for International Economic Affairs Mike Fromen.
   - Currently, the membership rules of NSG and MTCR required adherence to the Nuclear Non-Proliferation Treaty (NPT) or a Regional Nuclear Weapons Free Zone.
   - However, the US would encourage the evolution of a membership criteria of these regimes consistent with maintaining their core principles.
E. **India-US sign $10 billion worth deals:**
   - The US president Barack Obama announced in Mumbai that deals worth $10 billion had been reached between India and the US for creating more than 50,000 jobs back in the US.
F. **The US removed ISRO and DRDO from the Entity list (January 25, 2011):** The US removed India's space and defence research establishments from its punitive entity list, ending a 13-year ban on access to US high-tech exports.

Meeting between the Indian Prime Minister and the US President (Washington, September 27, 2013)

  A. **Issues of Concern:**

  India:
  - Concerns over the potential adverse impact that the comprehensive immigration reform bill currently with the US congress could have on businesses employing skilled Indian workers.
  - The US has said that Indian nationals were the largest recipients of H–1B and L-1 visas by a wide margin and, the legislation under consideration would bring significant benefits to Indian nationals.

  The US:
  - The US nuclear vendors Westinghouse and GE want section 17 (b) of civil liability for nuclear damage act, which holds the suppliers responsible in case of a nuclear accident caused by faulty products of services, amended or removed.
  - However, the Government of India has made it clear that there would be no dilution of the civil liability nuclear damage act stressing that the Government would act according to the law of the land and not take any decision which was against the nation's interest.
  - The US wants India to fall in line with the Montreal Protocol and scale back Indian companies use of refrigerant gases.
  - Analysts in India have pointed out that adoption of alternate technology would be 20 times more costly and in some cases untested for safety.

  B. **Issues Discussed at the Meeting:**
  - **Strategic Issues:** The strategic issues that dominated the bilateral discussions appeared to have focused on Syria and Iran.
  - **Areas of Co-operation:** Both leaders talked about a wide range of areas of cooperation including defence, clean energy, the civilian nuclear agreement, counter-terrorism and the Af-Pak region, Syria, Iran and East Asia.
  - **Indo-Pak Relations:** The Indian Prime Minister said that expectations about the meeting with his Pakistani counterpart had to be toned down as long as terror stalked the subcontinent and its epicenter remained focused in Pakistan.
  - **Terrorism:** Both leaders agreed to undertake more cooperation in intelligence sharing and homeland security cooperation and condemned the September 26, 2013, terrorist attack in Samba in Jammu and Kashmir. Both sides called upon Pakistan to work towards bringing the 2008 Mumbai terror attack perpetrators to justice.

- **Indo-US Civil Nuclear Agreement:** The joint statement welcomed the announcement that the Nuclear Power Cooperation in terms of defence technology transfer, joint research, co-development and co-production was by endorsing a joint declaration on defence cooperation.
- **Bilateral Trade and Investment:** Both leaders said that the best way to take forward the Indo-US defence cooperation in terms of defence technology transfer, joint research, co-development and co-production was by endorsing a joint declaration on defence cooperation.
- **Bilateral Trade and Investment:** Both leaders underscored the significant advances in bilateral trade and investment. The Indian Prime Minister said that the figure had touched $100 billion despite the slowdown in the global economy.
- **Climate Change:** Both leaders decided to convene the India-US Task Force on hydro fluorocarbons to discuss options based on economically viable and technically feasible alternatives.

Prime Minister Narendra Modi's Visit to the US

1. **September 27–October 01, 2014:**
    - Prime Minister Narendra Modi's speech at Madison Square Garden in New York to the Indian diaspora was a big success.
    - The mega public interaction was organized by the Indian American Community Foundation with around 186 organizations represented.
    - Indian diaspora from 48 US states and 5 Canadian provinces participated in the event.
    - Indian-American community about 3.2 million and accounts for 1 percent of the US population.
    - The Indian-American community is the most educated and richest minority, according to a survey conducted in 2013.
    - The Indian-American community is now part of the Democratic and Republican Parties and is also represented in the government.
    - The Indian diaspora is now an important input in the foreign policy initiat-ives of the NDA Government led by Prime Minister Narendra Modi.
    - In his speech at the Madison Square Garden in New York, Prime Minister Narendra Modi stressed on development and good governance and pointed out that he wanted to make the people of India a partner in the country's development.
    - Mr. Modi said that his dream was that by 2022, which would be the 75th anniversary of India's Independence, no one in India should be without a home.

- The Prime Minister announced that every person holding a PIO (Person of Indian Origin) card would get a life-long visa for India.

2. **Prime Minister Narendra Modi's Meeting with President Barack Obama (September 30, 2014):**
   - India's Prime Minister Narendra Modi and the US President Barack Obama decided to take the Indo-US relationship to the next level, stressing that the true potential of the relationship had yet to be realized.
   - The discussions with President Obama had confirmed that India and the US were natural global partners, according to Mr. Modi.
   - The US president said that he was impressed with the Indian Prime Minister's interest in not only addressing poverty in India and revitalizing the economy there but also his determination that India helped bring about peace and security in the world.
   - Prime Minister Narendra Modi and the US president Barack Obama unveiled a roadmap for Indo-US relations by issuing a vision document, wrote a joint editorial in Washington Post and issued a joint statement. The three documents covered all aspects of the relationship.
   - The vision statement "Chalein Saath Saath: Forward/Together We Go" stressed that their strategic partnership would work to combat terror threats and prevent the spread of Weapons of Mass Destruction (WMD).
   - The vision statement said that the Indo-US partnership would be a model for the rest of the world.

Significance of Prime Minister Narendra Modi's Visit to the US

- The Indian Prime Minister Narendra Modi's visit to the US was significant in deepening the bilateral relations as the two countries issued three key documents – the vision statement, joint editorial by the two leaders and a comprehensive joint statement.
- The US investment companies have signaled their desire to renew investments in India after the assurance given by Prime Minister Narendra Modi that his government would address the concerns of the business leaders and try to make the overall environment more business-friendly.
- India remained firm on the issue of WTO's Trade Facilitation Agreement (TFA) that was raised by the US President Barack Obama. Indian Prime Minister Narendra Modi said that India was not against the TFA, but wanted the full implementation of the Bali package.
- The Prime Minister's visit brought the faltering Indo-US relations back on track on all aspects of the comprehensive dialogue – energy, health, space, women's empowerment, trade, skills, strategy and security.

- India and the US had commonalities on a wide spectrum of issues including strategic partnership and trade.
- Indian Prime Minister and the US President said that as global partners, both countries were committed to enhancing their homeland security by sharing intelligence, through counter-terrorism and law-enforcement cooperation, while they jointly work to maintain freedom of navigation and lawful commerce across the seas.
- The health cooperation between India and the US would help tackle the toughest of challenges, whether combating the spread of Ebola, researching cancer cures or conquering diseases like tuberculosis, malaria and dengue, according to the vision statement.
- Both sides intended to expand their recent tradition of working together to empower women, build capacity and improve food security in Afghanistan and Africa, according to the vision statement.
- India and the US would expand collaboration in trade, investment and technology that harmonize with India's ambitious development agenda, while sustain the US as the global engine of growth, according to the vision statement.
- The leaders of both countries discussed ways to boost manufacturing and expand affordable renewable energy, while sustainably securing the future of their common environment, according to the vision document.
- The US would support the "Clean India" campaign, where it would leverage private and civil society innovation, expertise and technology to improve sanitation and hygiene throughout India, according to the vision document.
- Both sides agreed to address the problems in the implementation of the landmark Indo-US nuclear deal.
- The US agreed to support India's bid for membership of the Missile Technology Control Regime (MTCR) and the Nuclear Suppliers Group (NSG). The US President Barack Obama agreed that India met the eligibility criteria for these regimes.
- India and the US agreed to renew their 2005 Indo-US Defence Cooperation Framework Agreement. Analysts point out that although the US is the world's largest arms manufacturer, India wants joint manufacturing of arms with Prime Minister Modi inviting US defence companies to invest in India.
- Both sides agreed to make joint and concerted efforts to dismantle terror and crime networks like LeT, D-company and al-Qaeda, all of them based in Pakistan.

- The joint statement called on all parties to avoid the use, or threat of use, of force in advancing their claim on South China Sea. Vietnam and the Philippines have complained of China's increasing aggressive stance on advancing its territorial claim on South China Sea.
- The vision document said that the advent of a new Government in India was a natural opportunity to broaden and deepen the Indo-US relationship with a reinvigorated level of ambition and greater confidence. It stressed that it was time to set a new agenda that realized concrete benefits for the citizens of the two countries.

US President Barack Obama's Second Visit to India (January 25-27, 2015)

1. **First US President to be the Chief Guest on India's Republic Day:**
   - The US President Barack Obama visited India from January 25-27, 2015, to become the first US President to be the Chief Guest on India's Republic Day.
   - Mr. Obama also became the first President of the US to visit India twice in his tenure. His first visit was in November 2010.
   - Wing Commander Pooja Thakur became the first woman to lead a ceremonial tri-service guard of honour inspected by the US President Barack Obama.
   - The US President Barack Obama and the Indian Prime Minister Narendra Modi held a second summit within four months.

2. **Breakthrough Understanding on the Indo-US Civil Nuclear Deal:**
   - The second summit between the US President Barack Obama and India's Prime Minister Narendra Modi led to a breakthrough in the Indo-US Civil Nuclear deal launched in 2005.
   - Mr. Obama announced that both leaders had reached a "breakthrough understanding" on the Indo-US Civil Nuclear deal that would allow nuclear contracts to be signed between the US firms and India.
   - On July 18, 2005, India and the US launched the Civil Nuclear Cooperation Initiative.
   - On August 01, 2008, the International Atomic Energy Agency (IAEA) approved India's safeguards agreement.
   - On September 06, 2008, India got the Nuclear Suppliers Group (NSG) waiver to import nuclear fuel.
   - On October 01, 2008, the US congress approved the Indo-US Civil Nuclear Cooperation Initiative.
   - On October 10, 2008, India and the US signed the Indo-US Civil Nuclear Cooperation Initiative.

- On March 15, 2009, India signed the IAEA's Additional Protocol.
- On August 30, 2010, India's Parliament approved the Civil Liability for Nuclear Damage Bill.
- According to the Civil Liability for Nuclear Damage Bill, Nuclear operators to be strictly liable for damages resulting from an accident but their liability would be capped at Rs. 1,500 crore, unless a higher amount is notified by the government.
- The US objected to Sections 17 (b) and 46 of the civil liability for Nuclear Damage Act which open the door for legal action against nuclear suppliers if an accident was caused by faulty or defective equipment.
- The US felt that these provisions violated the International Atomic Energy Agency's (IAEA) Convention on Supplementary Compensation for Nuclear Damage (CSC).
- US companies like GE and Westinghouse insist that they would not be able to supply nuclear equipment to India unless they were fully insulated in the event of an accident.
- The Indian Government informed the US that the Act, as passed by the Parliament was final and that no changes in any of its provisions were possible.
- India's then Foreign Secretary Sujatha Singh said that the US had given up its reservations without any assurance from the Indian side on diluting the Civil Liability for Nuclear Damage Act in any way.
- To address the US concerns over Clause 17 of the Nuclear Liability law, India would set up an insurance pool of Rs. 750 crore led by General Insurance Company and four other insurance firms to indemnify companies that build nuclear reactors in India against liability in case of a nuclear accident. The remaining Rs. 750 crore of the total amount of Rs. 1500 crore to offset liability would be provided by the Government of India.

Significance of the US President's Visit to India

1. **Significance of the Breakthrough Understanding in the Indo-US Civil Nuclear Deal:**
    - The Civil Nuclear Agreement was the centre-piece of the transformed relations between India and the US, according to India's Prime Minister Narendra Modi.
    - The US President Barack Obama said that he was pleased that six years after India and the US signed the bilateral agreement, they were moving towards commercial cooperation, consistent with their law, international legal obligations, and technical and commercial viability.

- Analysts point out that the breakthrough understanding reached on the Indo-US civil nuclear deal was seen as a significant diplomatic victory for India's stand that it would not dilute its Nuclear Liability law.
- India's then Foreign Secretary Sujatha Singh said that no changes to the Civil Liability for Nuclear Damages (CLND) Act, 2010, had been made, and no assurances given to the US on its contentious Section 46 that opened suppliers to tort liability.
- Mr. Obama said that the breakthrough in the nuclear deal was an important step that showed how both countries could work together to elevate their relationship.
- Prime Minister Narendra Modi announced that India has also won US assurances of support for its membership in four nuclear regimes – the Nuclear Suppliers Group (NSG), Wassenaar Arrangement, Australian Group and the Missile Technology Control Regime (MTCR).

2. **The Joint Statement Pointed to Enhanced Counter-Terror Cooperation between India and the US:**
   - Both countries would deepen their bilateral security cooperation against terrorist groups and would further enhance their counter-terrorism capabilities, including in the area of technology, according to Mr. Modi.
   - The joint statement issued after talks between the US president and the Indian Prime Minister reflected enhanced cooperation between the two countries in counter-terrorism to dismantle terrorist safe havens in Pakistan.
   - The joint statement emphasized on the need for joint and concerted efforts to disrupt terror outfits like LeT, JeM, D Company and the Haqqani network. All these terror outfits were based in Pakistan.

3. **Joint Strategic Vision Statement for the Asia Pacific and the Indian Ocean Region Sent a Message to China:**
   - The Joint Strategic Vision Statement for the Asia Pacific and the Indian Ocean reaffirmed the concerns of India and the US on maritime disputes in the South China Sea.
   - The Vision Statement also recognized that India's Act Policy and the US rebalance provided opportunities for them and other Asia-Pacific countries to work together to safeguard regional ties.
   - The Vision Statement highlighted the close strategic relations between India and the US which could balance the growing strategic presence of Chine in the greater Indian Ocean region, according to observers.
   - Strategic affairs expert Brahma Chellaney, pointed out the Joint Strategic Vision Statement focuses on a key area of Indo-US convergence – the threat posed by an increasingly muscular China seeking to alter

the territorial status quo by stealthy force and shape a Chine-centric regional order.
- The Joint Strategic Vision Statement laid out the intent of the US and India to develop a roadmap to address the new challenges in the Asia-Pacific region, according to Mr. Chellaney.
- The Chinese official media cautioned India not to fall into the trap being laid to pit India against China by the US as part of its "Pivot to Asia" doctrine.

4. **Enhanced Economic Relations:**
   - The US President Barack Obama announced $4 billion of new initiatives to boost trade/investment ties, jobs in India through Exim Bank and Overseas Private Investment Corporation (OPIC).
   - India and the US declared their intention for enhanced cooperation in renewable energy for which $2 billion have been allotted out of the $4 billion loan announced by Mr. Obama.
   - Analysts point out that a significant outcome of the visit of the US President to India was to jointly step up climate action through clean energy, smart cities and improved air quality.

5. The Declaration of Friendship, the Joint Statement and the Strategic Vision Statement for the Asia-Pacific and Indian Ocean region lay out a clear roadmap of Indo-US relations.

Conclusion

1. **Deepening Indo-US Relations:**
   - The US President Barack Obama said that the Indo-US relationship was the "defining partnership of the century" and pointed to the similarities between the two countries – diversity, multi-religious, tolerant democracies that respect human rights.
   - India's President Pranab Mukherjee expressed happiness that India and the US were deepening strategic, security and defence cooperation. He stressed that the relationship between the two countries was a special one because it was forged in the hearts and minds of the two people, in the commercial ties between the two businesses, in the exchanges between their scientists and engineers and in the enduring linkages between hundreds of their institutions.
   - Deepening ties with India was a foreign policy priority for the US administration, according to the US President Barack Obama.
   - It has been pointed out that US President Barack Obama's visit to India was successful as most facets of bilateral relations were covered and deepened Indo-US strategic partnership.

2. **Five Key Areas of Indo-US Relationship:** The former US Ambassador to India Timothy J. Roemer identified the following five areas that would take the Indo-US relations forward:
   - **Indo-US Partnership Indispensable for Global Peace and Security:** The US and India would work together to ensure peace, stability and prosperity in South Asia. The new Counter-terrorism Cooperation Initiative would strengthen their transportation security. Both sides would also strengthen efforts to build a free and stable Afghanistan, expand defence cooperation and work of global non-proliferation.
   - **Energy Security, Food Security and Climate change would be pursued through Indo-US Green Partnership:** Energy security, food security and climate change are interlinked and would be pursued through the new Indo-US Green Partnership. That would ensure greater access to clean and affordable energy to all Indians, while producing economic opportunities for citizens of both countries.
   - **Cooperation between India and the US in Public Health:** Both India and the US stand committed to implementing a joint global disease detection programme to enhance detection of new health threats and better response to pandemic disease.
   - **21st Century Knowledge Initiative will further strengthen cooperation in Education:** A key area of Indo-US cooperation is education. The 21st Century Knowledge Initiative would further strengthen linkages between the US and Indian universities.
   - **Framework for Cooperation on Trade and Investment would push Technological Innovation and Promote Inclusive Growth and Job creation:** The US is the largest economy in the world and India is one of the fastest growing economies in the world. Both countries have potential for greater expansion to spur global economic growth. To increase trade between the two countries, a framework for cooperation on trade and investment was being developed. It would push technological innovation and collaboration while promoting inclusive growth and job creation.
3. **India Should Continue to Follow an Independent Foreign Policy:** Finally, a close working relationship with the US should be a priority in India's foreign policy. At the same time India should continue to follow an independent foreign policy retaining its freedom of options to exercise multifarious choices to meet its national interests.

4

Indian Ocean – Hub of Political & Economic Activities

The Indian Ocean, once regarded as a 'neglected ocean' has, today, become the hub of political, strategic and economic activities because of the presence of conventional and nuclear vessels of the major powers in the area and because of its own economic and strategic significance. The Indian Ocean has 36 States around its littoral belt. In addition, there are eleven hinterland states e.g., Nepal and Afghanistan, which though landlocked, are keenly interested in the Indian Ocean politics and trade. The ocean contains several important minerals: 80.7% of world extraction of gold, 56.6% of tin, 28.5% of manganese, 25.2% nickel and 77.3% natural rubber. Highest tonnage of the world goods, 65% of world oil, and 35% of the gas, located in the littoral states, passes through it. The region today is an arena of contemporary geopolitics.

Strategically the Indian Ocean occupies a crucial importance, especially because of the presence of major powers in the region and potential of the regional powers, three being nuclear powered: Pakistan, China and India. That is why key regional powers are placing great reliance on the deployment of fleet missile submarines and SLBMs for second strike capability as well as to maintain balance of power in order to deter hegemony of any power whether territorial or extra-territorial.

USA has established its naval base in the Indian Ocean at Diego Garcia which poses a threat to the regional states as well as stands to protect the US' vital interests in the region. Political relations in and around the Indian Ocean can have significant implications for the US as far as its new "Asia Pivot" strategy is concerned. The new US Strategic Guidance 2012 has linked the US economy and security to developments in the Indian Ocean, elevating India to the position of a long-term strategic partner serving "as a regional anchor" in the region. The official documents also declare Iran and China as two potential states most susceptible to using asymmetrical means to counter US' areas of interest. The Indo-US collusion in the Indian Ocean has made Pakistan and China wary of their semi-hostile overtures, hence ensuing strategic competition in the region and employment of resource-dependent strategies to counteract and counterbalance the enemy state's manoeuvers.

The world is said to be entering Geo-energy era in which questions of energy security (security of demand and security of supply) will condition both inter-state relations and may lead to re-configuration of world power hierarchy. Energy security will play decisive role in creating conflict and co-operation situations. The country which holds paramount position in the Indian Ocean is likely to control the flow of energy not only to the East Asia, the future center of the world economic power, but also to other regions. Currently, USA, the world's mightiest naval power is dominating the region and the regional states, especially China, is trying to balance US power in the region in order to protect its interests with regard to its growing economy and energy needs. The question why it is so important to dominate the Indian Ocean can also be answered by highlighting the fact that oil is shipped from the Persian Gulf to almost entire world via the Indian Ocean, and through the Straits of Malacca to China, Korea, and Japan. If another [power] holds the lifeline, oil-importing countries will suffer severe blows. Because the US strategy is to hold sway over the oil route, the US has in recent years showered attentions on India, Vietnam, and Singapore, all of which lie on that route.

New Maritime Challenges for India in the Indian Ocean

India, situated at the head of the Indian Ocean, shares the longest coastline of 7500 kms among the other nations surrounding it.

(A) China's presence in the Indian Ocean, building military naval bases.

(B) Security issues build over China's increasing cooperation with strategically important SL, Maldives, Pakistan.

(C) New maritime Silk Route of China with its ports along the Indian Ocean is a matter of concern

(D) China-US rivalry for dominance

(E) War of Terror in the Indian Ocean. Major wars like the Gulf Wars, Al shabab (Somalia), Horror of Africa, Axis of Evil, and even the ISIS camps are related to IO

(F) India is a major trade route to developing countries, the pirates of Africa are a source of major threat.

Significance of Indian Ocean

If one visualizes the map of South Asia upside down one would understand the importance of the Indian Ocean (IO). India situated at the head of the IO shares the longest coastline of 7500 kms among the other nations surrounding the IO.

(A) Oil trade – 60% of global trade

(B) Sea lanes of communication and choke points like Straits of Malacca.

(C) India's strategy to revive the old IOZOP is outdated.

India's Strategy to Address the IO Maritime Challenges

1. Build its naval strength, rapidly modernize its navy, develop civilian maritime infrastructure and island territories, undertake maritime operations across littoral states to expand capacity.

2. Deepen bilateral, trilateral and multilateral military security cooperation with US and France in the Indian Ocean.

3. Strengthen naval cooperation with maritime neighbours like SL, Maldives. Increase naval assistance and develop stronger relations with other island countries like Seychelles and Mauritius.
4. Start maritime dialogue with China on IO.
5. Expand its multilateral-ism through forums like IO Rim Association and IO Naval Symposium.

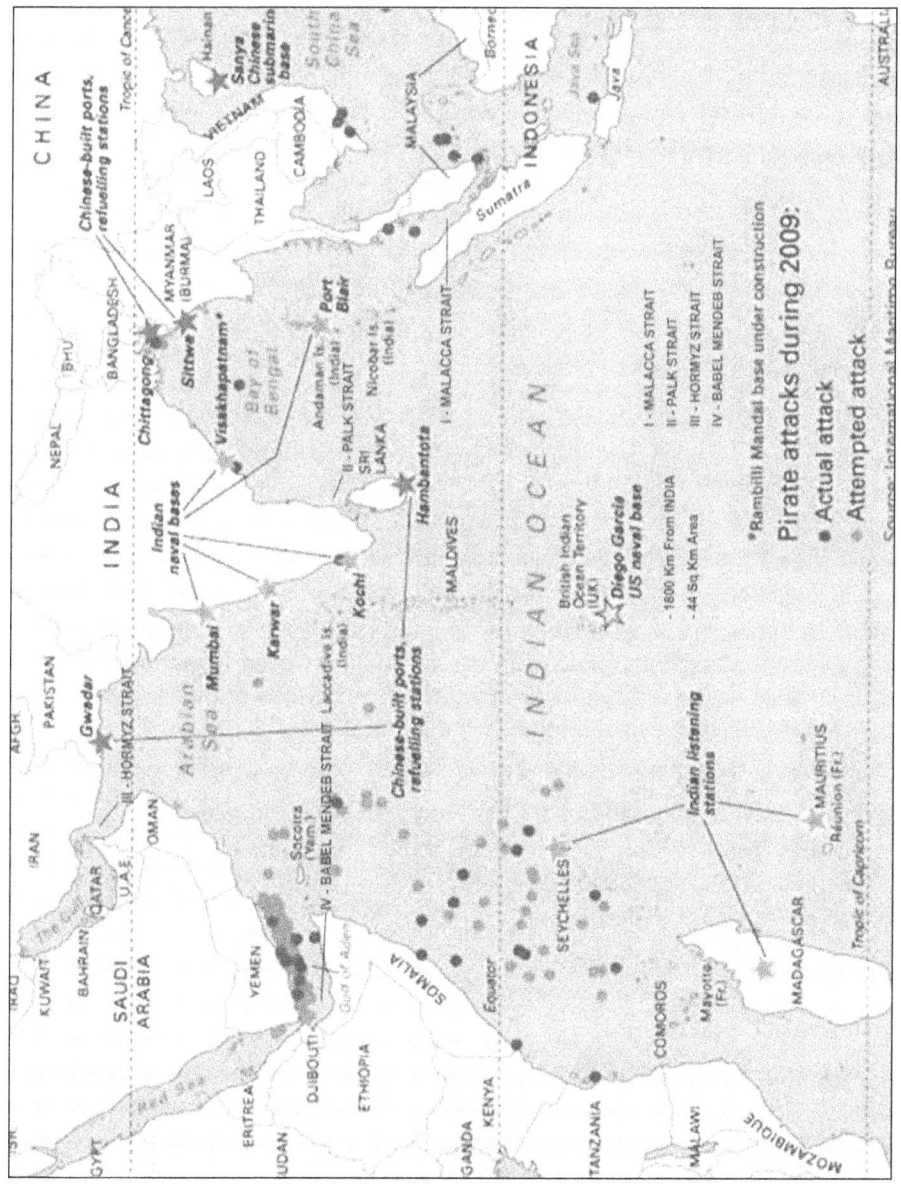

Importance of Indian Ocean to World

1. 70 percent of world trade from West to East and East to West.
2. Oil trade from Middle East to China, Japan, India, SE Asian countries.
3. Poly metallic nodules at ocean floor provide vital metals extraction sources from ocean.
4. Western powers involvement in security management against radical and fundamentalist Islamic groups in and around Iraq.
5. All the sea lanes leading to the Indian Ocean, particularly the Suez Canal and the Straits of Malacca be kept open at all the times.

Importance of Indian Ocean to India

1. 7,500 km coastline linking to Indian Ocean.
2. 80% of India's trade through sea route passes through Indian Ocean.
3. 85% of oil and gas imported through Indian Ocean into the country.
4. Fishing and tourism depends on it; due to huge marine resources it spreads prosperity in coastal plains of India.
5. Security of country after 26/11 and recent 1st January, 2015 (mid-sea blast of fishing boat incident). No industrial development, commercial growth, and stable political structure is possible unless our nation's shores are protected.
6. Vital for managing better relation with neighbours like Vietnam, Malaysia, Singapore, Thailand, Sri Lanka, Maldives, Seychelles, Mauritius, Iran, etc.
7. To maintain safer trade routes, and induce energy security for every party, India has recently pitched to declare Indian Ocean Region as "Region of Peace" at Galle dialogue (2014, Sri-Lanka), which provides enough reason that Indian Ocean is critical to India and the world.

India has recently announced a few projects in the Indian Ocean region

1. **Project Mausam** – India is using its history, culture and geography to compete with China's Maritime Silk Route project. India is uniquely placed to play a major role in Indian Ocean security and trade. India's location and power can serve to organize the states of the Indian Ocean littoral.

Project Mausam falls under the Ministry of Culture, and was launched in June, 2014 at the international audience at the 38th session of the World Heritage Committee at Doha, Qatar.

It is inspired by India's historical role as the focal point for trade in the Indian Ocean. In pre-modern times, sailors used seasonal monsoons (*mausam*, means weather or season in many South Asian languages) to swiftly journey across the Indian Ocean. This trip usually involved starting from one of the edges of the ocean, around today's Indonesia or east Africa, sailing to India, stopping, and allowing another crew to wait for another monsoon to sail to the other edge of the Indian

Ocean, as different monsoon winds blew in different directions at different times of the year.

Crews would frequently winter for months in India or at one of the edges of the ocean waiting for another season of monsoons. This allowed for significant cultural exchanges as diverse people from different places would often spend months at a time living in foreign countries (Islam is said to have entered Indonesia in this manner). Project Mausam would allow India to re-establish its ties with its ancient trade partners and re-establish an "Indian Ocean world" along the littoral of the Indian Ocean. This world would stretch from east Africa, along the Arabian Peninsula, past southern Iran to the major countries of South Asia and thence to Sri Lanka and Southeast Asia. The project is supposed to have both a cultural and serious strategic dimension. Perhaps one thing India could consider is seriously developing its Andaman and Nicobar Islands as a security and trade zone. This idea is sensible provided the island's close location to strategically important countries like the Straits of Malacca and Thailand. It is clear that India's government intends to expand its maritime presence, culturally, strategically and psychologically (in order to remind the region why the ocean is called the Indian Ocean). Despite the lack of details, Project Mausam seems like a positive step in that direction and one that will generally be well-received. It is to be hoped, however, that the project is meaningful and does not lack teeth, like many other Indian initiatives of the past. The fact that Narendra Modi's government is initiating Project Mausam, however, at least gives one assurance that the Indian government is not launching another arbitrary and half-hearted initiative.

2. **Sagar mala** – With the aim to promote India's connectivity to the Indian Ocean, in economic and security domains.

Along with these initiatives, multilateral platforms have been set up, such as,

- **Indian Ocean Rim Association** – to promote regional cooperation
- **Indian Ocean Naval Symposium** – which brings together chiefs of Navy every 2 years to discuss naval cooperation.
- **Joint mechanisms with Sri Lanka and Maldives** for shared maritime domain awareness. Further, projects launched in this region, like developing infrastructural assets in this region to match China's influence, are welcome steps.

However, there are crucial bottlenecks that have the potential to derail the initiative.

1. Inadequate civilian maritime infrastructure, which needs an overhaul.
2. Inadequate capacity or policy framework needed to bid for and execute major infrastructure projects in this region.
3. While several deals have been signed related to infrastructure, security and the provision of grants, the limitations lie in the defence budgetary grants,

constraints of funds and bureaucratic inefficiency in taking forward the opportunity.
4. Substantial investment in naval defence infrastructure, and cultivate capabilities, systems and attitudes required for India to be a 'net security provider', in this region.
5. Comparison with China - Intense competition can be seen in the aggressive Chinese policy of infrastructure, port development, formation of naval bases [through heavy loans and infrastructure] etc. While China has naval bases [String of Pearls] in rim countries like Myanmar, Sri Lanka, Pakistan and heavily investing in African [Tanzania, Sudan] and East Asian [Indonesia, Myanmar] countries, India lacks in such forwards posts and deep assets. Although recent measures for building defence assets in Mauritius, Seychelles are welcome, much depends upon pace of infrastructure development, joint cooperation and playing an aggressive role.
6. Importance of India Ocean has attracted countries like USA [already in Diego Garcia and latest talks for military base in Maldives], UK etc. Presence of any external military base near Indian coasts will undermine dominance of Indian Navy in this region.
7. Recent land border hostilities have attracted Indian attention towards strengthening and modernizing its military and air force which may result in budget cuts for navy, which is vital for dominance in Indian Ocean.
8. While defence cooperation with Indian Ocean countries like Vietnam, Singapore are welcome steps, the weak point is still majority of Indian defence equipment is imported with little high tech local presence, which often results in delays and supply of equipment to friendly countries.

Therefore the balance of power in Indian Ocean Region (IOR) is marked by the priorities of US, China and India. However, the emerging trends indicate that India is the biggest stakeholder and any instability in IOR could impact its national security. Why so?

Due to its geographic location and the growth trajectory, India occupies a strategic location in the turbulent IOR. India has a self interest in the security of this geostrategic maritime area as its long coastline, well-endowed EEZ (Exclusive Economy Zone), foreign trade over sea and the offshore installations need protection. Piracy, smuggling, illegal fishing, sea level rising, natural disasters, rampant poaching and terrorism will continue to demand maritime response and will remain critical to national security. It is important for India to create a secure maritime environment through a strong and effective military especially naval capability. Indian Navy today is a blue water navy with a sizable force projection capabilities. As its capabilities get further enhanced in future, so will its role as a net security provider in the IOR.

Andaman and Nicobar Islands provide India with potential to dominate the strategic sea lanes and choke points in the east, and makes them a cornerstone in Indian maritime strategy. Andaman and Nicobar Command, needs to be energised with resources to make it a viable military outreach into the IOR. The level of synergy and jointness achieved in the only Unified Command also has tremendous scope for improvement. In the true spirit of the Government's new policy of "Act East" the islands are to be looked at as a "Spring Board" towards furthering India's strategic outreach in the SE Asian region. This could be the first step towards a more robust Indian Ocean Strategy. India also needs to graduate to a maritime power; whose components include shipbuilding industry, modern port handling facilities and large merchant shipping fleet as all of them impinge either directly or indirectly, on maritime security.

It is said that "Humans always win, always get more if they collaborate". This is particularly valid for the IOR, which does not have region-wide security architectures, to deal with the security risks of the future. The maritime domain is where the collective interests and common security concerns of regional and extra-regional states converge. There is a compelling, imperative need to develop maritime security cooperation in the Indian Ocean region to address the massive human, economic, environmental, and energy security risks of the future. However, problems posed by the suspicion of intentions and doubts on viability of such a security structure have prevented formation of a collective security regime. Militarisation of IOR, proliferation of WMDs (Weapons of Mass Destruction), rise in non-traditional threats and power projection by extra regional powers demands greater security cooperation and enhancement of peace and stability in the region.

In conclusion, the interplay between China, India and the US – the three pillars would decide the reconfiguration of geopolitics in IOR. Other major powers and littorals will also influence the same. India needs to learn to deal with the Chinese emergence as a power, its growth, its interest and concerns in IOR along with US rebalancing. India with or without them must become the net security provider for the region.

The challenges are vast but then so are the opportunities presented by the emergence of strong political leaderships in New Delhi and a rising India under new leadership where everyone is considering it as an opportunity to interact with and cooperate with. India will need to anticipate the ever evolving security scenario in IOR and attempt to shape them in its favour.

5

Digital India Project

Prime Minister Narendra Modi, on July 1, 2015, formally launched the Digital India Project in two village panchayats of the district Indore, MP. The project, which will ensure an investment of Rs. 4.5 lakh crore and jobs for at least 18 lakh people, focuses on three objectives – infrastructure as a utility for every citizen, governance and services on demand, and digital empowerment of citizens. Here are the 10 important initiatives of Digital India:

1. **DIGI locker:** This initiative looks to minimize the usage of physical documents. It is a dedicated personal storage space for e-documents as well as Uniform Resource Identifier (URI) of e-documents issued by government departments. Individual locker will be linked to the resident's Aadhaar number, and enable sharing of e-documents across agencies whenever required.

2. **Bharat Net:** This initiative will work towards building high-speed digital highways to connect all 2.5 lakh Gram Panchayats of the country by next year. This would be the world's largest rural broadband connectivity project using optical fiber.

3. **MyGov app:** The PM launched the mobile versions of the MyGov.in website. This platform encourages citizen engagement in governance, and the app will do the same on mobile.

4. **eSign:** An initiative to eradicate forgery and fraudulent signature, the eSign framework would allow citizens to digitally sign a document online using Aadhaar authentication.

5. **National Scholarships Portal:** This new service is said to be one-stop-solution for end-to-end scholarship process right from submission of student application, verification, sanction and disbursal to end beneficiary for all the scholarships provided by the government.

6. **Swachh Bharat Mission (SBM) app:** To further the Swachh Bharat mission, the government has launched this app and would be used by people and government organizations.

7. **E-education:** The program looks to provide high-tech education using technology like smart phones, apps and internet services; it can also be used to provide education in far-flung areas where it may not be possible for teachers to be present in person.

8. **E-health:** This initiative aims at providing timely, effective and economical healthcare services to all, especially to the ones that have little access to healthcare services. This service too will be linked to Aadhaar numbers, and will make getting lab reports and OPD appointments easier.
9. **Next Generation Network (NGN):** A BSNL initiative, it looks to replace 30 year old exchanges, with this new IP-based technology to manage all types of services like voice, data, multimedia/video and other types of communication services.
10. **Wi-Fi hotspots:** BSNL has undertaken large scale development of Wi-fi hotspots throughout the country for Internet access on smart phones while on-the-go.

6

Smart Cities Mission and Amrut

Introduction

The government of India under Prime Minister Narendra Modi has a vision of developing 100 smart cities as financial services satellite towns of larger cities and by modernizing the existing mid-sized cities.

The government plans to identify 20 smart cities in 2015, 40 in 2016 and another 40 in 2017.

The 100 potential smart cities nominated by all the states and union territories based on Stage 1 criteria will prepare smart city plans which will be evaluated in Stage 2 of the competition for prioritizing cities for financing. In the first round of this stage, 20 top scorers will be chosen for financing during this financial year. The remaining will be asked to make up the deficiencies identified by the Apex Committee in the Ministry of Urban Development for participation in the next two rounds of competition. 40 cities each will be selected for financing during the next rounds of competition.

Smart cities are seen as a key to India's economic and social growth.

Financial Implication

A total of Rs. 980 billion (US$14 billion) has been approved by the Indian Cabinet for development of 100 smart cities and rejuvenation of 500 others. For the smart cities mission, Rs. 480 billion (US$ 7.1 billion) and for the Atal Mission for Rejuvenation and Urban Transformation (AMRUT), a total funding of 500 billion (US$7.4 billion) has been approved by the Cabinet.

Each city would get 1 billion (US$15 million) every year from the Centre for five years. The remaining money has to come from the states, urban bodies and the consortium that they form with corporate entities. Also, 10 per cent of budget allocation will be given to states/union territories as incentive based on achievement of reforms during the previous year.

In the 2014 Union budget of India, Finance Minister Arun Jaitley allocated Rs. 70.16 billion (US$1.0 billion) for the 100 smart cities. However, only Rs. 9.24 billion (US$140 million) could be spent out of the allocated amount till February 2015. Hence, the 2015 Union budget of India allocated only Rs. 1.43 billion (US$21 million) for the project.

Ninety-eight cities from all the states and Union Territories have so far been included in the Smart City Mission. This first round of selection of 98 cities was made based on competition among various urban local bodies in each state, based on a set of criteria.

In the second stage of 'City Challenge' competition, 20 top scoring mission cities will be selected from among the 98 city level Smart City Plans, for financing during the current financial year.

First batch of cities to be selected in the second stage of competition will be provided with central assistance of Rs.2 billion (US$30 million) each during this financial year followed by Rs.1 billion (US$15 million) per year during the next three years.

Urban Development Ministry had earlier released Rs.2 crore (US$300,000) each to mission cities for preparation of Smart City Plans.

Core Infrastructure Included

1. Adequate water supply
2. Assured electricity supply
3. Sanitation including solid waste management
4. Efficient urban mobility and public transport
5. Affordable housing (especially for the poor)
6. Robust IT connectivity and digitization
7. Good governance (especially e-governance and citizen participation)
8. Sustainable environment
9. Safety and security of citizens (particularly women, children and the elderly)
10. Health
11. Education

Jammu and Kashmir have asked for more time to decide on the potential smart city. Twelve cities have been shortlisted from Uttar Pradesh against 13 cities allocated to the state.

Selection Criteria

Given the challenges involved in developing 100 smart cities, only the capable cities will be chosen under the Smart Cities Mission through a two-stage competition. This was indicated in the Operation Guidelines for Smart Cities Mission released by Prime Minister Narendra Modi. The selection criteria to be used in both the stages of competition was elaborated in the Guidelines.

In the Stage-1 of City Challenge Competition, each State and Union Territory will score all their cities based on a set of criteria and nominate the top scorers as per the indicated number of potential smart cities for participation in the Stage 2 of competition.

Stage 1 of Selection

The list of nomination marks the first stage in the selection process of smart cities, in which the state governments nominated potential cities and the Centre shortlisted 100.

The evaluation criteria for Stage 1 of competition within the State/UT is as below:
1. Existing Service Levels (25 points): This includes Increase in service levels over Census 2011, an operational Online Grievance Redressal System, publication of at least first monthly newsletter and online publication of municipal budget expenditure details for the last two financial years on website.
2. Institutional Systems and Capacities (15 points): This covers imposition of penalties for delays in service delivery and improvement in internal resource generation over the last three years.
3. Self-financing (30 points): This would be reflected in payment of salaries by urban local bodies up to last month, auditing of accounts up to FY 2012-13, contribution of internal revenues to the budget for 2014-15 and percentage of establishment and maintenance cost of water supply met through user charges during 2014-15.
4. Past track record (30 points): Percentage of JNNURM projects completed which were sanctioned till 2012, percentage of city level reforms achieved under JNNURM and extent of capital expenditure met from internal resources.

Stage 2 of Selection

The Government on August 27, 2015 released the list of nominees for the ambitious smart city project. The list comprises 98 cities, including many state capitals.

Proposal Level Evaluation (70 points)

1. **Impact of proposal:** To what extent the proposal is inclusive in terms of benefits to the poor and disadvantaged, extent of employment generation, articulation of quantifiable outcomes based on citizen consultations, impact on environment etc.
2. **Cost effectiveness of Smart City Plan:** Application of smart solutions for doing more with less of resources, alternatives considered to enhance cost effectiveness of the proposal, firming up of resources required from various sources, provision for operation & maintenance costs, IT interventions to improve public service delivery.
3. **Innovation and Scalability:** Extent of adoption of best practices in consultation with citizens, applicability of project to the entire city, adoption of smart solutions and pan city developments.

4. **Processes followed:** Extent of citizen consultations, vulnerable sections like the differently abled, children, elderly etc., ward committees and area sabhas and important citizen groups, extent of use of social media and mobile governance during citizen consultations and accommodation of contrary voices in the strategy and planning.

7
India Building Relationship: PM Modi's Visits Abroad

Russia Visit

Prime Minister Narendra Modi went on his first official bilateral visit to Moscow on December 23-24, 2015 for the 16th India-Russia Annual Summit. During his two-day visit, Modi held talks with President Vladimir Putin, covering a wide range of sectors which included defence and nuclear cooperation.

The two nations inked 16 deals ranging from joint helicopter manufacture and Indian development of components for Russian nuclear reactors to oil and gas exploration and an easier visa regime for business persons from the nations to travel to each other's countries.

Putin gifted to the Indian Prime Minister an 18th century sword from Bengal and a page from Mahatma Gandhi's diary containing his handwritten notes. PM Modi laid a wreath at the tomb of the unknown soldier – a World War II monument just outside of the actual functioning and real-time monitoring operations of the centre.

Agreements between India and Russia include:

- Protocol amending the agreement on simplification of requirements for mutual travels of certain categories of citizens, Protocol amending agreement on mutual travel regime for holders of Diplomatic & Official Passports, Agreement on Co-operation on combating customs violations in 2015-2017, programme of action for Russian-designed nuclear reaction units, MOU on technical co-operation in railway sector, MOU on construction of solar energy plants in India, MOU for co-operation on heavy engineering design, MOU for co-operation for up gradation and modernization of HEC's manufacturing facilities, MOU pm co-operation in the field of Broadcasting, Tripartite MOU between C-Das, IISc and Moscow State University, Tripartite MOU between C-DAC, OJSC 'GLONASS' and GLONASS Union, MOU in the field of investment co-operation for geologic survey, exploration and production of hydrocarbons onshore, MOU between Rosneft Oil Company, Oil India and Indian Oil Corporation.

UK Visit

Prime Minister Narendra Modi paid a three-day official visit to the UK on November 12-14, 2015. This was the first bilateral visit after nine years. Former Prime Minister Dr. Manmohan Singh last visited in 2006. He was also there in 2009, but for the G20 Summit.

During the visit, PM Modi met his British counterpart David Cameron, held extensive talks on various important issues, signed key accords, addressed the British Parliament, and gave a speech to Indian diaspora and business community in London. He also paid homage to the statue of Mahatma Gandhi near Parliament Square and unveiled the statue of a great scholar Basaveshwara in London. Modi also inaugurated the memorial of Dr. B R Ambedkar at 10 King Henry's road.

India and Britain signed a civil nuclear co-operation agreement after the two sides held delegation level talks. They agreed on a comprehensive package of collaboration on energy and climate change which includes commercial deals worth 3.2 billion pounds. Britain also announced the UK climate investments joint venture with the Green Investment Bank. This will invest up to 200 million pounds in renewable energy and energy efficiency in India and Africa.

Both the leaders announced to deepen India-UK defence collaboration through capability partnerships in strategic areas. These areas include research, training, transfer of defence technologies and defence manufacturing in areas of mutual interest through Make in India.

PM Modi and Cameron announced the launch of a programme, named HSBC Skills in Life, for India, entailing an investment of Rs. 100 crore, which will impart skills to more than 75,000 people. Modi also launched the country's first low-income state infrastructure equity partnership (or the Neev fund) by State Bank of India (SBI) in London.

Malaysia and Singapore Visit

Prime Minister Narendra Modi paid an official visit to Malaysia and Singapore on November 21-24, 2015, during which several agreements were signed to bolster trade ties and attract investments to India.

• Modi in Malaysia

PM Modi reached Kuala Lumpur on November 21 on the first leg of his two-nation visit where he attended two crucial summits, East Asia and ASEAN-India, participated in bilateral meetings and sought greater investment to India.

He held talks with his Malaysian counterpart Najib Razak and signed three MOUs cultural exchange Programme agreement for 2015-2020, Co-operation project delivery and monitoring, and co-operation and Cyber Security at Putrajaya. They agreed to proceed with effort to develop the strategic partnership between the two countries. The two leaders jointly inaugurated the Torana Gate at Little India in Kuala Lumpur.

Modi unveiled a 12-ft bronze statue of Swami Vivekananda at the Ramkrishna Mission in Kuala Lumpur. He also addressed Indian diaspora in Kuala Lumpur where he announced that the Indian Cultural Centre in Kuala Lumpur will be named after freedom fighter and commander of the Indian National Army Netaji Subhas Chandra Bose.

Modi in Singapore

PM Modi reached Singapore on November 23 where he met his counterpart Lee Hsien Loong, President Tony Tan Keng Tam and Emeritus Senior Minister Goh Chok Tong. Modi and his Singaporean counterpart on November 24 elevated their ties to the 'strategic partnership' level and signed 10 bilateral agreements for enhanced defence co-operation and in areas like cyber security, shipping and civil aviation.

The other pacts included an agreement between the two countries on enhanced defence co-operation, which provides for defence ministers dialogue, joint exercises between armed forces, co-operation between defence industries to identify areas of co-production and co-development. They also signed an agreement on the extension of loan of artifacts to the Asian Civilizations Museum of Singapore and an MOU between Indian IT department and Singapore and an MOU between Indian Computer Emergency Response Team (CERT-In), the Indian IT department and Singapore Computer Emergency Response Team (SingCERT), Singapore's Cyber Security Agency on security co-operation.

They launched a joint postage stamp featuring the presidential residences of both the countries to mark the 50th anniversary of the establishment of diplomatic relations. Modi addressed Indian diaspora and also visited the campus of the Institute of Technical Education in Singapore. He paid homage at the Indian National Army Memorial Marker in Singapore.

UAE Visit

Prime Minister of India Narendra Modi visited United Arab Emirates (UAE) on August 16-17, 2015. He is the first Prime Minister of India to visit UAE after 34 years. The last Indian PM to visit the UAE was Indira Gandhi in 1981.

During the visit, the Prime Minister held talks with Crown Prince of Abu Dhabi Sheikh Mohamed bin Zayed Al Nahyan and Vice President and Prime Minister of UAE Sheikh Mohammed bin Rashid Al Maktoum.

The UAE agreed to increase investments in India to $75 billion (about Rs. 5 lakh crore) through a dedicated UAE – India Infrastructure Investment Fund, while the two nations will raise their bilateral trade to nearly $100 billion in five years. The two countries also agreed for strategic participation in petroleum sectors in India and tie-ups in the third-world countries.

He also visited the historic Sheikh Zayed Grand Mosque in Abu Dhabi, which is the third largest mosque in the world. Modi visited Masdar City, a zero carbon city, where he met with investors. He addressed Indian diaspora of the country at the Dubai Cricket Stadium.

He also interacted with Indian workers at the ICAD residential labour camping, Abu Dhabi. He announced a welfare fund for the welfare of Indian diaspora. It will be set up to help them legally so that they can deal with problems.

Central Asia Visit

Prime Minister Narendra Modi on July 6, 2015 started his visit to five central Asian nations and Russia.

• Uzbekistan

His first destination was Uzbekistan, which is the most populous country in Central Asia. Modi called on President Islam Karimov and Prime Minister Shavkat Miromonovich Mirziyoyev in Tashkent.

He paid tributes at the National Monument of Independence and Humanism in Tashkent. He released the first Uzbek-Hindi dictionary. Modi gifted Karimov a specially commissioned reproduction of the "Khamsa-i-Khusrau" quintet by Sufi poet Amir Khusrau.

• Kazakhstan

Modi was in Kazakhstan, the largest of the central Asian Nations, on July 7-8, 2015. Kazakhstan is India's largest trading partner in Central Asia. PM Modi inaugurated the India-Kazakh Centre for Excellence in Information and Communication Technology in Astana.

India and Kazakhstan inked five key agreements including a defence pact to enhance military co-operation and a contract for supply of uranium after Prime Minister Narendra Modi and Kazakh President Nursultan Nazarbayev held comprehensive talks in Astana. The two countries also agreed to work closely to expand bilateral trade by addressing structural impediments between India and hydrocarbon rich Kazakhstan.

Modi launched maiden drilling by ONGC Videsh Ltd. in the Satpayev oil block of Kazakhstan where the Indian firm is investing $400 million. The other agreements included treaty on transfer of sentenced persons, human resources, cultural exchanges and capacity building.

• Russia

Prime Minister Modi on July 8-10, 2015 visited Russia to take part in the 7th BRICS Summit and SCO Summit held in Ufa. Modi met Russian President Vladimir Putin in his first bilateral engagement after arriving in Ufa. He also met other foreign leaders including Chinese President, Pakistani PM and Iranian President and held talks with them.

• Turkmenistan

Modi reached Turkmenistan on July 11. He met President Gulbanguly Berdimuhamedov in Ashgabat. Modi inaugurated a traditional medicine and Yoga centre in Ashgabat. He also unveiled a bust of Mahatma Gandhi.

A total of seven pacts were signed between both the countries. An MOU was in the field of supply of chemical products between the Indian PSU Rashtriya Chemicals and Fertilizers Limited and the Turkmen State concern Turkmenhimiya. Another MOU was between India's Foreign Service Institute and Institute of International Relations of Turkmenistan. Other MOUs were for co-operation in the field of Sports, Science & Technology, Yoga & Traditional Medicine, Tourism and Defence.

• *Krygyzstan*

Modi met President Almazbek Atambayev on July 12. He laid a wreath at the Victory monument in Bishkek. India and Krygyzstan on July 12 signed agreements in four key areas, including defence co-operation and cultural preservation.

The two nations signed agreements to deepen co-operation in matters related to defence, security, military education and training. A MOU was signed in the field of elections, to enhance co-operation in matters related to legislation on elections and referendums. The Ministry of Economy of Krygyzstan and Bureau of Indian Standards (BIS) also signed a MOU in the sphere of standards.

Modi visited the Kyrgyz-India Mountain Biomedical Research Centre (KIMBMRC) at Bishkek. He unveiled a plaque commemorating the inauguration of the extreme high altitude test laboratory – Phase 2 of the KIMBMRC project, situated in the Syok Pass at 4000 meters height. He also inaugurated the first telemedicine link between India and Central Asia.

• *Tajikistan*

On July 12 and 13, the Prime Minister visited Tajikistan where he met President Emomali Rahmon in Dushanbe. The last prime ministerial visit to Tajikistan was by former prime minister Atal Bihari Vajpayee in November 2003. Agreements signed during the visit include a programme of co-operation (POC) between Ministries of Culture of India and Tajikistan in the field of Culture for the years 2016-18. Another agreement was an exchange of Note Verbala (NV) on setting up of computer labs in 37 schools in Tajikistan.

Bangladesh Visit

Prime Minister Narendra Modi paid an official visit to Bangladesh on June 6-7, 2015. This was Modi's first visit to Bangladesh during which he held discussions with Bangladeshi PM Sheikh Hasina.

India and Bangladesh on June 6 ratified an over 40-year-old land border swap agreement and flagged off two new trans-border buses as Modi announced a $2 billion line of credit to Dhaka. New Delhi and Dhaka also inked the exchange of letters on modalities for implementation of 1974 Land Boundary Agreement and its 2011 protocol; bilateral trade agreement (renewal). Both countries also inked 22 agreements.

Earlier, Modi also went to the National Martyrs' Memorial, or the Jatiyo Stiti Shoudho, to pay tribute to the soldiers who gave their lives in the Bangladesh Liberation War of 1971. Modi also received, on behalf of the former Prime Minister Atal Bihari Vajpayee, the 'Bangladesh Liberation War Honour' from Bangladesh President Abdul Hamid and Prime Minister Sheikh Hasina.

The agreements signed between India and Bangladesh include:
- Exchange of Instruments of Ratification of 1974 Land Boundary Agreement and its 2011 Protocol, Exchange of letters on Modalities for implementation of 1974 Land Boundary Agreement and its 2011 Protocol, Bilateral Trade Agreement (renewal), Agreement on Coastal Shipping, Protocol on Inland Water Transit and Trade (renewal), Agreement on Co-operation in the field of Standardization, Agreement on Dhaka-Shillong-Guwahati Bus Service, Agreement of Kolkata-Dhaka-Agartala Bus Service, MOU between Coast Guards, MOU on prevention of Human Trafficking, MOU on prevention of smuggling and circulation fake currency notes, MOU for $2 billion line of Credit (LOC), MOU on blue Economy and Maritime Co-operation in the Bay of Bengal and the Indian Ocean, MOU on use of Chittagong and Mongla Portsm MOU for a project under IECC (India Endowment for Climate Change) of SAARC, MOU on Indian Economic Zone, Cultural Exchange Programme for the years 2015-17, Statement of Intent on Education Co-operation (adoption), Agreement for leasing of international bandwidth for internet at Akhaura, MOU for Joint Research on Oceanography of the Bay of Bengal, MOU between University of Rajshahi, Bangladesh and Jamia Milia Islamia and Consent Letter between IDRA, Bangladesh and LIC, India.

China, Mangolia and Korea Visit

Prime Minister Narendra Modi paid a six-day, three-nation tour that took him to China, Mangolia and South Korea from May 14 to May 19, 2015.

• *China*

Prime Minister Narendra Modi reached Beijing on May 14, 2015 on his three-day China visit. He met Chinese President Xi Jinping, PM Li Keqiang and held extensive talks with them. The two sides signed a record 24 agreements covering railways, mining, outer space, earthquake science and engineering, tourism, sister-cities and establishments of consulates in Chengdu and Chennai.

Modi launched around 25 business plans and agreements worth $22 billion between Indian firms and Chinese business houses in Shanghai on May 16. The event saw Infosys unveiling a master plan of its new Shanghai campus. ICICI Bank inaugurated its first branch in China. The agreements between India and China include:
- Protocols on the establishment of consulates-general at Chengdu and Chennai and the extension of the consular district of the consulate general of India in

Guanzhou to include Jiangxi province, MOU on co-operation in vocational education and skill development, action plan on co-operation to set up Mahatma Gandhi National Institute for Skill Development and Entrepreneurship in Ahmedabad/ Gandhinagar in Gujarat, MOU on consultative mechanism for co-operation in trade negotiations, MOU on co-operation between MEA and international department of the central committee of the communist party of China, action plan on enhancing co-operation in the railway sector, MOU on education exchange programme, MOU on the co-operation in the mining and minerals sector, space co-operation outline (2015-2020), protocol on health and safety regulations on importing Indian rapeseed meal, MOU between on co-operation in the field of broadcasting, agreement on co-operation in the field of tourism, MOU on establishing India-China think-tanks forum, MOU between Niti Aayog and China's Development Research Centre, State Council, MOU on co-operation in earthquake science and earthquake engineering, MOU and co-operation in the field of ocean science, ocean technology, climate change, polar science and cryosphere, MOU on scientific co-operation between geological survey of India and the China Geological Survey, MOU on establishment of states/provincial leaders, forum, agreement on the establishment of sister-state/province relations between Karnataka and Sinhuan, agreement on establishment of sister-city relations between Chennai and Chongqing, Hyderabad and Qingdao and Aurangabad and Dunhuang, MOU on the establishment of a centre of Gandhian and Indian studies in Fudan University, MOU on the establishment of a yoga college in Yunnan Minzu University.

• Mongolia

Narendra Modi, the first Indian Prime Minister to visit Mongolia, started his Mongolian sojourn with a visit to the Gandan Monastery on May 17, 2015. Modi held wide ranging talks with his counterpart Chimed Saikhanbileg in capital Ulan Bator following which the two sides inked 14 agreements covering defence, cyber security, agriculture, renewable energy and health sector. India announced a credit line of $1 billion to Mongolia. He also addressed the Mongolian Parliament 'State Great Hural', the first foreign leader to do so on Sunday – a holiday.

• South Korea

Prime Minister Narendra Modi arrived in Seoul on May 18, 2015 and held talks with South Korean President Park Geun-hye in which the two countries decided to elevate their ties to a special strategic partnership.

Both sides agreed to increase their defence and security co-operation and also inked 7 agreements, including on avoidance of double taxation and for co-operation between their national security councils. South Korea offered on avoidance of double taxation and for co-operation between their national security councils. South Korea offered to provide $10 billion for infrastructure projects in India including smart cities and railways. Modi also visited Seoul National Cemetery where he joined a wreath-laying ceremony. He also addressed the Indian community.

France, Germany and Canada Visit

Prime Minister Narendra Modi on April 9-11, 2015 undertook a three-nation tour during which he met leaders of the three nations, namely French President Francois Hollande, German Chancellor Angela Markel and Canadian Prime Minister Stephen Harper.

• *France*

Modi reached France on April 9, 2015. He held wide-ranging consultations with French President Francois Hollande and conducted round-table discussions with French CEOs. Defence co-operation, fight against terrorism, infrastructure, nuclear reactor, renewable sources of energy, railways, smart cities and tourism were the major topics of discussions between Modi and Hollande after which 17 agreements were signed.

India asked France to supply 36 Rafale fighter jets in 'fly-away' condition. An agreement on proceeding forward on the stalled nuclear project in Jaitapur in Maharashtra was also among the 17 pacts signed. India and France also agreed that a Joint Working Group (JWG) on counter-terrorism will meet and formulate the modalities of greater co-operation on the matter.

Modi also addressed the UNESCO at the organisation's headquarters in Paris. He also paid homage to Indian soldiers martyred during World War I at a memorial in Neuve Chapelle.

• *Germany*

Prime Minister Modi, along with German Chancellor Angela Merkel, inaugurated the 2015 Hannover Messe industrial fair, for which India was a partner country. Both leaders spoke in favour of a free trade agreement between the European Union and India. PM Modi said that this was important for the expansion of India as a manufacturing hub.

The joint statement by both countries recognized the establishment of a working group on urban development. PM Modi promised to set up a mechanism to help German companies invest and do business in India – something that he has done only for Japan and the US.

• *Canada*

For the final leg of his nine-day tour, the Prime Minister travelled to Canada, the first stand-alone bilateral visit by an Indian Prime Minister in 42 years. Modi held talks with his Canadian counterpart Stephen Harper in Ottawa after which Canada agreed to supply 3,000 metric tonnes of uranium to India from this year under a five-year deal to power Indian atomic reactors.

Harper and Modi agreed to increase collaboration in the fields of energy efficiency, oil and gas development and renewable energy. They looked forward to an investment of CAD $ 2.5 million in five health innovations in India by Grand Challenges Canada and its Indian partner – the Department of Biotechnology, Ministry of Science and Technology.

Modi held a round table conference with heads of pension funds, banks and other financial leaders of Canada, assuring them that his government will facilitate their concerns regarding investment in India, adding that bureaucracy shall no longer be an issue.

Thirteen MOUs were signed between the National Skill Development Council of India and 13 Canadian colleges, institutes, and Sector Skill Councils in the fields such as agriculture, automotive, aviation, construction, healthcare, hydrocarbons and IT.

PM Modi addressed an 8000-strong audience of Indo-Canadians at Toronto's Ricoh Coliseum. He also visited the memorial to the Air India 'Kanishka' bombing and visited Gurdwara Khalsa Diwan and the Laxmo Narayan temple in Vancouver.

Seychelles, Mauritius and Sri Lanka Visit

Prime Minister Narendra Modi undertook a five-day tour of three Indian Ocean countries Seychelles, Mauritius and Sri Lanka from, March 10 to March 14, 2015.

• *Seychelles*

Modi on March 10 became the first Indian Prime Minister to visit Seychelles in 33 long years – the last was by Indira Gandhi in 1981. Modi held talks with the Seychelles President James Michel during which four agreements were signed including co-operation in hydrography, renewable energy, infrastructure development and sale of navigation charts and electronic navigational charts.

Modi also gifted a Dornier aircraft to Seychelles and unveiled the Plaque and Operationalisation of Radar for the CSRS India-Seychelles co-operation project in Seychelles. Prime Minister also announced to grant free visas for three months to the citizens of Seychelles. Modi and Michel also agreed to establish a JWG to expand co-operation on the blue economy to harness new possibilities of the ocean in a sustainable and balanced manner. Modi also delivered a public address before some 3000 guests.

• *Mauritius*

Modi reached Mauritius on March 11 and met Mauritius Prime Minister Sir Anerood Jugnauth. Modi held extensive meetings with the President of Mauritius, Rajkeswur Purryag. During the talks between Modi and his Mauritian counterpart, India and Mauritius signed five pacts.

The agreements cover the areas of ocean economy, cultural co-operation, the import of fresh mangoes from India, sea air transportation in the Agalega islands, medicine and homeopathy.

The MOU for the improvement in sea and air transportation facilities at Agalega Island of Mauritius provides for setting up and upgrade of infrastructure for improving sea and air connectivity at the outer island of Mauritius. Both leaders discussed the setting up of a specialized cancer hospital in Mauritius, discussed plans for water treatment, and to make Mauritius into a cyber-island.

Modi was the chief guest at the Mauritius National Day Celebrations on March 12. He also addressed the country's National Assembly and attended a public reception. Modi also attended the programme to mark the commissioning of the Barracuda, the first naval ship to be built by India for a foreign nation.

• *Sri Lanka*

Modi reached Sri Lanka on March 13. During his maiden trip to the island, the first bilateral tour by an Indian premier in 28 years, Modi held extensive talks with Sri Lankan President Maithripala Sirisena. The two sides signed four agreements on visa, customs, youth development and building Rabindranath Tagore memorial in Sri Lanka.

During the talks, Modi announced to provide a fresh Line of Credit of up to $318 million for the railways sector in Lanka. He also addressed the Sri Lankan Parliament and became the 4th Indian PM to do so: Jawaharlal Nehru, Indira Gandhi and Morarji Desai were the others.

PM Modi on March 14 visited Jaffna, becoming the first Indian premier to set foot in the war-ravaged town in Sri Lanka's Tamil dominated Northern Province. Modi also laid the foundation stone of a cultural centre in Jaffna. He also visited the North Central Province's capital city of Medawachchiya train service to Colombo.

8

ISIS – Terror Tentacles

What is ISIS?

ISIS (Islamic State of Iraq and Syria) is a radical Islamic group that has seized large swathes of territory in Syria and Iraq. The group aims to establish a 'caliphate' – a state ruled by Islamic law or sharia.

Formation of ISIS

ISIS can trace its roots back to 2002, when Abu Musab al-Zarqawi – a Jordanian who was to gain notoriety in the Iraqi insurgency from 2003-06, founded a jihadi organisation called Tawhid wal-Jihad in the north of Iraq. Zarqawi had been linked with al-Qaeda while in Afghanistan in the late '90s, but was not a member of the group and disagreed with the tactic of focusing on the 'far enemy' (the West) as opposed to the 'near enemy' (rulers in the Islamic world). Following the 2003 invasion of Iraq, Zarqawi's organisation grew more active and affiliated itself to al-Qaeda in 2004, becoming al-Qaeda in Iraq (AQI). Despite the tactical differences, this made a useful alliance of convenience: Zarqawi's organisation gained the recruiting and resourcing benefits of being part of a global and credible jihadi organisation, while al-Qaeda gained an affiliate in Iraq, already by that stage the global centre of jihad.

Zarqawi's AQI was an influential actor in Iraq's descent into chaos between 2003 and 2007. It had an explicit policy of stoking sectarian violence with the aim of rallying the Sunni community around Sunni jihadi groups, a tactic that ISIS is replicating now. This gained criticism from al-Qaeda's leaders, who felt that the indiscriminate and brutal violence risked alienating their supporters. However, it continued to support Zarqawi in public until he was killed in an airstrike in 2006.

In late 2006 AQI joined with eight other Islamist insurgent groups to form the Islamic State of Iraq (ISI), without permission from the al-Qaeda leadership. The name chosen for this new group indicated its ambitions: it was more than a mere jihadi group, but an embryonic caliphate, governed by Islamic law, to which all Muslims within its territory owed allegiance.

As the US surge took hold in 2007 and the so-called 'Anbar Awakening' or sahwa – the cooptation of Sunni tribes in Anbar province in the fight against the insurgency – diminished the group's support base, the notion of the Islamic State's 'territory' was a tenuous one. Successive ISI leaders were killed in airstrikes, and the group's capacity to launch attacks was severely diminished. But the accession in 2010 of its current leader, Abu Bakr al-Baghdadi, coincided with a change in the external pressures the group faced. The USA withdrew its forces in 2011 and the promised integration of the Anbar militias into the armed forces was abandoned, removing a significant counter to insurgent activity. Absent American restraint, Prime Minister Maliki gave vent to his more sectarian impulses, creating grievances that the Islamic State was quick to exploit. Moreover, the start of the Syrian civil war created a fertile new cause and battlefield for the group's recruitment, and moulded it into the military force it has become.

The Syrian war also facilitated the Islamic State's final break with al-Qaeda. Since 2006, the group's relationship with al-Qaeda had been ambiguous, possibly deliberately so: the mutual benefits that had first prompted Zarqawi to affiliate to the organisation remained. In 2011, Baghdadi created a Syrian subsidiary, Jabhat al-Nusra (JN), under Abu Mohammad al-Jolani, in order to gain a toehold in the war. In 2013, with JN showing unwelcome signs of independence, he announced their re-absorption into the expanded Islamic State of Iraq and al-Sham – 'al-Sham' being the Arabic name for Greater Syria, with connotations of earlier caliphates. However, Jolani appealed to al-Qaeda's central command, which ruled in his favour, ordering Baghdadi to confine his group to Iraq.

The alliance between al-Qaeda and ISIS was no longer convenient. ISIS could now claim a history and a support base that established its credibility, and al-Qaeda's central leadership was weak. An ISIS spokesman declared that al-Qaeda's leader, Ayman al-Zawahiri, was sinful, and Jolani nothing less than a traitor. Shortly afterwards, Zawahiri announced that ISIS had nothing to do with al-Qaeda.

In subsequent fighting in Syria, much of it with other rebels including JN and other jihadi groups, ISIS has gained and held significant amounts of territory. It captured the city of Raqqa from other rebels in early 2014, using it since as a base to launch attacks in Syria and Iraq. In Iraq, the group exploited botched Iraqi military operations in Fallujah in January 2014 to gain control of the city. Control of sparsely populated transport corridors allowed them to advance rapidly in the kind of surprise attacks that delivered them Mosul, among other cities, in June of the same year.

However, 2015 has brought setbacks for the group, with Kurdish forces, comprising mainly the Popular Protection Units in Syria and the Peshmerga in Iraq, emerging as key opponents. Iraqi security forces, aided by Shia militias supported by Iran, in March 2015 launched the first major government offensive against ISIS since June 2014, in Tikrit.

Regardless of these defeats, ISIS' development since 2013 changed the nature of the group. It is no longer a mere terrorist group, but an army that can hold and administer territory. It governs according to harshly interpreted principles of

Islamic law, including the imposition of dhimmi pacts on minorities – guaranteeing protection in exchange for the payment of a tax and the acceptance of second-class citizenship. Minorities, including Shia Muslims, have been subject to severe human rights abuses, including massacres and forced conversion, and the persecution of minorities in northern Iraq has been particularly brutal. ISIS has also provoked shock and condemnation worldwide for its brutal execution of foreign journalists and humanitarian aid workers, as well as captured combatants from opposing forces. Meanwhile, a further danger lies in the group's appeal beyond the borders of Iraq and Syria. While other jihadi groups, both in these countries and elsewhere, seek to establish an Islamic caliphate, ISIS claims to be one. Baghdadi has declared himself "Caliph Ibrahim," and goes by the title "Commander of the Faithful." In the language of his speeches and in his titles, he lays claim to a form of authority from the earliest days of Islam. This combined with the supposedly just cause of the fight against Assad in Syria has proved to be a powerful draw to young Islamists across the world, spread by means of an adept use of social media, and slickly presented propaganda such as the monthly magazine Dabiq. Some of these recruits will eventually return to their homes, taking with them their experiences as members of the most brutal jihadi group in the conflict.

By claiming responsibility for the November 2015 attacks in Paris and the downing of a Russian plane in Egypt, ISIS gives the impression that the group, ordinarily focused on targeting the near enemy, is keen to convey a broadening of its operational strategy and the pursuit of targets further afield.

The danger is not limited to individuals attracted to ISIS' flag. Recently, Baghdadi demanded that all Islamist and jihadi movements across the world be dissolved or absorbed into his 'caliphate.' Many groups have taken up the call, and new ones continue to do so. While some were previously unknown, others, including Boko Haram in Nigeria and Ansar Beit al-Maqdis in Egypt, have long been prominent actors in their own countries' conflicts. Moreover, the appeal of the universal caliphate is fracturing established groups that have not declared allegiance.

The US-led campaign against ISIS, known as Operation Inherent Resolve, has launched over 6,000 airstrikes against ISIS and has been killing about 1,000 militants every month, roughly the same number believed to be joining the group, leaving the group's manpower strength effectively capped at 30,000 to 40,000. ISIS has had to adopt a different strategy since the commencement of aerial attacks on the group in Iraq and Syria, no longer having the freedom of movement it once enjoyed. With Russia entering the foray and reportedly carrying out airstrikes against ISIS targets, the group's capabilities will be further diminished.

Territory Under Control

ISIS and its allies control about 40,000 sq. km of Iraq and Syria – roughly the size of Belgium. Others believe they control closer to 90,000 sq km about the size of Jordan.

Funding

ISIS has $2bn in cash & assets, making it the wealthiest militant group. It earns millions per month from oil and gas fields it controls, taxation, tolls, smuggling, extortion and kidnapping.

9

Nuclear Treaties & Disarmament

NUCLEAR TREATIES & DISARMAMENT

History

To date, over 2000 nuclear tests have been carried out at different locations all over the world. Arms control advocates had campaigned for the adoption of a treaty banning all nuclear explosions since the early 1950s, when public concern was aroused as a result of radioactive fall-out from atmospheric nuclear tests and the escalating arms race. Over 50 nuclear explosions were registered between July 16, 1945, when the first nuclear explosive test was conducted by the United States at White Sands Missile Range near Alamogordo, New Mexico, and December 31, 1953. Prime Minister Nehru of India voiced the heightened international concern in 1954, when he proposed the elimination of all nuclear test explosions worldwide. However, within the context of the Cold War, skepticism about the capability to verify compliance with a comprehensive nuclear test ban treaty posed a major obstacle to any agreement.

Partial Test Ban Treaty, 1963

Limited success was achieved with the signing of the Partial Test Ban Treaty in 1963, which banned nuclear tests in the atmosphere, underwater and in space, but not underground. Neither France nor China signed the PTBT. However, the treaty was still ratified by the United States after an 80 to 19 vote in the United States Senate. While the PTBT reduced atmospheric fallout, underground nuclear testing can also vent radioactivity into the atmosphere, and radioactivity released underground may seep into the ground water. Moreover, the PTBT had no restraining effects on the further development of nuclear warheads.

Treaty on the Non-Proliferation of Nuclear Weapons [npt]

Provisions: The Treaty on the Non-Proliferation of Nuclear Weapons, also referred to as the Nuclear Non-Proliferation Treaty (NPT), obligates the five acknowledged nuclear-weapon states (the United States, Russian Federation, United Kingdom, France, and China) not to transfer nuclear weapons, other nuclear explosive devices, or their technology to any non-nuclear-weapon state. Nuclear weapon states parties are also obligated, under Article VI, to "pursue negotiations in good faith on effective measures relating to cessation of the nuclear arms race at an early date and to nuclear disarmament, and on a treaty on general and complete disarmament under strict and effective international control." Non-nuclear-weapon states parties undertake not to acquire or produce nuclear weapons or nuclear explosive devices. They are required also to accept safeguards to detect diversions of nuclear materials from peaceful activities, such as power generation, to the production of nuclear weapons or other nuclear explosive devices. This must be done in accordance with an individual safeguards agreement, concluded between each non-nuclear-weapon State Party and the International Atomic Energy Agency (IAEA). Under these agreements, all nuclear materials in peaceful civil facilities under the jurisdiction of the state must be declared to the IAEA, whose inspectors have routine access to the facilities for periodic monitoring and inspections. If information from routine inspections is not sufficient to fulfill its responsibilities, the IAEA may consult with the state regarding special inspections within or outside declared facilities.

Status

The Treaty was opened for signature on July 1, 1968, and signed on that date by the United States, the United Kingdom, the Soviet Union, and 59 other countries. The Treaty entered into force with the deposit of US ratification on March 5, 1970. China acceded to the NPT on March 9, 1992, and France acceded on August 3, 1992. In 1996, Belarus joined Ukraine and Kazakhstan in removing and transferring to the Russian Federation the last of the remaining former Soviet nuclear weapons located within their territories, and each of these nations has become a State Party to the NPT, as a non-nuclear-weapon state. In June 1997 Brazil became a State Party to the NPT.

The NPT is the most widely accepted arms control agreement; only Israel, India, and Pakistan have never been signatories of the Treaty, and North Korea withdrew from the Treaty in 2003.

In accordance with the terms of the NPT, on May 11, 1995 more than 170 countries attended the 1995 NPT Review and Extension Conference (NPTREC) in New York. Three decisions and one resolution emanated from NPTREC. First, the NPT was extended for an indefinite duration and without conditions. Second, Principles and Objectives for Nuclear Non-Proliferation and Disarmament were worked out to guide the parties to the treaty in the next phase of its implementation. Third, an enhanced review process was established for future review conferences. Finally, a resolution endorsed the establishment of a zone free of weapons of mass destruction in the Middle East.

There have been no confirmed instances of official states party transfers of nuclear weapon technology or unsafeguarded nuclear materials to any non-nuclear-weapon states party. However, some non-nuclear-weapon states, such as Iraq, were able to obtain sensitive technology and/or equipment from private parties in states that are signatories to the NPT. South Africa conducted an independent nuclear weapons production program prior to joining the NPT; however, it dismantled all of its nuclear weapons before signing the Treaty. In 1994, the United States and North

Korea signed an "Agreed Framework" bringing North Korea into full compliance with its non-proliferation obligations under the NPT. In 2003 North Korea announced it was withdrawing from the Treaty effective immediately, and on October 9, 2006 became the eighth country to explode a nuclear device.

Comprehensive Nuclear Test-Ban Treaty (ctbt)

The Comprehensive Nuclear Test-Ban Treaty (CTBT) bans all nuclear explosions in all environments, for military or civilian purposes. It was adopted by the United Nations General Assembly on September 10, 1996 but has not entered into force as eight specific states have not ratified the treaty yet.

The Treaty was adopted by the United Nations General Assembly on September 10, 1996. It opened for signature in New York on September 24, 1996, when it was signed by 71 States, including five of the eight then nuclear-capable states. As of March 2015, 164 states have ratified the CTBT and another 19 states have signed but not ratified it.

The treaty will enter into force 180 days after the 44 states listed in Annex 2 of the treaty have ratified it. These "Annex 2 states" are states that participated in the CTBT's negotiations between 1994 and 1996 and possessed nuclear power reactors or research reactors at that time. As of 2015, eight Annex 2 states have not ratified the treaty: China, Egypt, Iran, Israel and the United States have signed but not ratified the Treaty; India, North Korea and Pakistan have not signed it.

In 1998 India said it would only sign the treaty if the United States presented a schedule for eliminating its nuclear stockpile, a condition the United States rejected.

Obligations

- Each State Party undertakes not to carry out any nuclear weapon test explosion or any other nuclear explosion, and to prohibit and prevent any such nuclear explosion at any place under its jurisdiction or control.
- Each State Party undertakes, furthermore, to refrain from causing, encouraging, or in any way participating in the carrying out of any nuclear weapon test explosion or any other nuclear explosion.

US Ratification of the CTBT

The US has signed the CTBT, but not ratified it. There is ongoing debate whether or not the US should ratify the CTBT.

The United states has stated that its ratification of the CTBT is conditional upon:

(A) The conduct of a Science Based Stockpile Stewardship Program to ensure a high level of confidence in the safety and reliability of nuclear weapons in the active stockpile, including the conduct of a broad range of effective and continuing experimental programs.

(B) The maintenance of modern nuclear laboratory facilities and programs in theoretical and exploratory nuclear technology which will attract, retain, and ensure the continued application of human scientific resources to those programs on which continued progress in nuclear technology depends.

(C) The maintenance of the basic capability to resume nuclear test activities prohibited by the CTBT should the United States cease to be bound to adhere to this treaty.

(D) Continuation of a comprehensive research and development program to improve the treaty monitoring capabilities and operations.

(E) The continuing development of a broad range of intelligence gathering and analytical capabilities and operations to ensure accurate and comprehensive information on worldwide nuclear arsenals, nuclear weapons development programs, and related nuclear programs.

(F) The understanding that if the President of the United States is informed by the Secretary of Defense and Secretary of Energy (DOE) – advised by the Nuclear Weapons Council, the Directors of DOE's nuclear weapons laboratories and the Commander of the US Strategic Command – that a high level of confidence in the safety or reliability of a nuclear weapon type which the two Secretaries consider to be critical to the US nuclear deterrent could no longer be certified, the President, in consultation with Congress, would be prepared to withdraw from the CTBT under the standard "supreme national interests" clause in order to conduct whatever testing might be required.

Proponents of ratification claim that it would:

- Establish an international norm that would push other nuclear-capable countries like North Korea, Pakistan, and India to sign.
- Constrain worldwide nuclear proliferation by vastly limiting a country's ability to make nuclear advancements that only testing can ensure.
- Not compromise US national security because the Science Based Stockpile Stewardship Program serves as a means for maintaining current US nuclear capabilities without physical detonation.

Opponents of ratification claim that

1. The treaty is unverifiable and that others nations could easily cheat.
2. The ability to enforce the treaty was dubious.
3. The US nuclear stockpile would not be as safe or reliable in the absence of testing.
4. The benefit to nuclear nonproliferation was minimal.

On October 13, 1999, the United States Senate rejected ratification of the CTBT. President Barack Obama stated during his 2008 election campaign that "As president, I will reach out to the Senate to secure the ratification of the CTBT at the earliest practical date." In his speech in Prague on April 5, 2009, he announced that "[To] achieve a global ban on nuclear testing, my administration will immediately and aggressively pursue US ratification of the Comprehensive Test Ban Treaty. After more than five decades of talks, it is time for the testing of nuclear weapons to finally be banned."

An article in Bulletin of the Atomic Scientists describes how a North Korean underground nuclear test on May 25, 2009 was detected and the source located by GPS satellites. The authors suggest that the effectiveness of GPS satellites for detecting nuclear explosions enhances the ability to verify compliance to the Comprehensive Nuclear Test Ban Treaty, giving the United States more reason to ratify it.

Monitoring of the CTBT

Geophysical and other technologies are used to monitor for compliance with the Treaty: forensic seismology, hydro acoustics, infrasound, and radionuclide monitoring. The technologies are used to monitor the underground, the waters and the atmosphere for any sign of a nuclear explosion. Statistical theories and methods are integral to CTBT monitoring providing confidence in verification analysis. Once the Treaty enters into force, onsite inspection will be provided for where concerns about compliance arise.

The Preparatory Commission for the Comprehensive Test Ban Treaty Organization (CTBTO), an international organization headquartered in Vienna, Austria, was created to build the verification regime, including establishment and provisional operation of the network of monitoring stations, the creation of an international data centre, and development of the On Site Inspection capability.

The monitoring network consists of 337 facilities located all over the globe. As of May 2012, more than 260 facilities have been certified. The monitoring stations register data that is transmitted to the international data centre in Vienna for processing and analysis. The data are sent to states that have signed the Treaty.

Nuclear Disarmament

Nuclear disarmament refers to both the act of reducing or eliminating nuclear weapons and to the end state of a nuclear-free world, in which nuclear weapons are completely eliminated.

Major nuclear disarmament groups include Campaign for Nuclear Disarmament, Greenpeace and International Physicians for the Prevention of Nuclear War. There have been many large anti-nuclear demonstrations and protests. On June 12, 1982, one million people demonstrated in New York City's Central Park against nuclear weapons and for an end to the cold war arms race. It was the largest anti-nuclear protest and the largest political demonstration in American history.

Proponents of nuclear disarmament say that it would lessen the probability of nuclear war occurring, especially accidentally. Critics of nuclear disarmament say that it would undermine deterrence.

After the Partial Test Ban Treaty (1963), which prohibited atmospheric testing, the movement against nuclear weapons somewhat subsided in the 1970s (and was replaced in part by a movement against nuclear power).

In the 1980s, a popular movement for nuclear disarmament again gained strength in the light of the weapons build-up and aggressive rhetoric of US President Ronald Reagan. Reagan had "a world free of nuclear weapons" as his personal mission, and was largely scorned for this in Europe. His officials tried to stop such talks but Reagan was able to start discussions on nuclear disarmament with Soviet Union. He changed the name "SALT" (Strategic Arms Limitation Talks) to "START" (Strategic Arms Reduction Talks).

After the 1986 Reykjavik summit between US President Ronald Reagan and the Soviet General Secretary Mikhail Gorbachev, the United States and the Soviet Union concluded two important nuclear arms reduction treaties: the INF Treaty (1987) and START I (1991). After the end of the Cold War, the United States and the Russian Federation concluded the Strategic Offensive Reductions Treaty (2003) and the New START Treaty (2010).

In the Soviet Union (USSR), voices against nuclear weapons were few and far between since there was no widespread Freedom of speech and Freedom of the press. Certain citizens who had become prominent enough to safely criticize the Soviet government, such as Andrei Sakharov, did speak out against nuclear weapons, but to little effect.

When the extreme danger intrinsic to nuclear war and the possession of nuclear weapons became apparent to all sides during the Cold War, a series of disarmament and nonproliferation treaties were agreed upon between the United States, the Soviet Union, and several other states throughout the world. Many of these treaties involved years of negotiations, and seemed to result in important steps in arms reduction and reducing the risk of nuclear war.

Summary

- Partial Test Ban Treaty (PTBT) 1963: Prohibited all testing of nuclear weapons except underground.
- Nuclear Non-Proliferation Treaty (NPT)—signed 1968, came into force 1970: An international treaty (currently with 189 member states) to limit the spread of nuclear weapons. The treaty has three main pillars: nonproliferation, disarmament, and the right to peacefully use nuclear technology.

- Interim Agreement on Offensive Arms (SALT I) 1972: The Soviet Union and the United States agreed to a freeze in the number of intercontinental ballistic missiles (ICBMs) and submarine (SLBMs) that they would deploy.
- Anti-Ballistic Missile Treaty (ABM) 1972: The United States and Soviet Union could deploy ABM interceptors at two sites, each with up to 100 ground-based launchers for ABM interceptor missiles. In a 1974 Protocol, the US and Soviet Union agreed to only deploy an ABM system to one site.
- Strategic Arms Limitation Treaty (SALT II) 1979: Replacing SALT I, SALT II limited both the Soviet Union and the United States to an equal number of ICBM launchers, SLBM launchers, and heavy bombers. Also placed limits on Multiple Independent Reentry Vehicles (MIRVS).
- Intermediate-Range Nuclear Forces Treaty (INF) 1987: Created a global ban on short-and long-range nuclear weapons systems, as well as an intrusive verification regime.
- Strategic Arms Reduction Treaty (START I)—signed 1991, ratified 1994: Limited long-range nuclear forces in the United States and the newly independent states of the former Soviet Union to 6,000 attributed warheads on 1,600 ballistic missiles and bombers.
- Strategic Arms Reduction Treaty II (START II)—signed 1993, never put into force: START II was a bilateral agreement between the US and Russia which attempted to commit each side to deploy no more than 3,000 to 3,500 warheads by December 2007 and also included a prohibition against deploying multiple independent reentry vehicles (MIRVs) on intercontinental ballistic missiles (ICBMs)
- Strategic Offensive Reductions Treaty (SORT or Moscow Treaty)—signed 2002, into force 2003: A very loose treaty that is often criticized by arms control advocates for its ambiguity and lack of depth, Russia and the United States agreed to reduce their "strategic nuclear warheads" (a term that remain undefined in the treaty) to between 1,700 and 2,200 by 2012.
- Comprehensive Test Ban Treaty (CTBT)—signed 1996, not yet in force: The CTBT is an international treaty (currently with 181 state signatures and 148 state ratifications) that bans all nuclear explosions in all environments. While the treaty is not in force, Russia has not tested a nuclear weapon since 1990 and the United States has not since 1992.
- New START Treaty—signed 2010, into force in 2011: replaces SORT treaty, reduces deployed nuclear warheads by about half, will remain into force until at least 2021.

Only one country has been known to ever dismantle their nuclear arsenal completely— the apartheid government of South Africa apparently developed half a dozen crude fission weapons during the 1980s, but they were dismantled in the early 1990s.

Nuclear Disarmament Movement

In 1954 Japanese peace movements converged to form a unified "Japanese Council against Atomic and Hydrogen Bombs". Japanese opposition to the Pacific nuclear weapons tests was widespread, and "an estimated 35 million signatures were collected on petitions calling for bans on nuclear weapons".

In the United Kingdom, the first Aldermaston March organised by the Campaign for Nuclear Disarmament took place at Easter 1958, when several thousand people marched for four days from Trafalgar Square, London, to the Atomic Weapons Research Establishment close to Aldermaston in Berkshire, England, to demonstrate their opposition to nuclear weapons. The Aldermaston marches continued into the late 1960s when tens of thousands of people took part in the four-day marches.

In 1959, a letter in the *Bulletin of Atomic Scientists* was the start of a successful campaign to stop the Commission dumping radioactive waste in the sea 19 kilometers from Boston. In 1962, Linus Pauling won the Nobel Peace Prize for his work to stop the atmospheric testing of nuclear weapons, and the "Ban the Bomb" movement spread.

In 1963, many countries ratified the Partial Test Ban Treaty prohibiting atmospheric nuclear testing. Radioactive fallout became less of an issue and the nuclear disarmament movement went into decline for some years.

On June 3, 1981, Thomas launched the longest running peace vigil in US history at Lafayette Square in Washington, DC. He was later joined on the White House Peace Vigil by anti-nuclear activists Concepcion Picciotto and Ellen Benjamin.

On June 12, 1982, one million people demonstrated in New York City's Central Park against nuclear weapons and for an end to the cold war arms race. It was the largest anti-nuclear protest and the largest political demonstration in American history. International Day of Nuclear Disarmament protests were held on June 20, 1983 at 50 sites across the United States. In 1986, hundreds of people walked from Los Angeles to Washington DC in the Great Peace March for Global Nuclear Disarmament. There were many Nevada Desert Experience protests and peace camps at the Nevada Test Site during the 1980s and 1990s.

On May 1, 2005, 40,000 anti-nuclear/anti-war protesters marched past the United Nations in New York, 60 years after the atomic bombings of Hiroshima and Nagasaki. This was the largest anti-nuclear rally in the US for several decades. In Britain, there were many protests about the government's proposal to replace the aging Trident weapons system with a newer model. The largest protest had 100,000 participants and, according to polls, 59 percent of the public opposed the move.

The International Conference on Nuclear Disarmament took place in Oslo in February, 2008, and was organized by The Government of Norway, the Nuclear Threat Initiative and the Hoover. The Conference was entitled *Achieving the Vision of a World Free of Nuclear Weapons* and had the purpose of building consensus between nuclear weapon states and non-nuclear weapon states in relation to the Nuclear Non-proliferation Treaty.

The Tehran International Conference on Disarmament and Non-Proliferation took place in Tehran in April 2010. The conference was held shortly after the signing of the New START, and resulted in a call of action toward eliminating all nuclear weapons. Representatives from 60 countries were invited to the conference. Non-governmental organizations were also present.

Among the prominent figures who have called for the abolition of nuclear weapons are the philosopher Bertrand Russell, the entertainer Steve Allen, CNN's Ted Turner, former Senator Claiborne Pell, Notre Dame president Theodore Hesburg, South African Bishop Desmond Tutu and the Dalai Lama.

10

Goods and Service Tax – GST

What is a 'Goods and Services Tax – GST'?

The Goods and Services Tax (GST) is a value-added tax levied on most goods and services sold for domestic comsumption. The GST is paid by consumers, but it is remitted to the government by the businesses selling the goods and services. In effect, GST provides revenue for the government.

GST Advantages:

1. GST is a transparent tax and also reduce number of indirect taxes.
2. GST will not be a cost to registered retailers therefore there will be no hidden taxes and the cost of doing business will be lower
3. Benefit people as price will come down which in turn will help companies as consumption will increase
4. There is no doubt that in production and distribution of goods, services are increasingly
5. Separate taxes for goods and services, which is the present taxation system, requires division of transaction value into value of goods and services for taxation, leading to greater complications, administration, including compliances costs.
6. In the GST system. When all the taxes are integrated, it would make possible the taxation burden to the split equitably, between manufacturing and services.
7. GST will be levied only at the final destination of consumption based on VAT principle and not at various points (from manufacturing to retail outlets). This will help in removing economic distortions and bring about development of a common national market.
8. GST will also help to build a transparent and corruption free tax administration.
9. Presently a tax is levied on when a finished product moves out from a factory which is paid by the manufacturer and it is again levied at the retail outlet when sold.

10. GST is backed by the GSTN, which is a fully integrated tax platform to deal with all aspects of GST.

GST Disadvantages:

1. Some Economist say that GST in India would impact negatively on the real estate market. It would add up to 8 percent to the cost of new homes and reduce demand by about 12 percent.
2. Some Expert says that GST(Central GST), are nothing but, new names for Central Excise/Service Tax VAT and CST. Hence, there is no major reduction in the number of tax layers
3. Some retail products currently have only four percent tax on them, After GST garments and clothes could become more expensive.
4. The aviation industry would be affected. Service taxes on airfares currently range from six to nine percent with GST, this rate will surpass fifteen percent and effectively double the tax rate.
5. Adoption and migration to the new GST system would involve teething troubles and learning for the entire ecosystem

Military Awards

Param Vir Chakra

- Awarded for most conspicuous bravery or some daring or pre-eminent act of valour or self-sacrifice, in the presence of the enemy, whether on land, at sea, or in the air. The decoration may be awarded posthumously. Maj. Som Nath Sharma is the 1st recipient of PVC.
- If any recipient of the Chakra shall again perform such an act of bravery as would have made him or her eligible to be recorded by a Bar to be attached to the riband by which the Chakra is suspended, and for every such additional act of bravery, an additional Bar shall be added, and any such Bar or Bars may also be awarded posthumously. For every Bar awarded a replica of the 'Indra's Vajra' in miniature shall be added to the riband when worn alone.
- Officers, men and women of all ranks of the Army, the Navy and the Air Force, of any of the Reserve Forces, of the Territorial Army Militia and of any other lawfully constituted Armed Forces.
- Matrons, Sisters, Nurses and the staff of the Nursing Services and other Service pertaining to Hospitals and Nursing, and Civilians of either sex serving regularly or temporarily under the orders, directions or supervision of any of the above-mentioned Forces.

Ashok Chakra

- Awarded for most conspicuous bravery, or some act of daring or pre-eminent act of valour or self-sacrifice otherwise than in the face of the enemy. The decoration may be awarded posthumously.
- If a recipient of the Chakra shall again perform such an act of gallantry as would have made him or her eligible to receive the Chakra, such further act of gallantry shall be recognized by a Bar to be attached to the riband by which the Chakra is suspended and, for every subsequent act of gallantry, an additional Bar shall be added and every such Bar, a replica of the Chakra in miniature shall be added to the riband when worn alone.
- Officers, men and women of all ranks of the Army, the Navy and the Air Force, of any of the Reserve Forces, of the Territorial Army, Militia and of any other lawfully constituted forces.

- Members of the Nursing Services of the Armed Forces.
- Civilian citizens of either sex in all walks of life, other than members of Police Forces and of recognized fire services.

Amendment: Civilian Citizens of either sex in all walks of life and members of Police Forces including Central Para-Military Forces and Railway Protection Force. (President's Secretariat Notification No. 94-Pres/99 – Published in Part I, Section I of the Gazette of India dated Saturday 10th July 1999).

Maha Vir Chakra

- For acts of gallantry in the presence of the enemy on land, at sea or in the air. The decoration may be awarded posthumously.
- If any recipient of the Chakra shall again perform such an act of bravery as would have made him or her eligible to receive the Chakra, such further act of bravery shall be recorded by a Bar to be attached to the riband by which the Chakra is suspended, and for every such additional act of bravery, an additional bar shall be added, and any such bar or bars may also be awarded posthumously. For every bar awarded a replica of the Chakra in miniature shall be added to the riband when worn alone.
- Officers, men and women of all ranks of the Army, the navy and the Air Force, of any of the Reserve Forces, of the Territorial Army, Militia and of any other lawfully constituted Armed forces.
- Matrons, Sisters, Nurses and the staff of the Nursing Services and other Services pertaining to Hospitals and Nursing, and Civilians of either sex serving regularly or temporarily under the orders, directions or supervision of any of the above-mentioned Forces.

Kirti Chakra

- Awarded for conspicuous gallantry otherwise than in the face of the enemy. The decoration may be awarded posthumously.
- If a recipient of the Chakra shall again perform such an act of gallantry as would have made him or her eligible to receive the Chakra, such further act of gallantry shall be recognized by a Bar to be attached to the riband by which the Chakra is suspended and, for every subsequent act of gallantry, an additional Bar shall be added and such bar or bars may also be awarded posthumously. For every such Bar, a replica of the Chakra in miniature shall be added to the riband when worn alone.
- Officers, men and women of all ranks of the Army, the Navy and the Air Force, of any of the Reserve Forces, of the Territorial Army, Militia and of any other lawfully constituted forces, members of the Nursing Services of the Armed Forces.

- Civilian citizens of either sex in all walks of life, other than members of Police Forces and of recognized Fire Services.

Amendment: Civilian Citizens of either sex in all walks of life and members of Police Forces including Central Para-Military Forces and Railway protection Force. (President's Secretariat Notification No 94-Pres/99 - Published in Part I, Section I of the Gazette of India dated Saturday 10th July 1999)

Vir Chakra

- For acts of gallantry in the presence of the enemy, whether on land or at sea or in the air. The decoration may be awarded posthumously.
- If any recipient of the Chakra shall again perform such an act of bravery as would have made him or her eligible to receive the Chakra, such further act of bravery shall be recorded by a Bar to be attached to the riband by which the Chakra is suspended, and for every such additional act of bravery, an additional Bar shall be added, and any such Bar or Bars may also be awarded posthumously. For every Bar awarded a replica of the Chakra in miniature shall be added to the riband when worn alone.
- Officers, men and women of all ranks of the Army, the Navy and the Air Force, of any of the Reserve Forces, of the Territorial Army, Militia and of any other lawfully constituted Armed Forces.
- Matrons, Sisters, Nurses and the staff of the Nursing Services and other Services pertaining to Hospitals and Nursing, and Civilians of either sex serving regularly or temporarily under the orders, directions or supervision of any of the above-mentioned Forces.

Shaurya Chakra

- Awarded for gallantry otherwise than in the face of the enemy. The decoration may be awarded posthumously.
- If a recipient of the Chakra shall again perform such an act of gallantry as would have made him or her eligible to receive the Chakra, such further act of gallantry shall be recognized by a Bar to be attached to the riband by which the Chakra is suspended and, for every subsequent act of gallantry, an additional Bar shall be added and such Bar or Bars may also be awarded posthumously. For every such Bar, a replica of the Chakra in miniature shall be added to the riband when worn alone.
- Officers and men and women of the Army, the Navy and the Air Force, of any of the Reserve Forces, of the Territorial Army, Militia, and of any other lawfully constituted Armed Forces.
- Members of the Nursing Services of the Armed Forces.
- Civilians of either sex in all walks of life, other than members of Police Forces and of recognized Fire Services.

Amendment: Civilian Citizens of either sex in all walks of life and members of Police Forces including Central Para-Military Forces and Railway Protection Force. (President's Secretariat Notification No 94-Pres/99 - Published in Part I, Section I of the Gazette of India dated Saturday 10th July 1999).

Sena Medal

- Awarded for such individual acts of exceptional devotion to duty or courage as have special significance for the Army. Awards may be made posthumously.
- A bar shall be given for every subsequent award of the medal to a person.
- All ranks of the Army.

Nao Sena Medal

- Awarded for such individual acts of exceptional devotion to duty or courage as have special significance for the Navy. Awards may be made posthumously.
- A bar shall be given for every subsequent award of the medal to a person.
- All ranks of the Navy.

Vayu Sena Medal

- Awarded for such individual acts of exceptional devotion to duty or courage as have special significance for the Air Force. Awards may be made posthumously.
- A bar shall be given for every subsequent award of the medal to a person.
- All ranks of the Air Force.

12 Defence Organisation-Army/Navy/Air Force

– Central Command – Lucknow

ARMY

Headquarters, Indian Army, New Delhi – 2nd largest army after China. Army Day – January 15.

Eastern Command, headquartered at Kolkata, West Bengal

South Western Command, headquartered at Jaipur, Rajasthan

Northern Command, headquartered at Udhampur, Jammu and Kashmir

Western Command, headquartered at Chandimandir

Training Command, headquartered at Shimla, Himachal Pradesh **Southern Command**, headquartered at Pune, Maharashtra

Regimental Organization

In addition to this (not to be confused with the Field Corps mentioned above) are the Regiments or Corps or departments of the Indian Army. The corps mentioned below are the functional divisions entrusted with specific pan-Army tasks.

Arms

Indian Infantry Regiments

Armoured Corps Regiments – The Armoured Corps Centre and School is at Ahmednagar.

Regiment of Artillery – The School of Artillery is at Deolali near Nasik.

Corps of Signals – Military College of Telecommunication Engineering (MCTE), Mhow is a premiere training institute of the Corps of Signals.

Corps of Engineers – The College of Military Engineering is at Dapodi, Pune. The Centers are located as follows – Madras Engineer Group at Bangalore, Bengal Engineer Group at Roorkee and Bombay Engineer Group at Khadki, Pune.

Corps of Army Air Defence – Center at Gopalpur in Orissa State.

Mechanised Infantry – Regimental Center at Ahmednagar.

Army aviation corps (India)

This is the flying branch of the Army (holding helicopters) The Territorial Army has battalions affiliated to the different infantry regiments and some department units which are either from the Corps of Engineers, Army Medical Corps or the Army Service Corps. They serve as a part-time reserve.

Services

Army Dental Corps – Centered at Lucknow.

Army Education Corps – Centered at Pachmarhi.

Army Medical Corps – Centered at Lucknow.

Army Ordnance Corps – Centered at Jabalpur and Secunderabad (HQ).

Army Postal Service Corps – Centered at Kamptee near Nagpur.

Army Service Corps – Centered at Bangalore and Gaya

Corps of Electronics and Mechanical Engineers – Centered at Bhopal and Secunderabad.

Corps of Military Police (India) – Centered at Bangalore Intelligence Corps – Centered at Pune.

Judge Advocate General's Dept. – Centered at the Institute of Military Law Kamptee, Nagpur.

Military Farms Service – Centered at the Military Farms School and Center, Meerut Cantt.

Military Nursing Service

Remount and Veterinary Corps

Pioneer Corps Bangalore

Division

An Army Division is an intermediate between a Corps and a Brigade. It is the largest strike force in the Army. Each Division is headed by a General Officer Commanding (GOC) in the rank of Major General. It usually consists of 15,000 combat troops and 8,000 support elements. Currently, the Indian Army has 37 Divisions including 4 RAPID (Re-organised Army Plains Infantry Divisions) Action Divisions, 18 Infantry Divisions, 10 Mountain Divisions, 3 Armoured Divisions and 2 Artillery Divisions. Each Division is composed of several Brigades.

Brigade

A Brigade generally consists of around 3,000 combat troops with supporting elements. An Infantry Brigade usually has 3 Infantry Battalions along with various Support Arms & Services. It is headed by a Brigadier, equivalent to a Brigadier General in some armies. In addition to the Brigades in various Army Divisions, the Indian Army also has 5 Independent Armoured Brigades, 15 Independent Artillery Brigades, 7 Independent Infantry Brigades, 1 Independent Parachute Brigade, 3 Independent Air Defence Brigades, 2 Independent Air Defence Groups and 4

Independent Engineer Brigades. These Independent Brigades operate directly under the Corps Commander (GOC Corps).

Battalion

A Battalion is commanded by a Colonel and is the Infantry's main fighting unit. It consists of more than 900 combat personnel.

Company

Headed by a Major, a Company comprises 120 soldiers.

Platoon

An intermediate between a Company and Section, a Platoon is headed by a Lieutenant or depending on the availability of Commissioned Officers, a Junior Commissioned Officer, with the rank of Subedar or Naib-Subedar. It has a total strength of about 32 troops.

Section

Smallest military outfit with a strength of 10 personnel. Commanded by a Non-commissioned officer of the rank of Havildar Major.

Future Development (Army)

- Futuristic Infantry Soldier as a system (F-INSAS) is the Indian Army's principal modernisation program from 2012 to 2020.
- India proposes to progressively induct as many as 248 Arjun MBT and develop and induct the Arjun MKII variant, 1657 Russian origin T-90S main-battle tanks (MBTs), apart from the ongoing upgrade of its T-72 fleet. The Army recently placed an order for 4100 French origin Milan-2T anti-tank guided missiles (ATGMs).
- The Army has proposed a mountain strike corps, two independent infantry brigades and two independent armoured brigades to plug its operational gaps along the entire Line of Actual Control (LAC) with China, as well as to acquire offensive capabilities. The proposed mountain strike corps, with over 40,000 soldiers and headquartered at Panagarhy in West Bengal, will for the first time give India the capability to also launch offensive action into Tibet Autonomous Region (TAR) in the event of Chinese attack. The corps will have two high-altitude divisions for rapid reaction (at Lekhapani and Missamari in Assam in 2009-10).
- Arjun MBT Mk – 2 – Trials started production by 2014.
- FMBT – Lighter tank of 50 tons at conceptual stage.
- FICV – Future Infantry Combat Vehicle program of DRDO. It is supposed to replace Indian Army's current regiment of BMP-2 infantry combat vehicle.
- Light Tank – 300 tanks (200 tracked wheeled) to be deployed on China border.
- Missiles – ICBM – Agni

- Cruise Missiles – Nirbhay and Brahmos
- Tactical Ballistic Missiles – Prahaar and Shaurya
- ATGM – Nag and Helina
- Army Aviation – 197 LUH
- Rustom -1 UAV

NAVY

The Indian Navy is the 7th largest Naval force of the world. Navy Day is celebrated on December 4. The first Indian CNS was Adm. R.D. Katari.

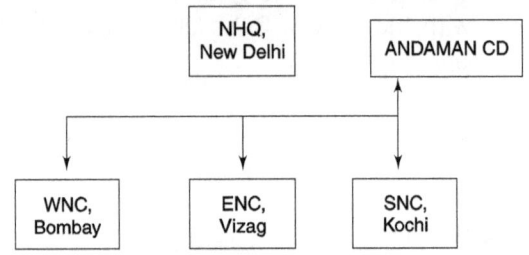

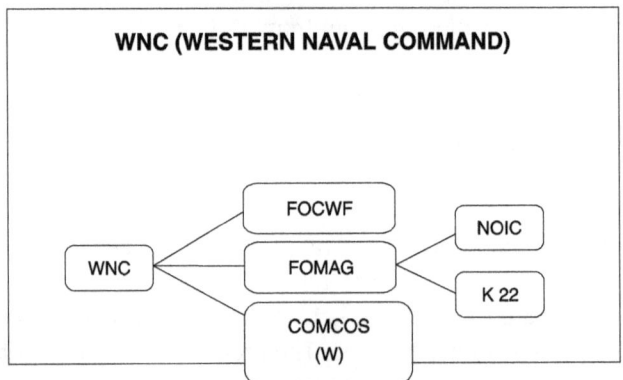

WESTERN FLEET

TYPES	NAMES OF SHIPS
• AIRCRAFT CARRIER	VIRAAT & VIKRAMADITYA
• DELHI CLASS	DELHI, MYSORE, MUMBAI
• TALWAR CLASS	TALWAR, TRISHUL, TABAR, TEG
• BRAHMPUTRA CLASS	BRAHMPUTRA, BETWA, BEAS
• GODAVARI CLASS	GODAVARI, GANGA, GOMATI
• LEANDERS	TARAGIRI
• TANKERS	DEEPAK, ADITYA
• OPV CLASS	SUBHADRA, SUVARNA
• LST(L)	SHARDUL

Defence Organisation-Army/Navy/Air Force

K 22 (Squadron - Check)

TYPES	NAME OF SHIPS
• PRABAL CLASS3	PRABAL, PRALAYA
• VEER CLASS	VEER, VIPUL, VIDYUT, NASHAK, NIPAT, NIRGHAT

NOIC (MH)
(Naval Officer Incharge)

TYPES	NAME OF SHIPS
• PE CLASS	ABHAY, AKSHAY, AJAY, AGRAY
• MINESWEEPER	ALLEPEY
• FACs	
• XFAC	T80, T81, T82

COMCOS (W)
(Commdore Commanding Submarine)

NAMES OF SUBMARINE
- Shankul
- Shankush
- Shalki
- Shishumar

ENC (Eastern Naval Command)

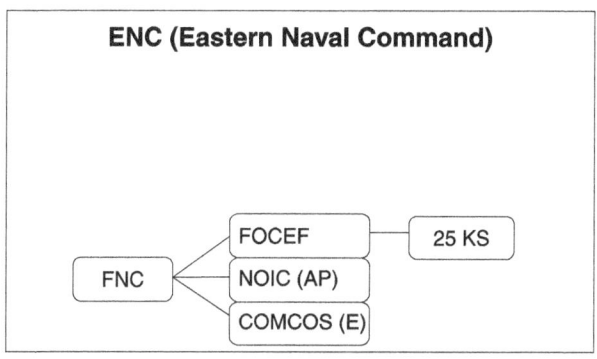

EASTERN FLEET

TYPES	NAME OF SHIPS
• R CLASS	RAJPUT, RANJIT, RANVIR, RANA, RANVIJAY
• SHIVALIK CLASS	SHIVALIK, SATPURA, SAHYADRI
• KHUKRI CLASS	KHUKRI, KIRPAN, KHANJAR, KUTHAR
• KORA CLASS	KORA, KIRCH, KULISH, KARMUKH
• LST(L)	MAGAR, GHARIAL, AIRAVAT
• TANKERS	SHAKTI, JYOTI
• OPV CLASS	SAVITRI, SUKANYA 25KS
• VEER CLASS	VIBHUTI, VINASH, NIRBHIK, NISHANK

NOIC (AP)
(Naval Officer Incharge)

TYPE	NAME OF SHIPS
• MINISWEEPERS	KARWAR, KAKINADA, CANNANORE, KONKAN, CUDDALORE, KOZHIKODE
• GAJ	
• ASTRAVAHINI	
• FACs	
• XFAC	T83, T84(BASED AT CHENNAI)

COMCOS (E)
(Commodore Commanding Submarine)

NAMES OF SUBMARINE

- Sinshudhwaj
- Sindhuraj
- Sindhuvir
- Sindhukirti & Arihant

SNC (Southern Naval Command)

NAME OF SHIPS
- TIR
- TARANGINI
- OPV CLASS – SHARDA, SUJATA
- SURVEY SHIPS

ANC (Andaman & Nicobar Command)

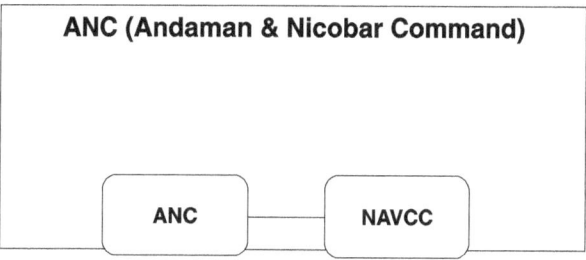

NAVCC (Naval Component Commander)

TYPE	NAME OF SHIPS
- LST(L)	KESARI
- LST(M)	KUMBHIR, CHEETAH, GULDAR
- LCUs	
- FACs	

Role of the Navy

Primary Role

1. To protect our country from external sea attacks.

Secondary Role

2. To maintain sea lanes of communication
3. To carry out search and rescue operations
4. Aid to civil administration during natural calamities
5. Improve foreign relations by diplomatic visits
6. Participate in Peace Keeping Mission.
7. Anti piracy ops

INDIAN AIR FORCE

It is the 4th largest Air Force of the World. October 8 is celebrated as Air Force Day. The various Commands of Air Force are given in succeeding paragraphs.

Central Air Command

The Central Air Command is one of the five operational commands of the Indian Air Force. Currently headquartered in Allahabad in Uttar Pradesh, it had its beginning as No. 1 Operational Group on May 27, 1958 at Rani Kuthee in Calcutta as a part of the government's increasing emphasis on defence of the eastern borders. Reorganisation of this Operational Group was created and upgraded to command on March 19, 1962 with headquarters at Rani Kuthee, Calcutta (now Kolkata). Calcutta was considered inappropriate location for the Central Air Command Headquarters and it was relocated at Allahabad in February 1966.

Eastern Air Command (EAC)

The Eastern Air Command is one of the five operational commands of the Indian Air Force. Currently headquartered in Shillong in Meghalaya, it had its beginning as No. 1 Operational Group on May 27, 1958 at Rani Kuthee in Calcutta as a part of the government's increasing emphasis on defence of the eastern borders. The Operational Group was upgraded as Command on December 1, 1959 with headquarters at Fort William, Calcutta and Air Vice Marshal K.L. Sondhi as the first AOC-in-C of the Eastern Command Indian Air Force # Rank structure. After the 1962 Indo-Chinese War, the decision was made to raise a full-fledged command at Shillong. The area of responsibility of the command now covers 11 states, and is bound by the international boundaries of Nepal, Bhutan, China, Myanmar and Bangladesh incorporating 6300 km of common border. Eastern Air Command now has permanent airbases at Chabua, Guwahati, Bagdogra, Barrackpore, Hasimara, Jorhat, Kalaikunda and Tezpur with forward airbases at Agartala, Calcutta, Panagarh and Shillong. Eastern Air Command consists of Air Defence squadrons consisting of the MiG-21 and Ground attack squadrons consisting of the MiG-27. It holds the motto Samareshu Parakramaha.

Southern Air Command (SAC)

The Southern Air Command (SAC) of the Indian Air Force (IAF) is headquartered in Thiruvananthapuram (Trivandrum), which is in the southern side of India. This is one among the five commands of IAF. This command was started on July 19, 1984 and is relatively new among the other commands. The conflicts in Sri Lanka and the need for establishing a strong base over the Indian Ocean resulted in the formation of this new command. The SAC was inaugurated by Indira Gandhi, the then Prime Minister of India.

From 1984 to 1999, the command grew from 5 lodger units to 17 lodger units under its jurisdiction. Air-sea rescue in the Indian Ocean may be among the command's tasks.

South Western Air Command (SWAC)

The South Western Air Command is one of the five operational commands of the Indian Air Force. It was raised in Jodhpur in July 1980 from the No. 1 Operations group of the Western Air Command. Its operations sector includes most of Rajasthan, through Gujarat and Saurashtra, as far south as Kutch and Pune. The SWAC moved to its current headquarters in Gandhinagar in May 1998, and incorporates the Indian airbases of Bhuj, Jaisalmer, Naliya, Jamnagar, Jodhpur, Uttarlai/Barmer and Poona. It controls air operations in the south western air sector, which includes most of Rajasthan, and south through Gujarat to Saurashtra, and Kutch to Pune. It also operates the forward airbases at Ahmedabad, Nal, Suratgarh and Uttarlai. The SWAC's role has historically been largely of air defence, although it has been reported to have incorporated a strike profile.

Western Air Command (WAC)

The Western Air Command (WAC) is the regional command of Indian Air Force headquartered in New Delhi. It is the largest and most important Air Command of the IAF, comprising sixteen Air Force Bases (AFBs) and is responsible for aerial defence of North India. The current Commander is Air Marshal Arup Raha AVSM VM, AOC-in-C, WAC.

WAC's Area of Responsibility extends from Kashmir to Rajasthan, covering the states of Jammu and Kashmir, Himachal Pradesh, Punjab, Haryana, New Delhi and some parts of Uttar Pradesh.

Training Command (TC)

Training Command is the Indian Air Force's command responsible for flying and ground training, located at Bangalore. In the 1930s the approaching threat and later advent of World War II and the leaning of Japan towards the Axis powers, the latter was considered as a potential enemy. Therefore, need was felt to make IAF a self-supporting force for the South Eastern threat of war. This led to the rapid expansion of the IAF. A target was fixed of 10 IAF Squadrons. With this expansion, the requirement of pilots and technical personnel increased. For the training of technical personnel, a technical training school was set up at Ambala in 1940.

In a 1949 reorganization of the Indian Air Force, while frontline units were put under the Operations Command, all the training institutions were placed under the jurisdiction of the Training Command.

Among Training Command's units is the Navigation Training School at Begumpet Air Force Station, Hyderabad. It flies the BAe HS.748.

Maintenance Command (MC)

Maintenance Command IAF is a command of the Indian Air Force. It was raised as Maintenance Group at Chakeri in Kanpur in 1950. In 1955, it was designated as Maintenance Command. Its current headquarters is located at Vayusena Nagar in Nagpur (Maharashtra); it handles the repair, overhaul and maintenance of all aircraft, helicopters and other equipment. MC has about nine base repair depots taking care of the overhaul and maintenance of various types of aircraft.

The command's Base Repair Depots include:
- 1 Base Repair Depot Kanpur-Chakeri for various overhaul
- 2 Base Repair Depot Gwalior-Maharajpur for various overhaul
- 3 Base Repair Depot Chandigarh Mi-8, Mi-17, Mi-25, Mi-35 for overhaul
- 4 Base Repair Depot Kanpur-Chakeri for various overhaul
- 5 Base Repair Depot Coimbatore-Sulur for various overhaul
- 11 Base Repair Depot Ojhar MiG-23, MiG-29 for overhaul
- Base Repair Depot Jodhpur MiG-21 for overhaul

Types of Aircraft

Fixed wing a/c And Rotary wing a/c.

Air Force Training Centres

1. Air Force Administrative College – Coimbatore
2. Air Force Flying College – Jodhpur
3. Air Force School – Jalahalli
4. Air Force Paratroopers Training School – Agra
5. Flying Instructors School – Tambaram
6. Air Force School – Sambra, Belgaun
7. Elementary Flying School – Bidar
8. Fighter Training & Transport Training Wings – Hakimpet and Yelahanka
9. Institute of Aviation Medicine – Bangalore
10. College of Air Warfare – Secunderabad

Army Training Institutes

1. National Defence Academy – Khadakvasla
2. National Defence College – New Delhi
3. Indian Military Academy – Dehradun
4. Defence Services Staff College – Wellington (TN)
5. Armed Forces Medical College – Pune

6. Infantry School – Mhow
7. Artillery Training – Deolali
8. Army Ordnance Corps School – Jabalpur
9. Army Cadet College – Dehradun
10. College of Defence Management – Secunderabad
11. College of Military Engineering – Kirkee, Pune
12. Armoured Corps Centre and School – Ahmednagar
13. College of Combat – Mhow
14. Officer's Training Academy – Chennai Gaya

Naval Training Centres
1. Indian Naval Academy – Ezimala
2. INS Valsura – Jamnagar (Electrical Training)
3. Dronacharya – Cochin
4. INS Shivaji – Lonavala (Engineering Training)
5. INS Circars – Vishakapatnam
6. INS Hamla – Mumbai (Logistic Training)

Naval Airbases
INS Rajali - Tu , Arakonam
INS Hansa - Goa
INS Garuda - Kochi
INS Dega - Vizag

Ranks of Commissioned Officers

Army	Air Force	Navy
General	Air Chief Marshal	Admiral
Lt. General	Air Marshal	Vice Admiral
Major General	Air Vice Marshal	Rear Admiral
Brigadier	Air Commodore	Commodore
Colonel	Group Captain	Captain
Lt. Colonel	Wing Commander	Commander
Major	Squadron Leader	Lt. Commander
Captain	Flt. Lieutenant	Lieutenant
Lieutenant	Flying Officer	Sub-Lieutenant

Defence Production Undertakings

Eight Public-Sector Undertakings (PSUs) currently function under the Department of Defence Production and Supplies. They are:

- **Hindustan Aeronautics Limited (HAL):** It has 12 factories out of which five are located at Bangalore, and one each at Koraput, Nasik, Karwar, Kanpur, Lucknow, Barrackpur and Hyderabad. It designs, manufactures and overhauls various types of aircrafts.
- **Bharat Electronics Limited (BEL):** It has nine factories located at Bangalore, Ghaziabad, Pune, Machhilipatnam, Taloja (Maharashtra), Panchkula (Haryana), Kotdwar (Uttaranchal), Hyderabad and Chennai. It is engaged in the design, development and manufacturing of electronic equipments.
- **Bharat Earth Movers Limited (BEML):** It has three factories located at Bangalore, Mysore and Kolar gold fields where heavy equipments like bulldozers, dumpers, loaders, cranes, etc. are manufactured.
- **Bharat Dynamics Limited (BDL):** It is located at Hyderabad to manufacture guided missiles.
- **Mazgaon Dock Limited (MDL):** It is located at Mumbai and its activities include shipbuilding apart from other works.
- **Garden Reach Shipbuilders and Engineering Limited (GRSE):** It was set up in Kolkata and is engaged in the construction and maintenance of warships and auxiliary vessels for Navy and Coast Guard.
- **Goa Shipyard Limited (GSL):** It comprises construction and repair/refit of ships/vessels.
- **Mishra Dhatu Nigam Limited (MIDHANI):** It is located at Hyderabad and manufactures sophisticated and strategic special metals and alloys for nuclear energy, aeronautics, space, etc.

Useful Topics for General Awareness which candidates must prepare before taking SSB Test:

1. Present state of India's missile programme.
2. Do we need a cut in the defence budget?
3. Over-involvement of media in the defence-related and national security matters have done more harm than good. Do you agree?
4. Was induction of women in armed forces a mistake?
5. Should there be any reservations in the armed forces?
6. Should India go for privatization of defence forces?
7. War is the best solution for peace.
8. Kargil – a debacle of Indian intelligence?
9. Should India have a Chief of Defence Services?
10. Should military be used to solve Sino-Indian border dispute?

11. Should all women officer's be granted permanent commission?
12. What in your opinion is the major problem faced by working women in India - sexual harassment, social discrimination or marital imbalance?
13. Do you agree that women today are being truthfully portrayed in the world of advertising?
14. In your opinion, the deterioration in the standard of sports in India is attributable to inherent lack of talents, politics in sports or extra importance to any other?
15. Which is the foremost problem which burdens India's progress – Corruption, Illiteracy or Criminalization of politics?
16. Should we go in for Presidential form of Government in India?
17. Indo-US renewed relationship
18. WMD
19. River cleaning & utilisation
20. Ethical hacking
21. Global oil crisis
22. Cyber crimes
23. Energy crisis & creation
24. Privatisation of education
25. Crime against women & their empowerment
26. Drug abuse
27. Swatch Bharat
28. Effective governance
29. Minimise red tape & maximise red carpet culture
30. National Judiciary Appointment Commission
31. Indo-China border dispute
32. Importance of Indian Ocean
33. Strategic importance of Andaman & Nicobar Islands
34. Incursions on East & West borders
35. FDI in Defence & Railway
36. Role of media - how fair are these?
37. GST
38. Gay rights
39. Euthanesia
40. Future energy
41. AI

13 Types of Entry & Eligibility for Armed Forces

"Success always comes when preparation meets opportunity."

– Henry Hartman

Recruitment in the armed forces is done though various schemes and is categorised into two main Commissions: Permanent Commission and Short Service Commission. A permanent commission is for those who want to make a career in the army until retirement, while a short-service commission allows one to join on a 10 contractual basis, after which one can exercise the option to continue.

Schemes under Permanent Commission For 10+2 (entry through NDA)

For entry through this scheme one has to take an entry level exam conducted by the UPSC to join the NDA, which is conducted twice a year in all major cities throughout India. The months of commencement of course are January and July. This mode of entry is only for boys between the ages of 16½ to 19½ years. Announcements are made in all leading newspapers. Those who clear the written exam go through a five-day interview process with the Services Selection Board (SSB). On completion of the NDA course, candidates are sent to the respective service academies for their pre-commission training: to the IMA (Dehradun) for Army, Naval Academy (Goa) for Indian Navy, Air Force Academy, Hyderabad for Air Force.

For Graduates

The UPSC also holds an all-India competitive examination known as the Combined Defence Services Examination (CDSE), twice a year for university graduates or equivalent. Successful candidates can join the Indian Military Academy (IMA) for their pre-commission training after they clear an interview conducted by the SSB and medical, depending on their merit list ranking. The age limit for this is between 19 to 24 years. The advertisement under this scheme is also given in all leading newspapers.

For Engineering Graduates

An engineering graduate can directly join the IMA after qualifying in SSB interview. The age at the time of joining under this scheme should be between 20 to 27 years.

For University Entry Scheme

Students who are in the final and pre-final years of engineering degree course can also apply to Indian army as an officer as they are eligible for induction into technical branches/services of the army as commissioned officers under the University Entry Scheme. The age limit under this scheme is between 18 to 25 years. The selection process is based on campus interview and SSB interview.

For 10+2 PCM (Tech.) scheme

Students who have 70% or more in PCM in their 12th board can apply directly for SSB and the age limit under this scheme is between 16½ to 19½ years.

Other Procedures for Recruitments

Apart from the above mentioned schemes, there is another scheme under the Special Commissioned Officers for serving NCO/JCO. For entry under this scheme the candidate should be between the age group of 30 to 35 years and a holder of Army Senior School Certificate Pass. Candidates under this scheme are sent for a screening test through SSB and Medical Board. Post this they are sent for a pre-commission training of one year duration.

Medical graduates from the Armed Forces Medical College (AFMC), Pune are directly inducted as permanent Commissioned Medical Officers in the Armed Forces. However, for recruitment under Regular Commissioned/Short Service Commissioned Medical Officers from the graduates/post graduates of Civil Medical Colleges, an all-India competitive exam is conducted.

Schemes under short service commission

Another Service option offered by the Indian Armed Forces is recruitment under the Short Service Commission and this gives an option of joining the forces as a Commissioned Officer for 10 years. Once the tenure of 10 years gets over the officers are allowed to opt for 4 years extension or a permanent commission. The short-service commission is also open to women.

For Graduates

Under this scheme, technical graduates have to apply through the SSB and after clearance at SSB they are sent to OTA Chennai. A medical test is done and later the candidates undergo a ten month course. The age limit for this scheme is between 19 to 24 years. On completion of training, the successful candidates are inducted as Short Service Commissioned Officers in the technical branches.

Women's special entry scheme (WSES)

Women are recruited usually in the support services and recruitments are done in non-technical, technical and specialist entry for unmarried females or issueless widow or divorcee candidates who are between 19 to 27 years of age. For entry under this scheme the candidate must have any of the following degrees - B.A., B.Com, BCA, B.Sc (physics, chemistry or maths) with a minimum aggregate of 60 per cent and above. NCC Cadets with 50 per cent marks and holders of C certificates can also apply in this category.

For Technical Entry, a degree in B.E./B.Tech in Civil/Electrical/Mechanical/Electronics/Computer Science/Telecommunications or Architecture is needed.

For the Special entry scheme candidate must be: a graduate B.Sc with a minimum one-year diploma in Computer Science, a graduate with a minimum one-year diploma in Communication or Journalism or Public Relations or Psychology, B.E. in Remote Sensing, a postgraduate degree in Earth Science/Computer Science/English/Geography/Maths/Physics/Computer Applications/Botany/Zoology/Biochemistry/Organic Chemistry or Statistics. The candidate must have an aggregate of 60 per cent marks in the above mentioned disciplines.

Selection is done on the basis of a written exam followed by SSB interview and medical examination.

NCC Special Entry Scheme

Under this scheme unmarried male/Female graduates with a total of 50 per cent marks and above and between 19 to 25 years of age and who have a minimum of B Grade in NCC **'C' Certificate** can apply. These cadets are exempted from appearing in the CDSE conducted by the UPSC and are directly selected through the SSB in Allahabad, Bhopal and Bangalore.

Short Service Commission Technical

Under this scheme unmarried male engineering graduates can apply. Educational qualification of the candidate should be a degree in engineering or equivalent degree from a recognised university in any discipline; Civil/Electrical/Mechanical/Tele-Communication/Electrical & Electronics/Computer Science/Engineering/Technology/Architecture/Industrial/Production.

For entry under this scheme candidates should be between the age group of 20 to 27 years. The selection process includes initial screening and the short-listing of applicants done at the Recruiting Directorate of the Army headquarters. Later the candidates have to undergo group test, psychological test and interview at SSB. This is followed by a medical test by the Medical Board and final selected candidates are sent to the OTA Chennai for a training of 49 weeks.

14

Call up Letter/Certificate

SAMPLE OF CALL-UP LETTER FOR CANDIDATES

INDIAN ARMY REGD/UPC

Selection Centre,
South, Cubbon Road,
Bangalore – 560042

Tele : 5591999
Extn. – 5643 Date _____
Fax. – 080 – 5096643
SCS/ /CU
To _____
  _____
  _____

Dear Candidate,

1. We are pleased to inform you that you have been nominated to attend SSB Interview for induction into the _____

2. You are required to report at this Centre at 1500 hours on _____. In case you are unable to attend on this date due to any unavoidable circumstances you should report at 1500 hours on _____. Kindly fill up the attached Acknowledgement Card and forward immediately by registered post. No further Call-up letter will be issued by Selection Centre. Please note that if you fail to report by the date confirmed by you, no further chances will be given for SSB interview. Neither the Selection Centre nor the Additional Directorate General of Recruiting, Adjutant General's Branch, West Block III, R.K. Puram, New Delhi – 110066 will entertain any correspondence in this regard.

3. Our representative wearing an arm band (top half red and bottom half black with inscription 'SSB') will be present at Movement Control Office (MCO)

location at Bangalore City Railway Station, who will arrange your reception and conveyance to this Centre. In case of difficulty you may contact the Call up Officer or the Duty Officer at the Telephone No. given above.

4. The testing will last for five days in two stages, excluding the day of arrival. If you secure the minimum acceptable grading in all tests, you will be detained at this centre for another three to four days or even longer for your medical examination.

"Candidates will be administered the stage one of the Selection Procedure on Day of their arrival. Candidates failing to make the grade in stage one will be returned back on the same day. Candidates recommended for Stage Two only will be retained for further testing".

5. Free boarding and lodging will be provided to you during your stay at the Selection Centre.
6. Joining instructions for your guidance and compliance are enclosed.
7. Please bring this letter with you and deposit the same at the Centre on arrival.
8. You are entitled to get traveling allowances in case you are coming for service selection board interview for the first time for this entry.
9. Please note that no lunch will be provided by the Selection Centre on the day you report at 1500 hours.
10. In your own interest you are advised to undergo a preliminary medical check-up for wax in ears, refractory error of eyes, fungal infections of skin and eosinophilia before reporting for SSB interview.
11. In case you are a candidate for 10+2 Navy Cadet Entry (Technical), a screening test will be administered on the next day of your arrival. Only those who make the grade will be detained for further tests and the rest will be directed to return on the same day.
12. Please bring with you a risk certificate duly completed and signed by your parents/guardian as per the format given below and submit the same at the time of the interview.
13. Candidate will adhere to laid down timings strictly.
14. Candidates will not visit testing areas or residences of testing officers and staff after testing hours.
15. The conduct of the candidates both in the Selection Centre as well as when visiting outside areas should be correct and gentleman like.
16. Candidates will not visit any area placed out of bound.
17. Any contravention of above orders or any act of indiscipline will result in immediate cancellation of candidature on disciplinary grounds.

18. Cases of serious breach of discipline and conduct will be handed over to civil police and FIR registered accordingly.

Yours faithfully,
Call up Officer
For Commander

Note: Candidate may get their call letter for SSB by emails/or on mobile as message as well.

RISK CERTIFICATE

I (Name) _____ father/guardian of (Name) _____ who is candidate for NDA Regular Commission of the Army hereby certify that I fully understand that my son/ward will, if required, attend Services Selection Board with my full and free consent and at my own risk and that I or my son/ward shall not be entitled to claim any compensation or other relief from the Government in respect of any injury which my son/ward may sustain in the course of or as a result of any of the test given to him at the said Services Selection Board whether due to negligence of any persons of or otherwise.

Place :

Date :   Signature of father/guardian

15

SSB Preparation By Services Candidates: ACC/SL/SCO

SSB PREPERATION BY SERVICES CANDIDATES : ACC/SL/SCO ETC.

"If you do not have Ambitions we can't cure that"

Service candidates have special privileges to get in to the Officer cadre. The primary reason is that there are special entries exclusively for Service candidates, how ever this opportunity is not being fully encashed by them. Individuals preparations are half baked. They are not doing any advance planning and priorities are not fixed accordingly. Majority of them have not accepted themselves that they can get Commission. It is a very casually set goal for them. Some of the ACC candidates even give up during the written exam itself.

After clearing the written exam, they are pooled in at the Regimental Centers where Service Officers who had a tenure at the SSB as assessors are given the task of training them. The point to keep in mind is that SSB assessors need not be effective Trainers. Training is a very highly skilled task and with experience a good trainer can make a lot of difference.

What is that a Service candidate need to clear the SSB. Three things needs to be kept in mind:

One – Save Two lakhs of rupees (approximately)

Two – 4 months leave

Three – Sheding time wasting activities; in other words making adjustments in daily activities.

Let us talk about the investment. Majority of Service candidates invest maximum money in the Provident fund so that it can come handy when they retire. This is what has been advised by their Superiors too. Remember, you are the most important person in your life. It is important that you invest in yourself, when your life needs it the most; when you are young and that is the time your real growth happens. In fact that set the platform for going up in life in every department. Today a good laptop with hi-speed internet is a necessity for any growing individual. It is a package of knowledge power house. Google God can tell you everything what you are looking for. Yes, it is a great source for self-development but one got to be careful how you want to use it and what you want to search in it.

A Majority of Service candidates have English language communication problem. There are numerous on line courses, join them. Listen to various high level talks on daily basis such as 'Ted talk'. It will improve your knowledge and proficiency in English language. Have a cell phone with internet connection. Down load Merrian websters dictionary where here you can learn English words, its usage and meaning. Set a target to learn five English words daily and use these words to make sentences. Try to read English novels where you will learn normal English conversation flow. "Communication takes place on two levels – what we say and how we say it"

From the allocated amount hire a personal English teacher and spend time in tution for 2 months. I assure your English language is set to take off. Rest your lap top with internet will do for you. Practice conversation that you need to initiate by talking to yourself in your mind in English language. Where ever possible speak out loud in your bed room or bath room etc, preferably facing a mirror There are numerous places and occasions where you can self-practice in a 24 hours' time period daily.

A suggested expenditure is as under:-

(a) Lap top with internet connection - 50,000
(b) Books - 5,000
(c) Cell Phone - 15,000
(d) Tution fee for English - 10,000
(e) SSB Coaching Fees &
 SSB book for reading - 14,000   (Rs 2 Lakhs approximately)
(f) Learning computers - 6,000
(g) Tution teacher - 20,000
(h) Good dress and Shoes - 15,000
(i) Misc - 15,000

 GRAND TOTAL   1,50,000
 BALANCE   50,000

Still you are left with 50 K may be you take SSB coaching at two places, spend some amount for guided learning. Besides your investment of Rs two lakhs and your will power you need to take two years annual leave with a one month gap (total 4 months).

There 4 months you can't afford to spend visiting relatives, watching movies etc. You need to lock yourself from outside interferences and remember you are on a Mission. Watching movies and wasting time on non-productive activities is not what you set your goal for. Movie, theatre, Cricket, TV serials. Visting astrologer and religious places etc have to be completely off from your daily activities. Out of 24 hours, sleep for 8 hours and rest of the time you are on mission. Do not spent too much time on a newspaper, maximum 15 mins is ideal.

A problem will be the start point. If you remain on your target for 10 days, you will get addicted to it and you will find how your life is getting transformed. You will start feeling that you are not ordinary but special and then you will get nailed to your target; it will be magic. You will see how your world is changing and how you are changing.

The most important step is the first step. Take it with determination. Getting to start will take you a head. If you don't start nothing can happen.

The other important aspect is to have confidence in your efforts that will give you results. Just going to religious places and wasting your time and effort will get you nothing. Understand all these are false. Nobody can tell you what they do not know. Be a thinking person. Knowledge gained will tell you what to do. Believe in science and evidence.

Your effort is the catch and you can make it. You can dine in the Officers mess. Your wife and children can say that you are an Officer. Your parents, villagers, friends and everyone else will be proud of you. Your life will change forever, so is the life for all your dear and near one's. You are not alone. You are an institution and your actions will have consequences in their lives too. You have far too many reasons to do what I explained in this book because the stakes are high.

Also be warned that you do not have any other option to reach the top as compared to Civilian candidates. You have only two options, retire as an OR/JCO or as a commissioned officer. The choice is yours. If you think the training activities organized by the Regimental Centre alone will get you Commission, then you will be sadly mistaken. There is no short cut. You need to invest that small amount and time while saying bye bye to low level activities and entertainments. Are you ready for it?

All that is required is willingness to spend little bit of money and bringing the best out of your potential. Presently you are not even using 20% of your potential for your personal growth. Your mind has to accept that you can be a Commissioned Officer. It is a realistic and achievable goal!

16

If you got rejected at the SSB then there is some thing special about you

"You can't change the past. But you can ruin the present by worrying about the future"

The SSB Selection procedure is basically extrovert oriented. Extroverts are the one who act fast without going into the details of the subject. Daniel Kheneman, the author of New York Times best seller "Thinking fast and slow" and the nobel price winner on economics clearly explains in his book the fallacies of thinking fast and how it effect human thinking and decision making. The first problem with extroverts are that they do not take time to think which is against all logics of leadership qualities.

Now here is the bomb shell, various researches have proved that introverts are more intelligent and they are the one who made maximum positive inputs in the world. Susain Cain in her bestselling book "Quiet" which sold over two millions copies in the world explains the power of introverts. Introverts are the one who sit quiet and take time to respond. Unfortunately the system in SSB is so designed that the extrovert take the initiative to talk first. Whenever opportunity comes the extroverts immediately jump in to the verbal warfare and Capture the attention of the assessors and the introverts take their time to respond and most of the time they do not get opportunity to participate in a discussion. Eventually the candidate get screened out or get rejected at the SSB.

This is a huge mistake of SSB Selection System. What these researches tell us is that those introverts get screened out are not all less intelligent and capable than those got selected. So here is the point to lift you up, if you got rejected at any time at the SSB then there is something to feel special about you. You are actually not the loser Susan Cain explains in her book that "Today introversion and extroversion are two of the most exhaustively researched subjects in personality psychology arousing the curiosity of hundreds of Scientists" She also indicates that there is Zero correlation between gift of the gab and good ideas. Some of the greatest inventions which changed the world and the way human life changed came from introverts. Had they were exposed to a screening system as being done at the SSB presently, surely they would have got rejected.

This talking world give an impression to an introvert that inherently there in something wrong with them which is not the fact. They initially fail to impress the class teacher, party crowd opposite sex, friends, colleagues and bosses. But eventually introverts builts stable relationships, emerges as strong leaders and succeed in every domain where they are involved. Essentially I am not saying all those selected candidates have something to worry about but bit of self-investigation of personal traits may be useful. However I am of the strong opinion that the extrovert oriented selection system at the SSB do not give a fair chance to introverts why do we punish someone who is soft spoken and gracious. Is it a bad leadership quality? I doubt why do we have to be excessively aggressive to impress some body. Excessive aggressiveness make the person to think fast, the outcome is wrong more often than not. Ignoring the unique power of an introvert is a costly error. Extroverts are eago centric and they get upset and become aggressive fast. Whereas introverts are calm and soft spoken majority times they are on target to the point. I think this is an important quality that a military officer should possess. Troops they commanding certainly would respond better to introvert officers who might treat them better and bring the best out of their team.

There is a feeling in the military Circle that anyone who yap too much is intelligent, capable and worthy of promotions. He gets better grades in the annual reports but has no correlation being a good officer for the organization and the troops he commands. Let me point out one thing very clear here. Every military officer will do everything possible to impress his/her seniors but how many genuinely tried to win the heart of the troops they command? Every military officer particularly Senior officers will yap out high end theories but execution is a different story.

Why I am mentioning this is that you after selection at the SSB have lots of thinking to do; To be able to control 21st century human being require different leadership qualities than what are being tested at the SSB. Therefore, this book is not only for anyone who is preparing to face the SSB but also for those who got rejected and selected and it is more valuable for them than the one preparing to face the SSB.

I reterate here that various researches clearly proved that introverts are more intelligent and well composed. They have produced better results in the world.

The extrovert oriented selection system has serious defects it fails to create an ideal pool of defence leaders for our defence forces. Extroverts are very good at getting their way but that doesn't mean they are going the right way. We see extroverts smarter than introverts but the studies about their intelligents points the other way. School grades and SAT score tells the story. "We also see talkers as leaders. The more a person talk, the more other group members direct their attention to him. Which means he becomes increasingly powerful as the proceeding goes on. All of these would be fine if talking were correlated with greater insight, but research suggests that there is no such link."

The US Army has a famous saying "Any Army officers can tell you what that means" But they understood this mistake long ago and corrected. Indian defence officers continue the same even today. "I worry that there are people who are put in positions of authority because they are good talkers but they don't have good ideas"

"It is worth noting here that highest – performing companies around the world every single one of them was lead by unassuming introverts. Those who worked with these leaders describe them with the following words. Quiet, humble, modest, reserved, shy, gracious, mild mannered, self – effaced and understated"

Jim Collins says, we need leader who build not their own egos but the institution they run. Ego centric Indian defence officers may like to take a lesson or two from this. Susan cain in her book explained her interaction with Wharton management professor Adam Grant who has spent considerable time consulting with Fortune 500 executives and military leaders from google to US Army & Navy. Grant narrated about a wing commander in the US Airforce, one rank below General in command of thousands of people, charged with protecting a high Security missile base. Who was one of the most classically introverted people as well as one of the finest leaders, Grant had ever met. He spoke quietly, without much variation in his vocal inflection or facial expressions. He was more interested in listening and gathering information than asserting his opinion or dominating a conversation.

"He was widely admired when he spoke, every one listened. This was not necessarily remarkable if you are at the top of the military hierarchy. People are supposed to listen to you. But in the case of this officer commander, says Grant, people respected not just his formal authority but also the way he led, by supporting his subordinate's effort to take the initiative."

He gave subordinates input in to key decisions, implementing the ideas that made sense, while making it clear that he had the final authority. He was not concerned with getting credit or even with being in charge. He simply assigned the task to those who could perform the best. This meant delegating some of his most interesting, meaningful and important task, work that other leaders would have kept for themselves. If the US defence could select such officers what is problem with our selection system?

She says in her book "The introvert leaders are 20% more likely to follow suggestions" Extrovert on the other hand "Often the leaders end up doing lot of talking and not listening to any of the ideas that the followers are trying to provides"

Extrovert oriented Indian defence forces leadership requires complete remodeling. Officers/Jawans relationship is not great in the defence Forces. The leaders imposes their views and Jawans obey them just out of fear nothing more. I have seen this in every department of defence. In an officer mess if there is a party hosted, the majority talking will be done by the Senior most officer. He completely ignores that the newly commissioned officer knows a thing or two more than him.

It is extremely difficult to strike a conversation with any senior defence officer, the talking will be done by him. The chapter of listening he forgotten the day he got commission and got troops under him if you are civilian had no military exposure meet a retired Indian defense officer and try to strike a conversation you will find it extremely difficult, he may not have any indepth knowledge about the topic but he will never let you talk.

Troops listen and obey them out of fear not because they accepted them from the heart as a leader.

I want you to understand the above if you are a selected candidate because you will not make the mistake others have been making. If you are a rejected candidate in an extrovert oriented selection system, you need not feel low because you may be superior than the one got selected.

17

Why SSB Selection System is not Perfect

"If I know exactly what I am going to do. What's the good in doing it" Pablo Picasso

We are often confident about our decisions when we are wrong. The SSB selection system is not fool proof. The system have many fallacies. The decisions that each assessor make can't be fully approved by decision research scientists. The system has strong heuristics and biases. There are various occasions in the decision making process where an individual can go wrong when influenced by various forms of emotions. Also the first impression extend to the future. If you like a film star all actions she/he does your mind automatically justify to a positive outcome. Mind is not ready to accept that the star is grossly wrong on a particular issue. This be the case the first impression has lots of impact in SSB selection system. All the three departments of SSB Selection System. Let us go little deep in to it. How possibly the first impression can effect the psych testing when the Assessor not even seing the Candidate? Yes it has impact. Let us assume that your first story that the psychologist read gave a very positive impact in his mind. Unconciously his mind already started processing that the 2nd story has to be good. The decision the brain has taken from the first story will extend to the future. It would be very rare that the brain endorsed the first story as excellent and then brain expect the 2nd story to be absolutely useless.

Daniel Kahneman in his book explains how brain access the stored information without our knowledge "We can be blind to the obvious, and we are also blind to our blindness. The knowledge is stored in memory and accessed without intention and without effort". If the psychologist read two stories and have to give the final grading he will be more aligned to the story which was read first.

Once I had a discussion with one of the psychologists who happened to access one of my trained candidates, during the discussion he told me that his way of reading the stories written by candidates is in reverse order. Out of twelve stories he starts with the twelfth one. Obviously this will have a negative impact in the final grading. When a Candidate has written twelve stories under stress more often than not the twelfth one will not be as strong as the first one. I feel it is a completely negative approach towards the Candidate, words and sentences spoken and written will have serious impacts on the final result. One should be careful and calculative while delivering them in written and verbal form. The impact of these words are processed by the brain without any effort on the part of all the assessors. Human beings have an habit of jumping in to conclusion without taking any effort to do bit of homework and deep thinking because it is painful and time consuming. We never spend time on thinking exercise. These days as it is people have no time for anything. Social media, Cricket and two thousand and more TV channels, newspapers etc, have made us slaves.

Nobody is out of the clutch of thinking and decision making fallacies as long as brain process information without prior permission. Let me give you an example. If you know driving while driving you do not think anything about the process of driving but concentrate on listening to music or talking on cell phone etc. The stored information inside your brain let you drive without any effort on your part.

I will use the same example when it comes to your preparation for facing the SSB. When you were learning driving your mind, body and brain were fully on the job of learning driving. It was a deep practice activity and that brain keep it forever. Now give a gap of five years for driving after five years if you get a vehicle you will drive with same comfort and ease. There were various other things you learnt in life but you forget them because it was not a deep learning. Formula is same for SSB preparations if you create depth in your preparations you will never forget them and it will be a natural and confidence performance at the SSB. Why do you fear the SSB because the preparations are not fully completed and it is shallow. You are scared of driving when you were learning because the learning process had not completed. Situation is dramatically different after having fully learnt. The depth has not been arrived at. This principle goes for everything important you do in your life. If you want to be a good friend create depth in friend ship. Take it to every domain of your life and see how your life changes forever. There is no point in knowing everything and knowing nothing.

It requires conscious efforts and making certain adjustments of daily activities. If you are a Cricket addict then this goal is far from you. Addictions are many and they steal your talents.

Getting back to the first impression magic "evaluating people as attractive or not is a basic assessment .You do that automatically whether or not you want to and it influences you. You like or dislike people long before you know much about them. We trust or distrust strangers without knowing"

If this be the case decision making can be hard and very much applicable for SSB Selection system too.

"Human beings are ignorant of their ignorance. The illusion that our past decisions were correct fosters over confidence in our ability to predict future. Favorable first impression influence later judgements."

Adequate weight should be given to the data we have on a candidate's past performance a PIQ form doesn't provide enough data. Focusing too much on the data provided in PIQ form neglect what is not provided in the PIQ form about the candidate. SSB Selection procedure leave a profound impact on all candidates rejection is stronger than success, losses will have more impact than gains. Selected candidates will never advertise how many in their batch got selected but the rejected candidate will always take the support of the rejected lot to advertise that i.e., 95% candidate got rejected they will not say 5% got selected that is how the system works after the announcement of SSB results.

There is no fixed value for human rationality and it get influenced by various emotional factors. Logical consistency may be at risk. We could say that his interview was the best because we compared other interviews. Same goes with every other SSB tests. Logical reasoning has many parameters to consider Daniel Kahneman gives an excellent example

"Dan is 5ft 2 inches tall

Tom is 5ft tall

Who is the tallest?

Obvious answer it is Dan

What if some more inputs are taken, Dan is 20 years old and Tom is 7 years old now see how the answer changes Tom is tall for a 7 year old.

Here it is obvious that an additional input can influence decision making so is the case when fail to take extra inputs which may be relevant. Logical reasoning requires every possible inputs. Bare mind can't do the job because human mind is not bound to reality.

Decision making is a serious affair and it requires in depth research. Study of decision making should be a subject in graduate studies and in military academics. Military leaders, politicians and manages in every level should be put to formal decision making studies. You are reading this book because you want to be a leader in life hence spending sometime on understanding the process of decision making could be worth an effort. Where to spend your time on is a decision, watching a TV serial or reading a book or going to GYM.

Whatever information we have our mind process that and whatever we don't have we do not know about it. How much we know I mean the public about defence forces is a big question mark.

> *"Experience is the name every one gives to his mistakes"*
>
> **Oscar Wilde**

Your aim should not be just to clear the SSB, become an officer and shut down your critical facilities or become a talking machine. In 21st century you will be privileged that the soldiers below you would listen to you and obey you without questioning. This situation make majority officers to be arrogant and over confident.

During my services in the Army I have seen a write up in the military set up

"Rule No. 1 – The boss is always right."

"Rule No. 2 – Whenever you find the boss is wrong apply rule no. 1"

This is the most popular writing in the offices of the Indian defence forces. In other words you can never be right that is the bottom line. Do you think any thinking person can accept a position like that? It is one of the worst teachings ever.

There is no surprise why there is frequent tension between officer community and the below officer rank personnel. There are many cases of Jawans shooting officers there has to be something to do with the extrovert and assertive leadership issues.

The point I am trying to bring home is that there is nothing extra ordinary if you got selected and nothing disastrous if got rejected by the SSB Selection system. It is not perfect and qualities of an individual is not permanent. It changes with time and circumstance that an individual faces during the discourse of living in the society.

Let us see how the behavior or qualities getting changed. I would like to start with SSB selection person 'A' get selected at the SSB. The selection system rated his honesty and integrity very high later on the same individual climb up to the top of the military ranking and get involved with various dishonest activities, not one huge number of senior defence officers got themselves involved in various grave dishonest activities.

How an honest officer become dishonest when reached high position in the services? Whatever information is available that we process and what about those information that we do not have?. Probably if all the information is made available, then the designers of the SSB selection system may have to hide their faces.

Here is my final advice to you that every quality can be developed and there is nothing called this person is better than you or you are inferior to him. It is all about developing all the required qualities as you build muscles in your body. These are inner muscles that can be constructed.

If you failed at the SSB, it is an event only nothing more than that and it has to be treated that way only.

"Everyone makes mistakes. Some people learn from them. Which others repeat them"

SSB SELECTION SYSTEM IS NOT ALIGNED WITH THE PRESENT AND FUTURE

"There is Difference Between Hero Of A Country And Hero Of The World"

Let us start with PIQ form. It is time to do away with PIQ forms. Taking the data from the Social media network of a candidate would give the true picture of a Candidate. It can't be cooked up overnight. Interviewing officer take PIQ form as the base data and which can be unreal on many aspects. IO will put in effort to verify the input given in the PIQ form and the Candidate will struggle to justify what is given out. Why to do this negative act. Let us get on to the original and let that be the thresh hold for everything at the SSB. Everything about a person is voluntarily without any pressure is posted in the internet let us use that data and move forward. Which can also be complicated a person with 1000 facebook friends and another guy closed the face book account being a time waste can be a catch 22 situation for assessor, of course every assessor will say the SSB Selection system is the absolute and perfect one. Then how come good number of defence officers got involved in various scams that includes the Chief of Air staff and other very senior officers?. I do not want to name them here. There are enough and more scams involving defence officers. I would say 80% of rejection in screening test is another mokery of human values. Conducting a test with an aim of rejecting human dignity is a crime. Stamping as failure a good number of young soul is an offence because the impact of these rejections they carry with them all their life and to the grave.

I have come across a good number of successful people who narrated the sad story of their rejection at the SSB. All those officers who completed their full services in the forces I did not find them saint either. Why I am saying this is because there are tons of appreciation for selected candidates but my sympathy goes to the rejected ones, all of them do not deserve a rejection, they deserve a better deal. When somebody is sleeping hungry do not wake him up and say there is no food for him. That is my definition for the screening test at the SSB. If the SSB has the assessors pool to test 50 candidates and calling 250 candidates to report clearly set the target. Only 50 have to be screened in. This happens at the cost of tax payers' money the expenses of so many candidates coming to SSB is borne by the tax payer.

If somebody has not jumped into discussion instantly on introducing the topic and remain gentle and polite he needs to be stamped as failure? My sympathy goes to thousands of candidates who were not given a fair chance at the SSB. Now let me get on to psychological series of testing. It is absolutely obsolete. It is a writing based test and writing is disappearing from the world and children of present advance countries do not write they carry tablet to School.

These days young Indians do not write love letters but they text. My First love letter I wrote at least twenty times and hugely wanted to improve handwriting. Now if the present generation is forced to write then their hand writing assessors will not be able to read. So the best option is reject them.

They have been shown 17th Century pictures and told to write stories. Why not show the picture of Elon musk and tell them to write story? Or an aircraft without pilot destroying a target?

Word association test why not we include words like Artificial intelligence, testla, Solar energy, space etc. These are relevant because future wars are going to be from the space stations. US will hit every nation on the earth from the space in 30 mins. Situation reaction test we have kiddish situations given to candidates as if they are completely dump and then grade them based on that. It is a very lazy system 19th Century Social situations are given and candidates are asked to respond. Why not we have situation like "All your friends are in face book and you are not in it"? "Your close friends have 1500 & more face book friends and you have only 15" "Your close friend find google a useless platform you would?" "Before the SSB interview your close friend consulted a famous astrologer and he said he will be selected provided he does a particular pooja costing Rs.1000, what you think he should do? "In order to reach the SSB he has to start the journey from home on an inauspicious day, His mother said, it is a bad omen he would_____?

The basic flaw is that you are tested as a local person. Infact you should be tested like a global person. Virtually everything is global now.

"Every person, every system, every product, every idea has faults"

18

SSB Interview Training & Development

SSB Coaching with a Training Institute

This book gives enough tools for you to clear the SSB; however, I personally recommend that you also undertake training and put all the ideas and techniques that you acquired from this book in action which will help you to seal your success hundred percent. Also you will come up in the order of merit.

However, it is extremely important that you undertake full training; taking partial training can be counter-productive. I would like to explain why partial training can be counter-productive. Since you have already read this book you know that at the SSB, psychological series of testing is spread over a time period of about 4 hours and the interview is for a period from 30 minutes to 45 minutes, both these techniques put together take about less than 5 hours to complete. Every training institute in the country is more or less equipped to give you training on the above two techniques, but When it comes to the GTO series of testing which is spread over a period of two days, it is extremely important that you get full training on GTO series. In order to have meaningful training on these techniques, the training institute should have facilities where the outdoor tasks are laid out on ground and where you are made to train on them. It is then only your training is complete and your performance in the SSB will be consistent and result oriented.

What is partial training and why it is dangerous?

There are numerous training institutes across the country. Let us take the biggest SSB coaching hub – New Delhi, where there are a number of training institutes but none of them has a full outdoor task area. However, they claim to be providing training for outdoor tasks too. Some of them have specimen outdoor task laid out on the building roof while others have a small portion of land where they have laid out few structures at random perhaps equal to one phase of the PGT out of 4 phases. The rest of the tests are theory-based.

One of the most important qualities that the SSB is looking for is your ability to think rationally i.e. Reasoning Ability, so let us discuss this. "Can you ever learn to swim without ever getting into the swimming pool?" The answer is 'No'. So is the case when it comes to SSB coaching about GTO task, practically without any actual on-ground exposure. This can't be taught in theory or in any kind of specimen-like models, roof structures or on a thousand square feet land with a few structures at random. To lay out a complete GTO task on ground you need large acres of land which to costs crores of rupees in Delhi and financially not viable for institutes to have them in reality. So one resorts to truncated arrangement which is dangerous for potential candidates arrangements.

Why is this ad hoc dangerous?

When a candidate is given partial exposure of outdoor tasks he may end up performing well at random tests and performance drastically drops in other tasks that he was not exposed to. Your performance is not gradually increasing in an ascending order but very erratic and failure is almost certain in this case. So one should either take full training or no training at all but follow this book.

How to ensure you get full training

Choose a training institute which has got complete outdoor task laid out on ground as it exists in the SSB. You must enquire at the chosen institute without mixing words; if they give you an honest answer then that is your criteria No. 1 to choose the institute.

Next question is: Who are the people teaching these techniques, are they former SSB posted officers or not? There are lots of quacks in every domain. In this industry too there are numerous such trainers. They can be counter- productive for your success. Even there are civilian individuals providing SSB coaching, which you need to filter out.

Also look at the websites of these coaching centers – taking pictures of fighter aircrafts, naval ships and fighting soldiers etc from the Internet and posting in the web site. Are they selling aircraft, naval ships and defence uniforms? They have nothing or very less to show about the product that they are selling. We should be very clear in our head when we see any such misleading input and advertisement. Let us take as an example the advertisement of a vest brand. It shows that just because the person is wearing that particular brand of garment everything is happening in his favour. Really?

What these organisations with partial training capabilities have done to thousands of candidates, particularly in Delhi. The market is large and thousands of candidates join training institutes merely on names and advertisement. Percentage of selection in these institutes is not even 7 per cent which is less than the SSB selection rate. The biggest damage they do is turn a good number of other wise selectable candidates to failure, due to partial training.

Let us see this rationally. An institute that advertises vigorously gets over 125 to 150 candidates in a month. There are at least three such organisations in Delhi, plus all the others who get lesser number. Let us take an average: all training institutes put together in Delhi alone account for training around 700 candidates, the lowest figure. So in a year 84000 candidates in Delhi alone and of all of them claim over 30 per cent selection. Let us take a low claim say 20 per cent selection; that means 16800 selection in Delhi alone; with this rate if we take all India a low figure of 20,000 selections. When we put together the total vacancies is never more than 4,500, that too I put a higher figure. From this data you can get a real picture about the false claims being propagated by these training institutes and how they trap innocent students. They are cultivating failures. A complete training in all aspects of SSB Selection techniques will hugely contribute to your success at SSB.

www.ingramcontent.com/pod-product-compliance
Lightning Source LLC
Chambersburg PA
CBHW031307150426
43191CB00005B/107